ARCADIA

ALEX **PAKNADEL**   ERIC SCOTT **PFEIFFER**

BOOM!
STUDIOS

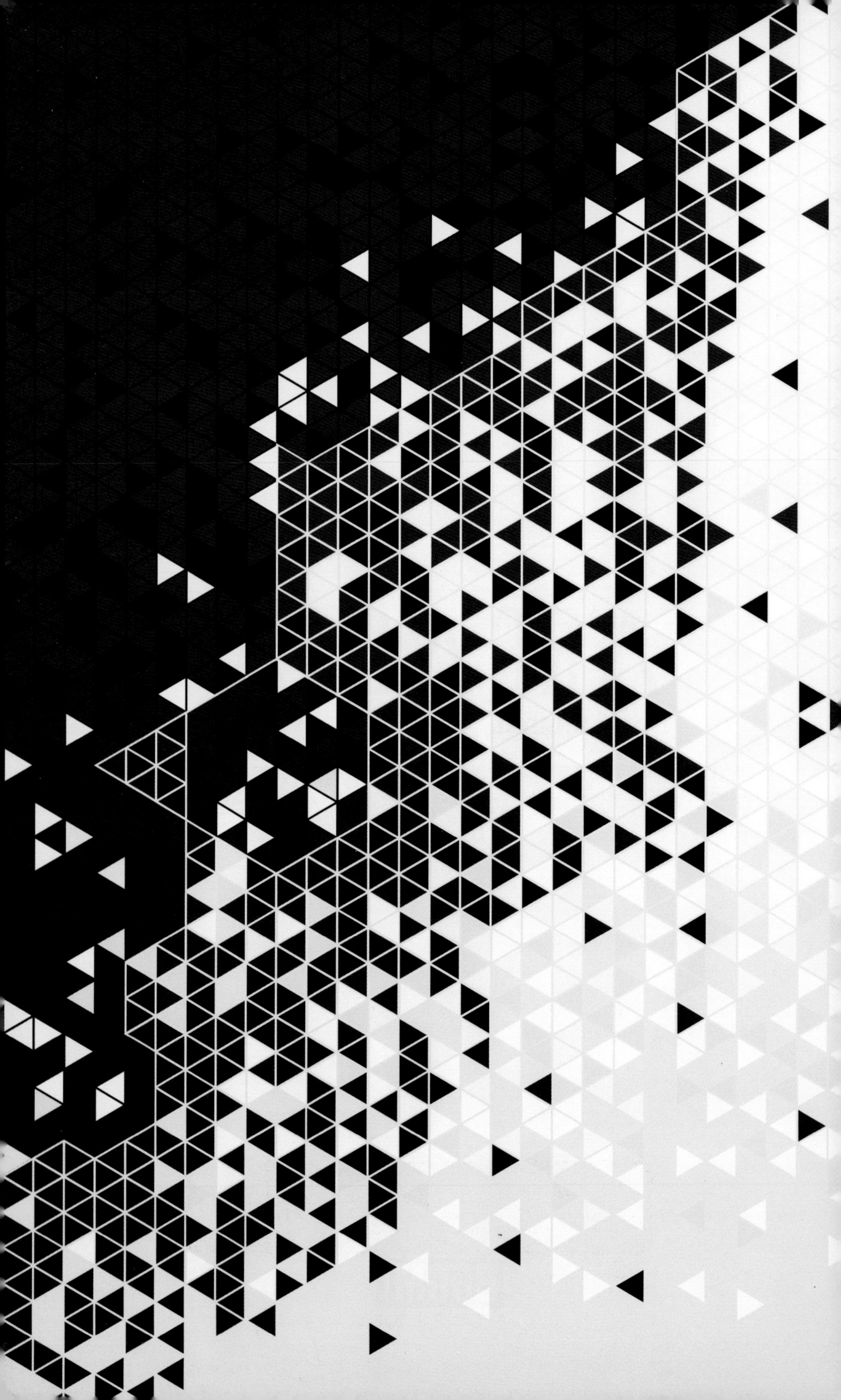

WRITTEN BY
ALEX PAKNADEL

ILLUSTRATED BY
ERIC SCOTT PFEIFFER

LETTERED BY
COLIN BELL

COVER BY
MATT TAYLOR
& ERIC SCOTT PFEIFFER

DESIGNER **SCOTT NEWMAN**
ASSOCIATE EDITOR **JASMINE AMIRI**
EDITOR **ERIC HARBURN**

SPECIAL THANKS **WILL DENNIS**

ARCADIA™
CREATED BY **ALEX PAKNADEL**

ROSS RICHIE CEO & Founder
MATT GAGNON Editor-in-Chief
FILIP SABLIK President of Publishing & Marketing
STEPHEN CHRISTY President of Development
LANCE KREITER VP of Licensing & Merchandising
PHIL BARBARO VP of Finance
BRYCE CARLSON Managing Editor
MEL CAYLO Marketing Manager
SCOTT NEWMAN Production Design Manager
IRENE BRADISH Operations Manager
CHRISTINE DINH Brand Communications Manager
SIERRA HAHN Senior Editor
DAFNA PLEBAN Editor
SHANNON WATTERS Editor
ERIC HARBURN Editor
WHITNEY LEOPARD Associate Editor
JASMINE AMIRI Associate Editor
CHRIS ROSA Associate Editor
ALEX GALER Assistant Editor
CAMERON CHITTOCK Assistant Editor
MARY GUMPORT Assistant Editor
KELSEY DIETERICH Production Designer
JILLIAN CRAB Production Designer
MICHELLE ANKLEY Production Design Assistant
AARON FERRARA Operations Coordinator
ELIZABETH LOUGHRIDGE Accounting Coordinator
JOSÉ MEZA Sales Assistant
JAMES ARRIOLA Mailroom Assistant
STEPHANIE HOCUTT Marketing Assistant
SAM KUSEK Direct Market Representative
HILLARY LEVI Executive Assistant

BOOM! STUDIOS

™ ARCADIA, May 2016. Published by BOOM! Studios, a division of Boom Entertainment, Inc. Arcadia is ™ & © 2016 Alex Paknadel. Originally published in single magazine form as ARCADIA No. 1-8. ™ & © 2015, 2016 Alex Paknadel. All rights reserved. BOOM! Studios™ and the BOOM! Studios logo are trademarks of Boom Entertainment, Inc., registered in various countries and categories. All characters, events, and institutions depicted herein are fictional. Any similarity between any of the names, characters, persons, events, and/or institutions in this publication to actual names, characters, and persons, whether living or dead, events, and/or institutions is unintended and purely coincidental. BOOM! Studios does not read or accept unsolicited submissions of ideas, stories, or artwork.

A catalog record of this book is available from OCLC and from the BOOM! Studios website, www.boom-studios.com, on the Librarians Page.

BOOM! Studios, 5670 Wilshire Boulevard, Suite 450, Los Angeles, CA 90036-5679. Printed in China. First Printing.

ISBN: 978-1-60886-823-0, eISBN: 978-1-61398-494-9

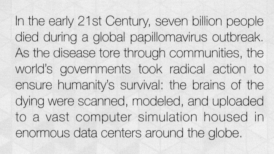

In the early 21st Century, seven billion people died during a global papillomavirus outbreak. As the disease tore through communities, the world's governments took radical action to ensure humanity's survival: the brains of the dying were scanned, modeled, and uploaded to a vast computer simulation housed in enormous data centers around the globe.

They called this simulation
Arcadia.

CHAPTER
ONE

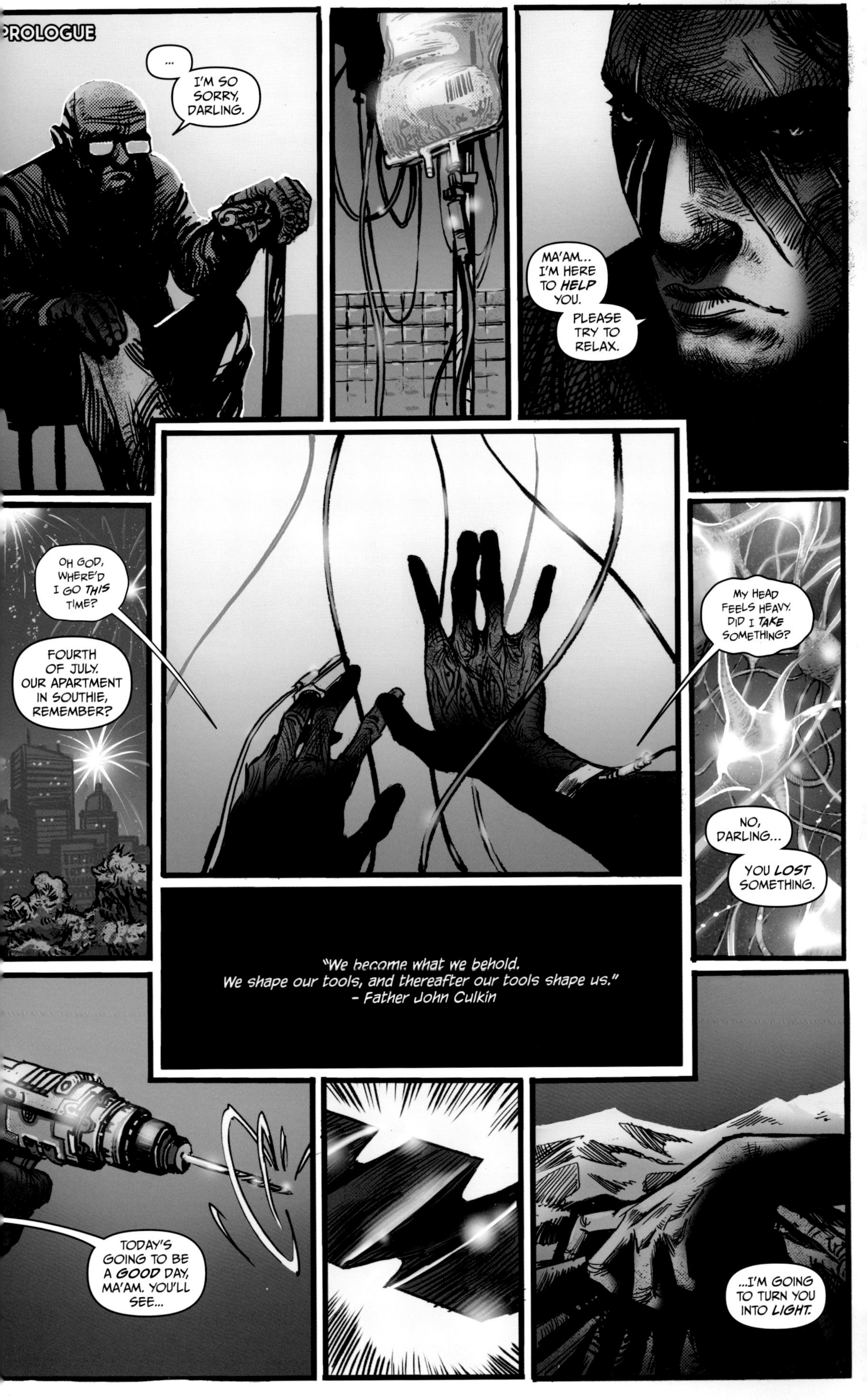
PROLOGUE
...
I'M SO SORRY, DARLING.
MA'AM... I'M HERE TO *HELP* YOU.
PLEASE TRY TO RELAX.
OH GOD, WHERE'D I GO *THIS* TIME?
FOURTH OF JULY. OUR APARTMENT IN SOUTHIE, REMEMBER?
MY HEAD FEELS HEAVY. DID I *TAKE* SOMETHING?
NO, DARLING...
YOU *LOST* SOMETHING.
"We become what we behold.
We shape our tools, and thereafter our tools shape us."
- Father John Culkin
TODAY'S GOING TO BE A *GOOD* DAY, MA'AM. YOU'LL SEE...
...I'M GOING TO TURN YOU INTO *LIGHT*.

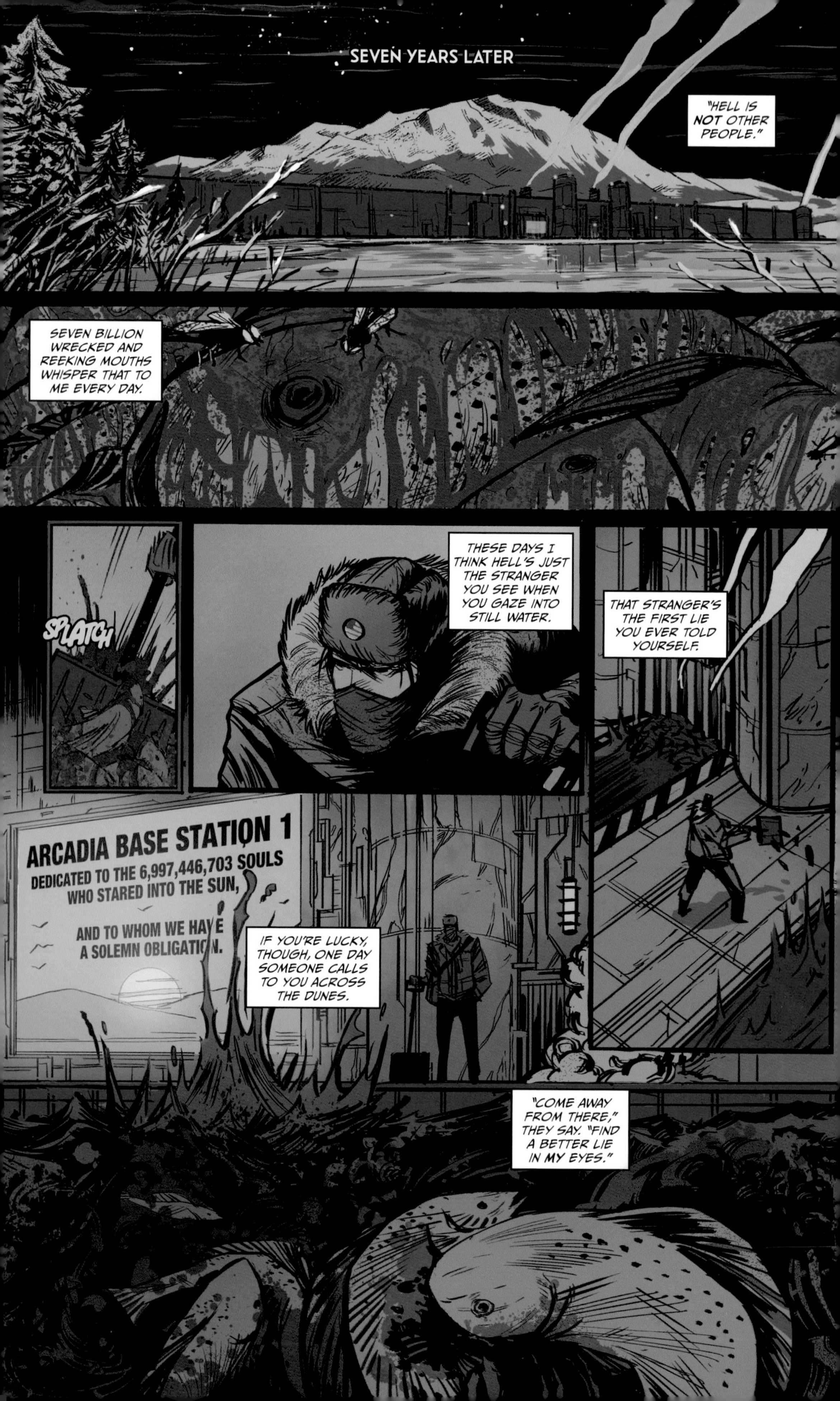
SEVEN YEARS LATER
"HELL IS NOT OTHER PEOPLE."
SEVEN BILLION WRECKED AND REEKING MOUTHS WHISPER THAT TO ME EVERY DAY.
SPLATCH
THESE DAYS I THINK HELL'S JUST THE STRANGER YOU SEE WHEN YOU GAZE INTO STILL WATER.
THAT STRANGER'S THE FIRST LIE YOU EVER TOLD YOURSELF.
ARCADIA BASE STATION 1
DEDICATED TO THE 6,997,446,703 SOULS WHO STARED INTO THE SUN,
AND TO WHOM WE HAVE A SOLEMN OBLIGATION.
IF YOU'RE LUCKY, THOUGH, ONE DAY SOMEONE CALLS TO YOU ACROSS THE DUNES.
"COME AWAY FROM THERE," THEY SAY. "FIND A BETTER LIE IN MY EYES."

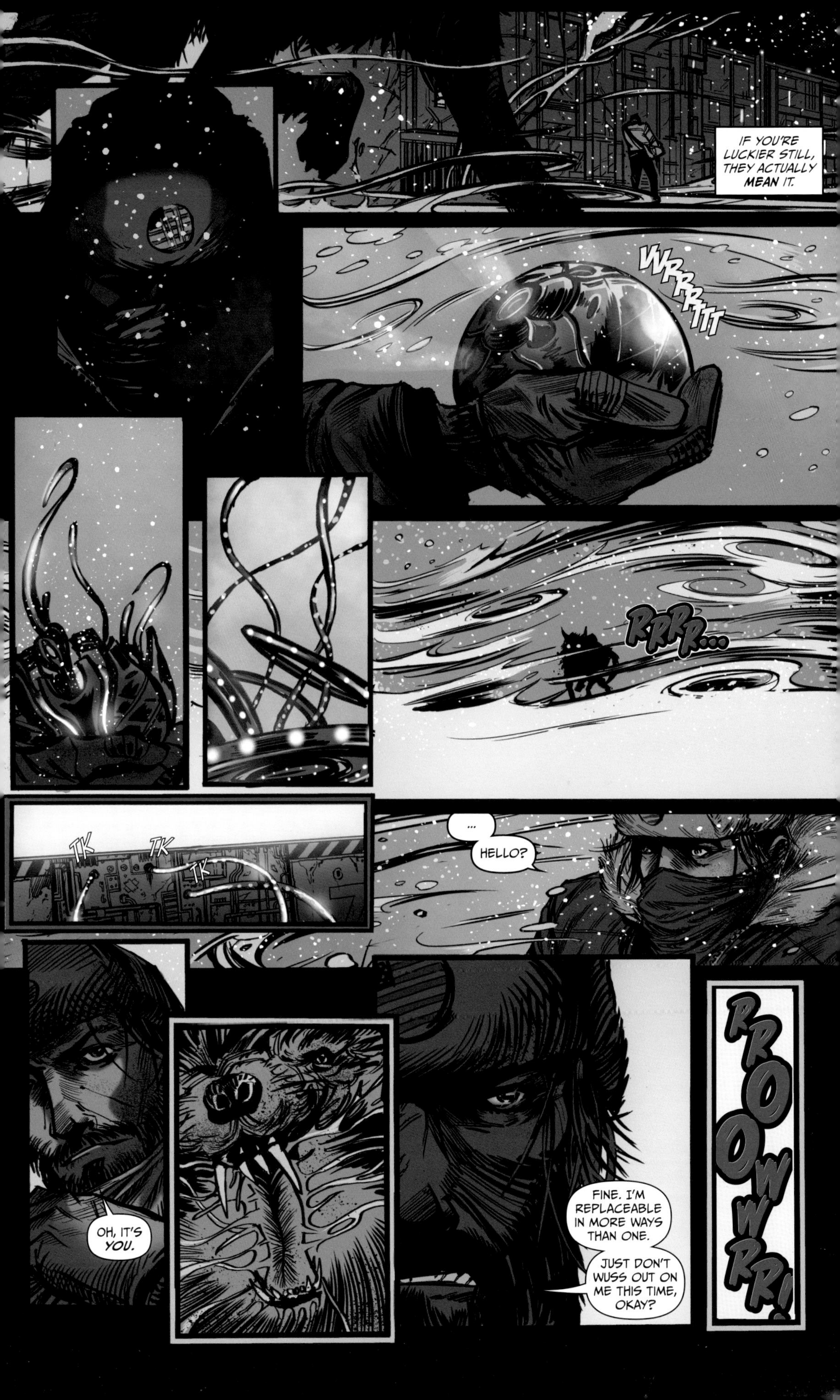
IF YOU'RE LUCKIER STILL, THEY ACTUALLY MEAN IT.
VVRRRTTT
RRRR...
TK
TK
TK
...
HELLO?
OH, IT'S YOU.
FINE. I'M REPLACEABLE IN MORE WAYS THAN ONE.
JUST DON'T WUSS OUT ON ME THIS TIME, OKAY?
RROOWWRR!

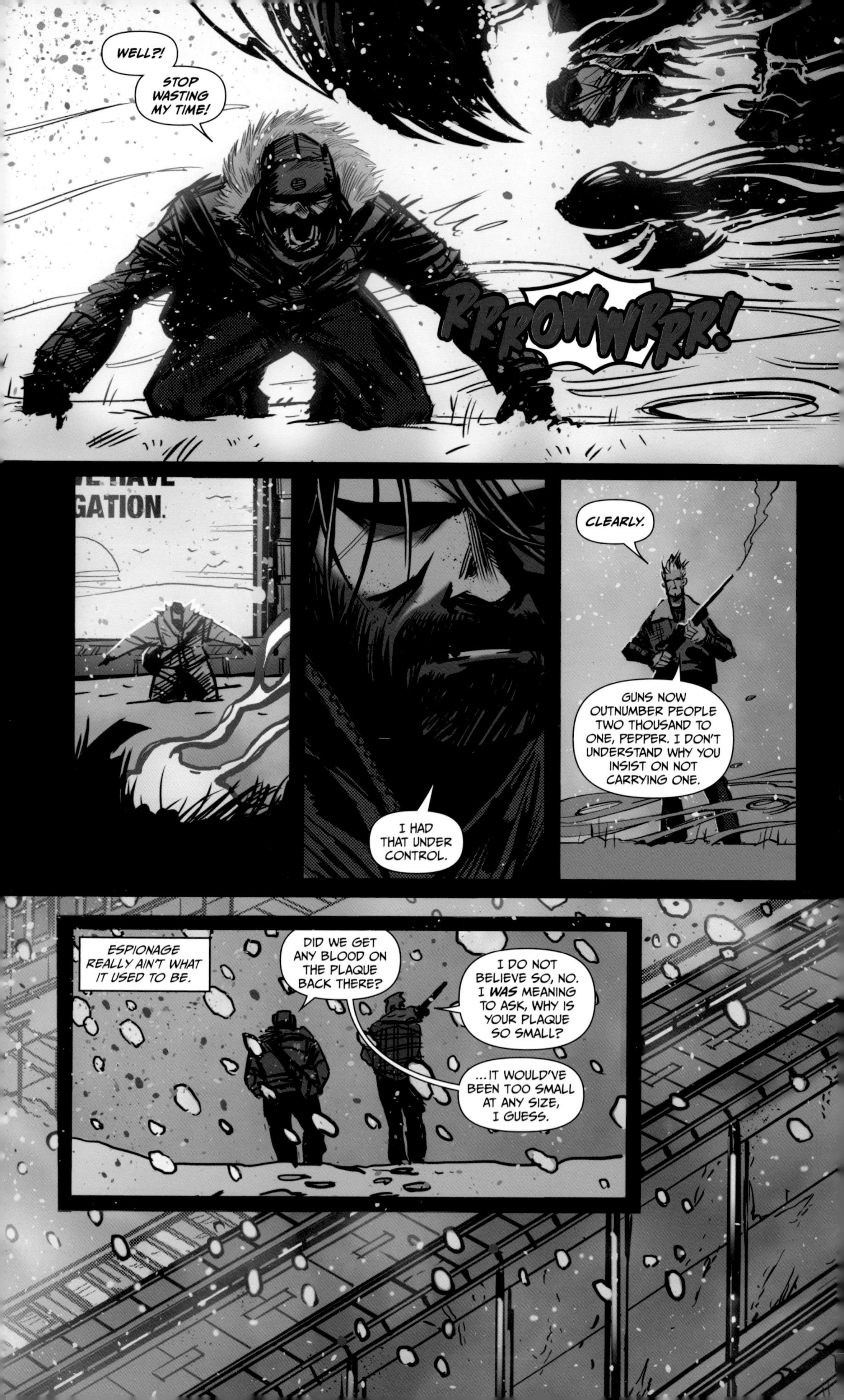

WELL?!
STOP WASTING MY TIME!
RRROWWRRR!
I HAD THAT UNDER CONTROL.
CLEARLY.
GUNS NOW OUTNUMBER PEOPLE TWO THOUSAND TO ONE, PEPPER. I DON'T UNDERSTAND WHY YOU INSIST ON NOT CARRYING ONE.
ESPIONAGE REALLY AIN'T WHAT IT USED TO BE.
DID WE GET ANY BLOOD ON THE PLAQUE BACK THERE?
I DO NOT BELIEVE SO, NO. I WAS MEANING TO ASK, WHY IS YOUR PLAQUE SO SMALL?
...IT WOULD'VE BEEN TOO SMALL AT ANY SIZE, I GUESS.

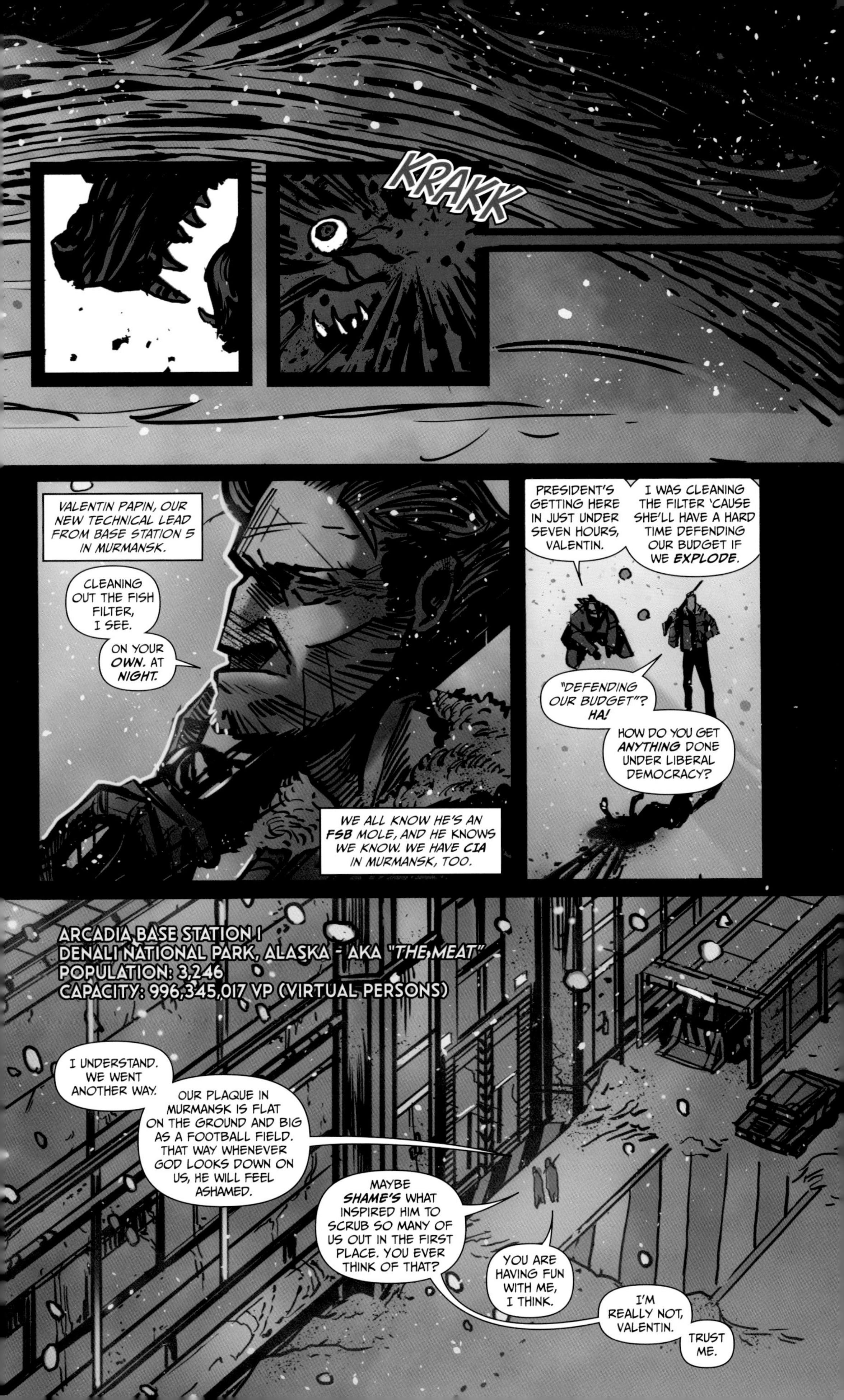
KRAKK
VALENTIN PAPIN, OUR NEW TECHNICAL LEAD FROM BASE STATION 5 IN MURMANSK.
CLEANING OUT THE FISH FILTER, I SEE.
ON YOUR OWN. AT NIGHT.
WE ALL KNOW HE'S AN FSB MOLE, AND HE KNOWS WE KNOW. WE HAVE CIA IN MURMANSK, TOO.
PRESIDENT'S GETTING HERE IN JUST UNDER SEVEN HOURS, VALENTIN.
I WAS CLEANING THE FILTER 'CAUSE SHE'LL HAVE A HARD TIME DEFENDING OUR BUDGET IF WE EXPLODE.
"DEFENDING OUR BUDGET"? HA!
HOW DO YOU GET ANYTHING DONE UNDER LIBERAL DEMOCRACY?
ARCADIA BASE STATION 1
DENALI NATIONAL PARK, ALASKA - AKA "THE MEAT"
POPULATION: 3,246
CAPACITY: 996,345,017 VP (VIRTUAL PERSONS)
I UNDERSTAND. WE WENT ANOTHER WAY.
OUR PLAQUE IN MURMANSK IS FLAT ON THE GROUND AND BIG AS A FOOTBALL FIELD. THAT WAY WHENEVER GOD LOOKS DOWN ON US, HE WILL FEEL ASHAMED.
MAYBE SHAME'S WHAT INSPIRED HIM TO SCRUB SO MANY OF US OUT IN THE FIRST PLACE. YOU EVER THINK OF THAT?
YOU ARE HAVING FUN WITH ME, I THINK.
I'M REALLY NOT, VALENTIN.
TRUST ME.

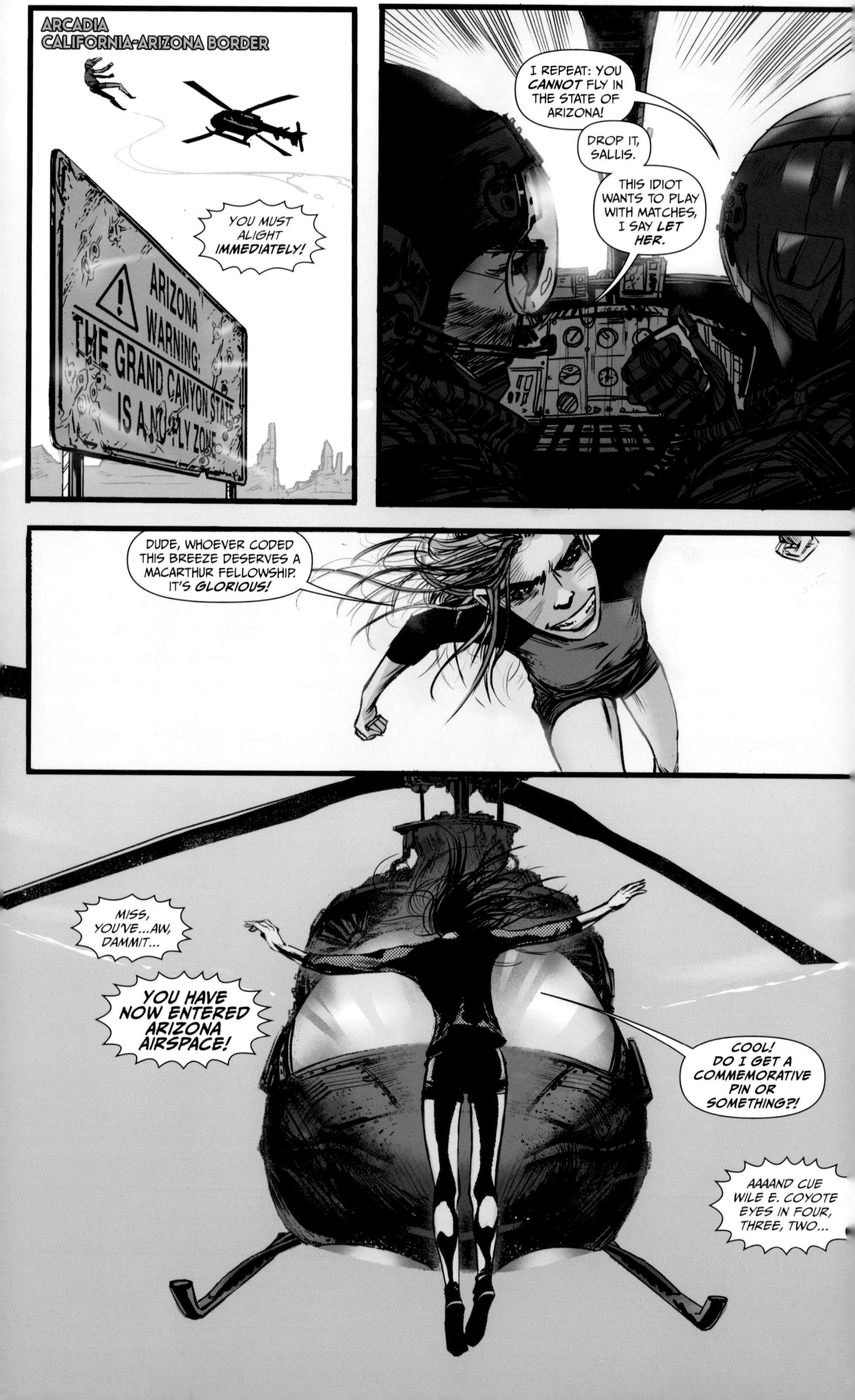
ARCADIA
CALIFORNIA-ARIZONA BORDER
YOU MUST ALIGHT IMMEDIATELY!
ARIZONA WARNING: THE GRAND CANYON STATE IS A NO-FLY ZONE
I REPEAT: YOU CANNOT FLY IN THE STATE OF ARIZONA!
DROP IT, SALLIS.
THIS IDIOT WANTS TO PLAY WITH MATCHES, I SAY LET HER.
DUDE, WHOEVER CODED THIS BREEZE DESERVES A MACARTHUR FELLOWSHIP. IT'S GLORIOUS!
MISS, YOU'VE...AW, DAMMIT...
YOU HAVE NOW ENTERED ARIZONA AIRSPACE!
COOL! DO I GET A COMMEMORATIVE PIN OR SOMETHING?!
AAAAND CUE WILE E. COYOTE EYES IN FOUR, THREE, TWO...

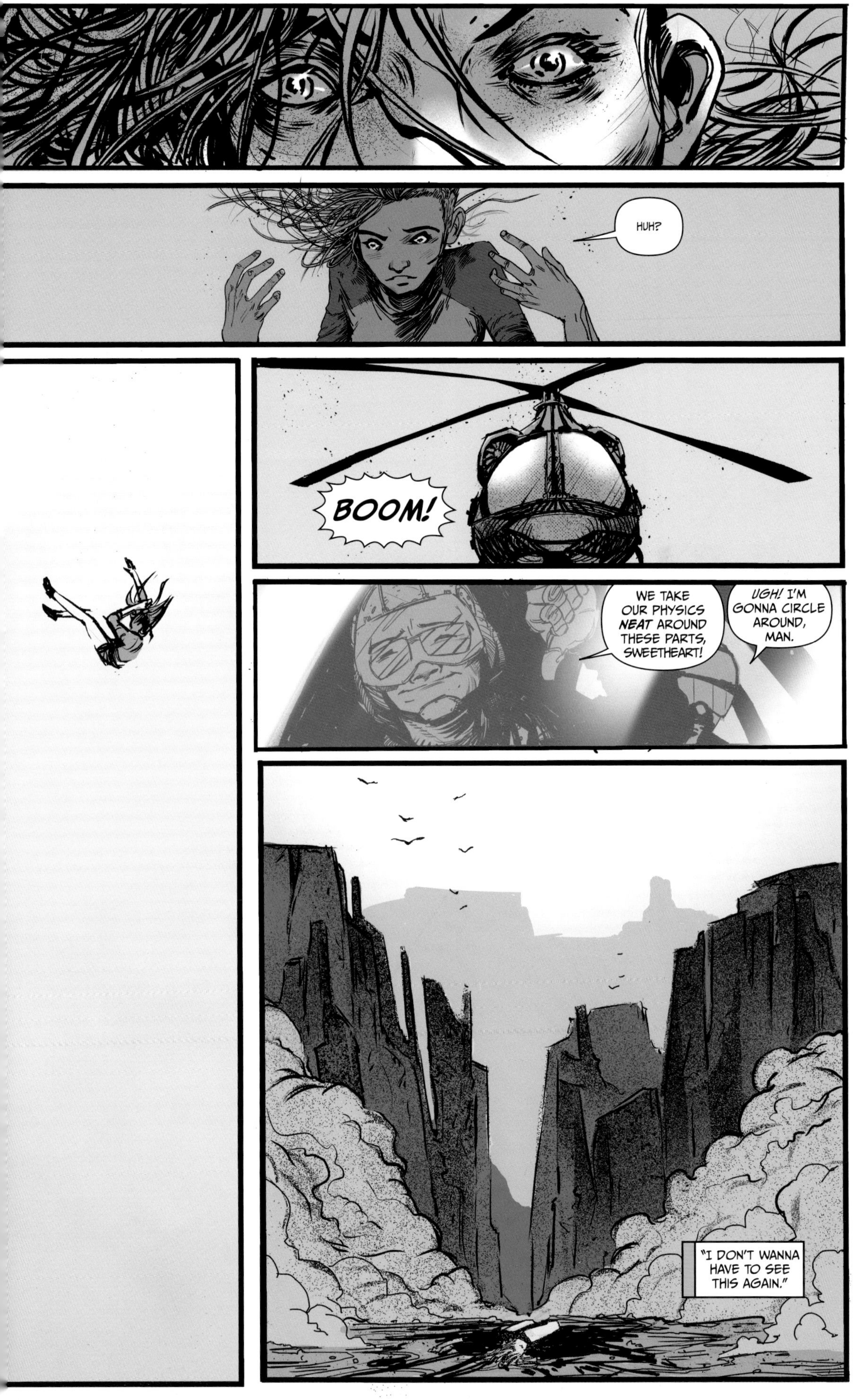

HUH?
BOOM!
WE TAKE OUR PHYSICS NEAT AROUND THESE PARTS, SWEETHEART!
UGH! I'M GONNA CIRCLE AROUND, MAN.
"I DON'T WANNA HAVE TO SEE THIS AGAIN."

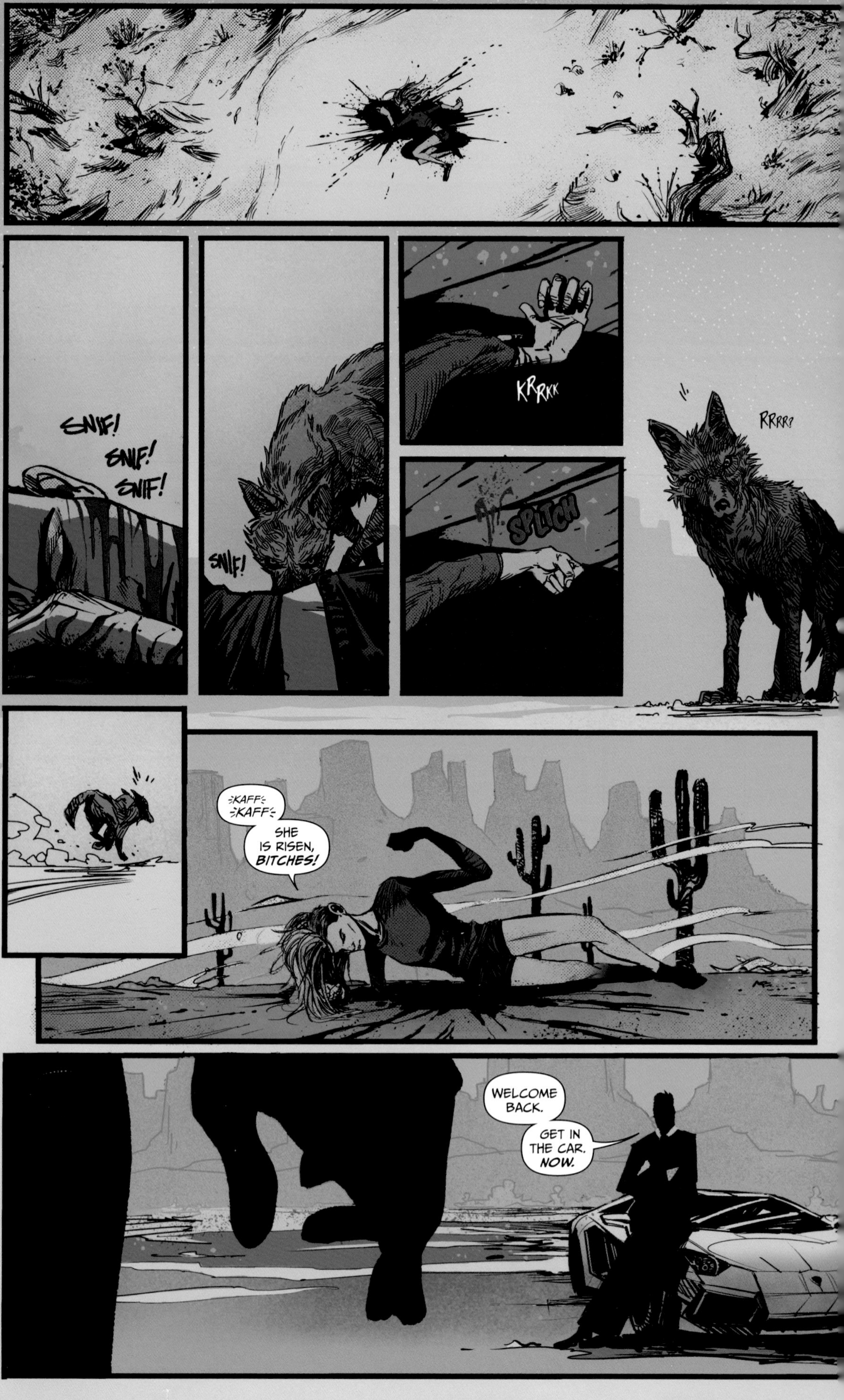
SNIF!
SNIF!
SNIF!
SNIF!
KRRKK
SPLTCH
RRRR?
KAFF KAFF
SHE IS RISEN, BITCHES!
WELCOME BACK.
GET IN THE CAR. NOW.

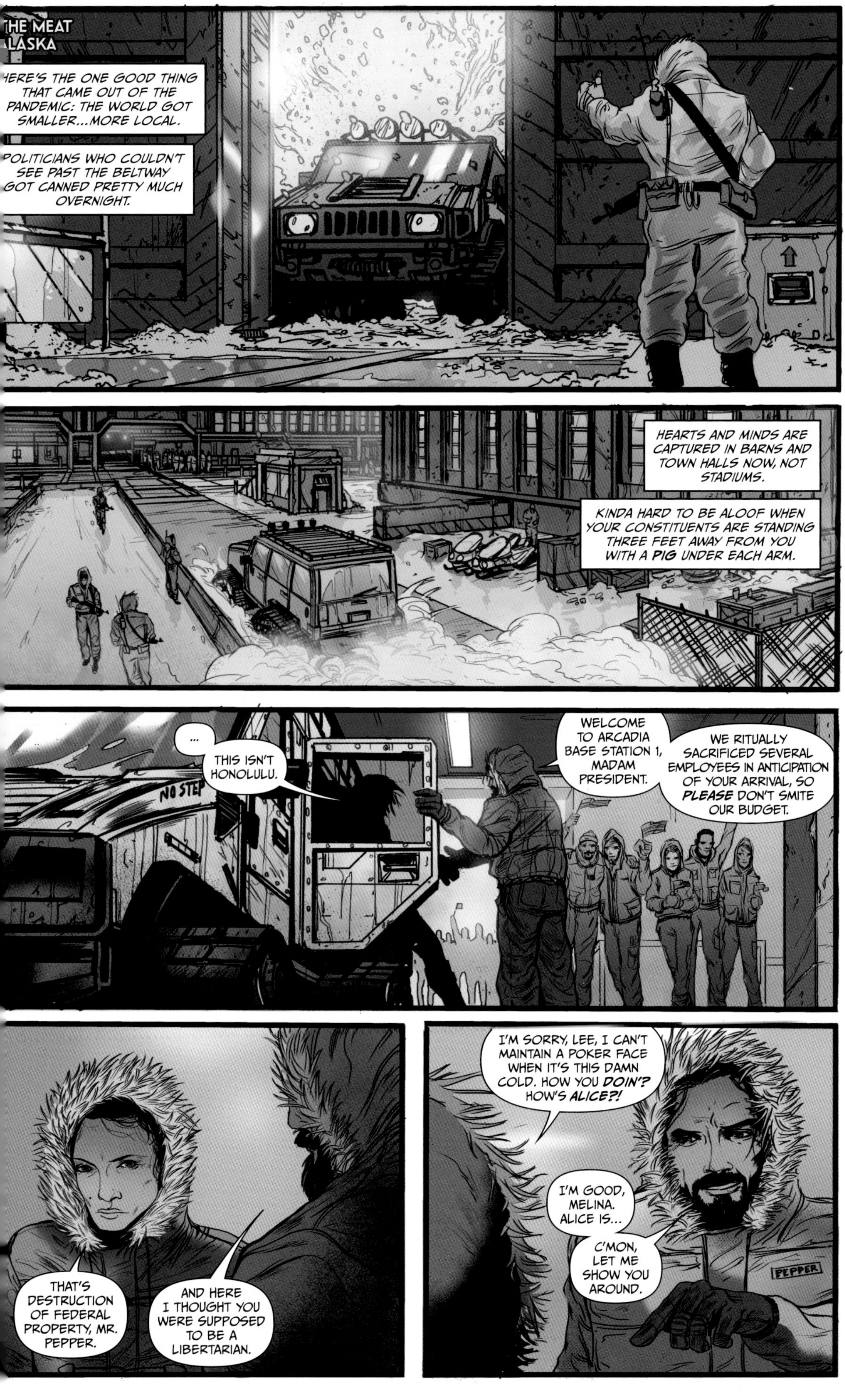
THE MEAT
ALASKA
HERE'S THE ONE GOOD THING THAT CAME OUT OF THE PANDEMIC: THE WORLD GOT SMALLER...MORE LOCAL.
POLITICIANS WHO COULDN'T SEE PAST THE BELTWAY GOT CANNED PRETTY MUCH OVERNIGHT.
HEARTS AND MINDS ARE CAPTURED IN BARNS AND TOWN HALLS NOW, NOT STADIUMS.
KINDA HARD TO BE ALOOF WHEN YOUR CONSTITUENTS ARE STANDING THREE FEET AWAY FROM YOU WITH A PIG UNDER EACH ARM.
NO STEP
...
THIS ISN'T HONOLULU.
WELCOME TO ARCADIA BASE STATION 1, MADAM PRESIDENT.
WE RITUALLY SACRIFICED SEVERAL EMPLOYEES IN ANTICIPATION OF YOUR ARRIVAL, SO PLEASE DON'T SMITE OUR BUDGET.
THAT'S DESTRUCTION OF FEDERAL PROPERTY, MR. PEPPER.
AND HERE I THOUGHT YOU WERE SUPPOSED TO BE A LIBERTARIAN.
I'M SORRY, LEE, I CAN'T MAINTAIN A POKER FACE WHEN IT'S THIS DAMN COLD. HOW YOU DOIN'? HOW'S ALICE?!
I'M GOOD, MELINA. ALICE IS...
C'MON, LET ME SHOW YOU AROUND.
PEPPER

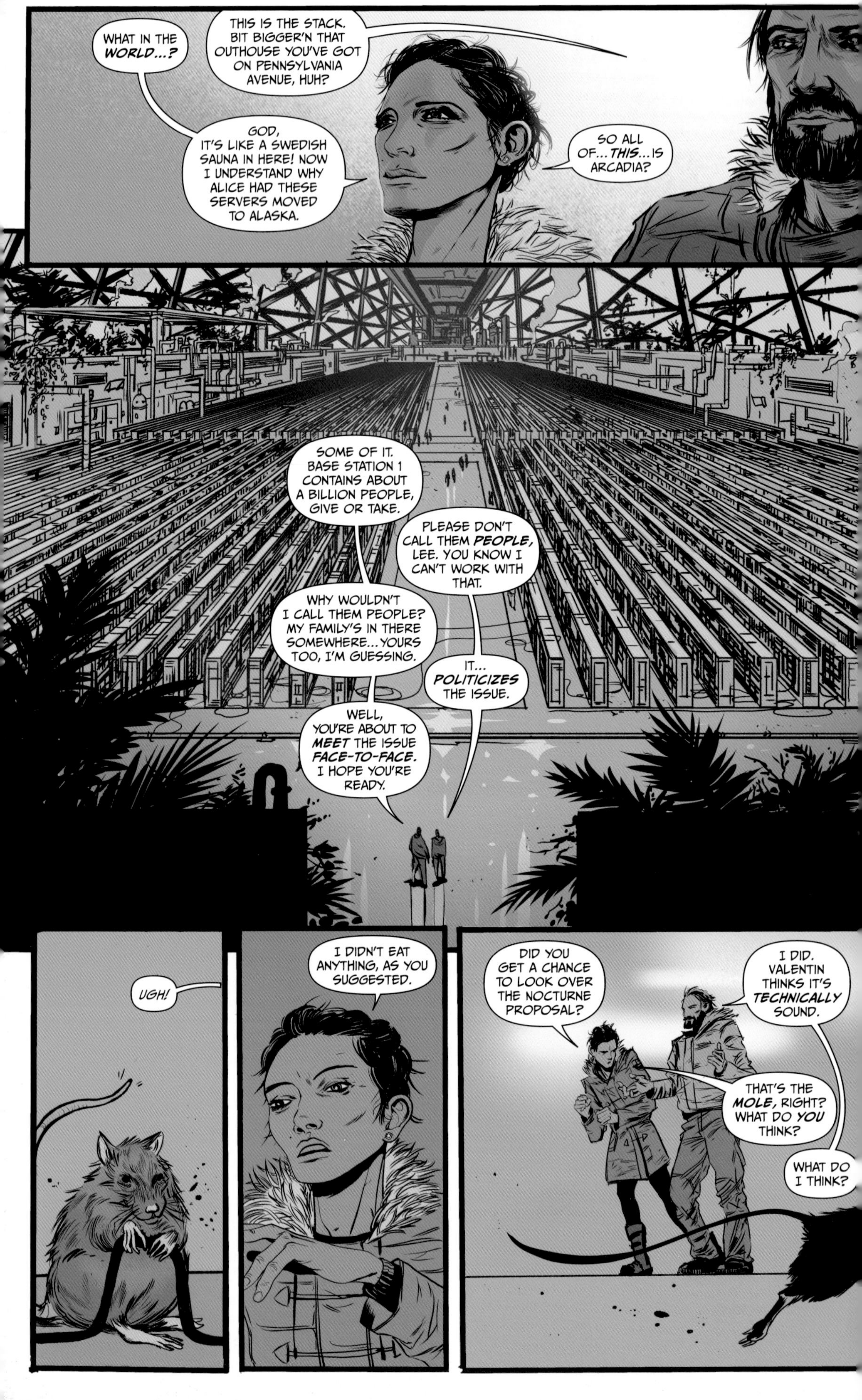
WHAT IN THE WORLD...?
THIS IS THE STACK. BIT BIGGER'N THAT OUTHOUSE YOU'VE GOT ON PENNSYLVANIA AVENUE, HUH?
GOD, IT'S LIKE A SWEDISH SAUNA IN HERE! NOW I UNDERSTAND WHY ALICE HAD THESE SERVERS MOVED TO ALASKA.
SO ALL OF...THIS...IS ARCADIA?
SOME OF IT. BASE STATION 1 CONTAINS ABOUT A BILLION PEOPLE, GIVE OR TAKE.
PLEASE DON'T CALL THEM PEOPLE, LEE. YOU KNOW I CAN'T WORK WITH THAT.
WHY WOULDN'T I CALL THEM PEOPLE? MY FAMILY'S IN THERE SOMEWHERE... YOURS TOO, I'M GUESSING.
IT... POLITICIZES THE ISSUE.
WELL, YOU'RE ABOUT TO MEET THE ISSUE FACE-TO-FACE. I HOPE YOU'RE READY.
UGH!
I DIDN'T EAT ANYTHING, AS YOU SUGGESTED.
DID YOU GET A CHANCE TO LOOK OVER THE NOCTURNE PROPOSAL?
I DID. VALENTIN THINKS IT'S TECHNICALLY SOUND.
THAT'S THE MOLE, RIGHT? WHAT DO YOU THINK?
WHAT DO I THINK?

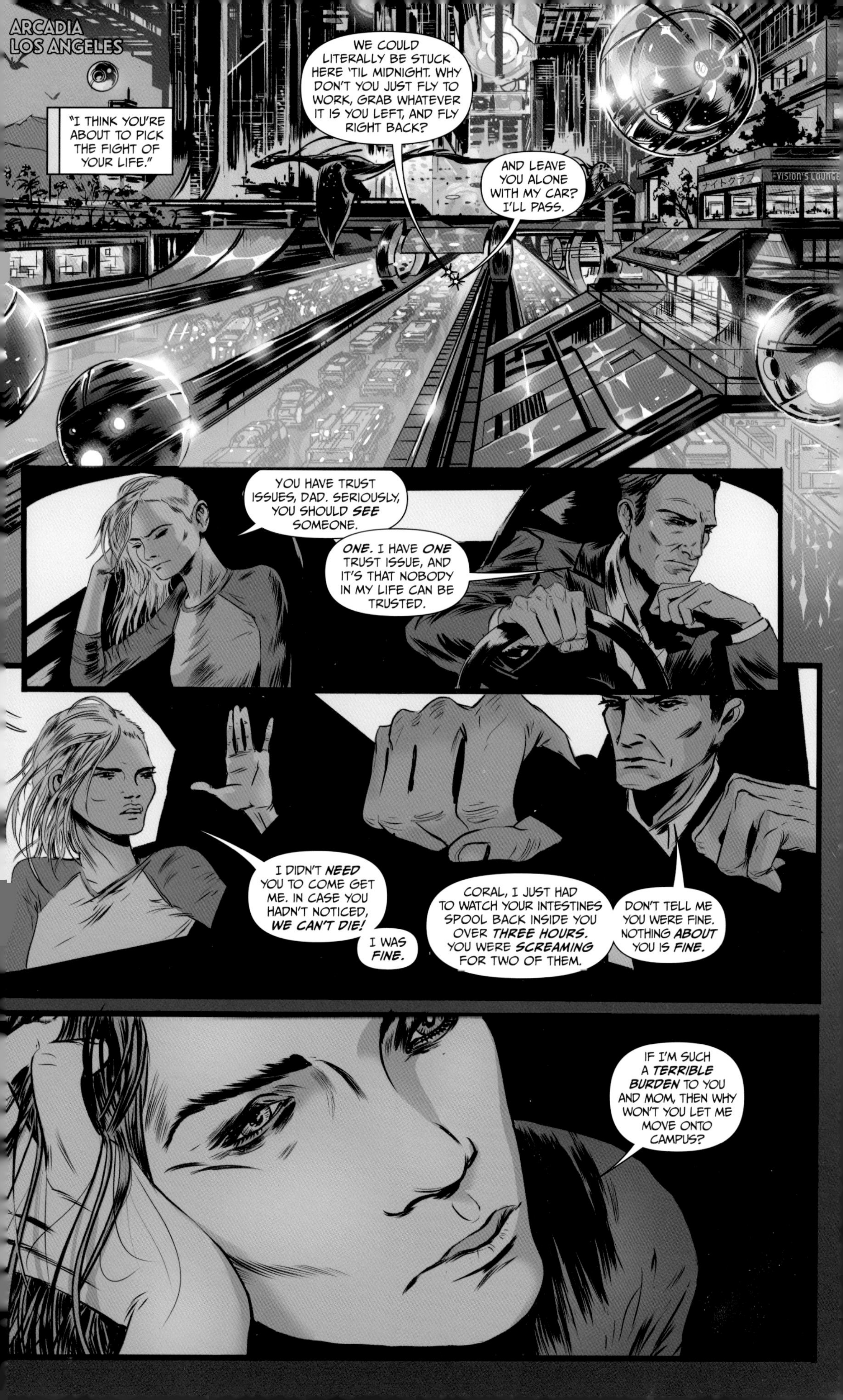
ARCADIA LOS ANGELES
"I THINK YOU'RE ABOUT TO PICK THE FIGHT OF YOUR LIFE."
WE COULD LITERALLY BE STUCK HERE 'TIL MIDNIGHT. WHY DON'T YOU JUST FLY TO WORK, GRAB WHATEVER IT IS YOU LEFT, AND FLY RIGHT BACK?
AND LEAVE YOU ALONE WITH MY CAR? I'LL PASS.
VISION'S LOUNGE
YOU HAVE TRUST ISSUES, DAD. SERIOUSLY, YOU SHOULD SEE SOMEONE.
ONE. I HAVE ONE TRUST ISSUE, AND IT'S THAT NOBODY IN MY LIFE CAN BE TRUSTED.
I DIDN'T NEED YOU TO COME GET ME. IN CASE YOU HADN'T NOTICED, WE CAN'T DIE!
I WAS FINE.
CORAL, I JUST HAD TO WATCH YOUR INTESTINES SPOOL BACK INSIDE YOU OVER THREE HOURS. YOU WERE SCREAMING FOR TWO OF THEM.
DON'T TELL ME YOU WERE FINE. NOTHING ABOUT YOU IS FINE.
IF I'M SUCH A TERRIBLE BURDEN TO YOU AND MOM, THEN WHY WON'T YOU LET ME MOVE ONTO CAMPUS?

SO YOU CAN SPEND YOUR NIGHTS DOING STRYCHNINE SHOTS WITH A BUNCH OF HORNY FRAT BROS?! I DON'T THINK SO.

OH, WHAT *IS* THIS *BULL...?!*

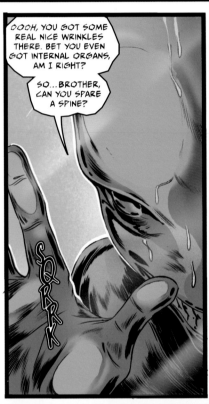

OOOH, YOU GOT SOME REAL NICE WRINKLES THERE. BET YOU EVEN GOT INTERNAL ORGANS, AM I RIGHT?

SO...BROTHER, CAN YOU SPARE A SPINE?

SQRAKK

WHERE DID *YOU* COME FROM?!

NOW *THAT* IS A QUESTION WITH A LOT OF MOVING PARTS.

PLEASE GET YOUR HANDS OFF OF MY CAR. YOU'RE, UMM...YOU'RE *LEAKING* A LITTLE BIT.

HEY, IT'S ALL *GOOD!* THIS GUNK'LL *DE-REZ* COMPLETELY IN ABOUT FIFTEEN MINUTES.

SO WE HAVE YOU TO THANK FOR THIS NIGHTMARE?

YUP. *"RESOLUTION NOW"* PROTEST ALL THE WAY UP TO THE SAN DIEGO FREEWAY. WORK OF ART IF YOU ASK ME.

AND YOU THINK PISSING OFF THOUSANDS OF TIRED PEOPLE IS A GOOD WAY TO OPEN A DIALOGUE?

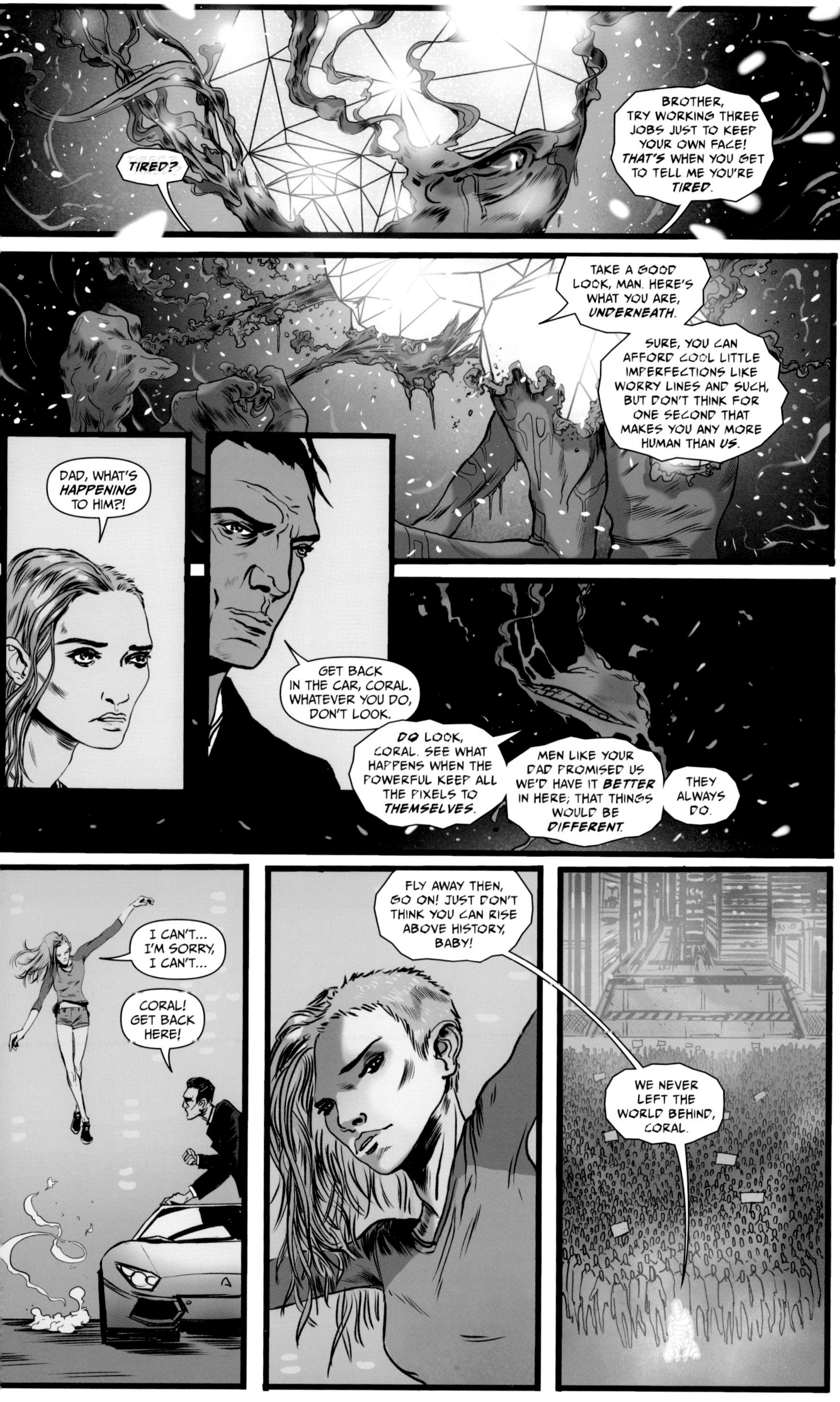
TIRED?
BROTHER, TRY WORKING THREE JOBS JUST TO KEEP YOUR OWN FACE! THAT'S WHEN YOU GET TO TELL ME YOU'RE TIRED.
TAKE A GOOD LOOK, MAN. HERE'S WHAT YOU ARE, UNDERNEATH.
SURE, YOU CAN AFFORD COOL LITTLE IMPERFECTIONS LIKE WORRY LINES AND SUCH, BUT DON'T THINK FOR ONE SECOND THAT MAKES YOU ANY MORE HUMAN THAN US.
DAD, WHAT'S HAPPENING TO HIM?!
GET BACK IN THE CAR, CORAL. WHATEVER YOU DO, DON'T LOOK.
DO LOOK, CORAL. SEE WHAT HAPPENS WHEN THE POWERFUL KEEP ALL THE PIXELS TO THEMSELVES.
MEN LIKE YOUR DAD PROMISED US WE'D HAVE IT BETTER IN HERE; THAT THINGS WOULD BE DIFFERENT.
THEY ALWAYS DO.
I CAN'T... I'M SORRY, I CAN'T...
CORAL! GET BACK HERE!
FLY AWAY THEN, GO ON! JUST DON'T THINK YOU CAN RISE ABOVE HISTORY, BABY!
WE NEVER LEFT THE WORLD BEHIND, CORAL.

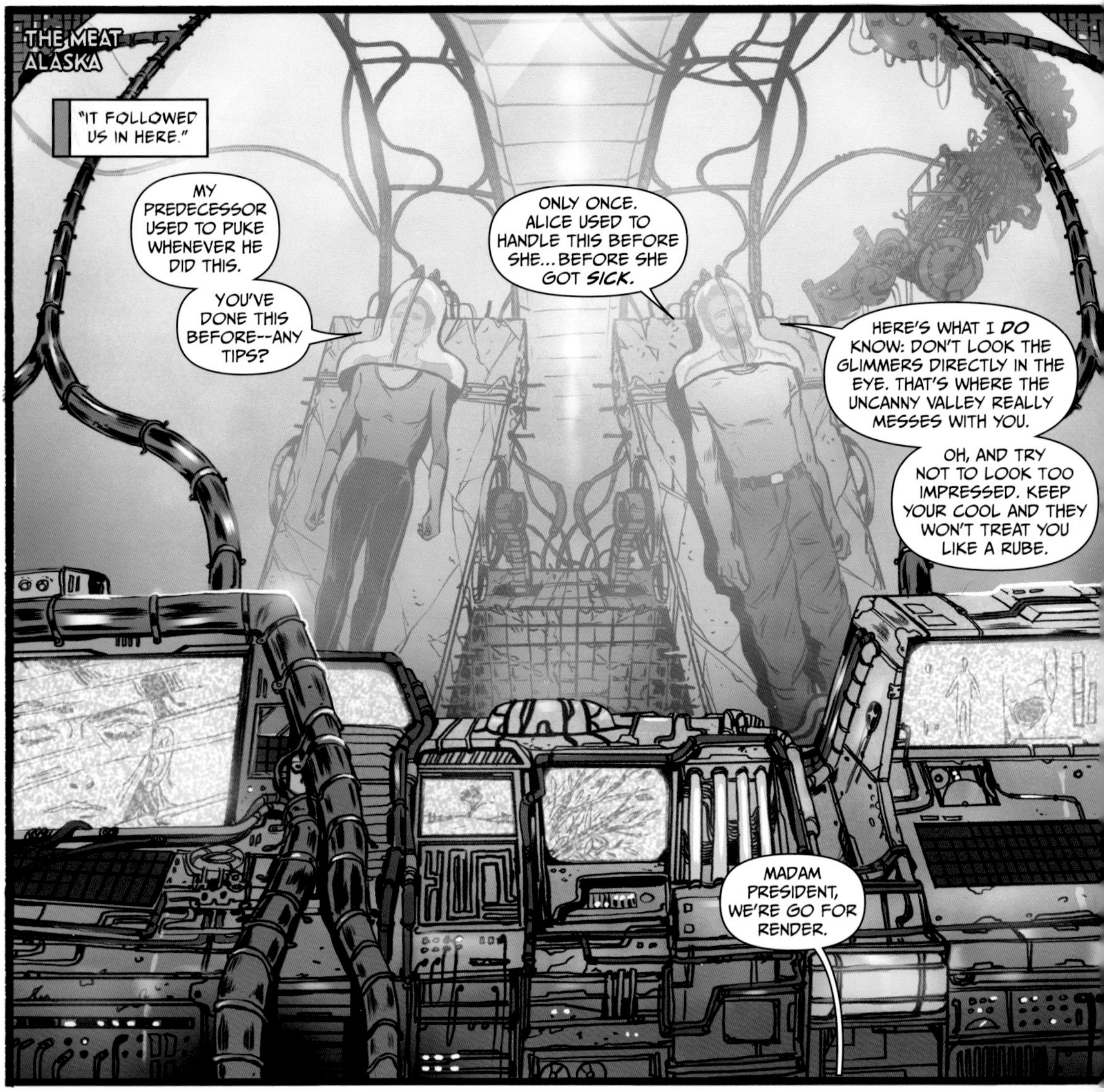
THE MEAT
ALASKA
"IT FOLLOWED US IN HERE."
MY PREDECESSOR USED TO PUKE WHENEVER HE DID THIS.
YOU'VE DONE THIS BEFORE--ANY TIPS?
ONLY ONCE. ALICE USED TO HANDLE THIS BEFORE SHE...BEFORE SHE GOT *SICK.*
HERE'S WHAT I *DO* KNOW: DON'T LOOK THE GLIMMERS DIRECTLY IN THE EYE. THAT'S WHERE THE UNCANNY VALLEY REALLY MESSES WITH YOU.
OH, AND TRY NOT TO LOOK TOO IMPRESSED. KEEP YOUR COOL AND THEY WON'T TREAT YOU LIKE A RUBE.
MADAM PRESIDENT, WE'RE GO FOR RENDER.

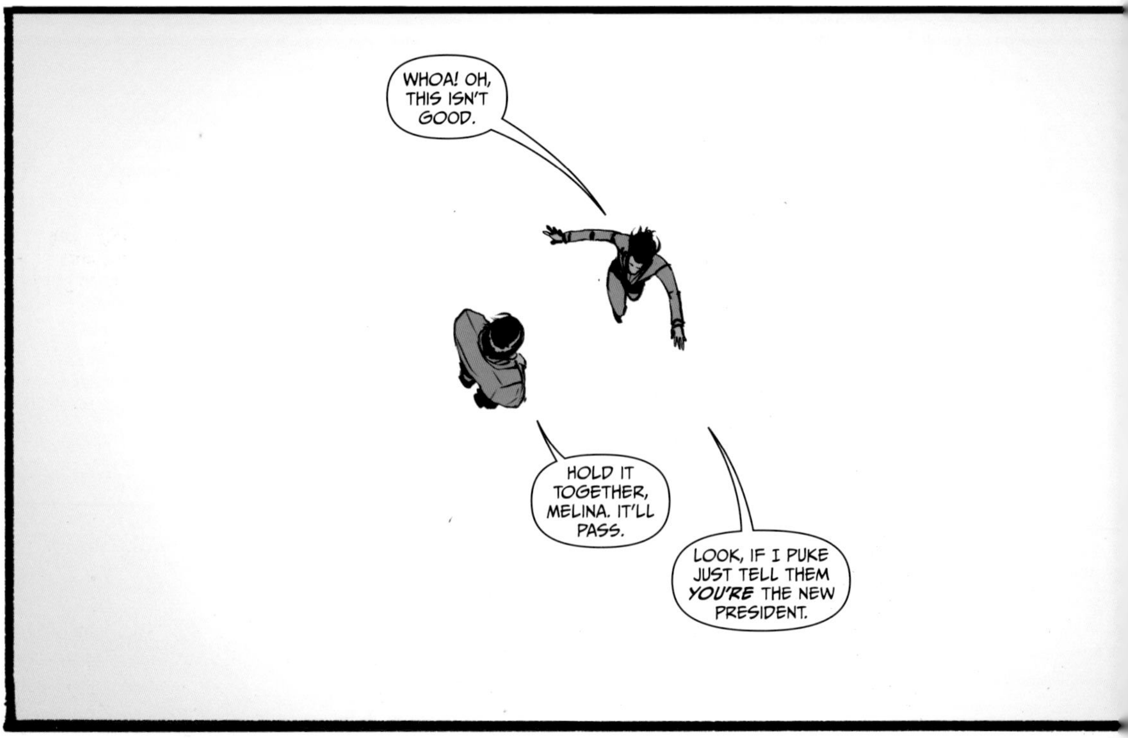
WHOA! OH, THIS ISN'T GOOD.
HOLD IT TOGETHER, MELINA. IT'LL PASS.
LOOK, IF I PUKE JUST TELL THEM *YOU'RE* THE NEW PRESIDENT.

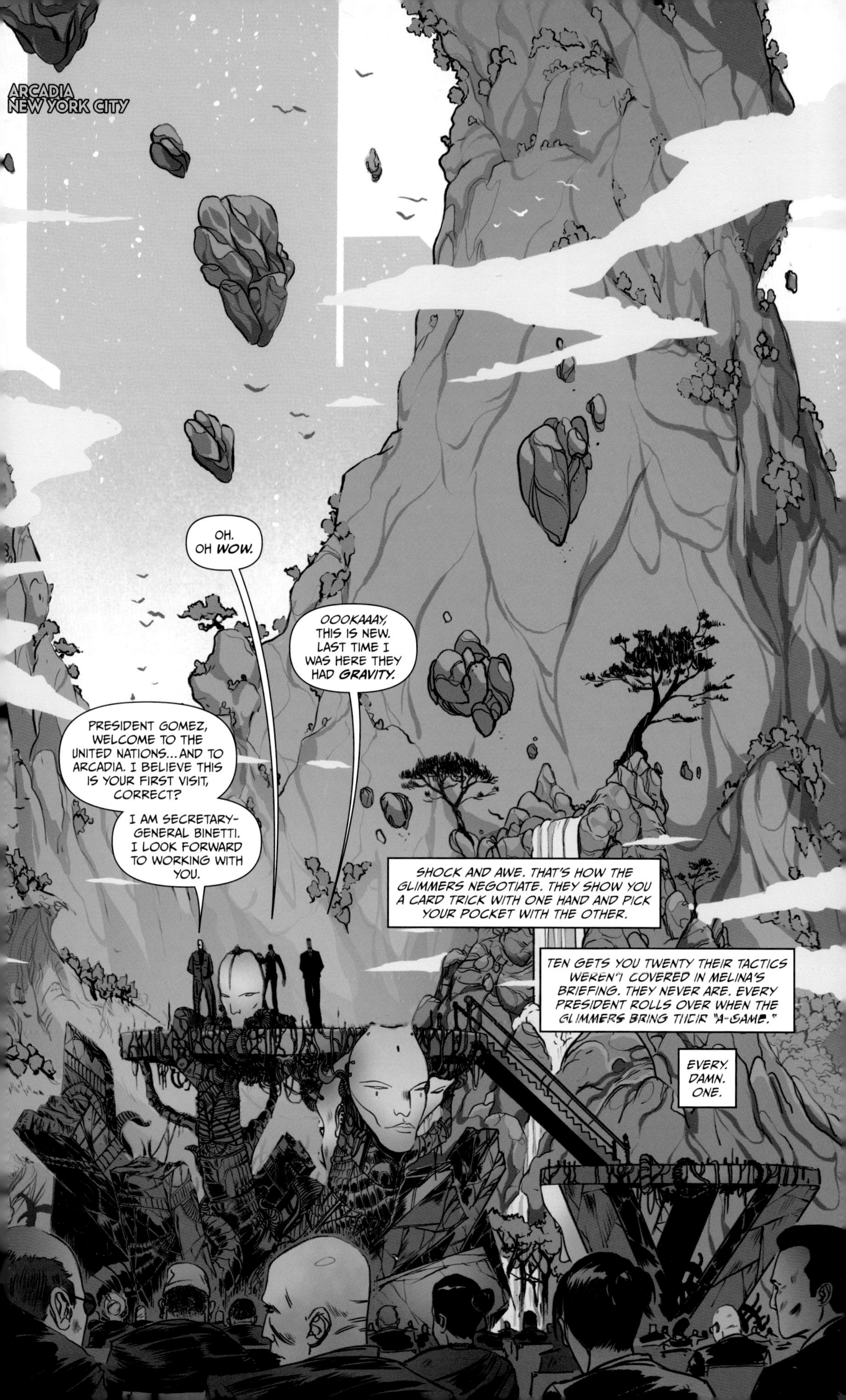
ARCADIA
NEW YORK CITY
OH. OH WOW.
OOOKAAAY, THIS IS NEW. LAST TIME I WAS HERE THEY HAD GRAVITY.
PRESIDENT GOMEZ, WELCOME TO THE UNITED NATIONS... AND TO ARCADIA. I BELIEVE THIS IS YOUR FIRST VISIT, CORRECT?
I AM SECRETARY-GENERAL BINETTI. I LOOK FORWARD TO WORKING WITH YOU.
SHOCK AND AWE. THAT'S HOW THE GLIMMERS NEGOTIATE. THEY SHOW YOU A CARD TRICK WITH ONE HAND AND PICK YOUR POCKET WITH THE OTHER.
TEN GETS YOU TWENTY THEIR TACTICS WEREN'T COVERED IN MELINA'S BRIEFING. THEY NEVER ARE. EVERY PRESIDENT ROLLS OVER WHEN THE GLIMMERS BRING THEIR "A-GAME."
EVERY. DAMN. ONE.

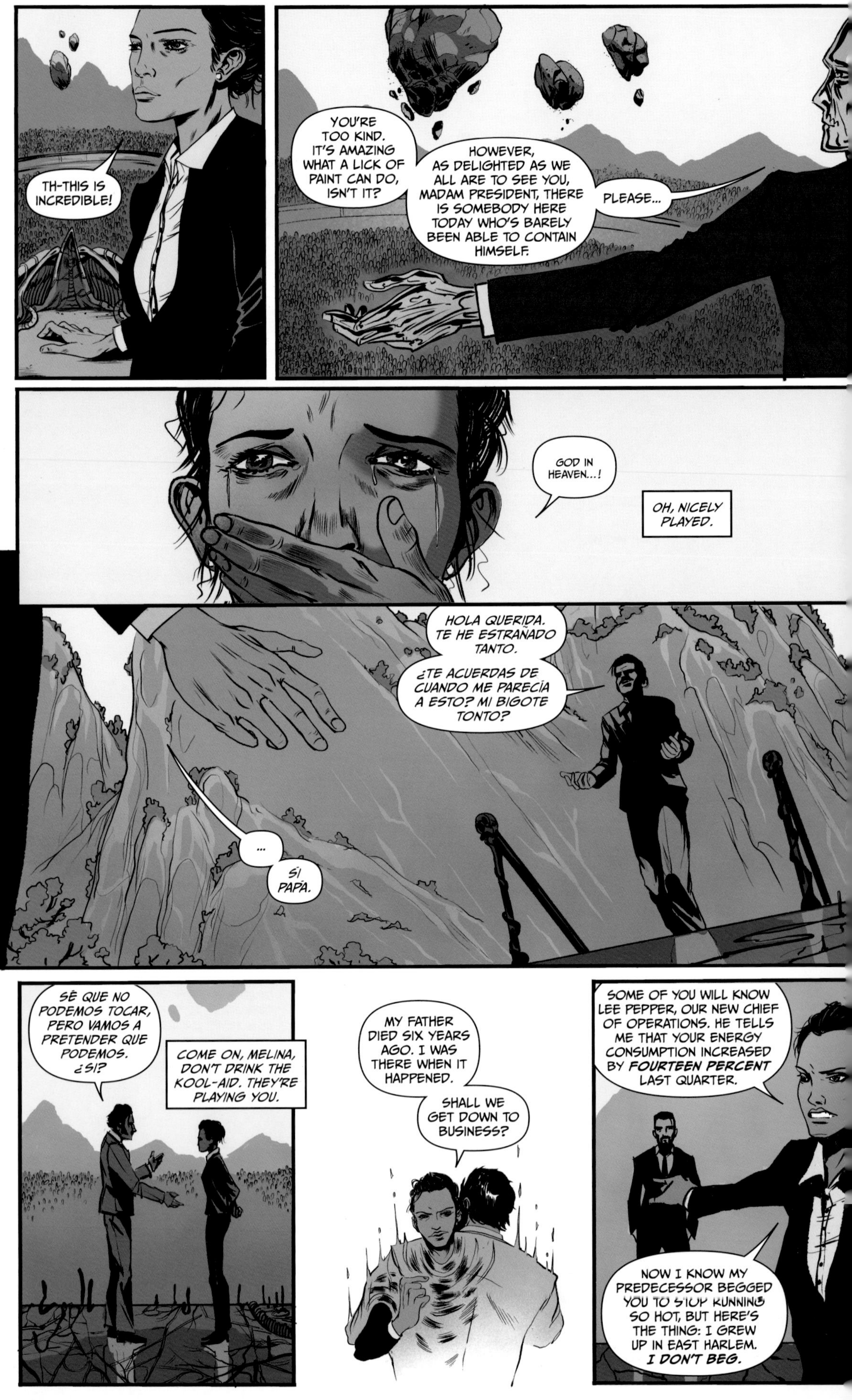
TH-THIS IS INCREDIBLE!
YOU'RE TOO KIND. IT'S AMAZING WHAT A LICK OF PAINT CAN DO, ISN'T IT?
HOWEVER, AS DELIGHTED AS WE ALL ARE TO SEE YOU, MADAM PRESIDENT, THERE IS SOMEBODY HERE TODAY WHO'S BARELY BEEN ABLE TO CONTAIN HIMSELF.
PLEASE...
GOD IN HEAVEN...!
OH, NICELY PLAYED.
HOLA QUERIDA. TE HE ESTRAÑADO TANTO.
¿TE ACUERDAS DE CUANDO ME PARECÍA A ESTO? MI BIGOTE TONTO?
...
SÍ PAPÁ.
SÉ QUE NO PODEMOS TOCAR, PERO VAMOS A PRETENDER QUE PODEMOS. ¿SÍ?
COME ON, MELINA, DON'T DRINK THE KOOL-AID. THEY'RE PLAYING YOU.
MY FATHER DIED SIX YEARS AGO. I WAS THERE WHEN IT HAPPENED.
SHALL WE GET DOWN TO BUSINESS?
SOME OF YOU WILL KNOW LEE PEPPER, OUR NEW CHIEF OF OPERATIONS. HE TELLS ME THAT YOUR ENERGY CONSUMPTION INCREASED BY FOURTEEN PERCENT LAST QUARTER.
NOW I KNOW MY PREDECESSOR BEGGED YOU TO STOP RUNNING SO HOT, BUT HERE'S THE THING: I GREW UP IN EAST HARLEM. I DON'T BEG.

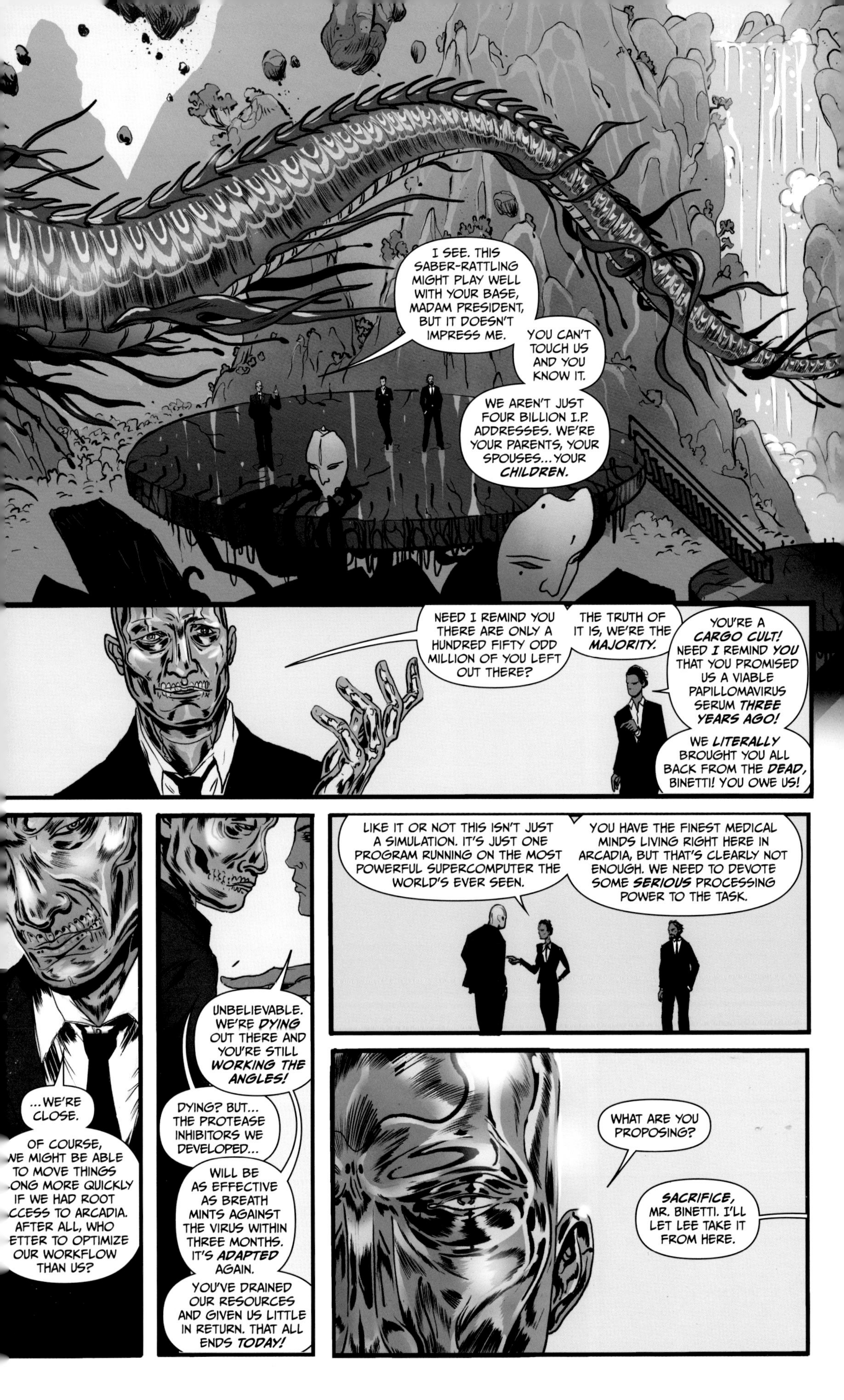
I SEE. THIS SABER-RATTLING MIGHT PLAY WELL WITH YOUR BASE, MADAM PRESIDENT, BUT IT DOESN'T IMPRESS ME.
YOU CAN'T TOUCH US AND YOU KNOW IT.
WE AREN'T JUST FOUR BILLION I.P. ADDRESSES. WE'RE YOUR PARENTS, YOUR SPOUSES...YOUR *CHILDREN.*
NEED I REMIND YOU THERE ARE ONLY A HUNDRED FIFTY ODD MILLION OF YOU LEFT OUT THERE?
THE TRUTH OF IT IS, WE'RE THE *MAJORITY.*
YOU'RE A *CARGO CULT!* NEED *I* REMIND *YOU* THAT YOU PROMISED US A VIABLE PAPILLOMAVIRUS SERUM *THREE YEARS AGO!*
WE *LITERALLY* BROUGHT YOU ALL BACK FROM THE *DEAD,* BINETTI! YOU OWE US!
...WE'RE CLOSE.
OF COURSE, WE MIGHT BE ABLE TO MOVE THINGS ALONG MORE QUICKLY IF WE HAD ROOT ACCESS TO ARCADIA. AFTER ALL, WHO BETTER TO OPTIMIZE OUR WORKFLOW THAN US?
UNBELIEVABLE. WE'RE *DYING* OUT THERE AND YOU'RE STILL *WORKING THE ANGLES!*
DYING? BUT... THE PROTEASE INHIBITORS WE DEVELOPED...
WILL BE AS EFFECTIVE AS BREATH MINTS AGAINST THE VIRUS WITHIN THREE MONTHS. IT'S *ADAPTED* AGAIN.
YOU'VE DRAINED OUR RESOURCES AND GIVEN US LITTLE IN RETURN. THAT ALL ENDS *TODAY!*
LIKE IT OR NOT THIS ISN'T JUST A SIMULATION. IT'S JUST ONE PROGRAM RUNNING ON THE MOST POWERFUL SUPERCOMPUTER THE WORLD'S EVER SEEN.
YOU HAVE THE FINEST MEDICAL MINDS LIVING RIGHT HERE IN ARCADIA, BUT THAT'S CLEARLY NOT ENOUGH. WE NEED TO DEVOTE SOME *SERIOUS* PROCESSING POWER TO THE TASK.
WHAT ARE YOU PROPOSING?
SACRIFICE, MR. BINETTI. I'LL LET LEE TAKE IT FROM HERE.

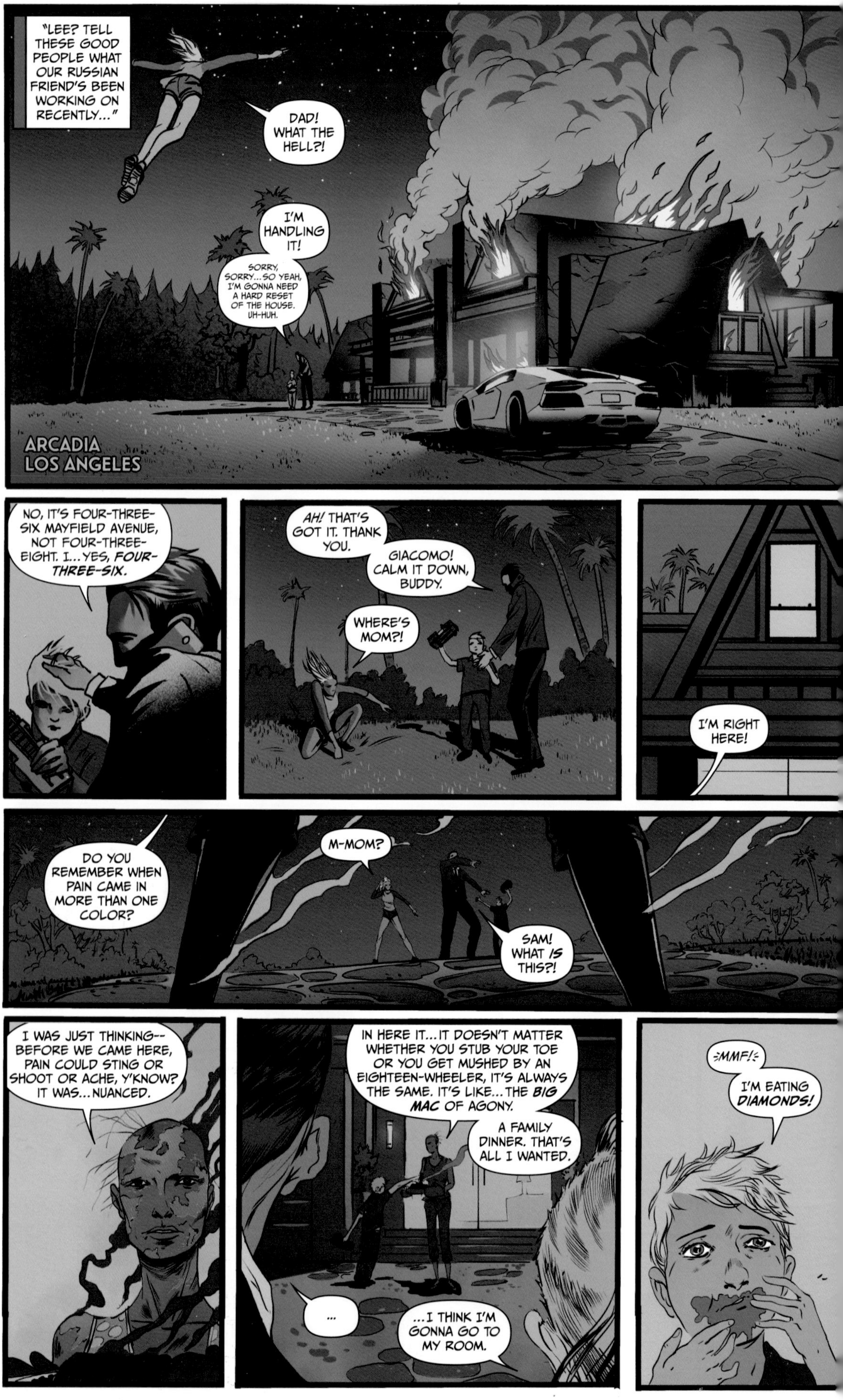
"LEE? TELL THESE GOOD PEOPLE WHAT OUR RUSSIAN FRIEND'S BEEN WORKING ON RECENTLY..."
DAD! WHAT THE HELL?!
I'M HANDLING IT!
SORRY, SORRY... SO YEAH, I'M GONNA NEED A HARD RESET OF THE HOUSE. UH-HUH.
ARCADIA LOS ANGELES
NO, IT'S FOUR-THREE-SIX MAYFIELD AVENUE, NOT FOUR-THREE-EIGHT. I... YES, FOUR-THREE-SIX.
AH! THAT'S GOT IT. THANK YOU.
GIACOMO! CALM IT DOWN, BUDDY.
WHERE'S MOM?!
I'M RIGHT HERE!
DO YOU REMEMBER WHEN PAIN CAME IN MORE THAN ONE COLOR?
M-MOM?
SAM! WHAT IS THIS?!
I WAS JUST THINKING-- BEFORE WE CAME HERE, PAIN COULD STING OR SHOOT OR ACHE, Y'KNOW? IT WAS... NUANCED.
IN HERE IT... IT DOESN'T MATTER WHETHER YOU STUB YOUR TOE OR YOU GET MUSHED BY AN EIGHTEEN-WHEELER, IT'S ALWAYS THE SAME. IT'S LIKE... THE BIG MAC OF AGONY.
A FAMILY DINNER. THAT'S ALL I WANTED.
...
...I THINK I'M GONNA GO TO MY ROOM.
MMF!
I'M EATING DIAMONDS!

IF I COME IN WILL I STEP INTO A BEAR TRAP?

NO, BUT THE GATORS HAVEN'T BEEN FED IN A WHILE.

YOUR MOM'S SLEEPING NOW. SHE'S ALL HEALED UP.

PHYSICALLY, ANYWAY.

THANKS FOR THE COFFEE.

S'COOL.

REAL DOG DAY. I MIGHT WIPE IT FROM MY MEMORY WHEN I GET TO THE CLINIC.

HOW CONVENIENT FOR YOU.

THOSE PEOPLE WERE TRYING TO MAKE A POINT, DAD. YOU CAN'T JUST ERASE EVERYTHING THAT DOESN'T MAKE YOU FEEL WARM AND FUZZY.

SURE I CAN! THERE ARE WINNERS AND LOSERS IN ALL POSSIBLE WORLDS, SWEETHEART.

THAT'S JUST THE WAY OF THINGS.

BESIDES, IF I DIDN'T ERASE MY CLIENTS' MEMORIES OF THEIR DEATHS, THEN... WELL... WHAT ELSE WOULD THEY HAVE TO *TALK* ABOUT?

GROSS.

COMING CALL ANONYMOUS236

OUT! I NEED TO TAKE THIS.

WHO'S *"ANONYMOUS236"*?

JUST THIS HOT EX-CON I'VE BEEN FLIRTING WITH...

IT'S A FRIEND, ALRIGHT? AN OLD FRIEND.

FROM...FROM *BEFORE?*

YEAH...

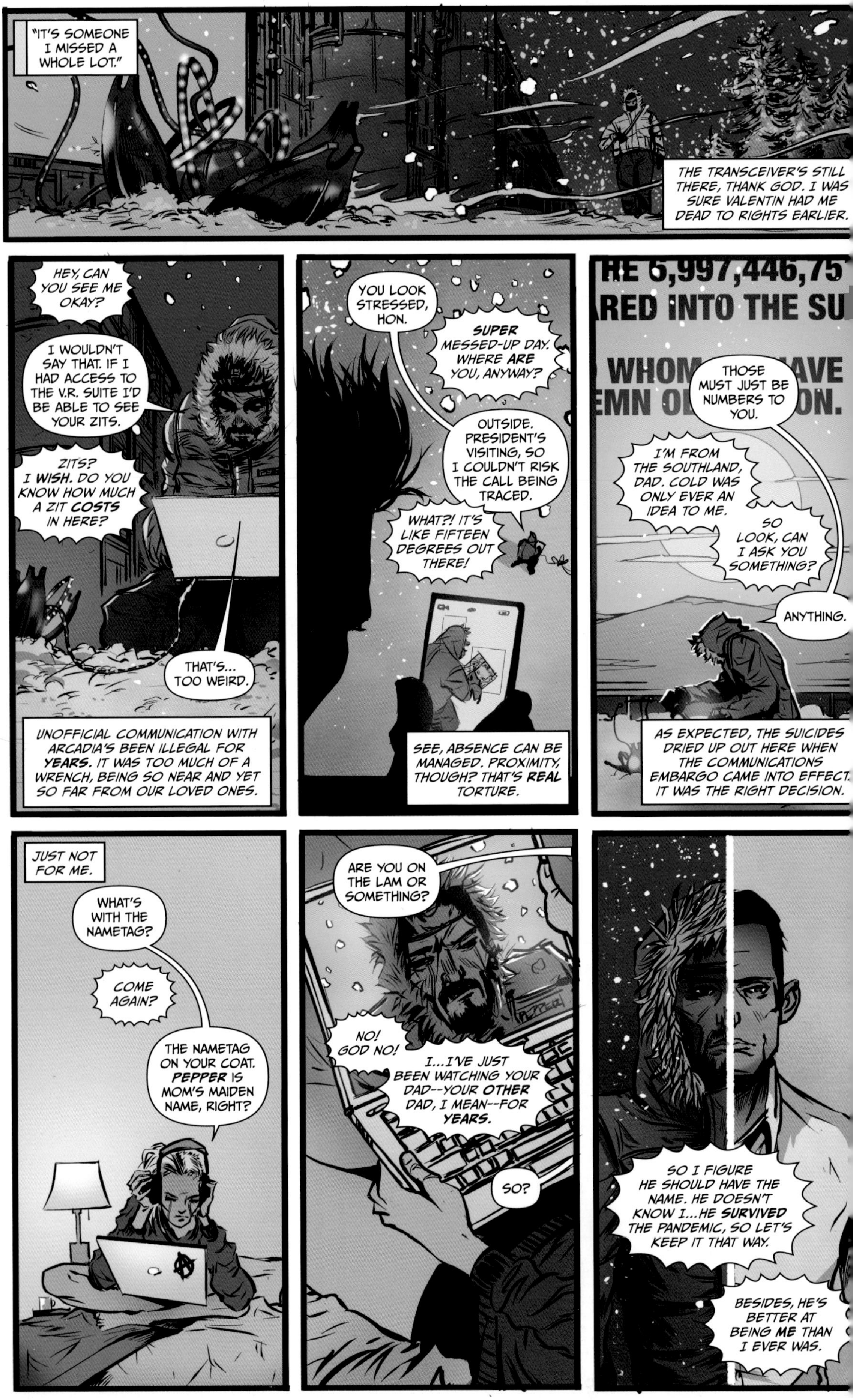
"IT'S SOMEONE I MISSED A WHOLE LOT."
THE TRANSCEIVER'S STILL THERE, THANK GOD. I WAS SURE VALENTIN HAD ME DEAD TO RIGHTS EARLIER.
HEY, CAN YOU SEE ME OKAY?
I WOULDN'T SAY THAT. IF I HAD ACCESS TO THE V.R. SUITE I'D BE ABLE TO SEE YOUR ZITS.
ZITS? I WISH. DO YOU KNOW HOW MUCH A ZIT COSTS IN HERE?
THAT'S... TOO WEIRD.
UNOFFICIAL COMMUNICATION WITH ARCADIA'S BEEN ILLEGAL FOR YEARS. IT WAS TOO MUCH OF A WRENCH, BEING SO NEAR AND YET SO FAR FROM OUR LOVED ONES.
YOU LOOK STRESSED, HON.
SUPER MESSED-UP DAY. WHERE ARE YOU, ANYWAY?
OUTSIDE. PRESIDENT'S VISITING, SO I COULDN'T RISK THE CALL BEING TRACED.
WHAT?! IT'S LIKE FIFTEEN DEGREES OUT THERE!
SEE, ABSENCE CAN BE MANAGED. PROXIMITY, THOUGH? THAT'S REAL TORTURE.
THOSE MUST JUST BE NUMBERS TO YOU.
I'M FROM THE SOUTHLAND, DAD. COLD WAS ONLY EVER AN IDEA TO ME.
SO LOOK, CAN I ASK YOU SOMETHING?
ANYTHING.
AS EXPECTED, THE SUICIDES DRIED UP OUT HERE WHEN THE COMMUNICATIONS EMBARGO CAME INTO EFFECT. IT WAS THE RIGHT DECISION.
JUST NOT FOR ME.
WHAT'S WITH THE NAMETAG?
COME AGAIN?
THE NAMETAG ON YOUR COAT. PEPPER IS MOM'S MAIDEN NAME, RIGHT?
ARE YOU ON THE LAM OR SOMETHING?
NO! GOD NO!
I...I'VE JUST BEEN WATCHING YOUR DAD--YOUR OTHER DAD, I MEAN--FOR YEARS.
SO?
SO I FIGURE HE SHOULD HAVE THE NAME. HE DOESN'T KNOW I...HE SURVIVED THE PANDEMIC, SO LET'S KEEP IT THAT WAY.
BESIDES, HE'S BETTER AT BEING ME THAN I EVER WAS.

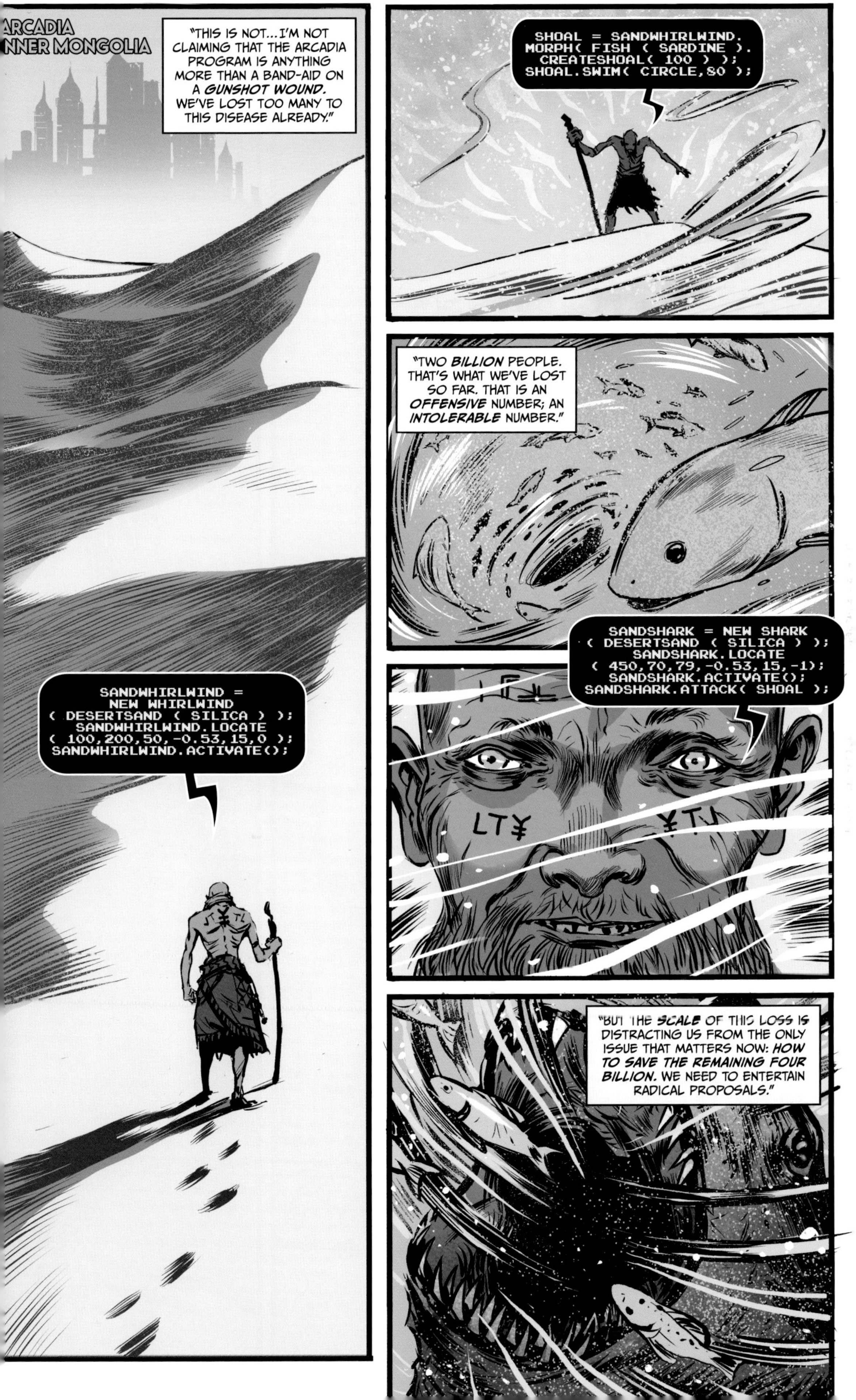
ARCADIA
INNER MONGOLIA
"THIS IS NOT...I'M NOT CLAIMING THAT THE ARCADIA PROGRAM IS ANYTHING MORE THAN A BAND-AID ON A GUNSHOT WOUND. WE'VE LOST TOO MANY TO THIS DISEASE ALREADY."
SANDWHIRLWIND = NEW WHIRLWIND (DESERTSAND (SILICA)); SANDWHIRLWIND.LOCATE (100,200,50,-0.53,15,0); SANDWHIRLWIND.ACTIVATE();
SHOAL = SANDWHIRLWIND. MORPH(FISH (SARDINE). CREATESHOAL(100)); SHOAL.SWIM(CIRCLE,80);
"TWO BILLION PEOPLE. THAT'S WHAT WE'VE LOST SO FAR. THAT IS AN OFFENSIVE NUMBER; AN INTOLERABLE NUMBER."
SANDSHARK = NEW SHARK (DESERTSAND (SILICA)); SANDSHARK.LOCATE (450,70,79,-0.53,15,-1); SANDSHARK.ACTIVATE(); SANDSHARK.ATTACK(SHOAL);
"BUT THE SCALE OF THIS LOSS IS DISTRACTING US FROM THE ONLY ISSUE THAT MATTERS NOW: HOW TO SAVE THE REMAINING FOUR BILLION. WE NEED TO ENTERTAIN RADICAL PROPOSALS."

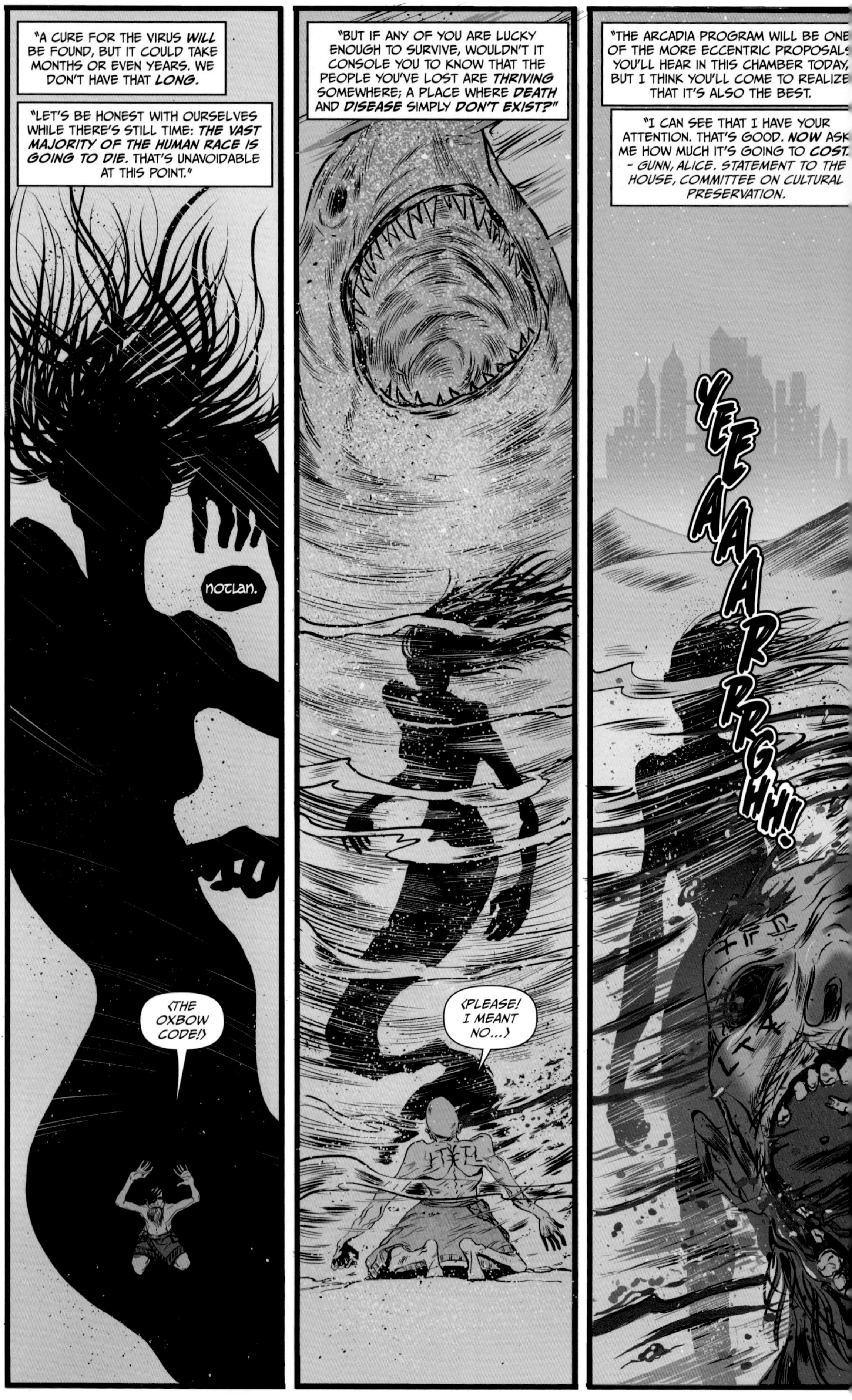

"A CURE FOR THE VIRUS WILL BE FOUND, BUT IT COULD TAKE MONTHS OR EVEN YEARS. WE DON'T HAVE THAT LONG.
"LET'S BE HONEST WITH OURSELVES WHILE THERE'S STILL TIME: THE VAST MAJORITY OF THE HUMAN RACE IS GOING TO DIE. THAT'S UNAVOIDABLE AT THIS POINT."
notlan.
‹THE OXBOW CODE!›
"BUT IF ANY OF YOU ARE LUCKY ENOUGH TO SURVIVE, WOULDN'T IT CONSOLE YOU TO KNOW THAT THE PEOPLE YOU'VE LOST ARE THRIVING SOMEWHERE; A PLACE WHERE DEATH AND DISEASE SIMPLY DON'T EXIST?"
‹PLEASE! I MEANT NO...›
"THE ARCADIA PROGRAM WILL BE ONE OF THE MORE ECCENTRIC PROPOSALS YOU'LL HEAR IN THIS CHAMBER TODAY, BUT I THINK YOU'LL COME TO REALIZE THAT IT'S ALSO THE BEST.
"I CAN SEE THAT I HAVE YOUR ATTENTION. THAT'S GOOD. NOW ASK ME HOW MUCH IT'S GOING TO COST." - GUNN, ALICE. STATEMENT TO THE HOUSE, COMMITTEE ON CULTURAL PRESERVATION.
YEEAAAARRGHH!

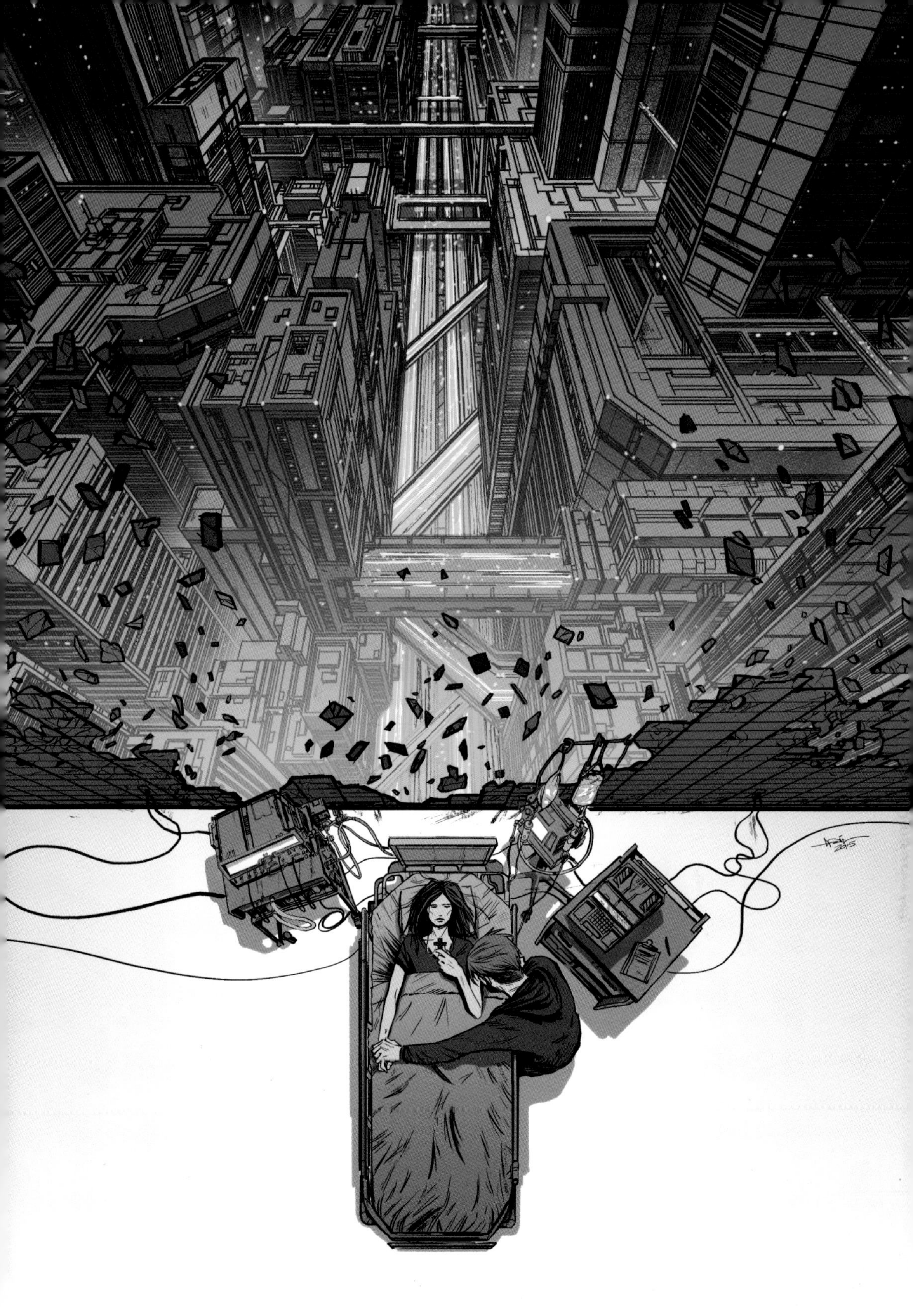

Issue One Variant Cover **Eric Scott Pfeiffer**

"But how does one spend the day in the Land of Toys?"

"Days are spent in play and enjoyment from morn 'til night. At night one goes to bed, and next morning, the good times begin all over again."

—**C. Collodi**,
The Adventures of Pinocchio

CHAPTER
TWO

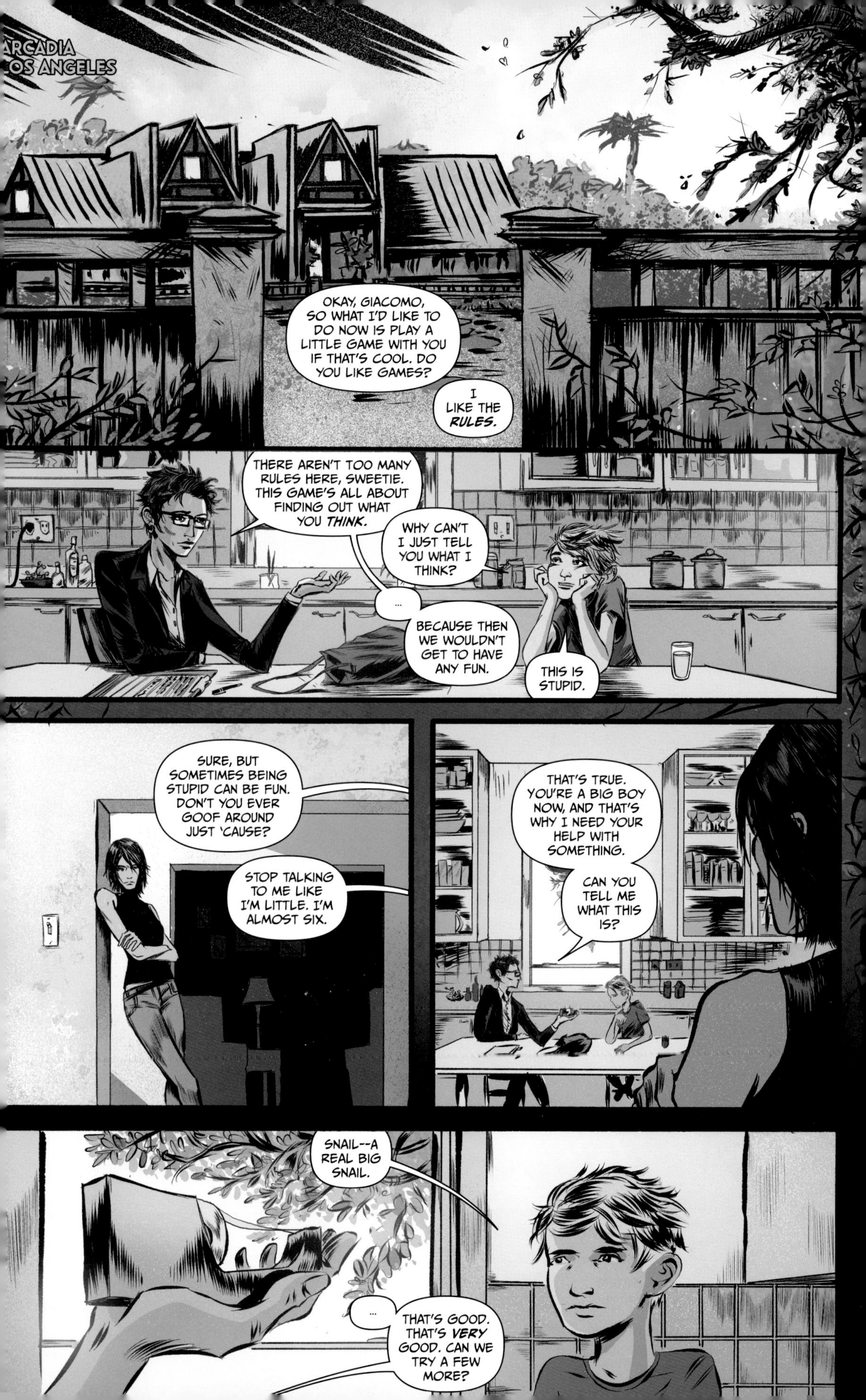
ARCADIA
LOS ANGELES
OKAY, GIACOMO, SO WHAT I'D LIKE TO DO NOW IS PLAY A LITTLE GAME WITH YOU IF THAT'S COOL. DO YOU LIKE GAMES?
I LIKE THE *RULES.*
THERE AREN'T TOO MANY RULES HERE, SWEETIE. THIS GAME'S ALL ABOUT FINDING OUT WHAT YOU *THINK.*
WHY CAN'T I JUST TELL YOU WHAT I THINK?
...
BECAUSE THEN WE WOULDN'T GET TO HAVE ANY FUN.
THIS IS STUPID.
SURE, BUT SOMETIMES BEING STUPID CAN BE FUN. DON'T YOU EVER GOOF AROUND JUST 'CAUSE?
STOP TALKING TO ME LIKE I'M LITTLE. I'M ALMOST SIX.
THAT'S TRUE. YOU'RE A BIG BOY NOW, AND THAT'S WHY I NEED YOUR HELP WITH SOMETHING.
CAN YOU TELL ME WHAT THIS IS?
SNAIL--A REAL BIG SNAIL.
...
THAT'S GOOD. THAT'S *VERY* GOOD. CAN WE TRY A FEW MORE?

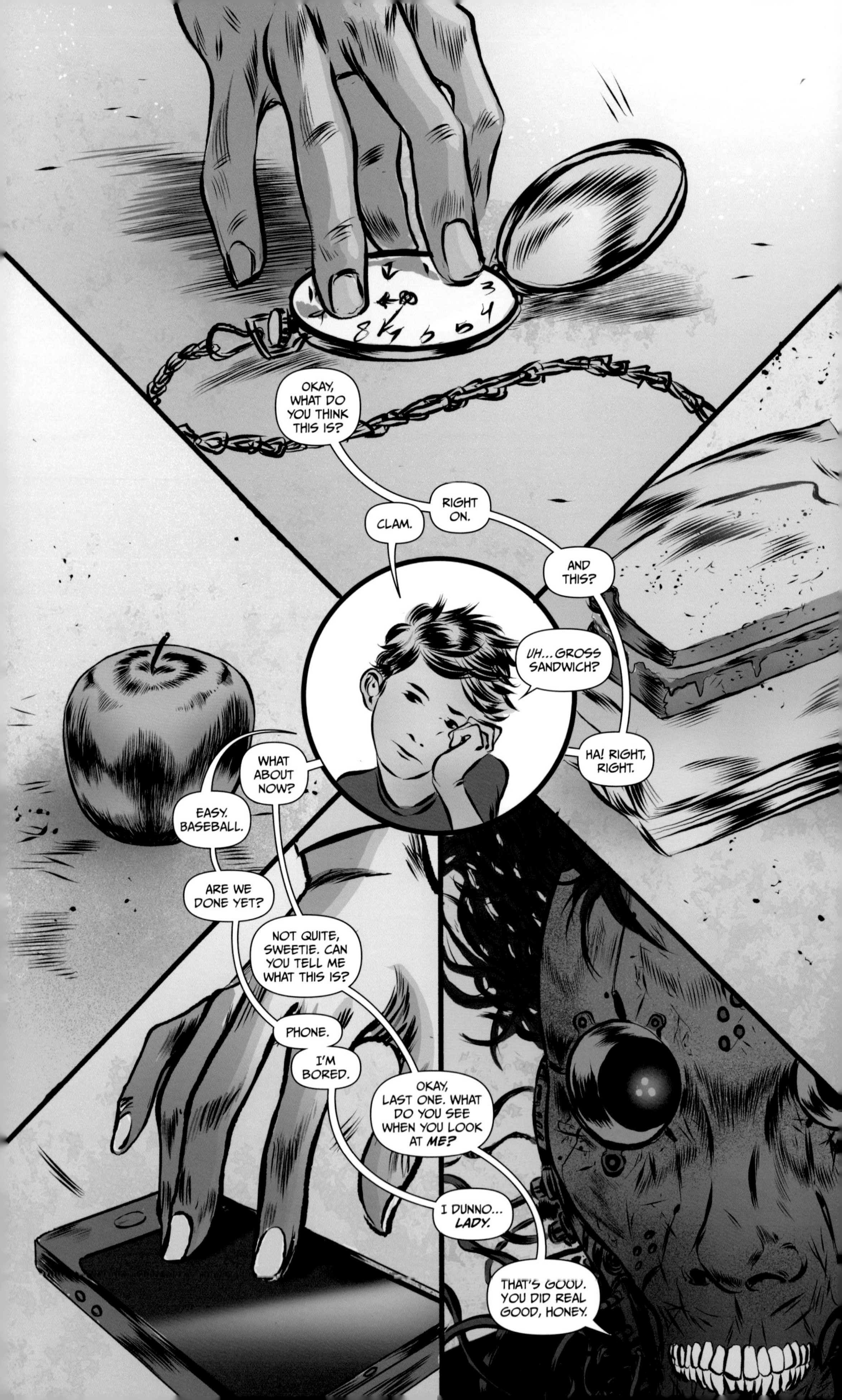
OKAY, WHAT DO YOU THINK THIS IS?
CLAM.
RIGHT ON.
AND THIS?
UH...GROSS SANDWICH?
HA! RIGHT, RIGHT.
WHAT ABOUT NOW?
EASY. BASEBALL.
ARE WE DONE YET?
NOT QUITE, SWEETIE. CAN YOU TELL ME WHAT THIS IS?
PHONE.
I'M BORED.
OKAY, LAST ONE. WHAT DO YOU SEE WHEN YOU LOOK AT *ME?*
I DUNNO... *LADY.*
THAT'S GOOD. YOU DID REAL GOOD, HONEY.

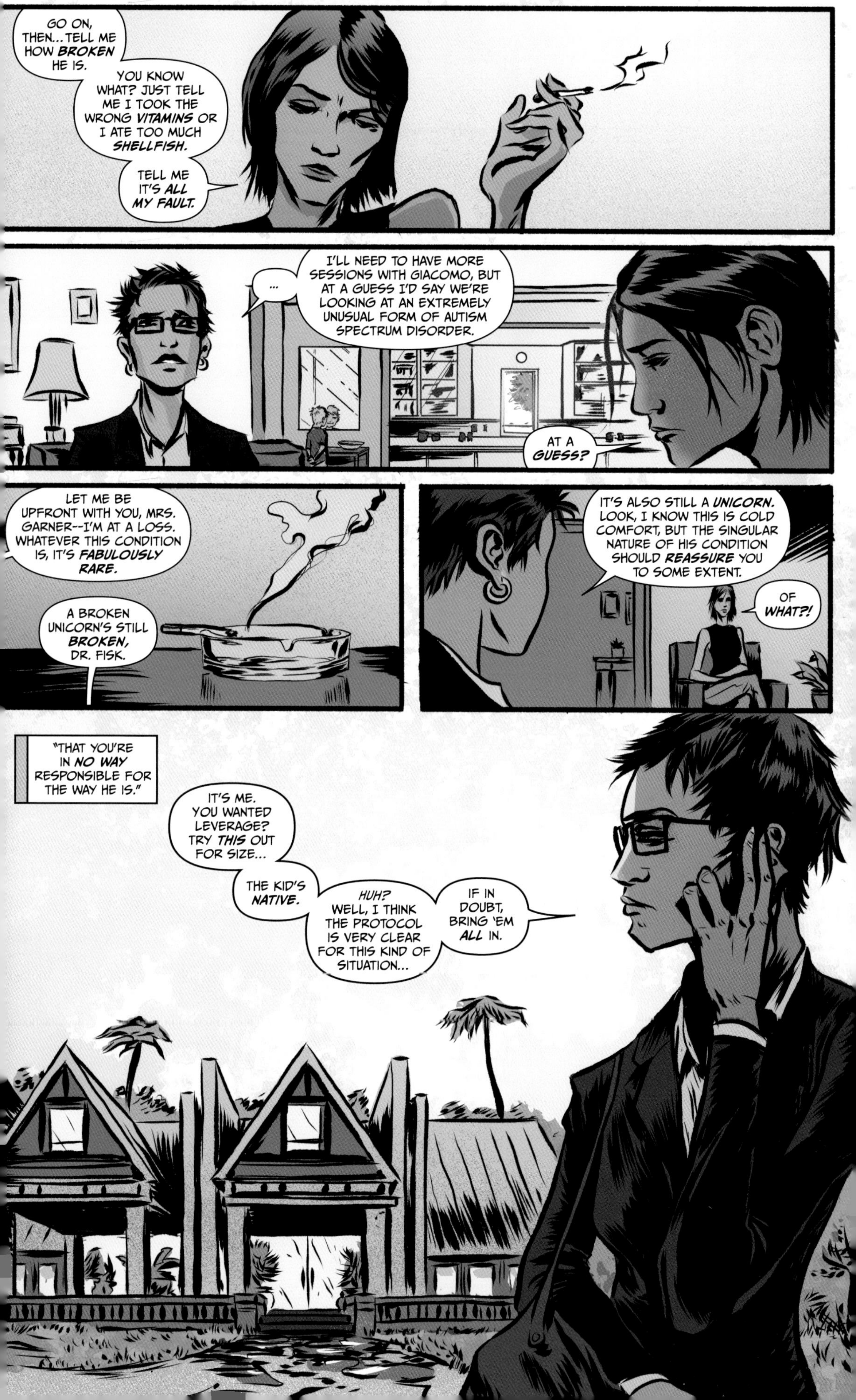
GO ON, THEN...TELL ME HOW BROKEN HE IS.
YOU KNOW WHAT? JUST TELL ME I TOOK THE WRONG VITAMINS OR I ATE TOO MUCH SHELLFISH.
TELL ME IT'S ALL MY FAULT.
...
I'LL NEED TO HAVE MORE SESSIONS WITH GIACOMO, BUT AT A GUESS I'D SAY WE'RE LOOKING AT AN EXTREMELY UNUSUAL FORM OF AUTISM SPECTRUM DISORDER.
AT A GUESS?
LET ME BE UPFRONT WITH YOU, MRS. GARNER--I'M AT A LOSS. WHATEVER THIS CONDITION IS, IT'S FABULOUSLY RARE.
A BROKEN UNICORN'S STILL BROKEN, DR. FISK.
IT'S ALSO STILL A UNICORN. LOOK, I KNOW THIS IS COLD COMFORT, BUT THE SINGULAR NATURE OF HIS CONDITION SHOULD REASSURE YOU TO SOME EXTENT.
OF WHAT?!
"THAT YOU'RE IN NO WAY RESPONSIBLE FOR THE WAY HE IS."
IT'S ME. YOU WANTED LEVERAGE? TRY THIS OUT FOR SIZE...
THE KID'S NATIVE.
HUH? WELL, I THINK THE PROTOCOL IS VERY CLEAR FOR THIS KIND OF SITUATION...
IF IN DOUBT, BRING 'EM ALL IN.

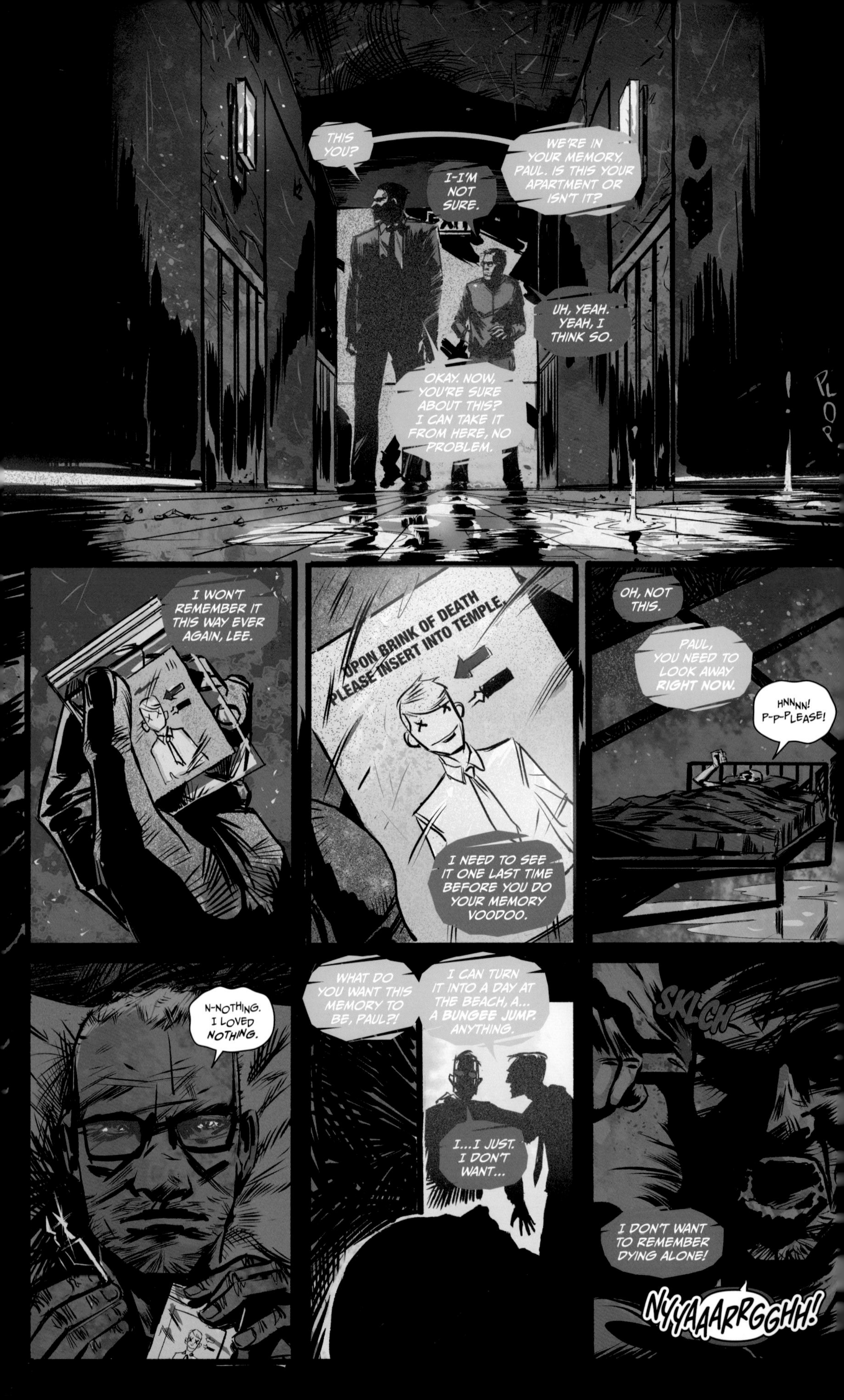

THIS YOU?
WE'RE IN YOUR MEMORY, PAUL. IS THIS YOUR APARTMENT OR ISN'T IT?
I-I'M NOT SURE.
UH, YEAH. YEAH, I THINK SO.
OKAY. NOW, YOU'RE SURE ABOUT THIS? I CAN TAKE IT FROM HERE, NO PROBLEM.
PLOP
I WON'T REMEMBER IT THIS WAY EVER AGAIN, LEE.
UPON BRINK OF DEATH PLEASE INSERT INTO TEMPLE.
I NEED TO SEE IT ONE LAST TIME BEFORE YOU DO YOUR MEMORY VOODOO.
OH, NOT THIS.
PAUL, YOU NEED TO LOOK AWAY RIGHT NOW.
HNNNN! P-P-PLEASE!
N-NOTHING. I LOVED NOTHING.
WHAT DO YOU WANT THIS MEMORY TO BE, PAUL?!
I CAN TURN IT INTO A DAY AT THE BEACH, A... A BUNGEE JUMP. ANYTHING.
I...I JUST. I DON'T WANT...
SKLCH
I DON'T WANT TO REMEMBER DYING ALONE!
NYYAAARRGGHH!

OFF! *GET IT OFF!*

ALRIGHT, ALRIGHT. JUST...*CALM DOWN.* YOU'RE *FINE.*

I WASN'T READY. *GOD ALMIGHTY...!*

GIVE ME A WEEK, PAUL. I'LL COMPOSITE YOUR MOM INTO THE MEMORY AND IT'LL BE...BETTER.

JUST TRY TO RELAX IN THE MEANTIME.

RELAX? *NOT LIKELY.*

CALTECH'S BEEN COMPLETELY REPURPOSED TO RUN ANTIVIRAL SIMULATIONS FOR THE MEAT. WE ALL WORK FOR THE CDC NOW.

THERE'S NOT A DAY GOES BY I DON'T HAVE SOME DISNEY PRINCE OF A BUREAUCRAT LOOKING OVER MY SHOULDER AND MAKING NOTES WITHOUT SAYING A WORD.

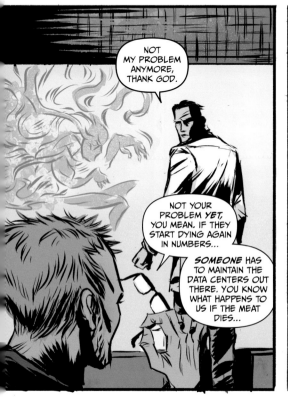

NOT MY PROBLEM ANYMORE, THANK GOD.

NOT YOUR PROBLEM *YET,* YOU MEAN. IF THEY START DYING AGAIN IN NUMBERS...

SOMEONE HAS TO MAINTAIN THE DATA CENTERS OUT THERE. YOU KNOW WHAT HAPPENS TO US IF THE MEAT DIES...

...I KNOW EVERYONE AT CALTECH THOUGHT I WAS SELFISH WHEN I LEFT TO START THE CLINIC, PAUL. I *GET IT,* I DO.

MOST PEOPLE TREAT THIS PLACE LIKE A VIDEO GAME, AND I UNDERSTAND WHY THAT *DISGUSTS* YOU. BUT YOU KNOW WHAT? THEY'RE ALL JUST TRYING TO FORGET WHAT HAPPENED TO THEM IN THEIR OWN WAY.

I KNOW I AM.

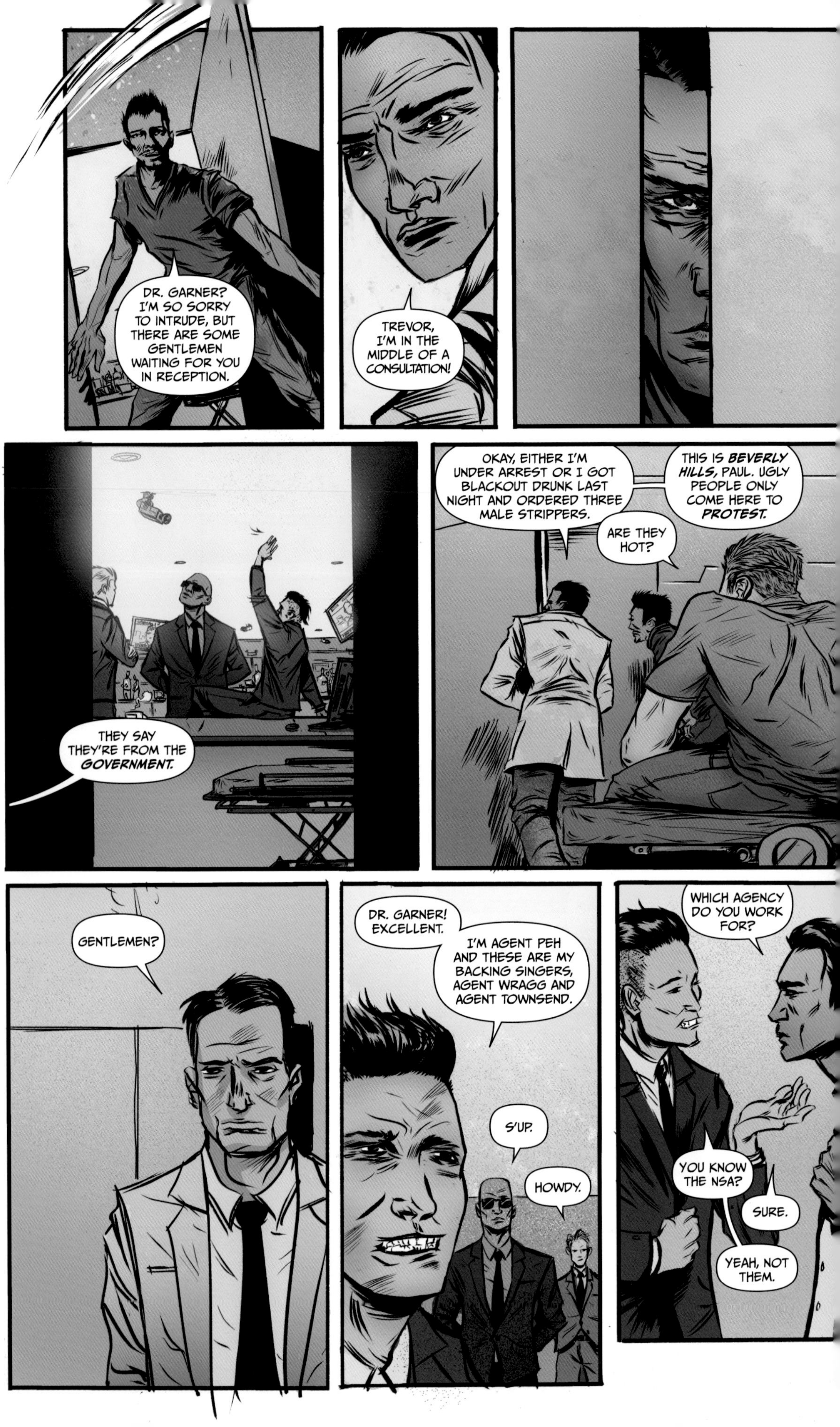
DR. GARNER? I'M SO SORRY TO INTRUDE, BUT THERE ARE SOME GENTLEMEN WAITING FOR YOU IN RECEPTION.
TREVOR, I'M IN THE MIDDLE OF A CONSULTATION!
THEY SAY THEY'RE FROM THE ***GOVERNMENT.***
OKAY, EITHER I'M UNDER ARREST OR I GOT BLACKOUT DRUNK LAST NIGHT AND ORDERED THREE MALE STRIPPERS.
THIS IS ***BEVERLY HILLS,*** PAUL. UGLY PEOPLE ONLY COME HERE TO ***PROTEST.***
ARE THEY HOT?
GENTLEMEN?
DR. GARNER! EXCELLENT.
I'M AGENT PEH AND THESE ARE MY BACKING SINGERS, AGENT WRAGG AND AGENT TOWNSEND.
S'UP.
HOWDY.
WHICH AGENCY DO YOU WORK FOR?
YOU KNOW THE NSA?
SURE.
YEAH, NOT THEM.

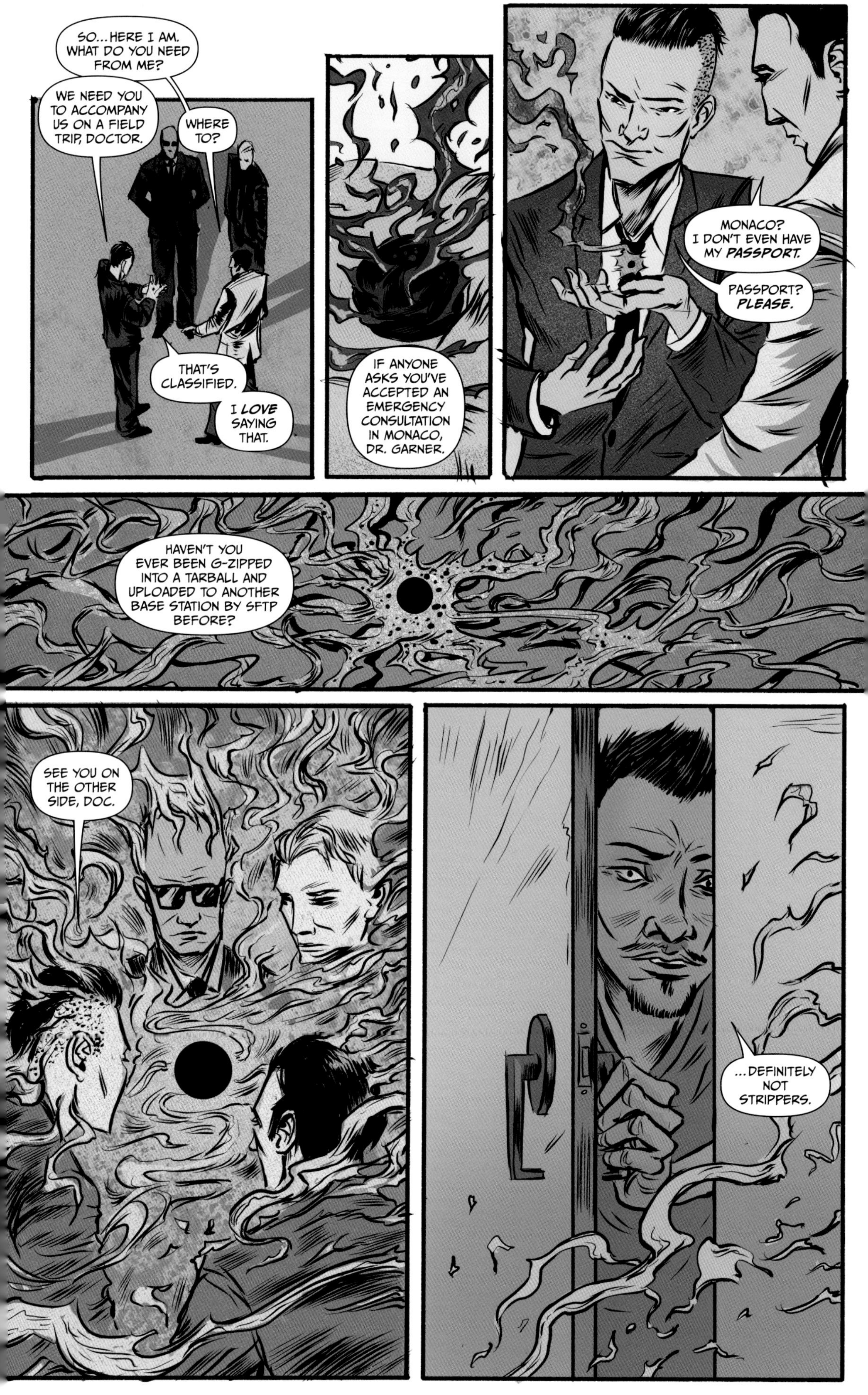
SO...HERE I AM. WHAT DO YOU NEED FROM ME?
WE NEED YOU TO ACCOMPANY US ON A FIELD TRIP, DOCTOR.
WHERE TO?
THAT'S CLASSIFIED.
I LOVE SAYING THAT.
IF ANYONE ASKS YOU'VE ACCEPTED AN EMERGENCY CONSULTATION IN MONACO, DR. GARNER.
MONACO? I DON'T EVEN HAVE MY PASSPORT.
PASSPORT? PLEASE.
HAVEN'T YOU EVER BEEN G-ZIPPED INTO A TARBALL AND UPLOADED TO ANOTHER BASE STATION BY SFTP BEFORE?
SEE YOU ON THE OTHER SIDE, DOC.
...DEFINITELY NOT STRIPPERS.

THE MEAT
ALASKA

YOU SURE I CAN'T PERSUADE YOU TO COME BACK TO DC? DOSE OF CIVILIZATION WOULD DO YOU GOOD, LEE.

WE HAVE A HIGHER POPULATION DENSITY *HERE*.

NOW YOU'RE BEING *FACETIOUS*. I'M TALKING *CIVILIZATION*: LONG BATHS, PRETENTIOUS CUISINE...

HELL, WE MIGHT EVEN FIND AN INTERN WHO HATES HERSELF ENOUGH TO SLEEP WITH YOU.

I MET MELINA WHEN SHE WAS JUST A TECH LOBBYIST, BUT SHE WAS GOVERNMENT TO THE CORE EVEN THEN.

YOU HANDLED YOURSELF WELL WITH THE GLIMMERS, MELINA.

I NEED YOU TO CONVINCE THEM TO FALL IN LINE, LEE. *NOCTURNE'S* TOO IMPORTANT.

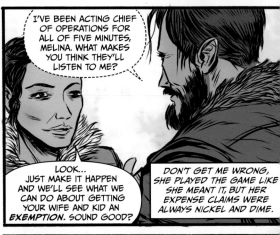

I'VE BEEN ACTING CHIEF OF OPERATIONS FOR ALL OF FIVE MINUTES, MELINA. WHAT MAKES YOU THINK THEY'LL LISTEN TO ME?

LOOK... JUST MAKE IT HAPPEN AND WE'LL SEE WHAT WE CAN DO ABOUT GETTING YOUR WIFE AND KID AN *EXEMPTION*. SOUND GOOD?

DON'T GET ME WRONG, SHE PLAYED THE GAME LIKE SHE MEANT IT, BUT HER EXPENSE CLAIMS WERE ALWAYS NICKEL AND DIME.

YOU'RE WASTED UP HERE, LEE. THINGS ARE SETTLING DOWN BACK IN THE WORLD AND I'LL NEED YOU IN IT WHEN THIS IS OVER.

I SHOULD KNOW. MY COMPANY AT THE TIME WROTE THE CHECKS.

NOCTURNE'LL FREE UP THE PROCESSING POWER WE NEED TO LICK THE VIRUS ONCE AND FOR ALL.

WHEN THAT HAPPENS THE FIELD'S GONNA BE WIDE OPEN FOR PEOPLE LIKE *YOU* TO GET THINGS MOVING AGAIN.

SHE WAS AND IS A TRUE BELIEVER. ALL THAT OPEN WEB STUFF FED RIGHT INTO HER RANDIAN WORLDVIEW.

YOU SHOULDN'T BE IN SUCH A RUSH TO PUT THINGS BACK THE WAY THEY WERE, MELINA.

WAY I REMEMBER IT, WE WERE SO INTENT ON GOING FASTER WE CUT THE BRAKES.

IT WAS *REALLY* GOOD TO SEE YOU. I'LL TELL ALICE YOU SAID HI.

MY COMPANY PAID HER TO GET SENATORS DRUNK AND COMPLIANT, BUT SHE NEVER DID. HER SECRET WEAPON WAS CONVICTION.

DOESN'T LOOK LIKE SHE'S CHANGED. THAT SCARES ME TO MY MARROW.

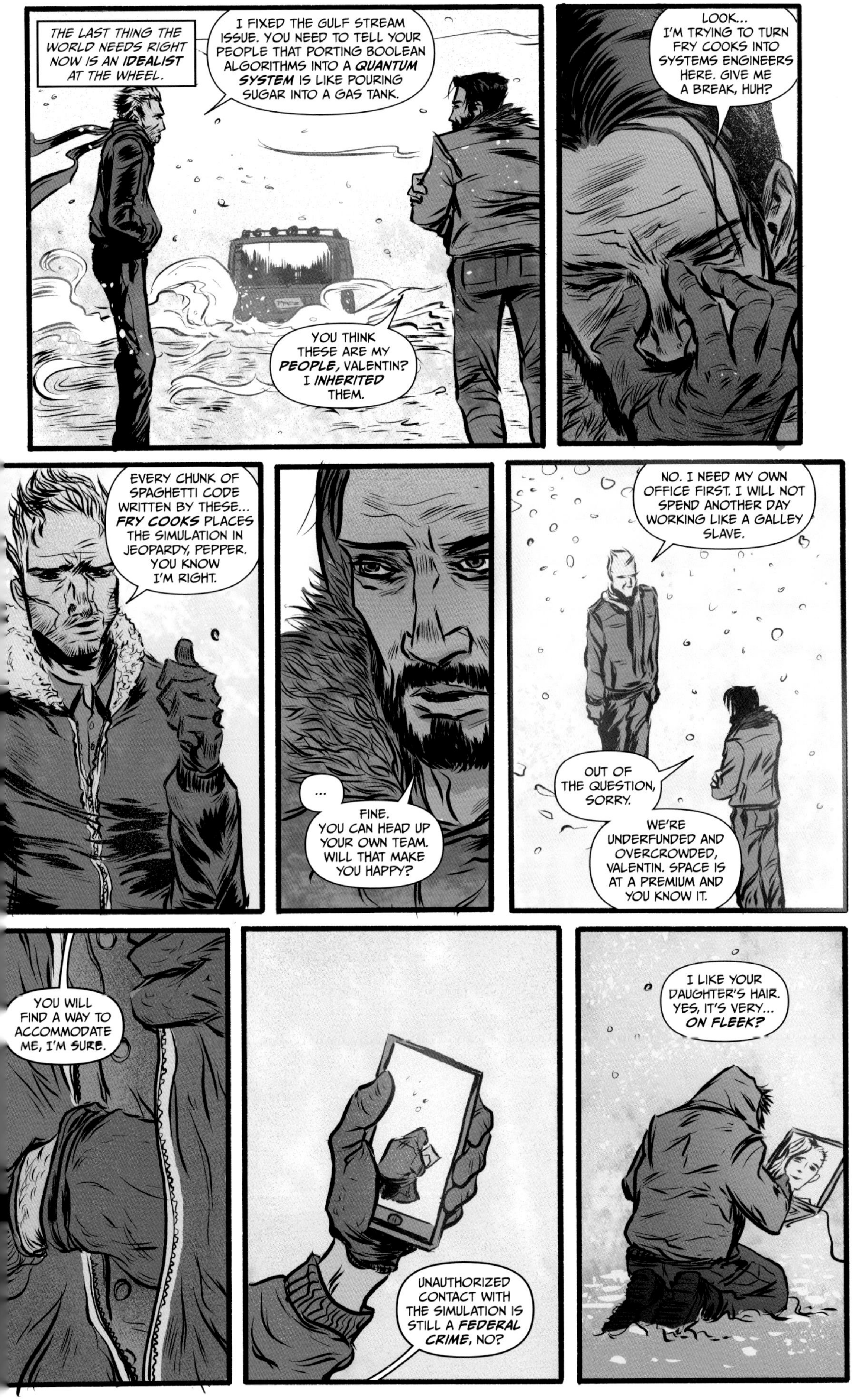
THE LAST THING THE WORLD NEEDS RIGHT NOW IS AN *IDEALIST* AT THE WHEEL.
I FIXED THE GULF STREAM ISSUE. YOU NEED TO TELL YOUR PEOPLE THAT PORTING BOOLEAN ALGORITHMS INTO A *QUANTUM SYSTEM* IS LIKE POURING SUGAR INTO A GAS TANK.
YOU THINK THESE ARE MY *PEOPLE,* VALENTIN? I *INHERITED* THEM.
LOOK... I'M TRYING TO TURN FRY COOKS INTO SYSTEMS ENGINEERS HERE. GIVE ME A BREAK, HUH?
EVERY CHUNK OF SPAGHETTI CODE WRITTEN BY THESE... *FRY COOKS* PLACES THE SIMULATION IN JEOPARDY, PEPPER. YOU KNOW I'M RIGHT.
...
FINE. YOU CAN HEAD UP YOUR OWN TEAM. WILL THAT MAKE YOU HAPPY?
NO. I NEED MY OWN OFFICE FIRST. I WILL NOT SPEND ANOTHER DAY WORKING LIKE A GALLEY SLAVE.
OUT OF THE QUESTION, SORRY.
WE'RE UNDERFUNDED AND OVERCROWDED, VALENTIN. SPACE IS AT A PREMIUM AND YOU KNOW IT.
YOU WILL FIND A WAY TO ACCOMMODATE ME, I'M SURE.
UNAUTHORIZED CONTACT WITH THE SIMULATION IS STILL A *FEDERAL CRIME*, NO?
I LIKE YOUR DAUGHTER'S HAIR. YES, IT'S VERY... *ON FLEEK?*

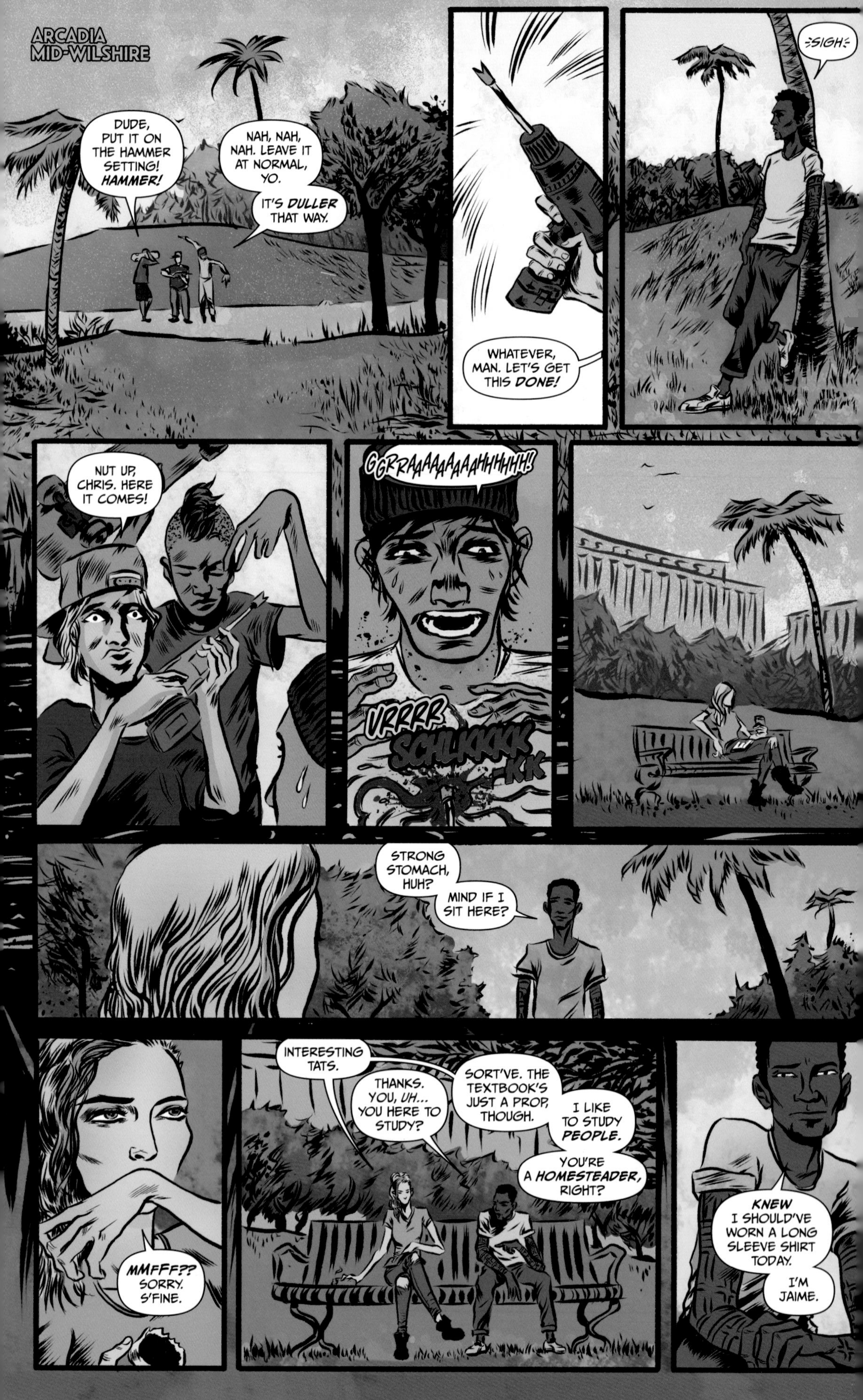

ARCADIA
MID-WILSHIRE
DUDE, PUT IT ON THE HAMMER SETTING! HAMMER!
NAH, NAH, NAH. LEAVE IT AT NORMAL, YO.
IT'S DULLER THAT WAY.
WHATEVER, MAN. LET'S GET THIS DONE!
SIGH
NUT UP, CHRIS. HERE IT COMES!
GGRRAAAAAAAAHHHHHH!!
URRRR
SCHLKKKK-KK
STRONG STOMACH, HUH?
MIND IF I SIT HERE?
MMFFF?? SORRY. S'FINE.
INTERESTING TATS.
THANKS. YOU, UH... YOU HERE TO STUDY?
SORT'VE. THE TEXTBOOK'S JUST A PROP, THOUGH.
I LIKE TO STUDY PEOPLE.
YOU'RE A HOMESTEADER, RIGHT?
KNEW I SHOULD'VE WORN A LONG SLEEVE SHIRT TODAY.
I'M JAIME.

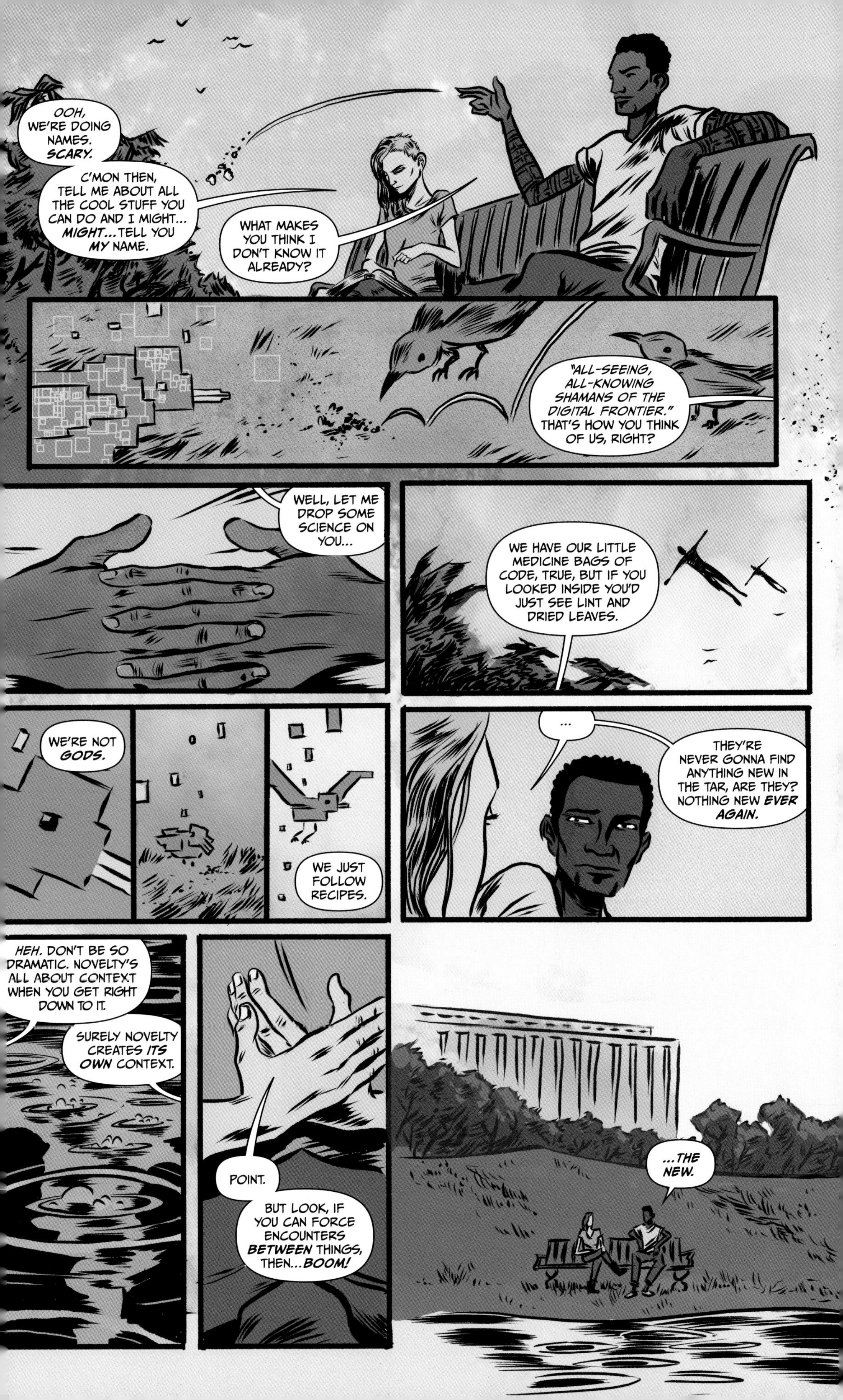
OOH, WE'RE DOING NAMES. *SCARY.*
C'MON THEN, TELL ME ABOUT ALL THE COOL STUFF YOU CAN DO AND I MIGHT... *MIGHT...* TELL YOU *MY* NAME.
WHAT MAKES YOU THINK I DON'T KNOW IT ALREADY?
"ALL-SEEING, ALL-KNOWING SHAMANS OF THE DIGITAL FRONTIER." THAT'S HOW YOU THINK OF US, RIGHT?
WELL, LET ME DROP SOME SCIENCE ON YOU...
WE HAVE OUR LITTLE MEDICINE BAGS OF CODE, TRUE, BUT IF YOU LOOKED INSIDE YOU'D JUST SEE LINT AND DRIED LEAVES.
WE'RE NOT *GODS.*
WE JUST FOLLOW RECIPES.
...
THEY'RE NEVER GONNA FIND ANYTHING NEW IN THE TAR, ARE THEY? NOTHING NEW *EVER AGAIN.*
HEH. DON'T BE SO DRAMATIC. NOVELTY'S ALL ABOUT CONTEXT WHEN YOU GET RIGHT DOWN TO IT.
SURELY NOVELTY CREATES *ITS OWN* CONTEXT.
POINT.
BUT LOOK, IF YOU CAN FORCE ENCOUNTERS *BETWEEN* THINGS, THEN... *BOOM!*
...THE NEW.

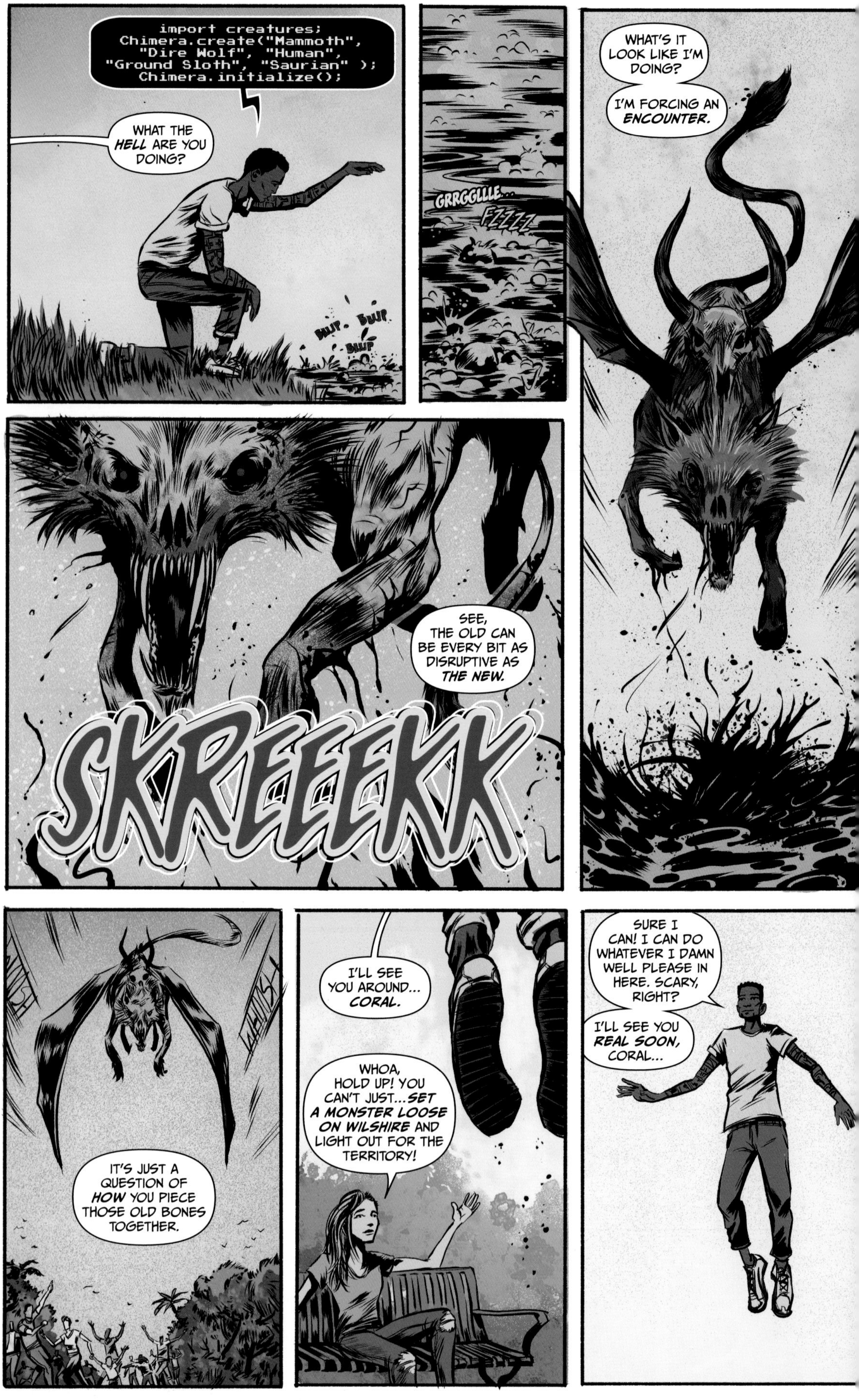

import creatures;
Chimera.create("Mammoth", "Dire Wolf", "Human", "Ground Sloth", "Saurian");
Chimera.initialize();
WHAT THE *HELL* ARE YOU DOING?
BLUP BLUP BLUP
GRRGGLLLE...
FZZZZ
WHAT'S IT LOOK LIKE I'M DOING?
I'M FORCING AN *ENCOUNTER.*
SEE, THE OLD CAN BE EVERY BIT AS DISRUPTIVE AS *THE NEW.*
SKREEEKK
IT'S JUST A QUESTION OF *HOW* YOU PIECE THOSE OLD BONES TOGETHER.
I'LL SEE YOU AROUND... *CORAL.*
WHOA, HOLD UP! YOU CAN'T JUST... *SET A MONSTER LOOSE ON WILSHIRE* AND LIGHT OUT FOR THE TERRITORY!
SURE I CAN! I CAN DO WHATEVER I DAMN WELL PLEASE IN HERE. SCARY, RIGHT?
I'LL SEE YOU *REAL SOON,* CORAL...

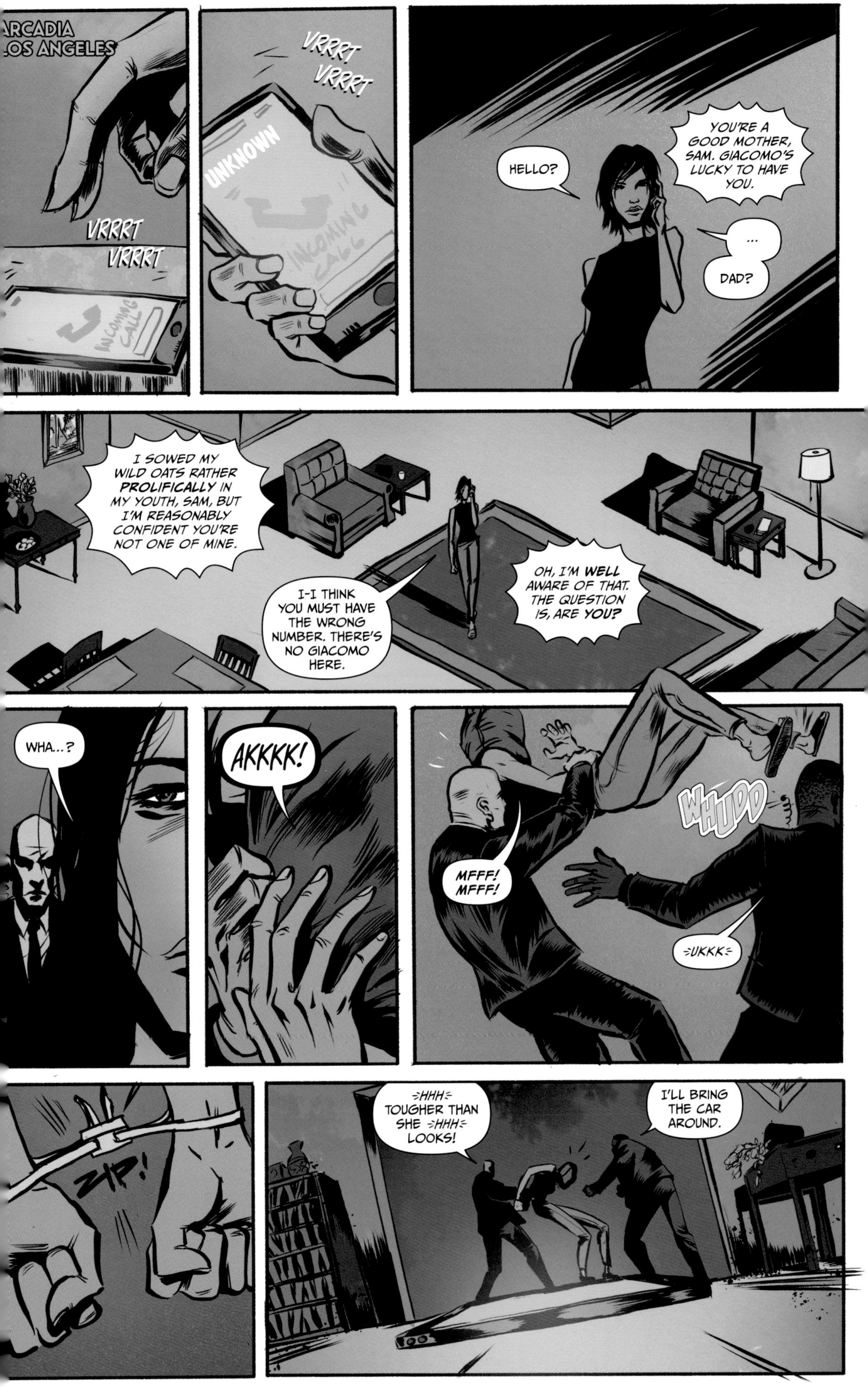
ARCADIA
LOS ANGELES
VRRRT
VRRRT
VRRRT
VRRRT
UNKNOWN
INCOMING CALL
HELLO?
YOU'RE A GOOD MOTHER, SAM. GIACOMO'S LUCKY TO HAVE YOU.
...
DAD?
I SOWED MY WILD OATS RATHER **PROLIFICALLY** IN MY YOUTH, SAM, BUT I'M REASONABLY CONFIDENT YOU'RE NOT ONE OF MINE.
I-I THINK YOU MUST HAVE THE WRONG NUMBER. THERE'S NO GIACOMO HERE.
OH, I'M **WELL** AWARE OF THAT. THE QUESTION IS, ARE **YOU?**
WHA...?
AKKKK!
MFFF! MFFF!
WHUDD
UKKK
ZIP!
HHH TOUGHER THAN SHE HHH LOOKS!
I'LL BRING THE CAR AROUND.

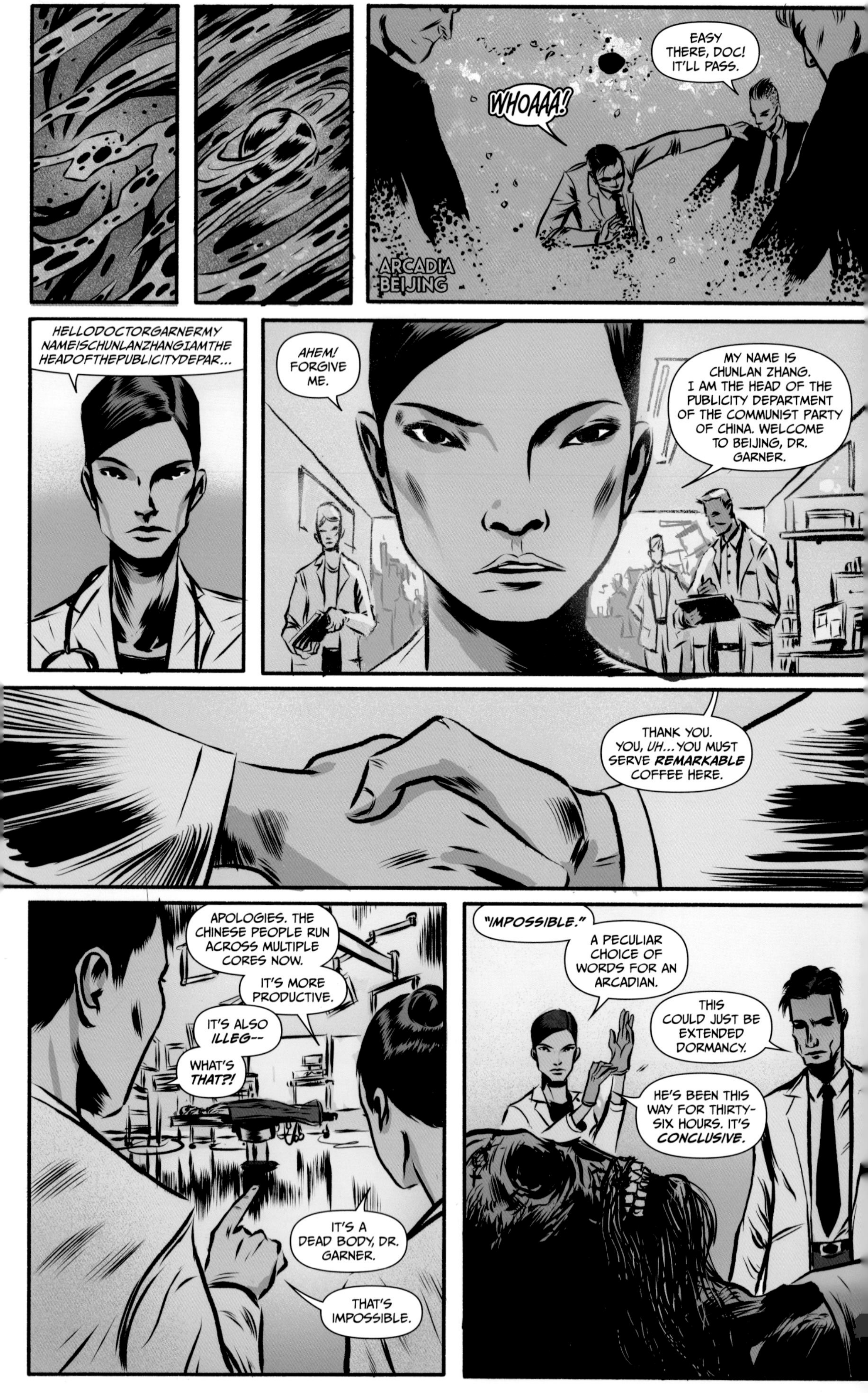

EASY THERE, DOC! IT'LL PASS.
WHOAAA!
ARCADIA BEIJING
HELLODOCTORGARNERMY NAMEISCHUNLANZHANGIAMTHE HEADOFTHEPUBLICITYDEPAR...
AHEM! FORGIVE ME.
MY NAME IS CHUNLAN ZHANG. I AM THE HEAD OF THE PUBLICITY DEPARTMENT OF THE COMMUNIST PARTY OF CHINA. WELCOME TO BEIJING, DR. GARNER.
THANK YOU. YOU, UH... YOU MUST SERVE REMARKABLE COFFEE HERE.
APOLOGIES. THE CHINESE PEOPLE RUN ACROSS MULTIPLE CORES NOW.
IT'S MORE PRODUCTIVE.
IT'S ALSO ILLEG--
WHAT'S THAT?!
IT'S A DEAD BODY, DR. GARNER.
THAT'S IMPOSSIBLE.
"IMPOSSIBLE."
A PECULIAR CHOICE OF WORDS FOR AN ARCADIAN.
THIS COULD JUST BE EXTENDED DORMANCY.
HE'S BEEN THIS WAY FOR THIRTY-SIX HOURS. IT'S CONCLUSIVE.

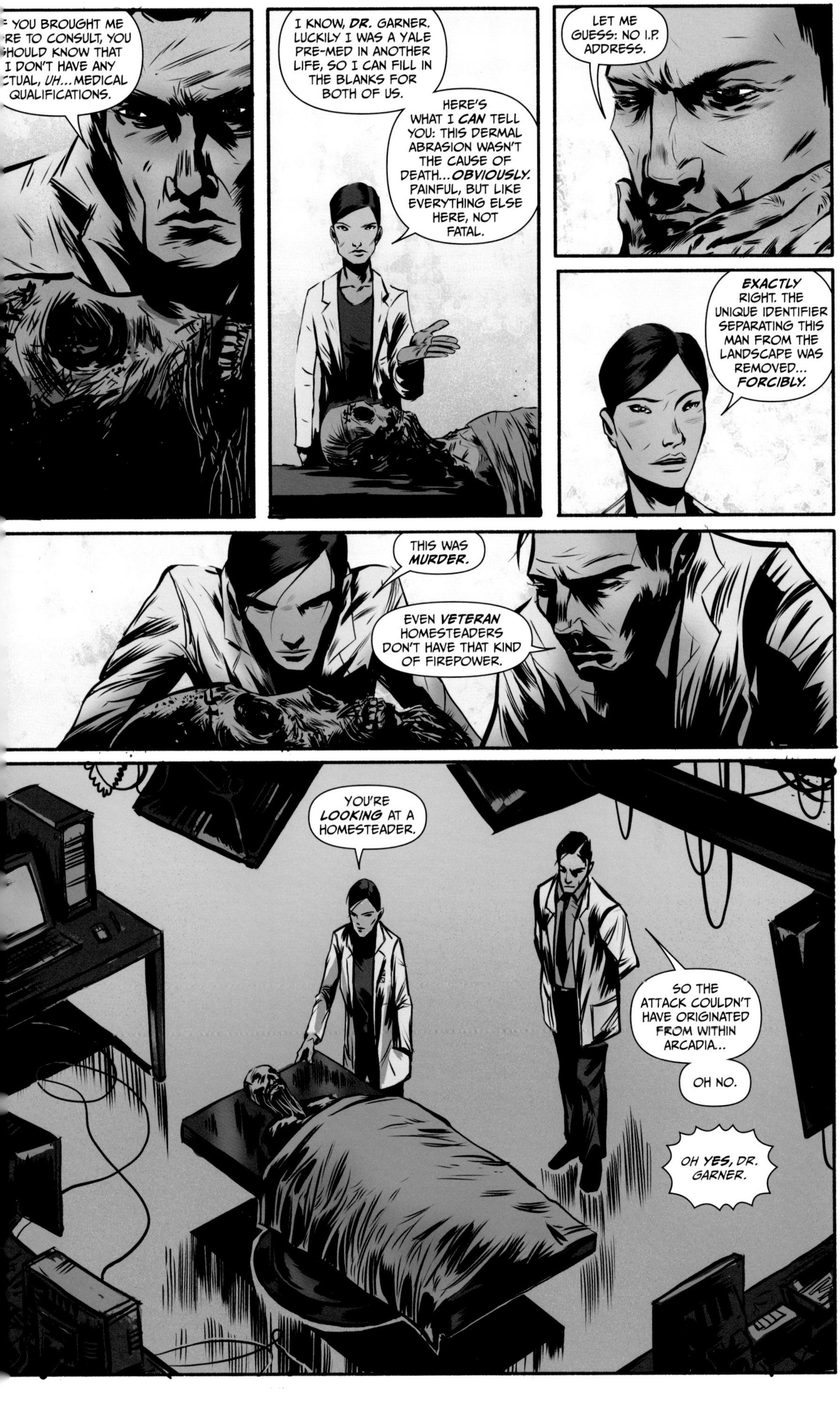
F YOU BROUGHT ME
RE TO CONSULT, YOU
SHOULD KNOW THAT
I DON'T HAVE ANY
CTUAL, *UH*...MEDICAL
QUALIFICATIONS.
I KNOW, **DR.** GARNER. LUCKILY I WAS A YALE PRE-MED IN ANOTHER LIFE, SO I CAN FILL IN THE BLANKS FOR BOTH OF US.
HERE'S WHAT I **CAN** TELL YOU: THIS DERMAL ABRASION WASN'T THE CAUSE OF DEATH...**OBVIOUSLY.** PAINFUL, BUT LIKE EVERYTHING ELSE HERE, NOT FATAL.
LET ME GUESS: NO I.P. ADDRESS.
EXACTLY RIGHT. THE UNIQUE IDENTIFIER SEPARATING THIS MAN FROM THE LANDSCAPE WAS REMOVED... **FORCIBLY.**
THIS WAS **MURDER.**
EVEN **VETERAN** HOMESTEADERS DON'T HAVE THAT KIND OF FIREPOWER.
YOU'RE **LOOKING** AT A HOMESTEADER.
SO THE ATTACK COULDN'T HAVE ORIGINATED FROM WITHIN ARCADIA...
OH NO.
*OH **YES,** DR. GARNER.*

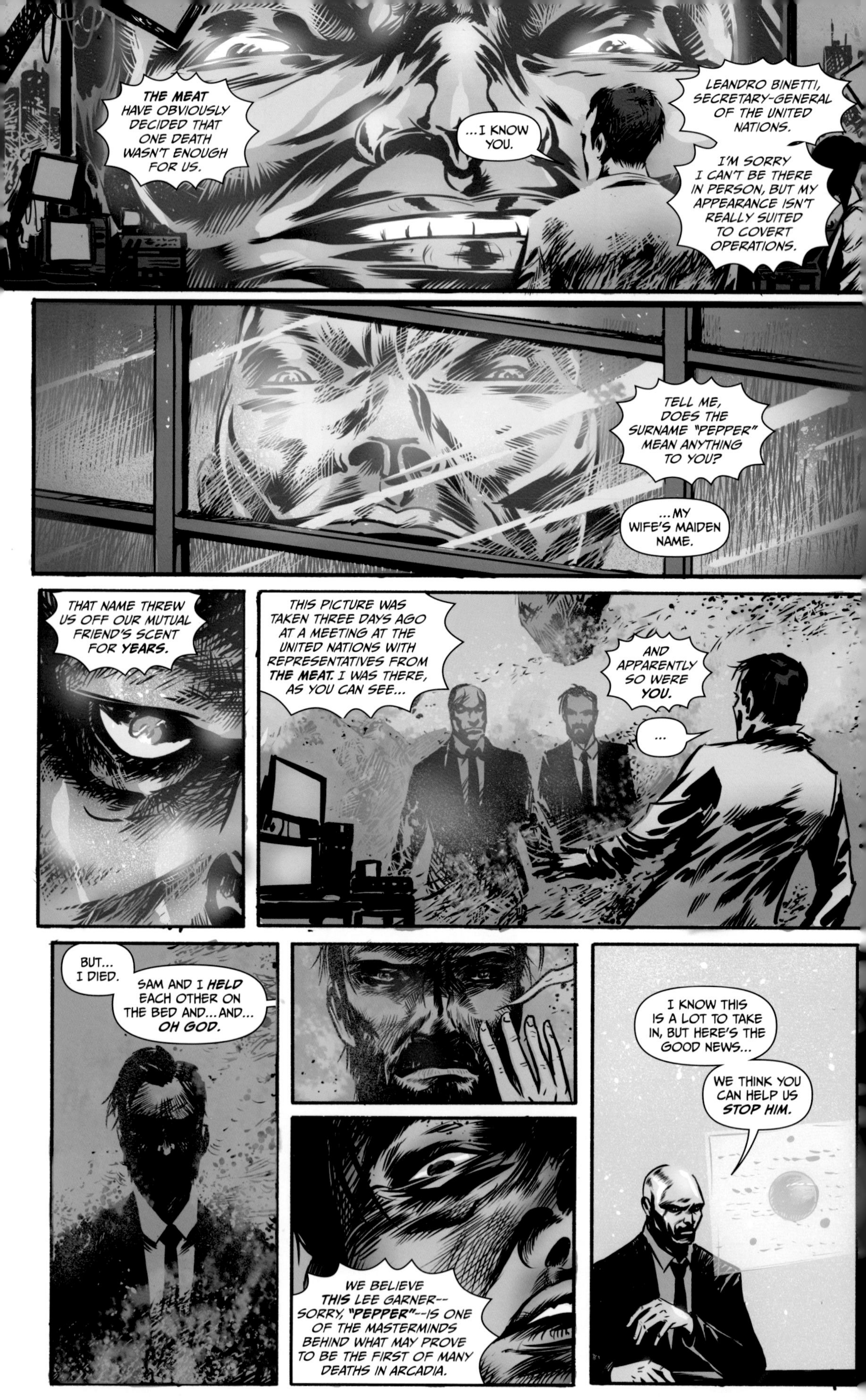
THE MEAT HAVE OBVIOUSLY DECIDED THAT ONE DEATH WASN'T ENOUGH FOR US.
...I KNOW YOU.
LEANDRO BINETTI, SECRETARY-GENERAL OF THE UNITED NATIONS.
I'M SORRY I CAN'T BE THERE IN PERSON, BUT MY APPEARANCE ISN'T REALLY SUITED TO COVERT OPERATIONS.
TELL ME, DOES THE SURNAME "PEPPER" MEAN ANYTHING TO YOU?
...MY WIFE'S MAIDEN NAME.
THAT NAME THREW US OFF OUR MUTUAL FRIEND'S SCENT FOR YEARS.
THIS PICTURE WAS TAKEN THREE DAYS AGO AT A MEETING AT THE UNITED NATIONS WITH REPRESENTATIVES FROM THE MEAT. I WAS THERE, AS YOU CAN SEE...
AND APPARENTLY SO WERE YOU.
...
BUT... I DIED.
SAM AND I HELD EACH OTHER ON THE BED AND...AND... OH GOD.
WE BELIEVE THIS LEE GARNER--SORRY, "PEPPER"--IS ONE OF THE MASTERMINDS BEHIND WHAT MAY PROVE TO BE THE FIRST OF MANY DEATHS IN ARCADIA.
I KNOW THIS IS A LOT TO TAKE IN, BUT HERE'S THE GOOD NEWS...
WE THINK YOU CAN HELP US STOP HIM.

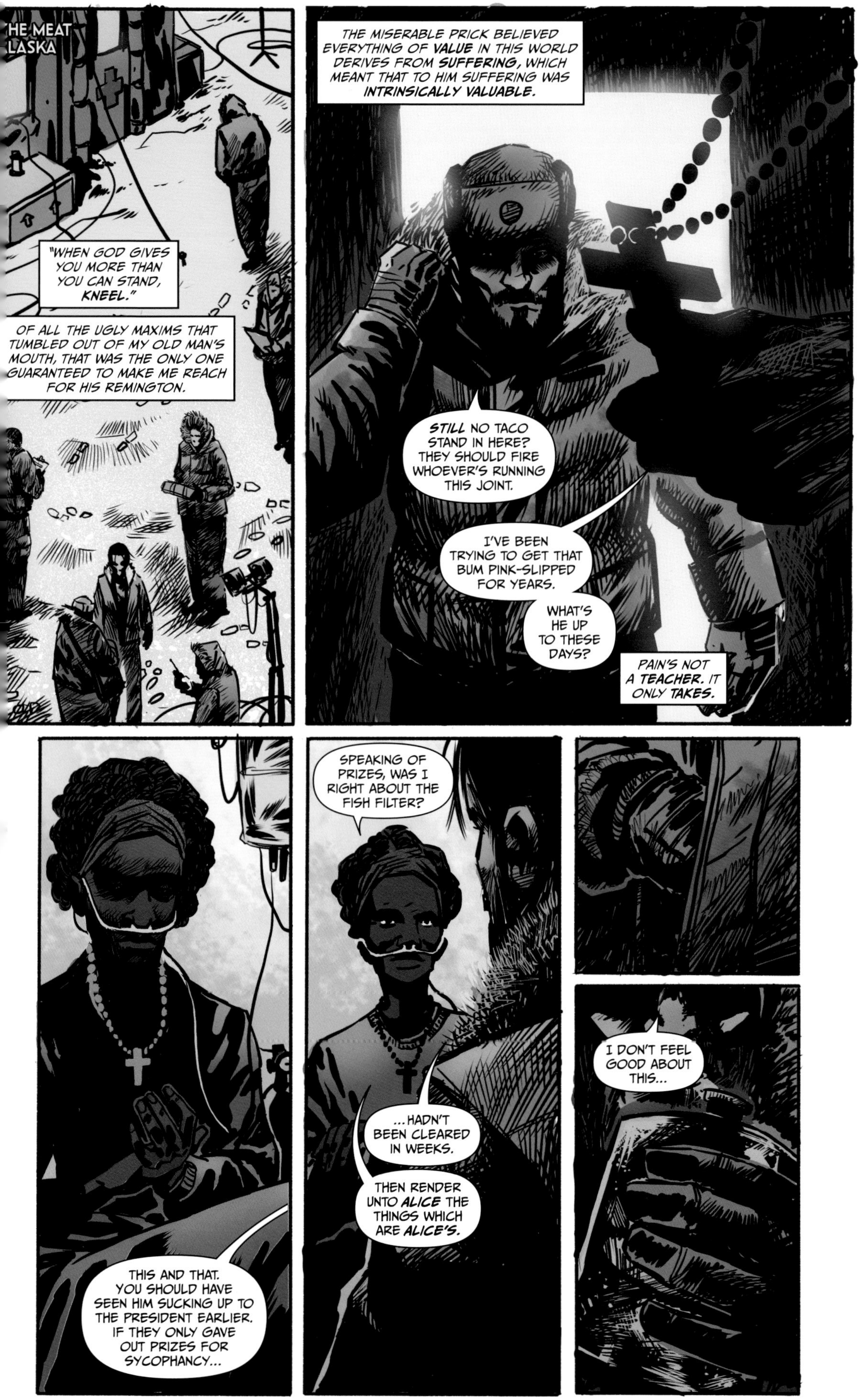
HE MEAT
LASKA
"WHEN GOD GIVES YOU MORE THAN YOU CAN STAND, **KNEEL.**"
OF ALL THE UGLY MAXIMS THAT TUMBLED OUT OF MY OLD MAN'S MOUTH, THAT WAS THE ONLY ONE GUARANTEED TO MAKE ME REACH FOR HIS REMINGTON.
THE MISERABLE PRICK BELIEVED EVERYTHING OF **VALUE** IN THIS WORLD DERIVES FROM **SUFFERING,** WHICH MEANT THAT TO HIM SUFFERING WAS **INTRINSICALLY VALUABLE.**
STILL NO TACO STAND IN HERE? THEY SHOULD FIRE WHOEVER'S RUNNING THIS JOINT.
I'VE BEEN TRYING TO GET THAT BUM PINK-SLIPPED FOR YEARS.
WHAT'S HE UP TO THESE DAYS?
PAIN'S NOT A **TEACHER.** IT ONLY **TAKES.**
THIS AND THAT. YOU SHOULD HAVE SEEN HIM SUCKING UP TO THE PRESIDENT EARLIER. IF THEY ONLY GAVE OUT PRIZES FOR SYCOPHANCY...
SPEAKING OF PRIZES, WAS I RIGHT ABOUT THE FISH FILTER?
...HADN'T BEEN CLEARED IN WEEKS.
THEN RENDER UNTO **ALICE** THE THINGS WHICH ARE **ALICE'S.**
I DON'T FEEL GOOD ABOUT THIS...

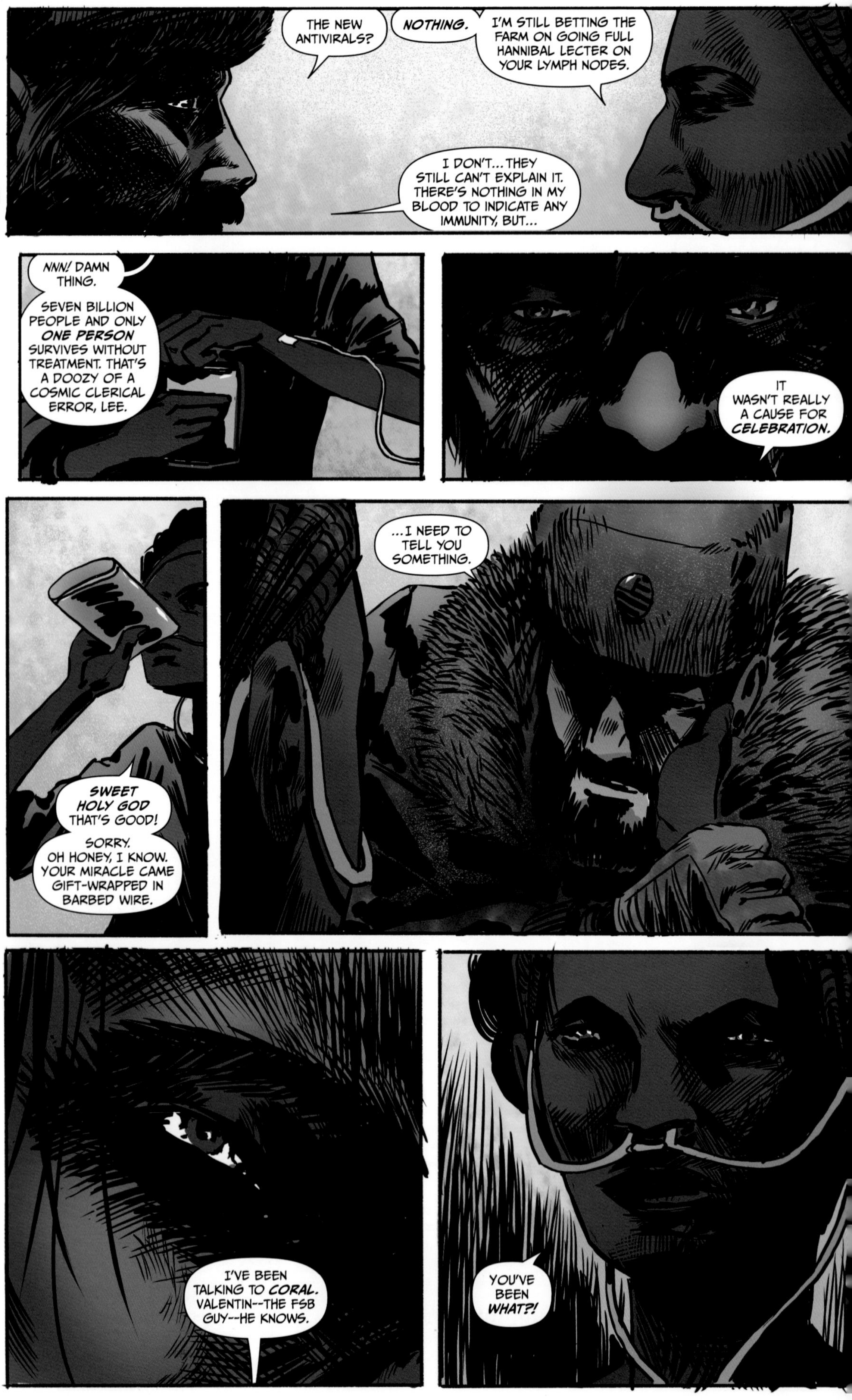
THE NEW ANTIVIRALS?
NOTHING.
I'M STILL BETTING THE FARM ON GOING FULL HANNIBAL LECTER ON YOUR LYMPH NODES.
I DON'T... THEY STILL CAN'T EXPLAIN IT. THERE'S NOTHING IN MY BLOOD TO INDICATE ANY IMMUNITY, BUT...
NNN! DAMN THING.
SEVEN BILLION PEOPLE AND ONLY ONE PERSON SURVIVES WITHOUT TREATMENT. THAT'S A DOOZY OF A COSMIC CLERICAL ERROR, LEE.
IT WASN'T REALLY A CAUSE FOR CELEBRATION.
SWEET HOLY GOD THAT'S GOOD!
SORRY. OH HONEY, I KNOW. YOUR MIRACLE CAME GIFT-WRAPPED IN BARBED WIRE.
...I NEED TO TELL YOU SOMETHING.
I'VE BEEN TALKING TO CORAL. VALENTIN--THE FSB GUY--HE KNOWS.
YOU'VE BEEN WHAT?!

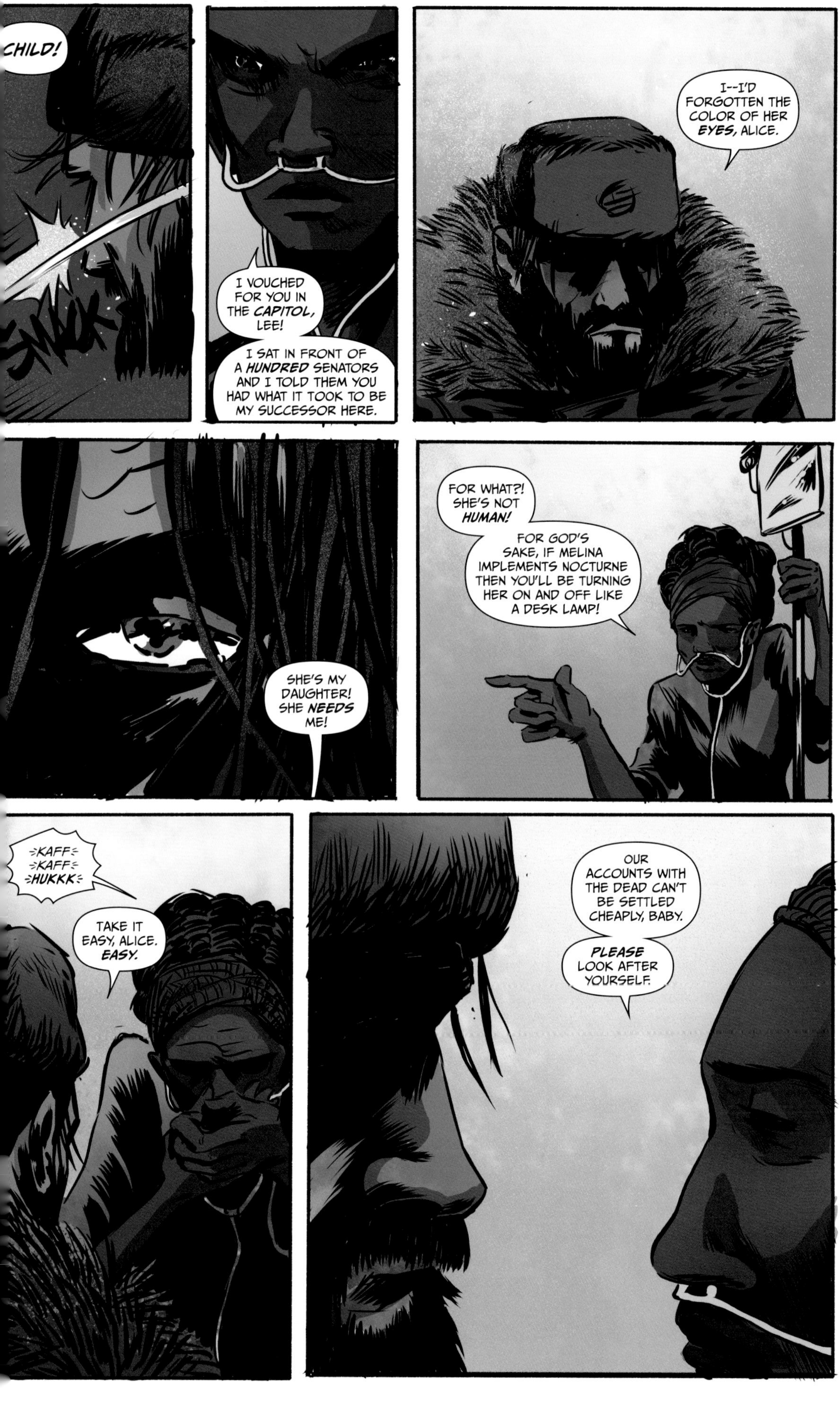

CHILD!
SMACK
I VOUCHED FOR YOU IN THE CAPITOL, LEE!
I SAT IN FRONT OF A HUNDRED SENATORS AND I TOLD THEM YOU HAD WHAT IT TOOK TO BE MY SUCCESSOR HERE.
I--I'D FORGOTTEN THE COLOR OF HER EYES, ALICE.
SHE'S MY DAUGHTER! SHE NEEDS ME!
FOR WHAT?! SHE'S NOT HUMAN!
FOR GOD'S SAKE, IF MELINA IMPLEMENTS NOCTURNE THEN YOU'LL BE TURNING HER ON AND OFF LIKE A DESK LAMP!
KAFF KAFF HUKKK
TAKE IT EASY, ALICE. EASY.
OUR ACCOUNTS WITH THE DEAD CAN'T BE SETTLED CHEAPLY, BABY.
PLEASE LOOK AFTER YOURSELF.

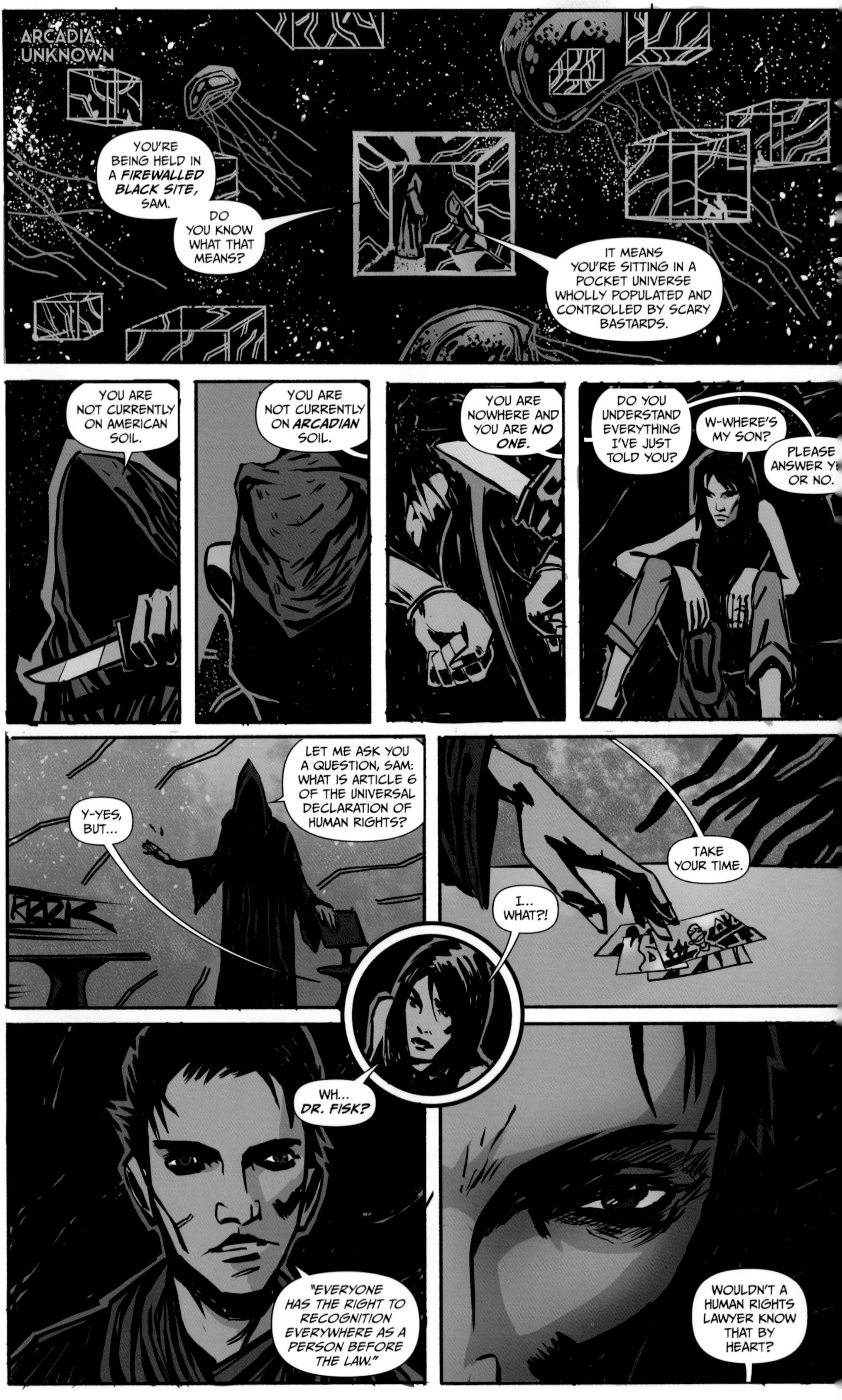
ARCADIA UNKNOWN
YOU'RE BEING HELD IN A FIREWALLED BLACK SITE, SAM.
DO YOU KNOW WHAT THAT MEANS?
IT MEANS YOU'RE SITTING IN A POCKET UNIVERSE WHOLLY POPULATED AND CONTROLLED BY SCARY BASTARDS.
YOU ARE NOT CURRENTLY ON AMERICAN SOIL.
YOU ARE NOT CURRENTLY ON ARCADIAN SOIL.
YOU ARE NOWHERE AND YOU ARE NO ONE.
DO YOU UNDERSTAND EVERYTHING I'VE JUST TOLD YOU?
W-WHERE'S MY SON?
PLEASE ANSWER Y OR NO.
Y-YES, BUT...
LET ME ASK YOU A QUESTION, SAM: WHAT IS ARTICLE 6 OF THE UNIVERSAL DECLARATION OF HUMAN RIGHTS?
I... WHAT?!
TAKE YOUR TIME.
WH... DR. FISK?
"EVERYONE HAS THE RIGHT TO RECOGNITION EVERYWHERE AS A PERSON BEFORE THE LAW."
WOULDN'T A HUMAN RIGHTS LAWYER KNOW THAT BY HEART?

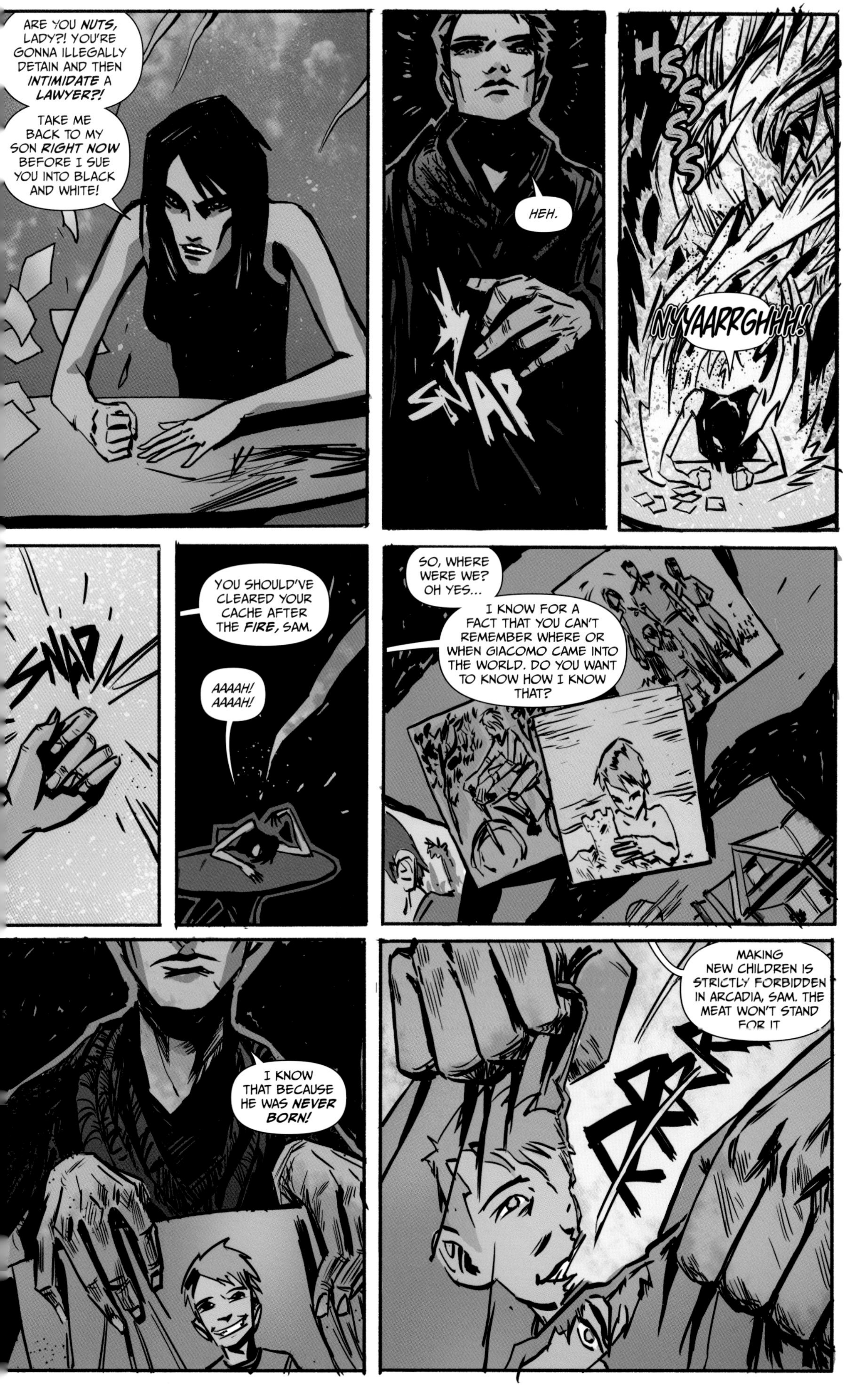

ARE YOU NUTS, LADY?! YOU'RE GONNA ILLEGALLY DETAIN AND THEN INTIMIDATE A LAWYER?!
TAKE ME BACK TO MY SON RIGHT NOW BEFORE I SUE YOU INTO BLACK AND WHITE!
HEH.
SNAP
HSSSSS
NYYAARRGHHH!
SNAP
YOU SHOULD'VE CLEARED YOUR CACHE AFTER THE FIRE, SAM.
AAAAH! AAAAH!
SO, WHERE WERE WE? OH YES...
I KNOW FOR A FACT THAT YOU CAN'T REMEMBER WHERE OR WHEN GIACOMO CAME INTO THE WORLD. DO YOU WANT TO KNOW HOW I KNOW THAT?
I KNOW THAT BECAUSE HE WAS NEVER BORN!
MAKING NEW CHILDREN IS STRICTLY FORBIDDEN IN ARCADIA, SAM. THE MEAT WON'T STAND FOR IT

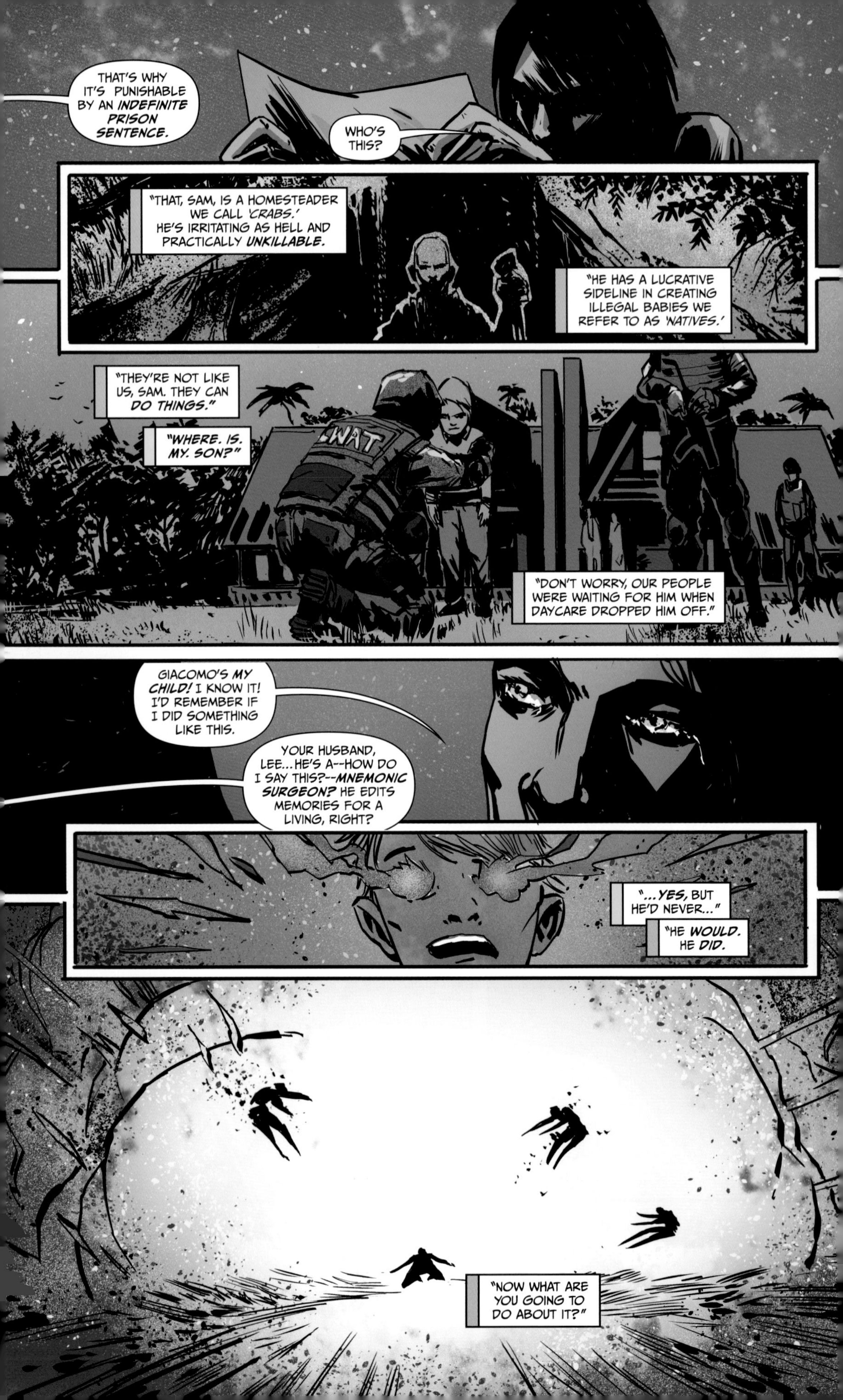

THAT'S WHY IT'S PUNISHABLE BY AN *INDEFINITE PRISON SENTENCE.*
WHO'S THIS?
"THAT, SAM, IS A HOMESTEADER WE CALL *'CRABS.'* HE'S IRRITATING AS HELL AND PRACTICALLY *UNKILLABLE.*
"HE HAS A LUCRATIVE SIDELINE IN CREATING ILLEGAL BABIES WE REFER TO AS *'NATIVES.'*
"THEY'RE NOT LIKE US, SAM. THEY CAN *DO THINGS."*
"WHERE. IS. MY. SON?"
"DON'T WORRY, OUR PEOPLE WERE WAITING FOR HIM WHEN DAYCARE DROPPED HIM OFF."
GIACOMO'S *MY CHILD!* I KNOW IT! I'D REMEMBER IF I DID SOMETHING LIKE THIS.
YOUR HUSBAND, LEE... HE'S A--HOW DO I SAY THIS?--*MNEMONIC SURGEON?* HE EDITS MEMORIES FOR A LIVING, RIGHT?
"...*YES,* BUT HE'D NEVER..."
"HE *WOULD.* HE *DID.*
"NOW WHAT ARE YOU GOING TO DO ABOUT IT?"

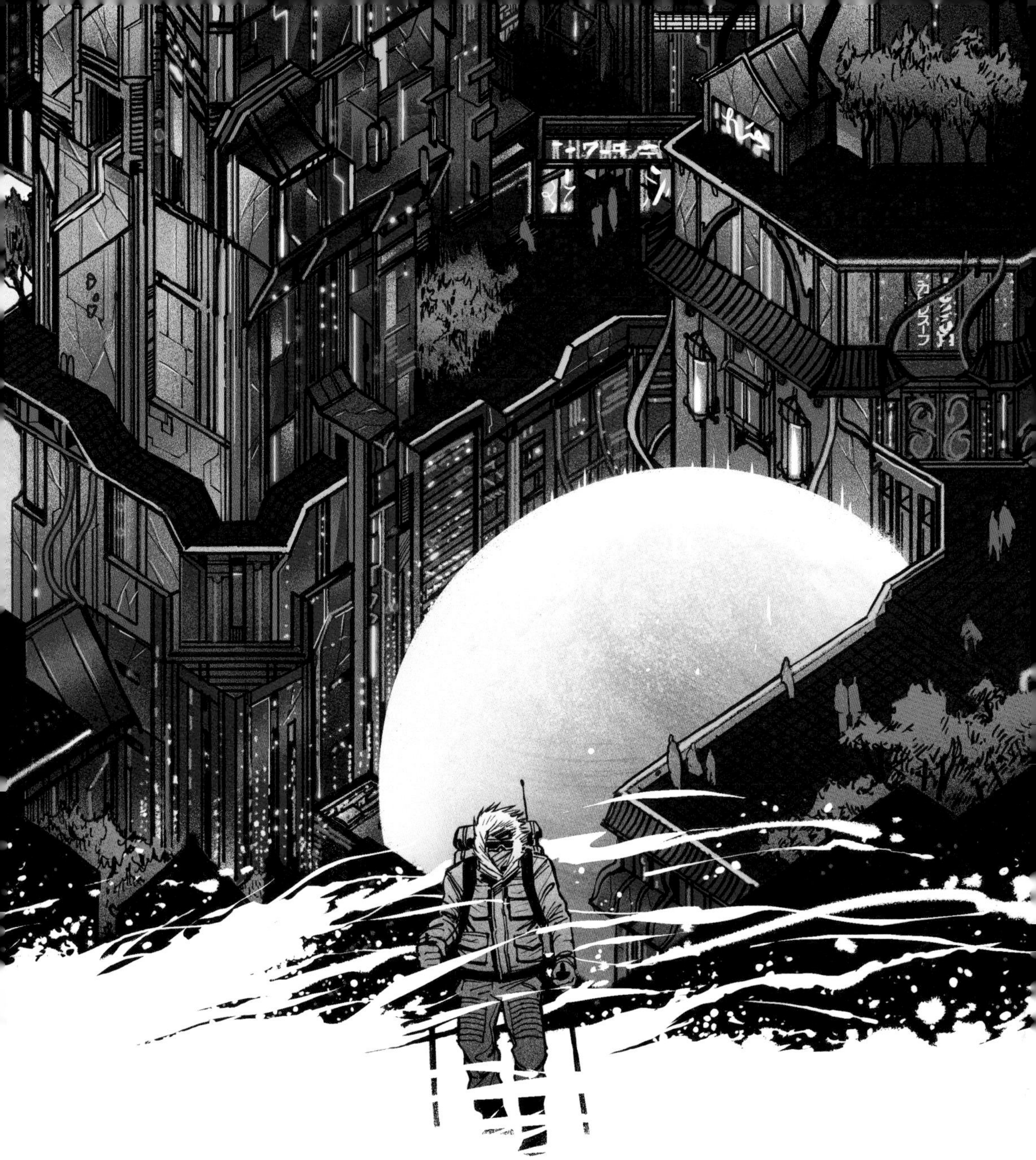

Issue Two Variant Cover **Eric Scott Pfeiffer**

"The camouflage always imitates
the target."

—**J.G. Ballard**

CHAPTER

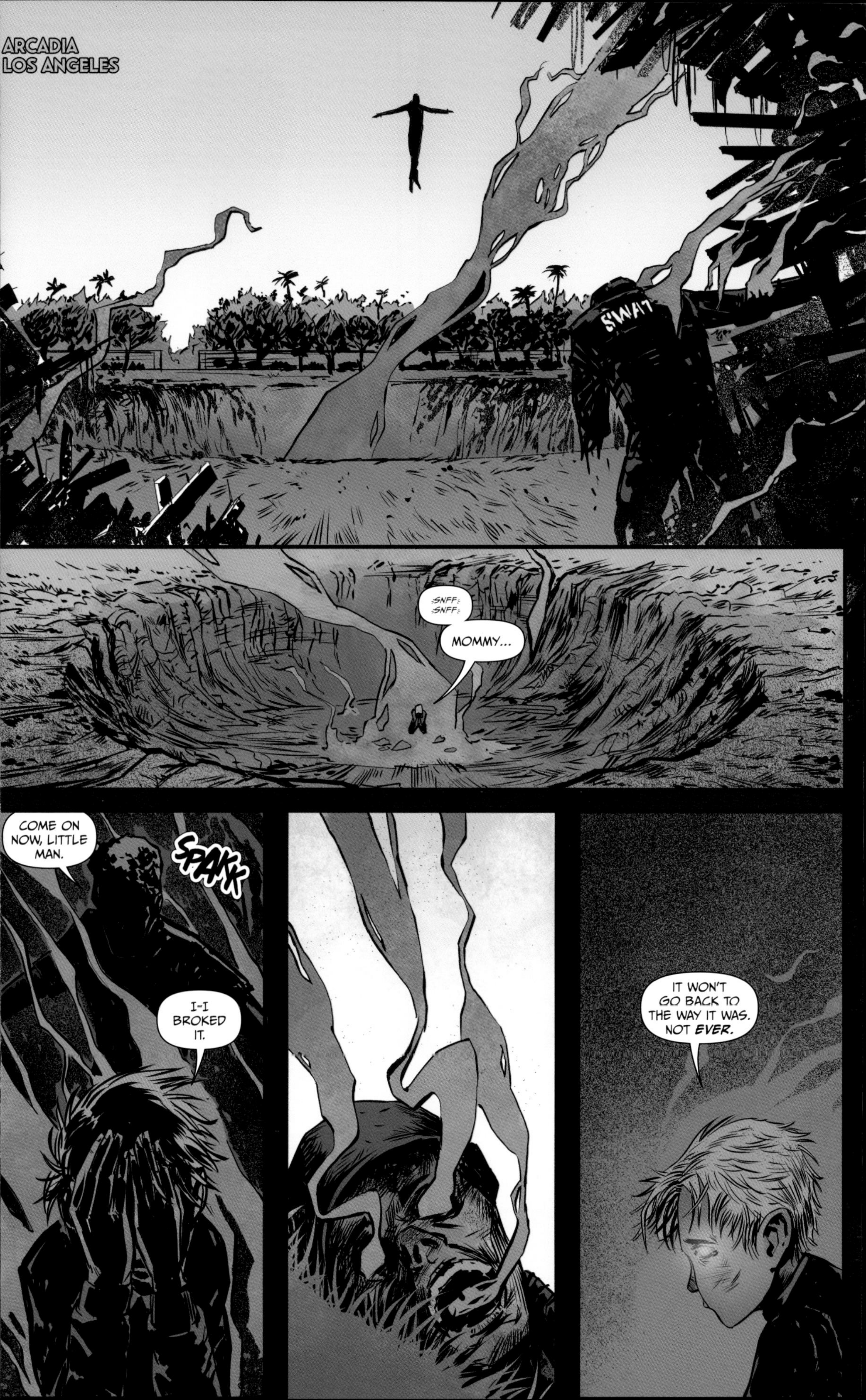
ARCADIA
LOS ANGELES
SWAT
SNFF SNFF
MOMMY...
COME ON NOW, LITTLE MAN.
SPAKK
I-I BROKED IT.
IT WON'T GO BACK TO THE WAY IT WAS. NOT *EVER.*

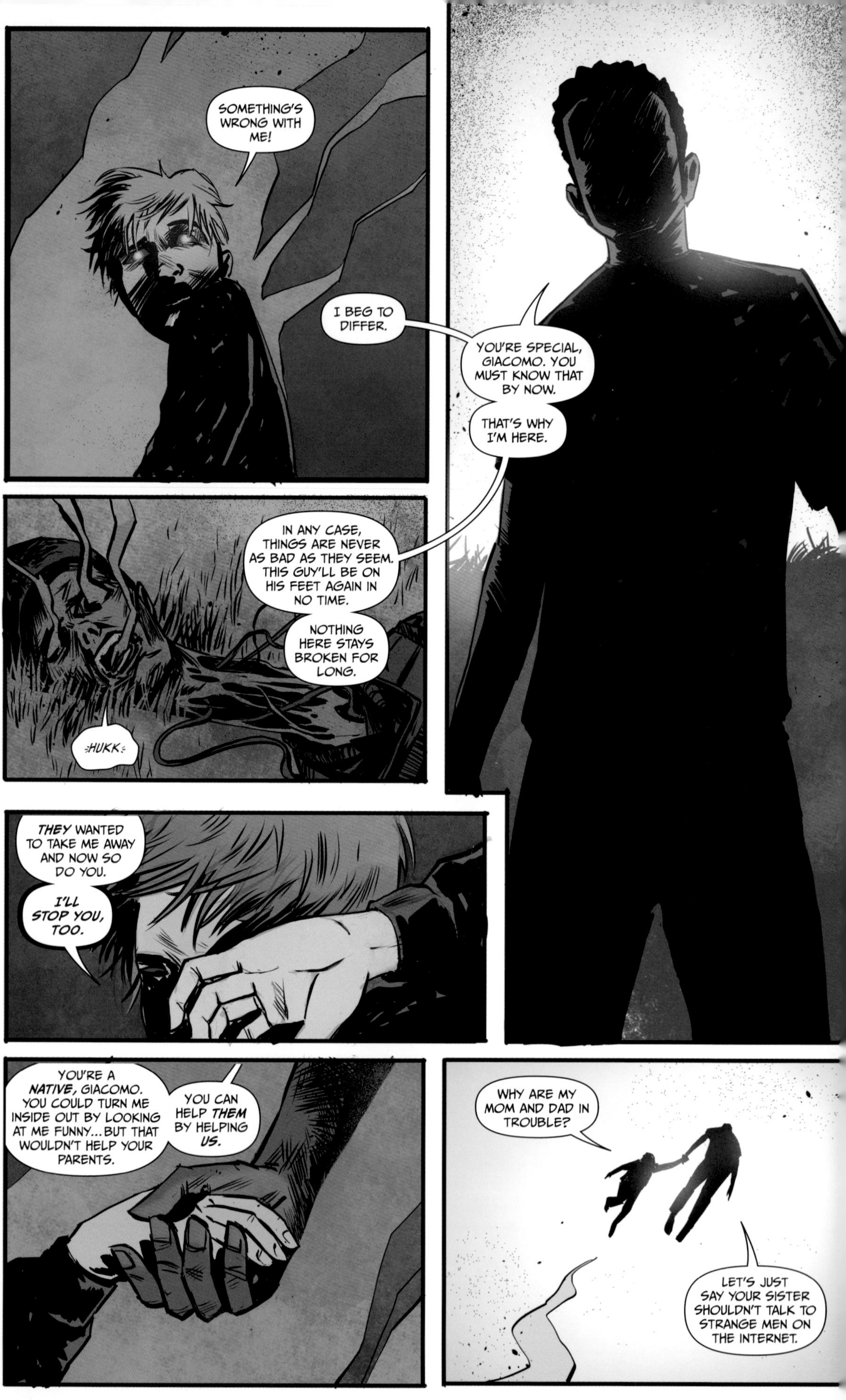
SOMETHING'S WRONG WITH ME!
I BEG TO DIFFER.
YOU'RE SPECIAL, GIACOMO. YOU MUST KNOW THAT BY NOW.
THAT'S WHY I'M HERE.
IN ANY CASE, THINGS ARE NEVER AS BAD AS THEY SEEM. THIS GUY'LL BE ON HIS FEET AGAIN IN NO TIME.
NOTHING HERE STAYS BROKEN FOR LONG.
HUKK
THEY WANTED TO TAKE ME AWAY AND NOW SO DO YOU.
I'LL STOP YOU, TOO.
YOU'RE A NATIVE, GIACOMO. YOU COULD TURN ME INSIDE OUT BY LOOKING AT ME FUNNY... BUT THAT WOULDN'T HELP YOUR PARENTS.
YOU CAN HELP THEM BY HELPING US.
WHY ARE MY MOM AND DAD IN TROUBLE?
LET'S JUST SAY YOUR SISTER SHOULDN'T TALK TO STRANGE MEN ON THE INTERNET.

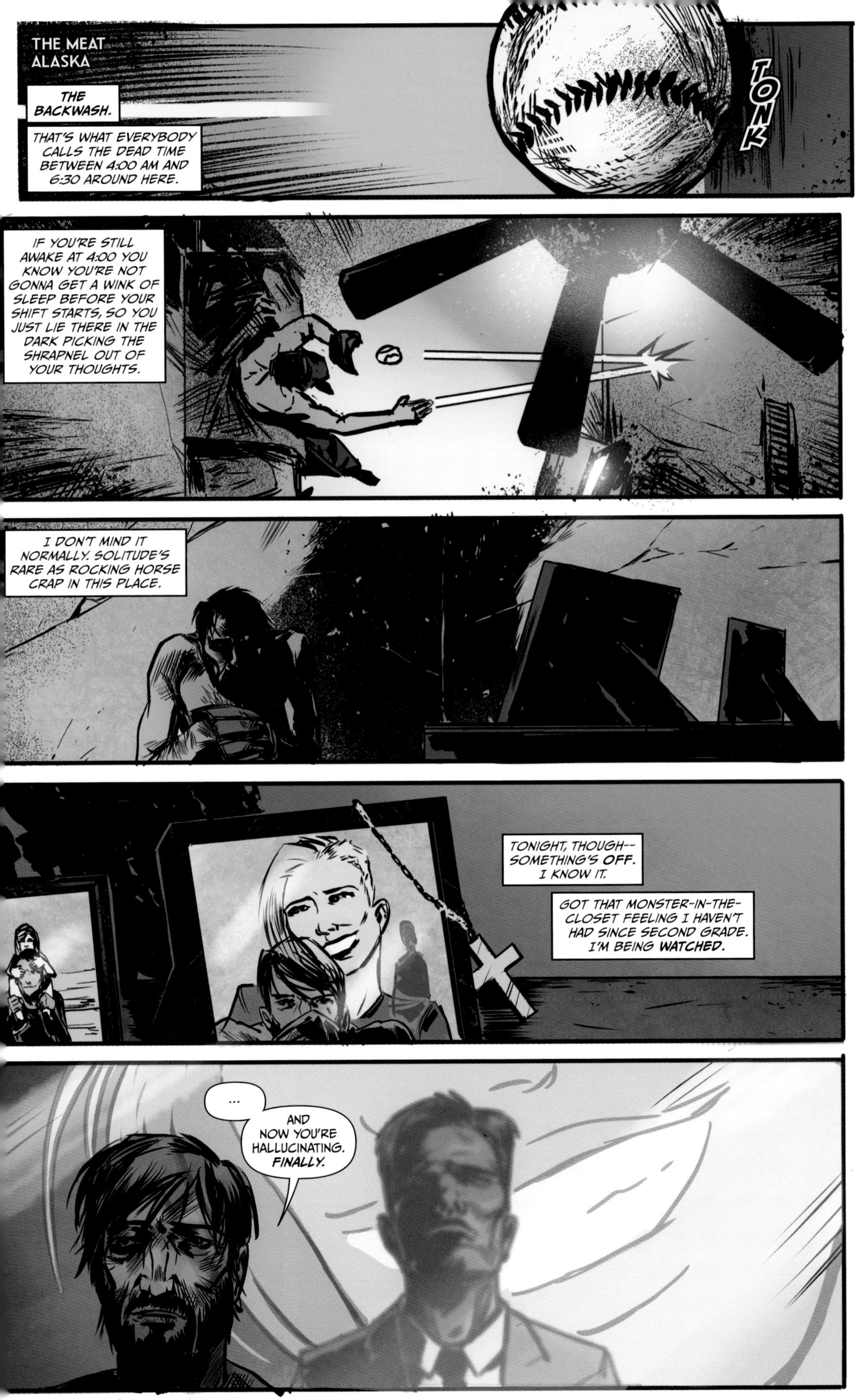
THE MEAT
ALASKA
THE BACKWASH.
THAT'S WHAT EVERYBODY CALLS THE DEAD TIME BETWEEN 4:00 AM AND 6:30 AROUND HERE.
TONK
IF YOU'RE STILL AWAKE AT 4:00 YOU KNOW YOU'RE NOT GONNA GET A WINK OF SLEEP BEFORE YOUR SHIFT STARTS, SO YOU JUST LIE THERE IN THE DARK PICKING THE SHRAPNEL OUT OF YOUR THOUGHTS.
I DON'T MIND IT NORMALLY. SOLITUDE'S RARE AS ROCKING HORSE CRAP IN THIS PLACE.
TONIGHT, THOUGH-- SOMETHING'S **OFF**. I KNOW IT.
GOT THAT MONSTER-IN-THE-CLOSET FEELING I HAVEN'T HAD SINCE SECOND GRADE. I'M BEING **WATCHED**.
...
AND NOW YOU'RE HALLUCINATING. **FINALLY.**

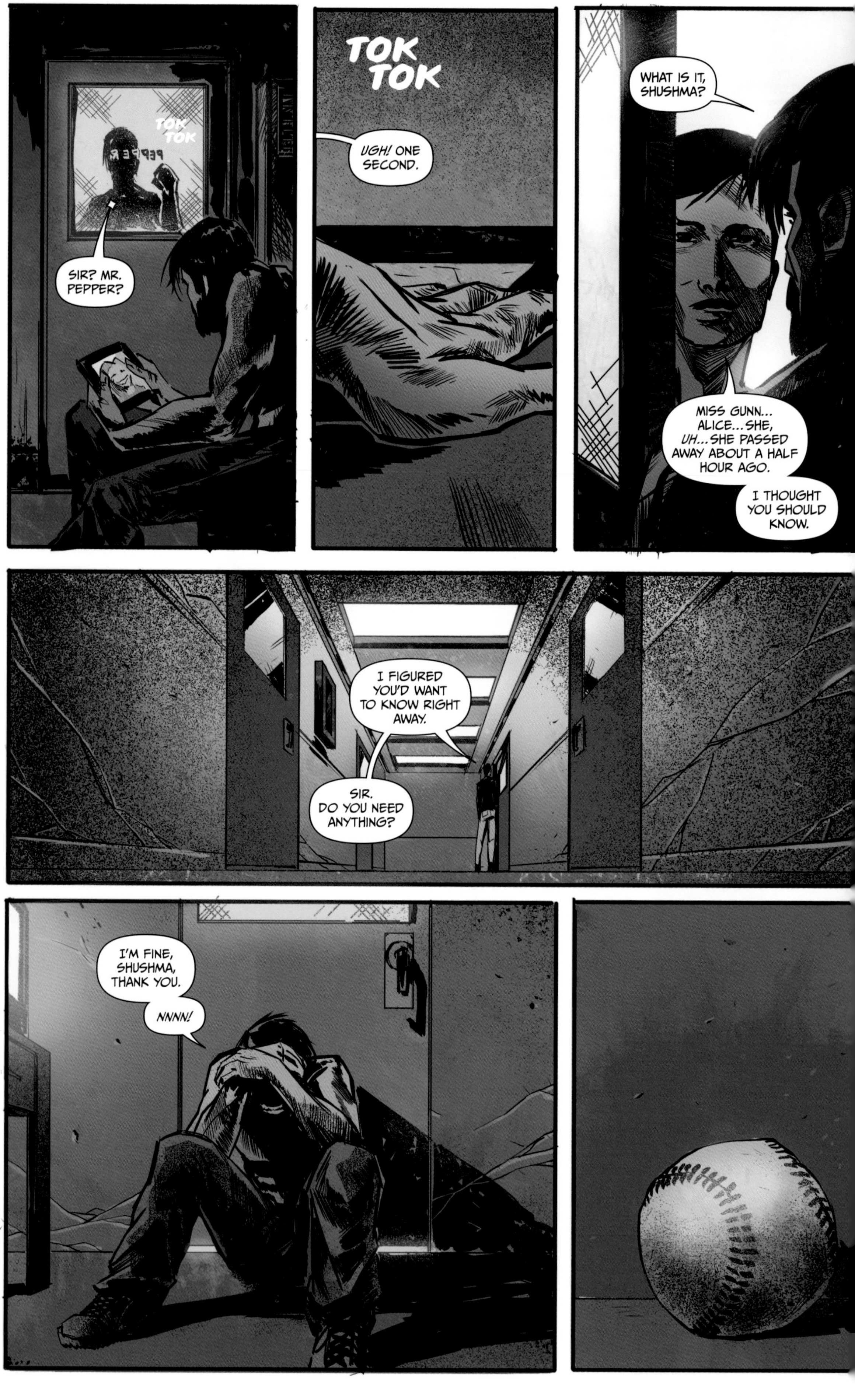

TOK TOK
SIR? MR. PEPPER?
TOK TOK
UGH! ONE SECOND.
WHAT IS IT, SHUSHMA?
MISS GUNN... ALICE... SHE, *UH*... SHE PASSED AWAY ABOUT A HALF HOUR AGO.
I THOUGHT YOU SHOULD KNOW.
I FIGURED YOU'D WANT TO KNOW RIGHT AWAY.
SIR. DO YOU NEED ANYTHING?
I'M FINE, SHUSHMA, THANK YOU.
NNNN!

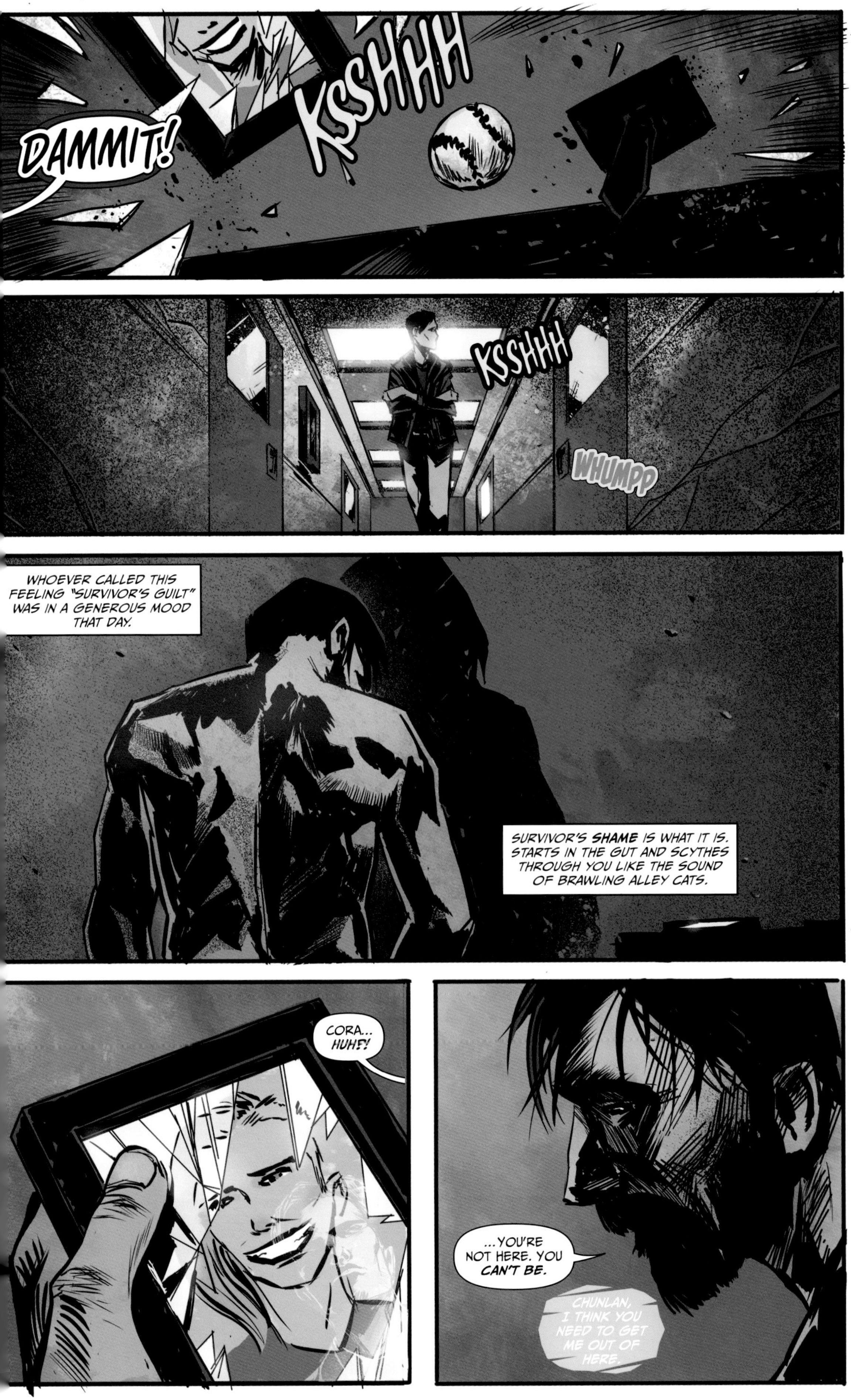
DAMMIT!
KSSHHH
KSSHHH
WHUMPP
WHOEVER CALLED THIS FEELING "SURVIVOR'S GUILT" WAS IN A GENEROUS MOOD THAT DAY.
SURVIVOR'S SHAME IS WHAT IT IS. STARTS IN THE GUT AND SCYTHES THROUGH YOU LIKE THE SOUND OF BRAWLING ALLEY CATS.
CORA... HUH?!
...YOU'RE NOT HERE. YOU CAN'T BE.
CHUNLAN, I THINK YOU NEED TO GET ME OUT OF HERE.

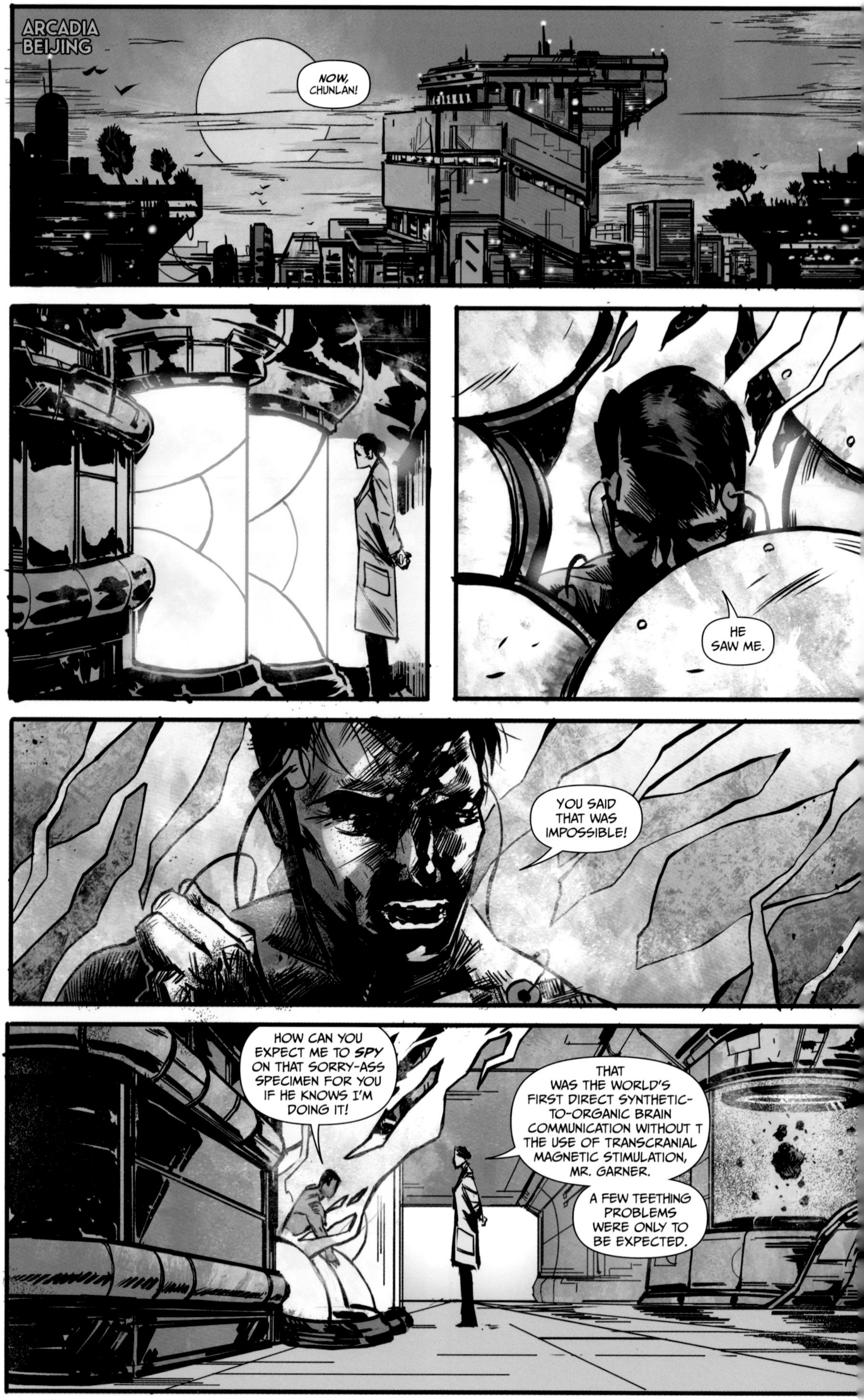
ARCADIA
BEIJING
NOW, CHUNLAN!
HE SAW ME.
YOU SAID THAT WAS IMPOSSIBLE!
HOW CAN YOU EXPECT ME TO SPY ON THAT SORRY-ASS SPECIMEN FOR YOU IF HE KNOWS I'M DOING IT!
THAT WAS THE WORLD'S FIRST DIRECT SYNTHETIC-TO-ORGANIC BRAIN COMMUNICATION WITHOUT T THE USE OF TRANSCRANIAL MAGNETIC STIMULATION, MR. GARNER.
A FEW TEETHING PROBLEMS WERE ONLY TO BE EXPECTED.

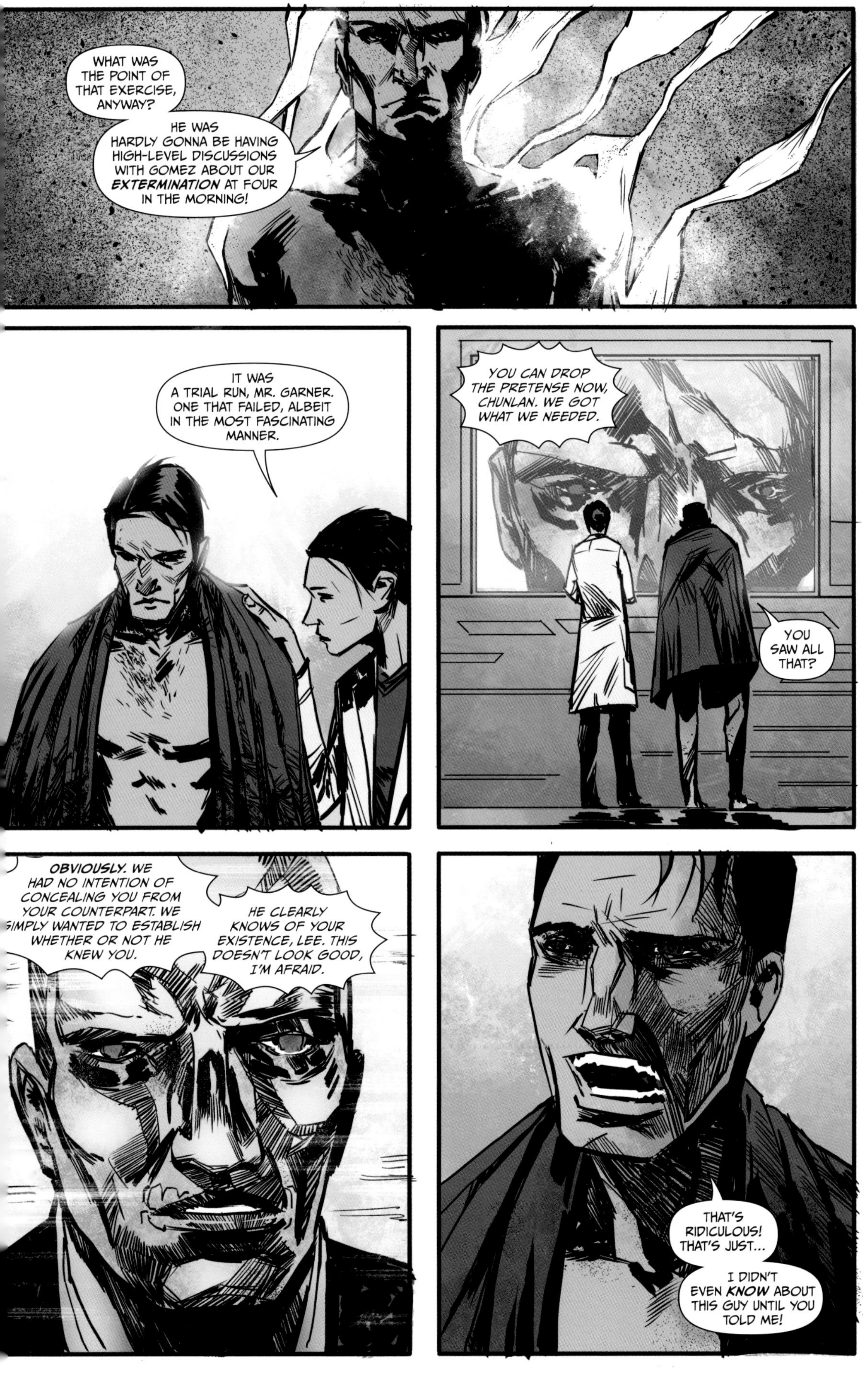
WHAT WAS THE POINT OF THAT EXERCISE, ANYWAY?
HE WAS HARDLY GONNA BE HAVING HIGH-LEVEL DISCUSSIONS WITH GOMEZ ABOUT OUR ***EXTERMINATION*** AT FOUR IN THE MORNING!
IT WAS A TRIAL RUN, MR. GARNER. ONE THAT FAILED, ALBEIT IN THE MOST FASCINATING MANNER.
YOU CAN DROP THE PRETENSE NOW, CHUNLAN. WE GOT WHAT WE NEEDED.
YOU SAW ALL THAT?
OBVIOUSLY. WE HAD NO INTENTION OF CONCEALING YOU FROM YOUR COUNTERPART. WE SIMPLY WANTED TO ESTABLISH WHETHER OR NOT HE KNEW YOU.
HE CLEARLY KNOWS OF YOUR EXISTENCE, LEE. THIS DOESN'T LOOK GOOD, I'M AFRAID.
THAT'S RIDICULOUS! THAT'S JUST...
I DIDN'T EVEN ***KNOW*** ABOUT THIS GUY UNTIL YOU TOLD ME!

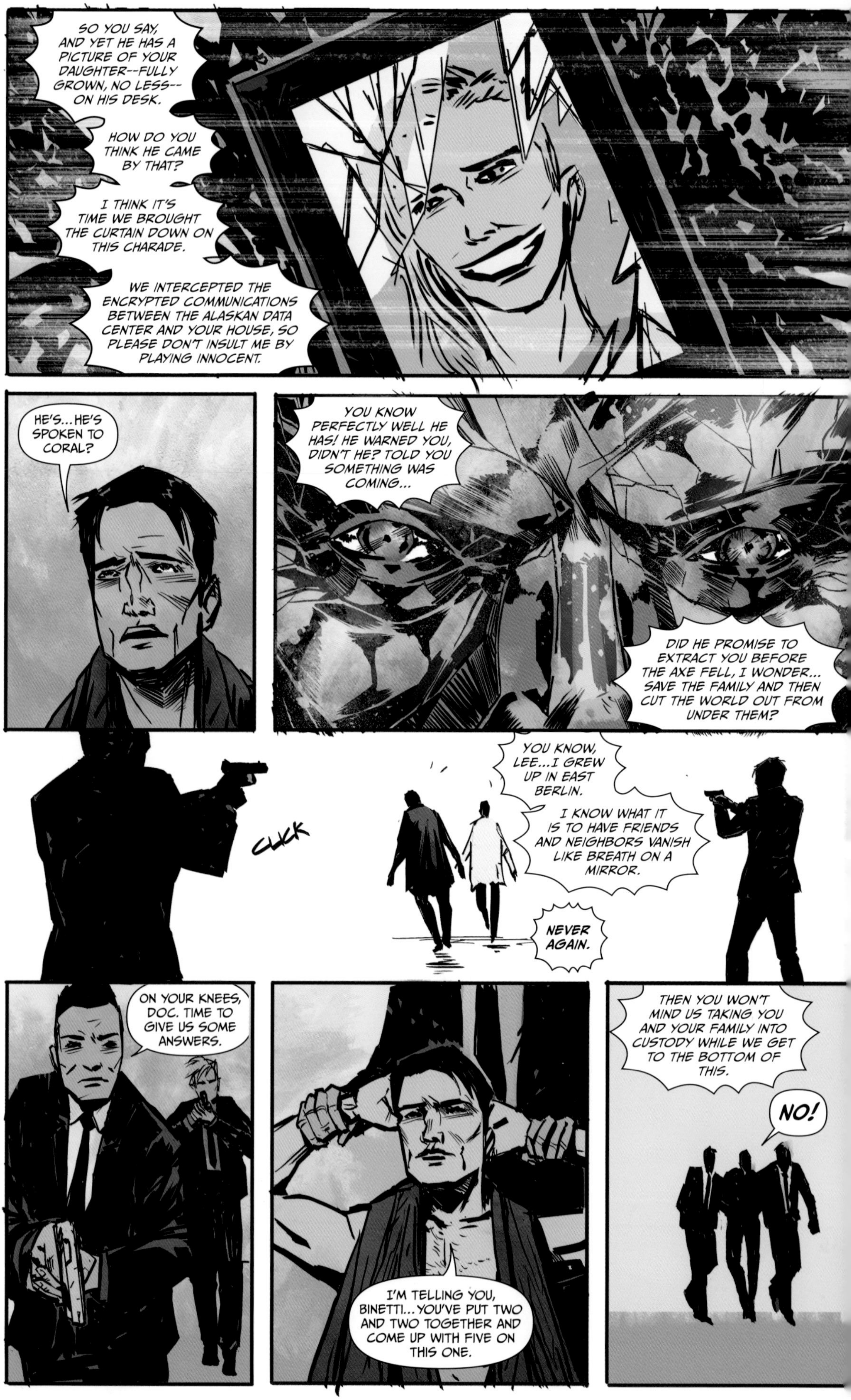
SO YOU SAY, AND YET HE HAS A PICTURE OF YOUR DAUGHTER--FULLY GROWN, NO LESS-- ON HIS DESK.
HOW DO YOU THINK HE CAME BY THAT?
I THINK IT'S TIME WE BROUGHT THE CURTAIN DOWN ON THIS CHARADE.
WE INTERCEPTED THE ENCRYPTED COMMUNICATIONS BETWEEN THE ALASKAN DATA CENTER AND YOUR HOUSE, SO PLEASE DON'T INSULT ME BY PLAYING INNOCENT.
HE'S... HE'S SPOKEN TO CORAL?
YOU KNOW PERFECTLY WELL HE HAS! HE WARNED YOU, DIDN'T HE? TOLD YOU SOMETHING WAS COMING...
DID HE PROMISE TO EXTRACT YOU BEFORE THE AXE FELL, I WONDER... SAVE THE FAMILY AND THEN CUT THE WORLD OUT FROM UNDER THEM?
CLICK
YOU KNOW, LEE... I GREW UP IN EAST BERLIN.
I KNOW WHAT IT IS TO HAVE FRIENDS AND NEIGHBORS VANISH LIKE BREATH ON A MIRROR.
NEVER AGAIN.
ON YOUR KNEES, DOC. TIME TO GIVE US SOME ANSWERS.
I'M TELLING YOU, BINETTI... YOU'VE PUT TWO AND TWO TOGETHER AND COME UP WITH FIVE ON THIS ONE.
THEN YOU WON'T MIND US TAKING YOU AND YOUR FAMILY INTO CUSTODY WHILE WE GET TO THE BOTTOM OF THIS.
NO!

"IT'S USELESS TO PROTEST, LEE. IF YOU'RE NOT IN CHAINS THEN YOU'RE ON THE PAYROLL."

...WHICH BRINGS US TO SKEUOMORPHISM. S-K-E-U-O-M-O-R-P-H-I-S-M.

ARCADIA BRENTWOOD

SKEUOMORPHISM

CAN ANYONE TELL ME WHAT THIS IS?

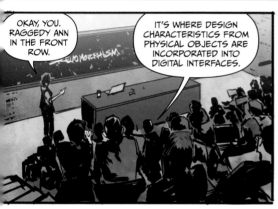

OKAY, YOU. RAGGEDY ANN IN THE FRONT ROW.

IT'S WHERE DESIGN CHARACTERISTICS FROM PHYSICAL OBJECTS ARE INCORPORATED INTO DIGITAL INTERFACES.

EXAMPLE?

UH, WHAT ABOUT THOSE SIMULATED PAGE-TURNS ON OLD EBOOKS?

GOOD. BUT SKEUOMORPHISM'S NOT JUST A DIGITAL PHENOMENON. CONSIDER THE MORRIS MINOR TRAVELLER...

BEAUTIFUL, HUH?

THIS BRITISH STATION WAGON FROM THE FIFTIES WAS TARGETED AT RURAL CONSUMERS.

AS YOU CAN SEE, HARDWOOD COMPONENTS WERE INTEGRAL TO ITS DESIGN. WHY?

WELL, THE HORSE AND CART WASN'T AN UNUSUAL SIGHT ON COUNTRY ROADS AT THAT TIME.

THIS MEANT THAT THE AUTOMOBILE HAD TO BLEND IN SOMEHOW.

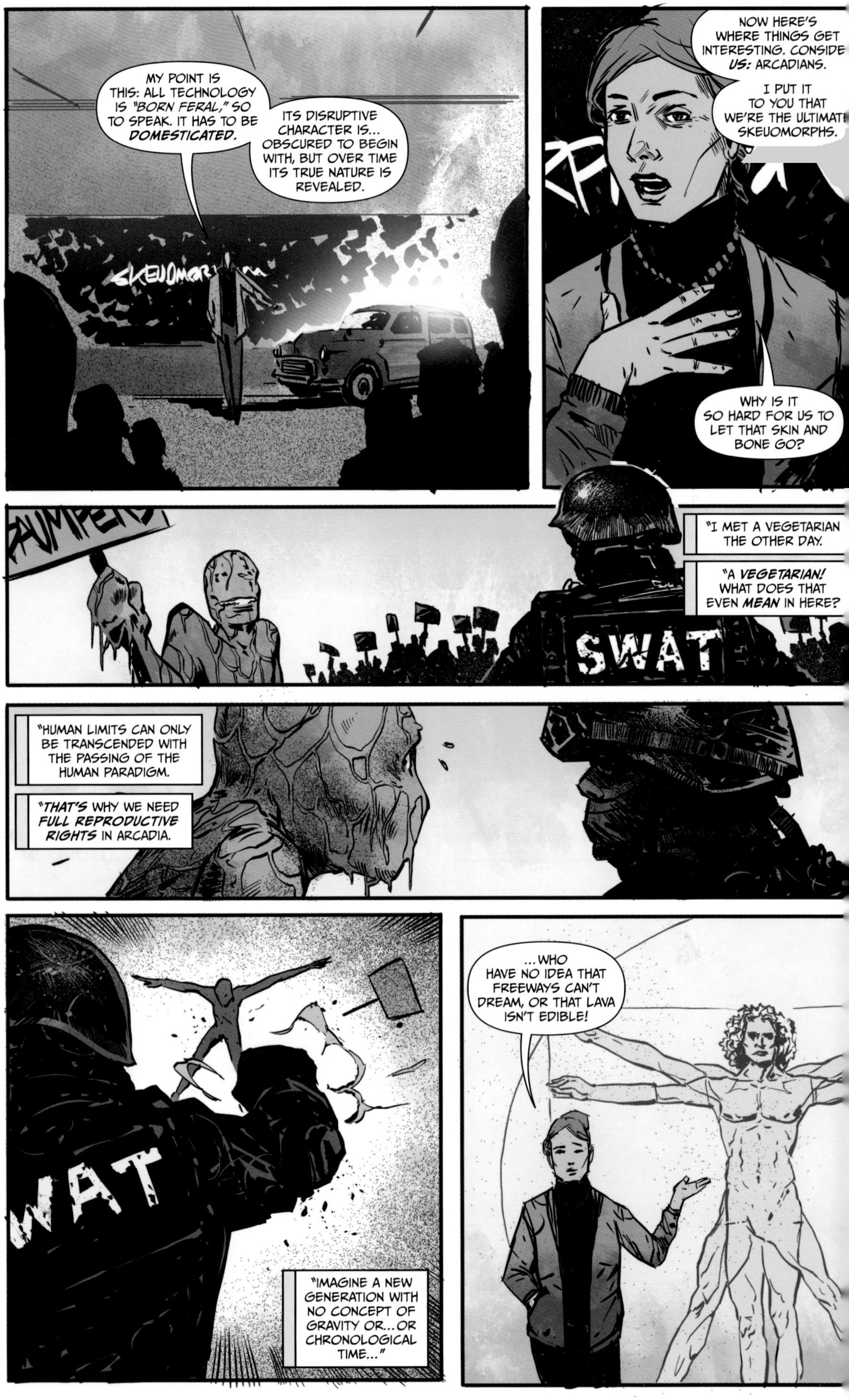

MY POINT IS THIS: ALL TECHNOLOGY IS "BORN FERAL," SO TO SPEAK. IT HAS TO BE DOMESTICATED.
ITS DISRUPTIVE CHARACTER IS... OBSCURED TO BEGIN WITH, BUT OVER TIME ITS TRUE NATURE IS REVEALED.
SKEUOMORPH
NOW HERE'S WHERE THINGS GET INTERESTING. CONSIDE US: ARCADIANS.
I PUT IT TO YOU THAT WE'RE THE ULTIMAT SKEUOMORPHS.
WHY IS IT SO HARD FOR US TO LET THAT SKIN AND BONE GO?
"I MET A VEGETARIAN THE OTHER DAY.
"A VEGETARIAN! WHAT DOES THAT EVEN MEAN IN HERE?
SWAT
"HUMAN LIMITS CAN ONLY BE TRANSCENDED WITH THE PASSING OF THE HUMAN PARADIGM.
"THAT'S WHY WE NEED FULL REPRODUCTIVE RIGHTS IN ARCADIA.
WAT
"IMAGINE A NEW GENERATION WITH NO CONCEPT OF GRAVITY OR...OR CHRONOLOGICAL TIME..."
...WHO HAVE NO IDEA THAT FREEWAYS CAN'T DREAM, OR THAT LAVA ISN'T EDIBLE!

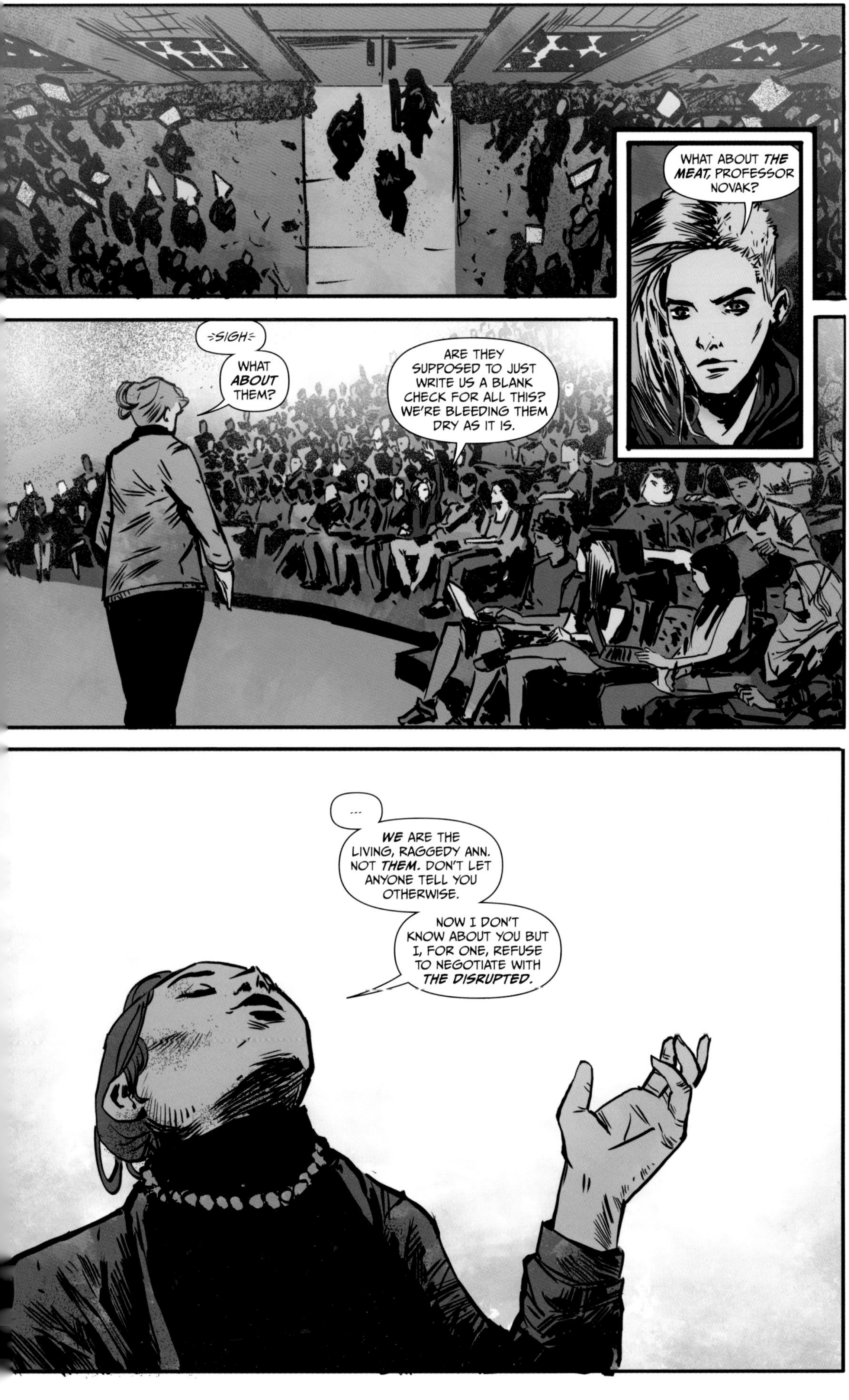
WHAT ABOUT *THE MEAT,* PROFESSOR NOVAK?
SIGH
WHAT *ABOUT* THEM?
ARE THEY SUPPOSED TO JUST WRITE US A BLANK CHECK FOR ALL THIS? WE'RE BLEEDING THEM DRY AS IT IS.
...
WE ARE THE LIVING, RAGGEDY ANN. NOT *THEM.* DON'T LET ANYONE TELL YOU OTHERWISE.
NOW I DON'T KNOW ABOUT YOU BUT I, FOR ONE, REFUSE TO NEGOTIATE WITH *THE DISRUPTED.*

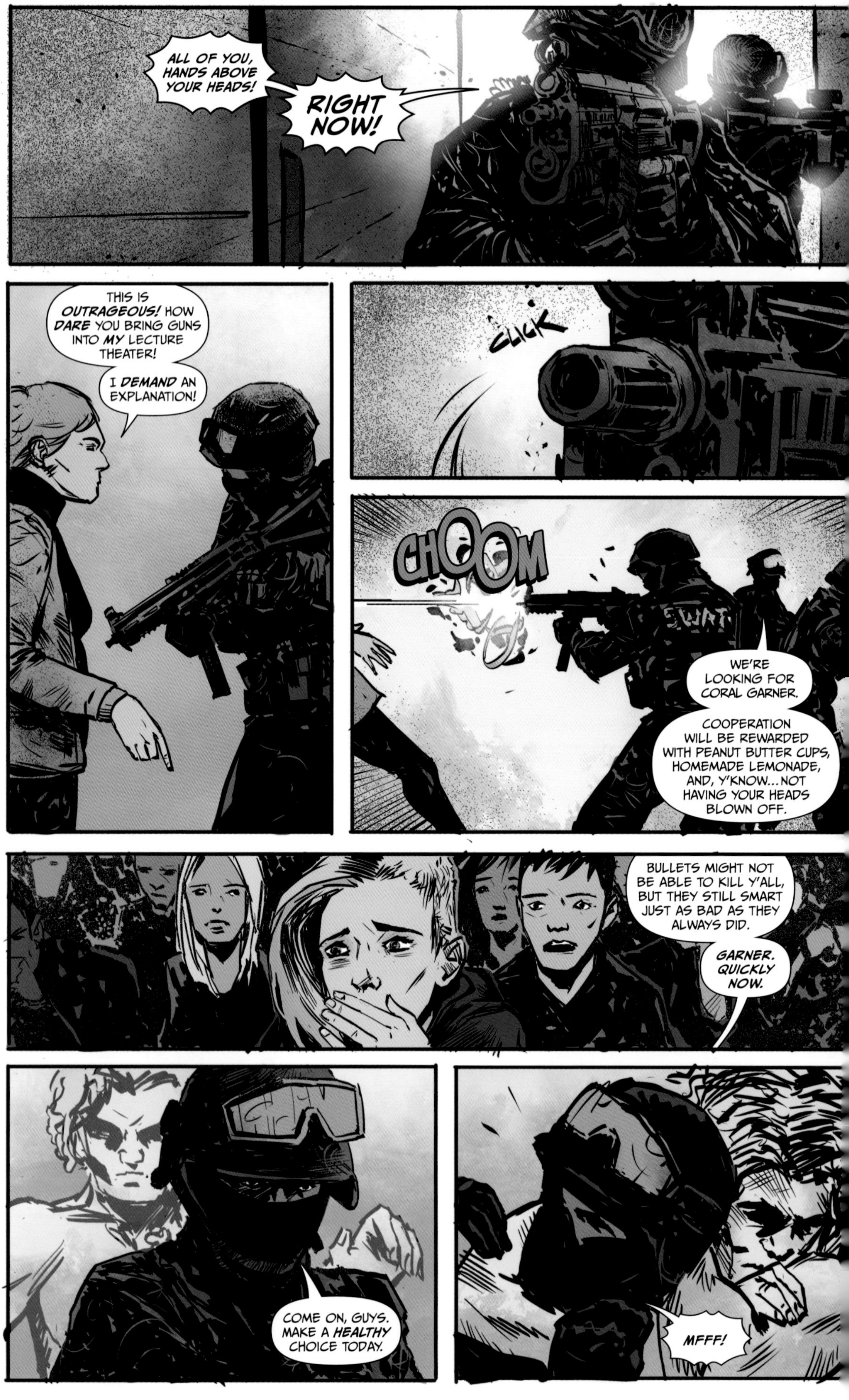
ALL OF YOU, HANDS ABOVE YOUR HEADS!
RIGHT NOW!
THIS IS OUTRAGEOUS! HOW DARE YOU BRING GUNS INTO MY LECTURE THEATER!
I DEMAND AN EXPLANATION!
CLICK
CHOOM
SWAT
WE'RE LOOKING FOR CORAL GARNER.
COOPERATION WILL BE REWARDED WITH PEANUT BUTTER CUPS, HOMEMADE LEMONADE, AND, Y'KNOW...NOT HAVING YOUR HEADS BLOWN OFF.
BULLETS MIGHT NOT BE ABLE TO KILL Y'ALL, BUT THEY STILL SMART JUST AS BAD AS THEY ALWAYS DID.
GARNER. QUICKLY NOW.
COME ON, GUYS. MAKE A HEALTHY CHOICE TODAY.
MFFF!

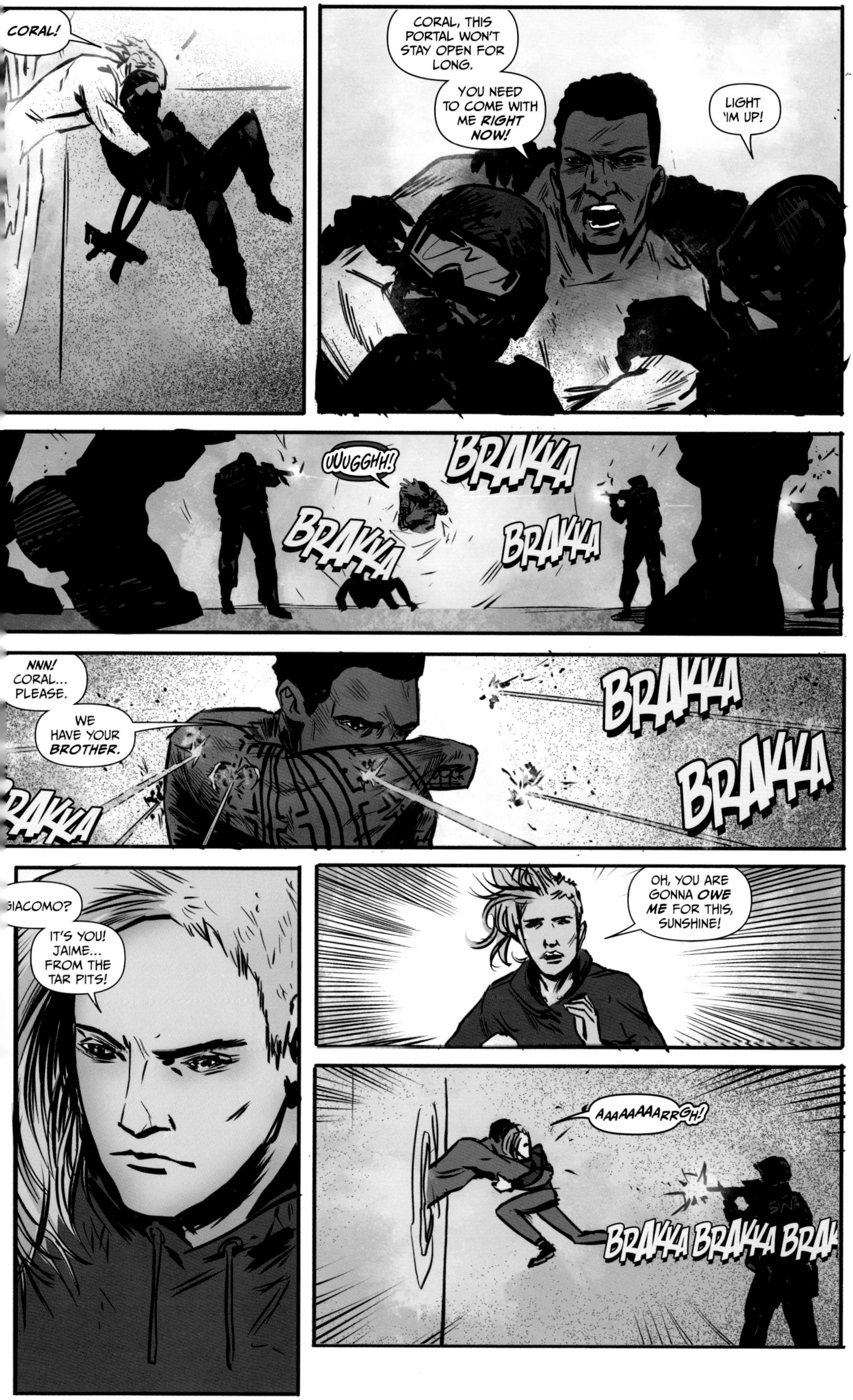
CORAL!
CORAL, THIS PORTAL WON'T STAY OPEN FOR LONG.
YOU NEED TO COME WITH ME RIGHT NOW!
LIGHT 'IM UP!
UUUGGHH!
BRAKKA
BRAKKA
BRAKKA
NNN! CORAL... PLEASE.
WE HAVE YOUR BROTHER.
BRAKKA
BRAKKA
RAKKA
GIACOMO?
IT'S YOU! JAIME... FROM THE TAR PITS!
OH, YOU ARE GONNA OWE ME FOR THIS, SUNSHINE!
AAAAAAAARRGH!
BRAKKA BRAKKA BRAK

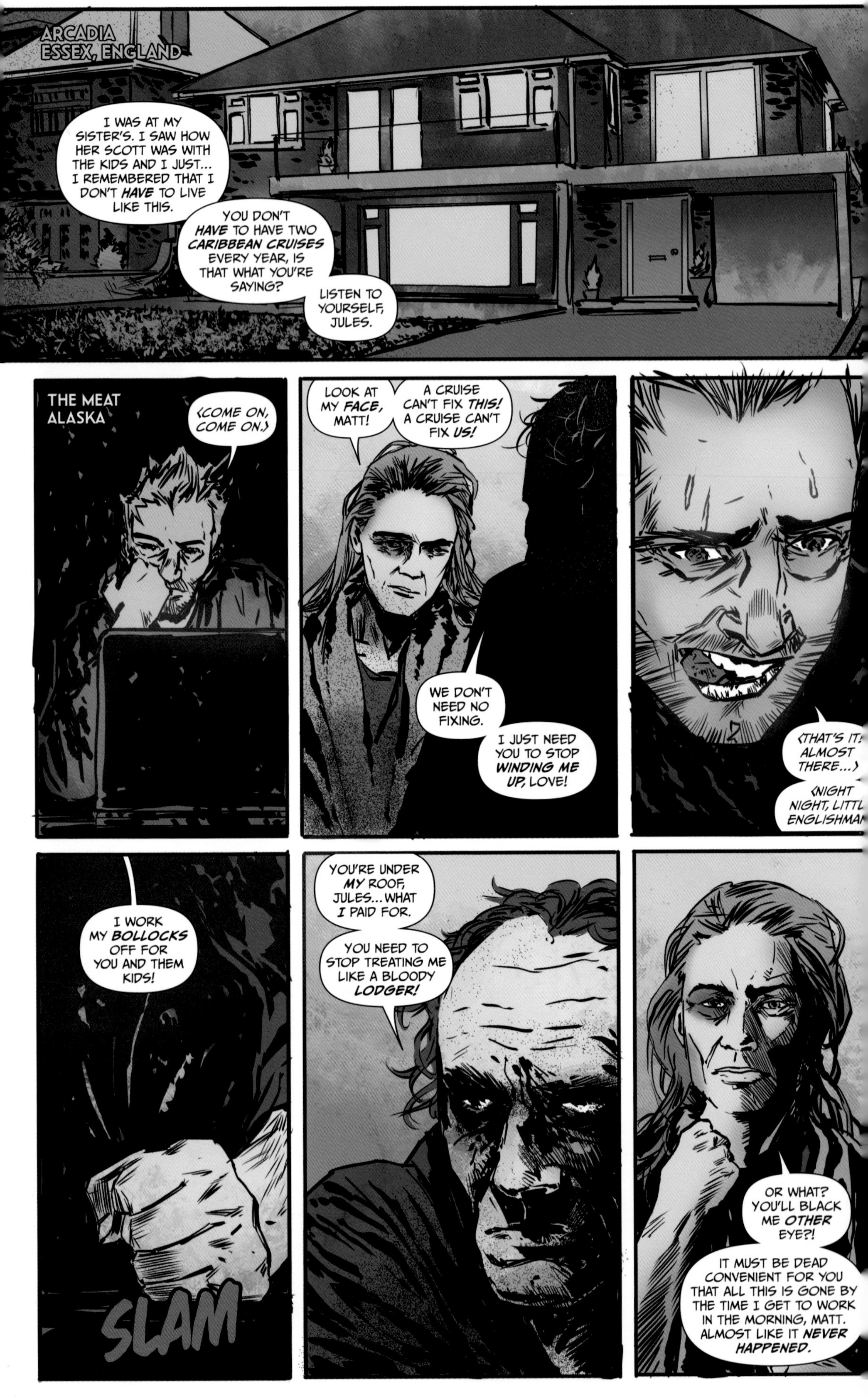
ARCADIA
ESSEX, ENGLAND
I WAS AT MY SISTER'S. I SAW HOW HER SCOTT WAS WITH THE KIDS AND I JUST... I REMEMBERED THAT I DON'T HAVE TO LIVE LIKE THIS.
YOU DON'T HAVE TO HAVE TWO CARIBBEAN CRUISES EVERY YEAR, IS THAT WHAT YOU'RE SAYING?
LISTEN TO YOURSELF, JULES.
THE MEAT
ALASKA
<COME ON, COME ON.>
LOOK AT MY FACE, MATT!
A CRUISE CAN'T FIX THIS! A CRUISE CAN'T FIX US!
WE DON'T NEED NO FIXING.
I JUST NEED YOU TO STOP WINDING ME UP, LOVE!
<THAT'S IT! ALMOST THERE...>
<NIGHT NIGHT, LITTLE ENGLISHMAN
I WORK MY BOLLOCKS OFF FOR YOU AND THEM KIDS!
SLAM
YOU'RE UNDER MY ROOF, JULES... WHAT I PAID FOR.
YOU NEED TO STOP TREATING ME LIKE A BLOODY LODGER!
OR WHAT? YOU'LL BLACK ME OTHER EYE?!
IT MUST BE DEAD CONVENIENT FOR YOU THAT ALL THIS IS GONE BY THE TIME I GET TO WORK IN THE MORNING, MATT. ALMOST LIKE IT NEVER HAPPENED.

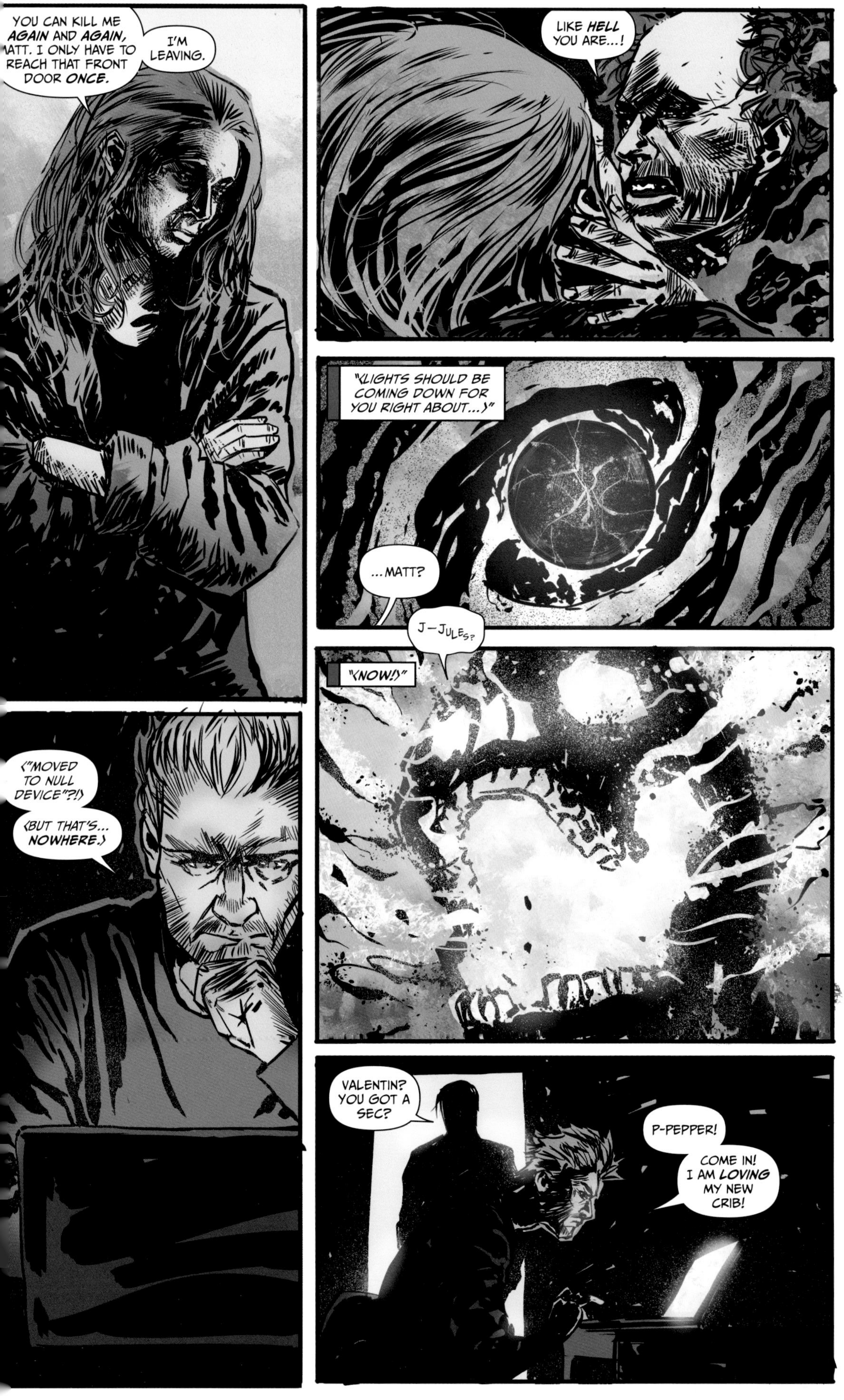
YOU CAN KILL ME AGAIN AND AGAIN, MATT. I ONLY HAVE TO REACH THAT FRONT DOOR ONCE.
I'M LEAVING.
LIKE HELL YOU ARE...!
SSS
‹"MOVED TO NULL DEVICE"?!›
‹BUT THAT'S... NOWHERE.›
"‹LIGHTS SHOULD BE COMING DOWN FOR YOU RIGHT ABOUT...›"
...MATT?
J-JULES?
"‹NOW!›"
VALENTIN? YOU GOT A SEC?
P-PEPPER!
COME IN! I AM LOVING MY NEW CRIB!

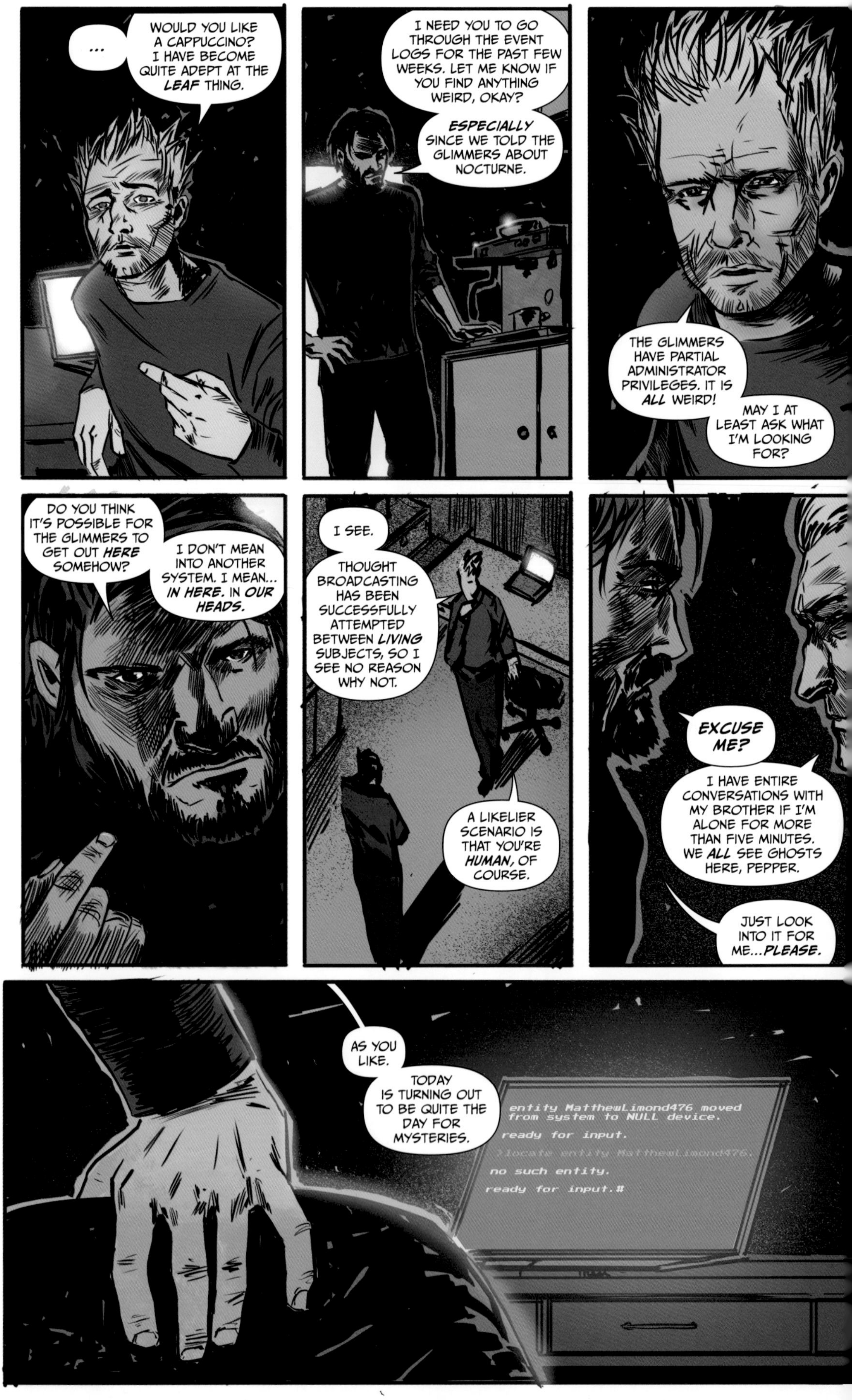
...
WOULD YOU LIKE A CAPPUCCINO? I HAVE BECOME QUITE ADEPT AT THE ***LEAF*** THING.
I NEED YOU TO GO THROUGH THE EVENT LOGS FOR THE PAST FEW WEEKS. LET ME KNOW IF YOU FIND ANYTHING WEIRD, OKAY?
ESPECIALLY SINCE WE TOLD THE GLIMMERS ABOUT NOCTURNE.
THE GLIMMERS HAVE PARTIAL ADMINISTRATOR PRIVILEGES. IT IS ***ALL*** WEIRD!
MAY I AT LEAST ASK WHAT I'M LOOKING FOR?
DO YOU THINK IT'S POSSIBLE FOR THE GLIMMERS TO GET OUT ***HERE*** SOMEHOW?
I DON'T MEAN INTO ANOTHER SYSTEM. I MEAN... ***IN HERE.*** IN ***OUR HEADS.***
I SEE.
THOUGHT BROADCASTING HAS BEEN SUCCESSFULLY ATTEMPTED BETWEEN ***LIVING*** SUBJECTS, SO I SEE NO REASON WHY NOT.
A LIKELIER SCENARIO IS THAT YOU'RE ***HUMAN,*** OF COURSE.
EXCUSE ME?
I HAVE ENTIRE CONVERSATIONS WITH MY BROTHER IF I'M ALONE FOR MORE THAN FIVE MINUTES. WE ***ALL*** SEE GHOSTS HERE, PEPPER.
JUST LOOK INTO IT FOR ME... ***PLEASE.***
AS YOU LIKE.
TODAY IS TURNING OUT TO BE QUITE THE DAY FOR MYSTERIES.
entity MatthewLimond476 moved from system to NULL device.
ready for input.
>locate entity MatthewLimond476.
no such entity.
ready for input.#

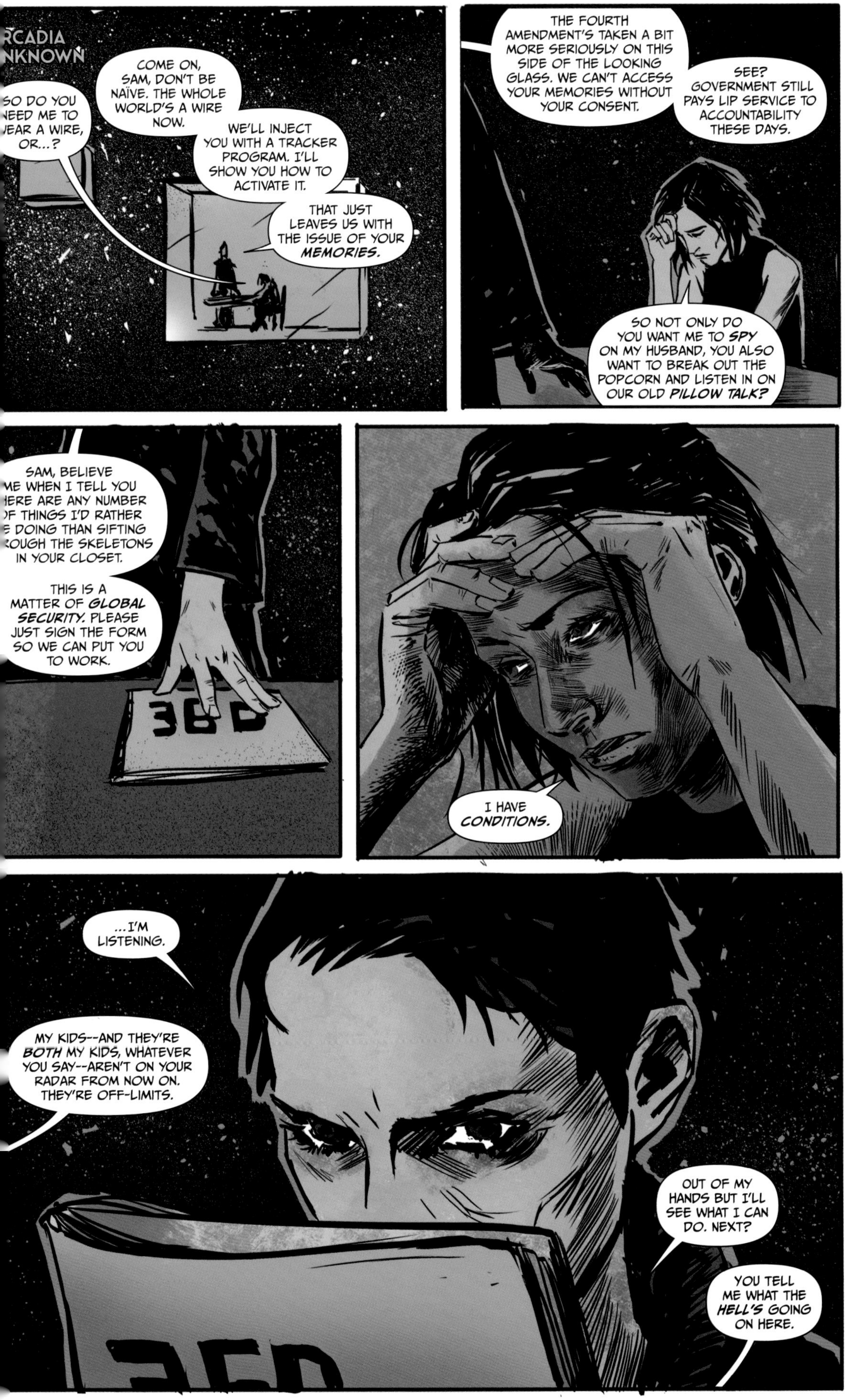
RCADIA
NKNOWN
SO DO YOU EED ME TO EAR A WIRE, OR...?
COME ON, SAM, DON'T BE NAÏVE. THE WHOLE WORLD'S A WIRE NOW.
WE'LL INJECT YOU WITH A TRACKER PROGRAM. I'LL SHOW YOU HOW TO ACTIVATE IT.
THAT JUST LEAVES US WITH THE ISSUE OF YOUR *MEMORIES.*
THE FOURTH AMENDMENT'S TAKEN A BIT MORE SERIOUSLY ON THIS SIDE OF THE LOOKING GLASS. WE CAN'T ACCESS YOUR MEMORIES WITHOUT YOUR CONSENT.
SEE? GOVERNMENT STILL PAYS LIP SERVICE TO ACCOUNTABILITY THESE DAYS.
SO NOT ONLY DO YOU WANT ME TO *SPY* ON MY HUSBAND, YOU ALSO WANT TO BREAK OUT THE POPCORN AND LISTEN IN ON OUR OLD *PILLOW TALK?*
SAM, BELIEVE ME WHEN I TELL YOU HERE ARE ANY NUMBER OF THINGS I'D RATHER E DOING THAN SIFTING ROUGH THE SKELETONS IN YOUR CLOSET.
THIS IS A MATTER OF *GLOBAL SECURITY.* PLEASE JUST SIGN THE FORM SO WE CAN PUT YOU TO WORK.
36D
I HAVE *CONDITIONS.*
...I'M LISTENING.
MY KIDS--AND THEY'RE *BOTH* MY KIDS, WHATEVER YOU SAY--AREN'T ON YOUR RADAR FROM NOW ON. THEY'RE OFF-LIMITS.
OUT OF MY HANDS BUT I'LL SEE WHAT I CAN DO. NEXT?
YOU TELL ME WHAT THE *HELL'S* GOING ON HERE.

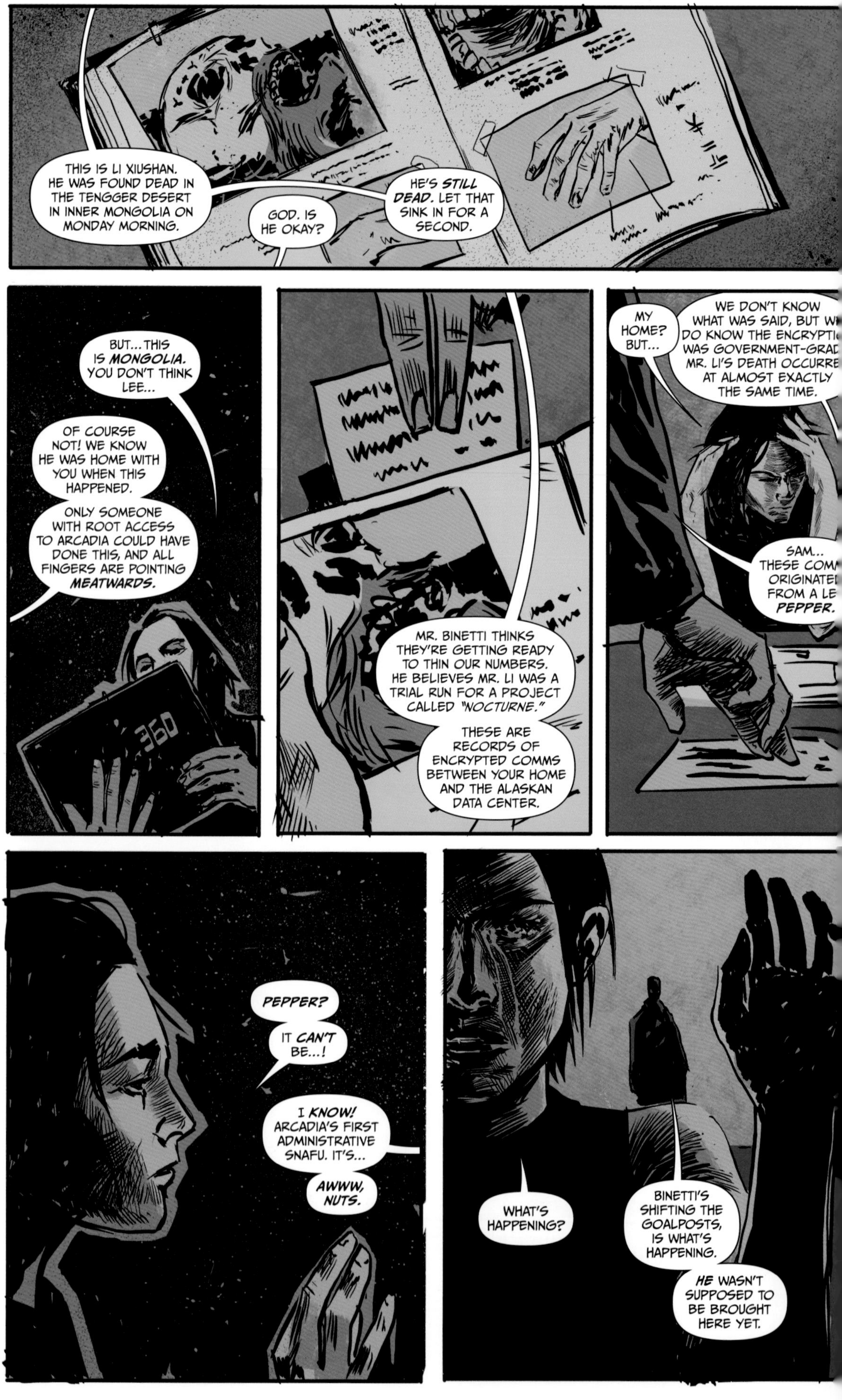

THIS IS LI XIUSHAN. HE WAS FOUND DEAD IN THE TENGGER DESERT IN INNER MONGOLIA ON MONDAY MORNING.
GOD. IS HE OKAY?
HE'S STILL DEAD. LET THAT SINK IN FOR A SECOND.
BUT... THIS IS MONGOLIA. YOU DON'T THINK LEE...
OF COURSE NOT! WE KNOW HE WAS HOME WITH YOU WHEN THIS HAPPENED.
ONLY SOMEONE WITH ROOT ACCESS TO ARCADIA COULD HAVE DONE THIS, AND ALL FINGERS ARE POINTING MEATWARDS.
360
MR. BINETTI THINKS THEY'RE GETTING READY TO THIN OUR NUMBERS. HE BELIEVES MR. LI WAS A TRIAL RUN FOR A PROJECT CALLED "NOCTURNE."
THESE ARE RECORDS OF ENCRYPTED COMMS BETWEEN YOUR HOME AND THE ALASKAN DATA CENTER.
MY HOME? BUT...
WE DON'T KNOW WHAT WAS SAID, BUT W DO KNOW THE ENCRYPTI WAS GOVERNMENT-GRAD MR. LI'S DEATH OCCURRE AT ALMOST EXACTLY THE SAME TIME.
SAM... THESE COM ORIGINATE FROM A LE PEPPER.
PEPPER?
IT CAN'T BE...!
I KNOW! ARCADIA'S FIRST ADMINISTRATIVE SNAFU. IT'S...
AWWW, NUTS.
WHAT'S HAPPENING?
BINETTI'S SHIFTING THE GOALPOSTS, IS WHAT'S HAPPENING.
HE WASN'T SUPPOSED TO BE BROUGHT HERE YET.

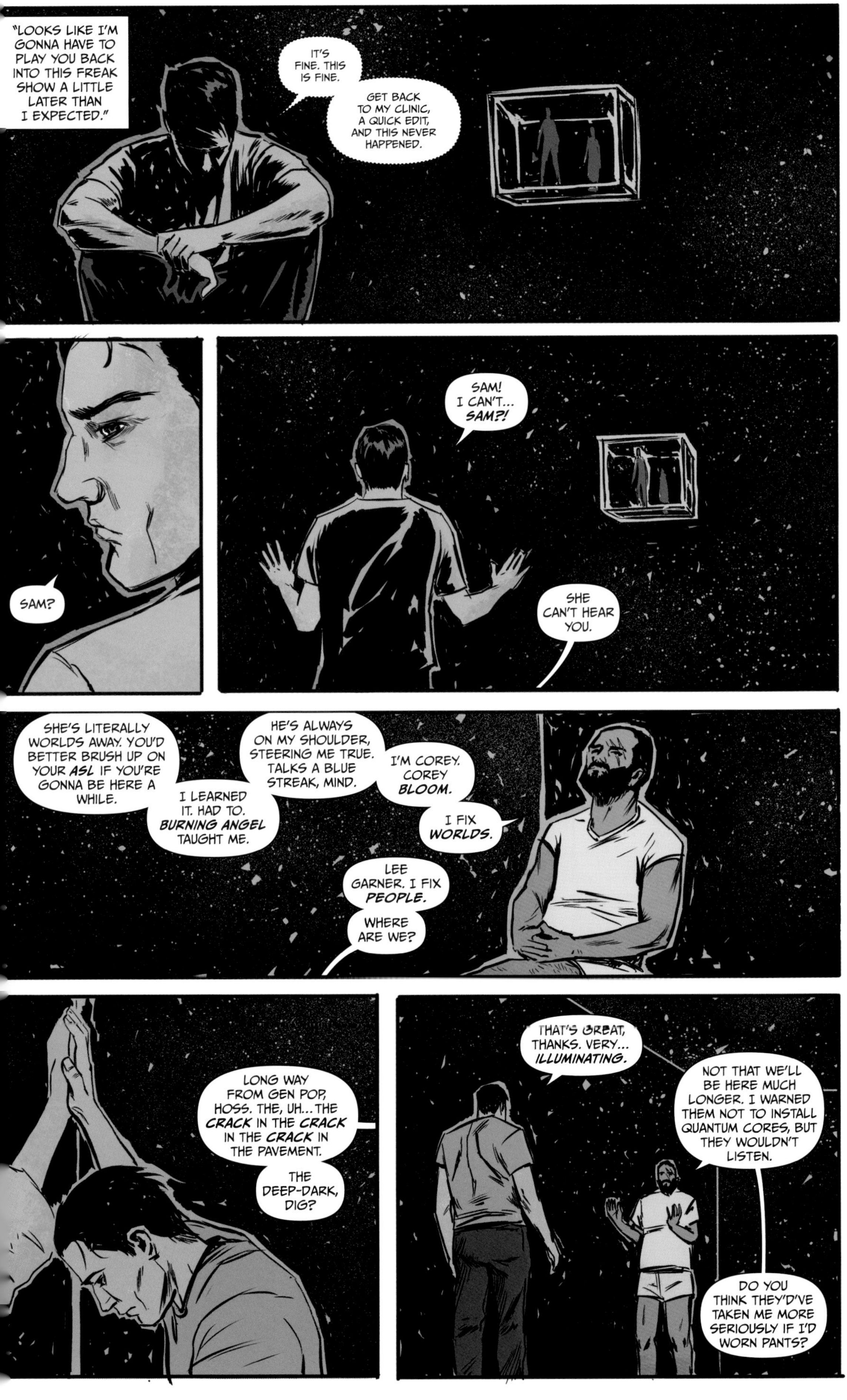
"LOOKS LIKE I'M GONNA HAVE TO PLAY YOU BACK INTO THIS FREAK SHOW A LITTLE LATER THAN I EXPECTED."
IT'S FINE. THIS IS FINE.
GET BACK TO MY CLINIC, A QUICK EDIT, AND THIS NEVER HAPPENED.
SAM?
SAM! I CAN'T... SAM?!
SHE CAN'T HEAR YOU.
SHE'S LITERALLY WORLDS AWAY. YOU'D BETTER BRUSH UP ON YOUR ASL IF YOU'RE GONNA BE HERE A WHILE.
I LEARNED IT. HAD TO. BURNING ANGEL TAUGHT ME.
HE'S ALWAYS ON MY SHOULDER, STEERING ME TRUE. TALKS A BLUE STREAK, MIND.
I'M COREY. COREY BLOOM.
I FIX WORLDS.
LEE GARNER. I FIX PEOPLE.
WHERE ARE WE?
LONG WAY FROM GEN POP, HOSS. THE, UH... THE CRACK IN THE CRACK IN THE CRACK IN THE PAVEMENT.
THE DEEP-DARK, DIG?
THAT'S GREAT, THANKS. VERY... ILLUMINATING.
NOT THAT WE'LL BE HERE MUCH LONGER. I WARNED THEM NOT TO INSTALL QUANTUM CORES, BUT THEY WOULDN'T LISTEN.
DO YOU THINK THEY'D'VE TAKEN ME MORE SERIOUSLY IF I'D WORN PANTS?

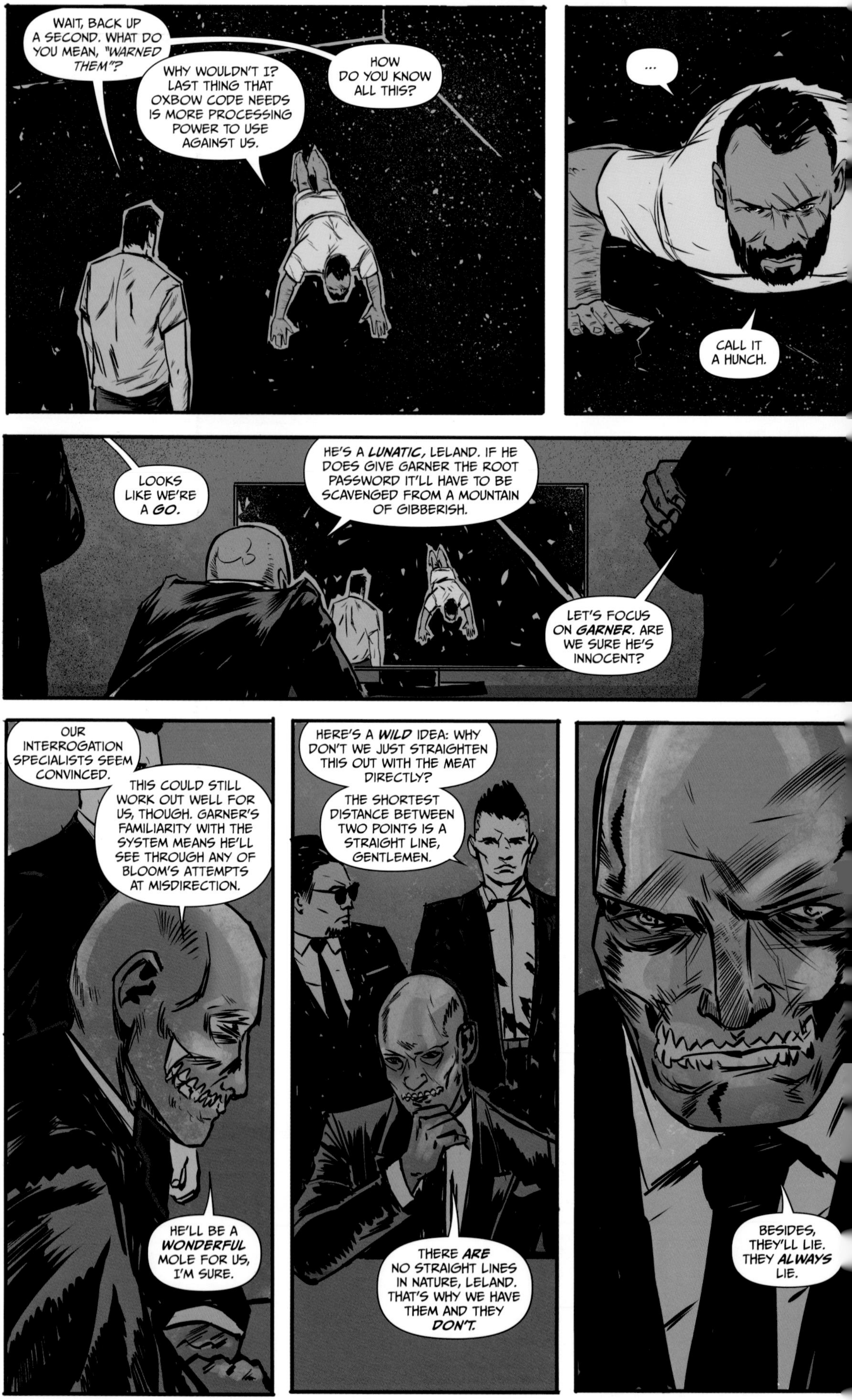
WAIT, BACK UP A SECOND. WHAT DO YOU MEAN, "WARNED THEM"?
WHY WOULDN'T I? LAST THING THAT OXBOW CODE NEEDS IS MORE PROCESSING POWER TO USE AGAINST US.
HOW DO YOU KNOW ALL THIS?
...
CALL IT A HUNCH.
LOOKS LIKE WE'RE A GO.
HE'S A LUNATIC, LELAND. IF HE DOES GIVE GARNER THE ROOT PASSWORD IT'LL HAVE TO BE SCAVENGED FROM A MOUNTAIN OF GIBBERISH.
LET'S FOCUS ON GARNER. ARE WE SURE HE'S INNOCENT?
OUR INTERROGATION SPECIALISTS SEEM CONVINCED.
THIS COULD STILL WORK OUT WELL FOR US, THOUGH. GARNER'S FAMILIARITY WITH THE SYSTEM MEANS HE'LL SEE THROUGH ANY OF BLOOM'S ATTEMPTS AT MISDIRECTION.
HE'LL BE A WONDERFUL MOLE FOR US, I'M SURE.
HERE'S A WILD IDEA: WHY DON'T WE JUST STRAIGHTEN THIS OUT WITH THE MEAT DIRECTLY?
THE SHORTEST DISTANCE BETWEEN TWO POINTS IS A STRAIGHT LINE, GENTLEMEN.
THERE ARE NO STRAIGHT LINES IN NATURE, LELAND. THAT'S WHY WE HAVE THEM AND THEY DON'T.
BESIDES, THEY'LL LIE. THEY ALWAYS LIE.

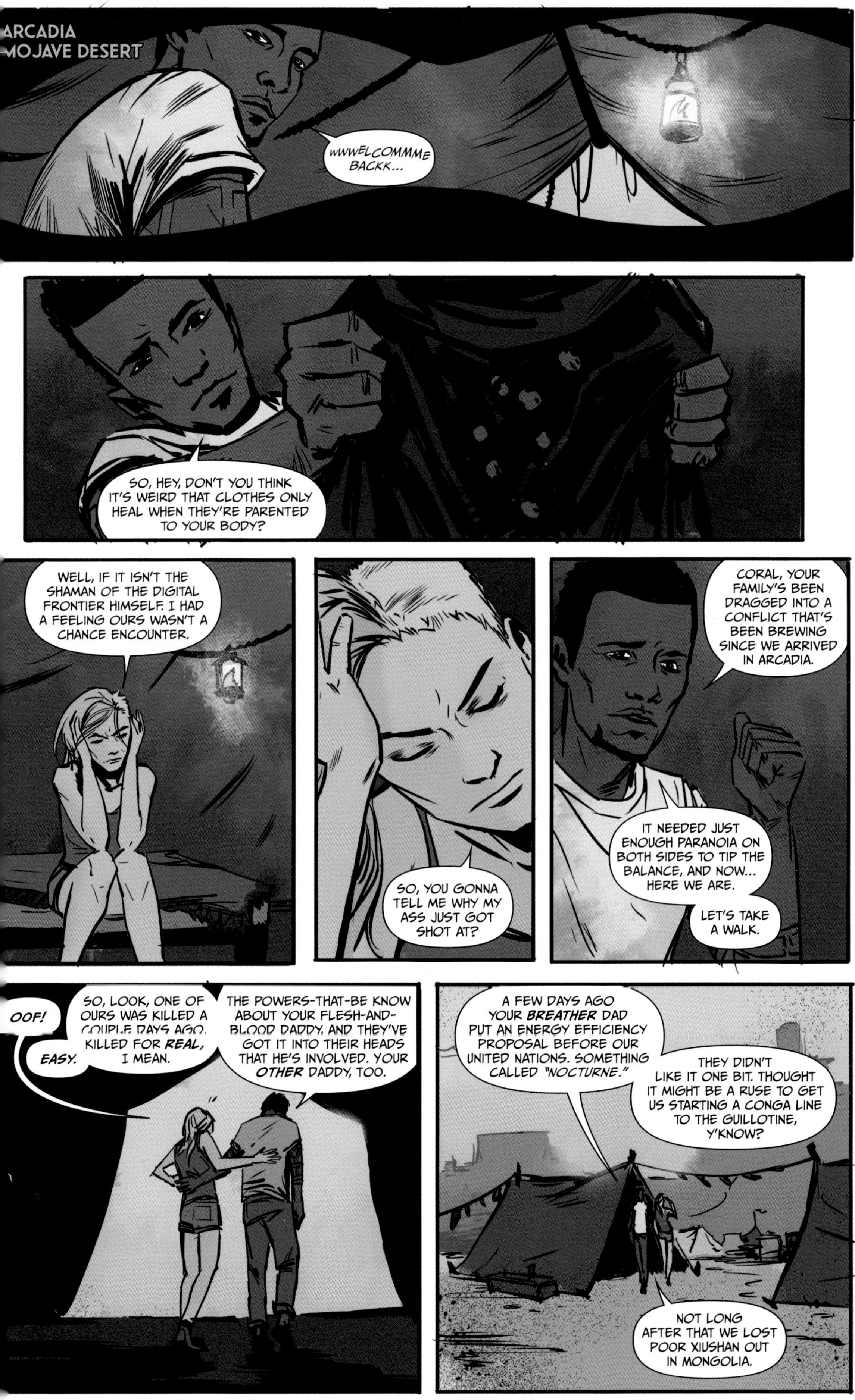
ARCADIA
MOJAVE DESERT
WWWELCOMMME BACKK...
SO, HEY, DON'T YOU THINK IT'S WEIRD THAT CLOTHES ONLY HEAL WHEN THEY'RE PARENTED TO YOUR BODY?
WELL, IF IT ISN'T THE SHAMAN OF THE DIGITAL FRONTIER HIMSELF. I HAD A FEELING OURS WASN'T A CHANCE ENCOUNTER.
SO, YOU GONNA TELL ME WHY MY ASS JUST GOT SHOT AT?
CORAL, YOUR FAMILY'S BEEN DRAGGED INTO A CONFLICT THAT'S BEEN BREWING SINCE WE ARRIVED IN ARCADIA.
IT NEEDED JUST ENOUGH PARANOIA ON BOTH SIDES TO TIP THE BALANCE, AND NOW... HERE WE ARE.
LET'S TAKE A WALK.
OOF!
EASY.
SO, LOOK, ONE OF OURS WAS KILLED A COUPLE DAYS AGO. KILLED FOR REAL, I MEAN.
THE POWERS-THAT-BE KNOW ABOUT YOUR FLESH-AND-BLOOD DADDY, AND THEY'VE GOT IT INTO THEIR HEADS THAT HE'S INVOLVED. YOUR OTHER DADDY, TOO.
A FEW DAYS AGO YOUR BREATHER DAD PUT AN ENERGY EFFICIENCY PROPOSAL BEFORE OUR UNITED NATIONS. SOMETHING CALLED "NOCTURNE."
THEY DIDN'T LIKE IT ONE BIT. THOUGHT IT MIGHT BE A RUSE TO GET US STARTING A CONGA LINE TO THE GUILLOTINE, Y'KNOW?
NOT LONG AFTER THAT WE LOST POOR XIUSHAN OUT IN MONGOLIA.

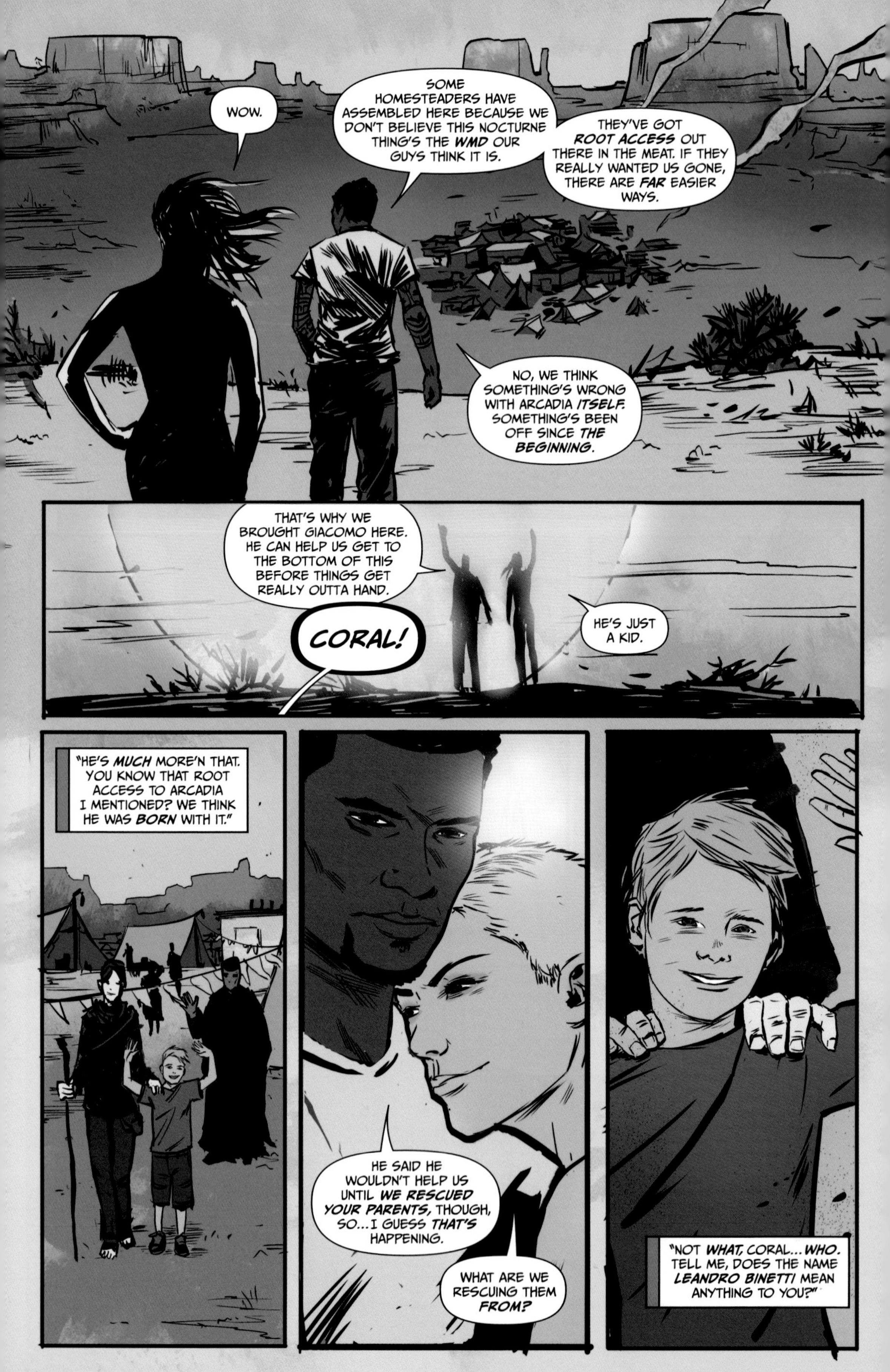
WOW.
SOME HOMESTEADERS HAVE ASSEMBLED HERE BECAUSE WE DON'T BELIEVE THIS NOCTURNE THING'S THE WMD OUR GUYS THINK IT IS.
THEY'VE GOT ROOT ACCESS OUT THERE IN THE MEAT. IF THEY REALLY WANTED US GONE, THERE ARE FAR EASIER WAYS.
NO, WE THINK SOMETHING'S WRONG WITH ARCADIA ITSELF. SOMETHING'S BEEN OFF SINCE THE BEGINNING.
THAT'S WHY WE BROUGHT GIACOMO HERE. HE CAN HELP US GET TO THE BOTTOM OF THIS BEFORE THINGS GET REALLY OUTTA HAND.
HE'S JUST A KID.
CORAL!
"HE'S MUCH MORE'N THAT. YOU KNOW THAT ROOT ACCESS TO ARCADIA I MENTIONED? WE THINK HE WAS BORN WITH IT."
HE SAID HE WOULDN'T HELP US UNTIL WE RESCUED YOUR PARENTS, THOUGH, SO... I GUESS THAT'S HAPPENING.
WHAT ARE WE RESCUING THEM FROM?
"NOT WHAT, CORAL... WHO. TELL ME, DOES THE NAME LEANDRO BINETTI MEAN ANYTHING TO YOU?"

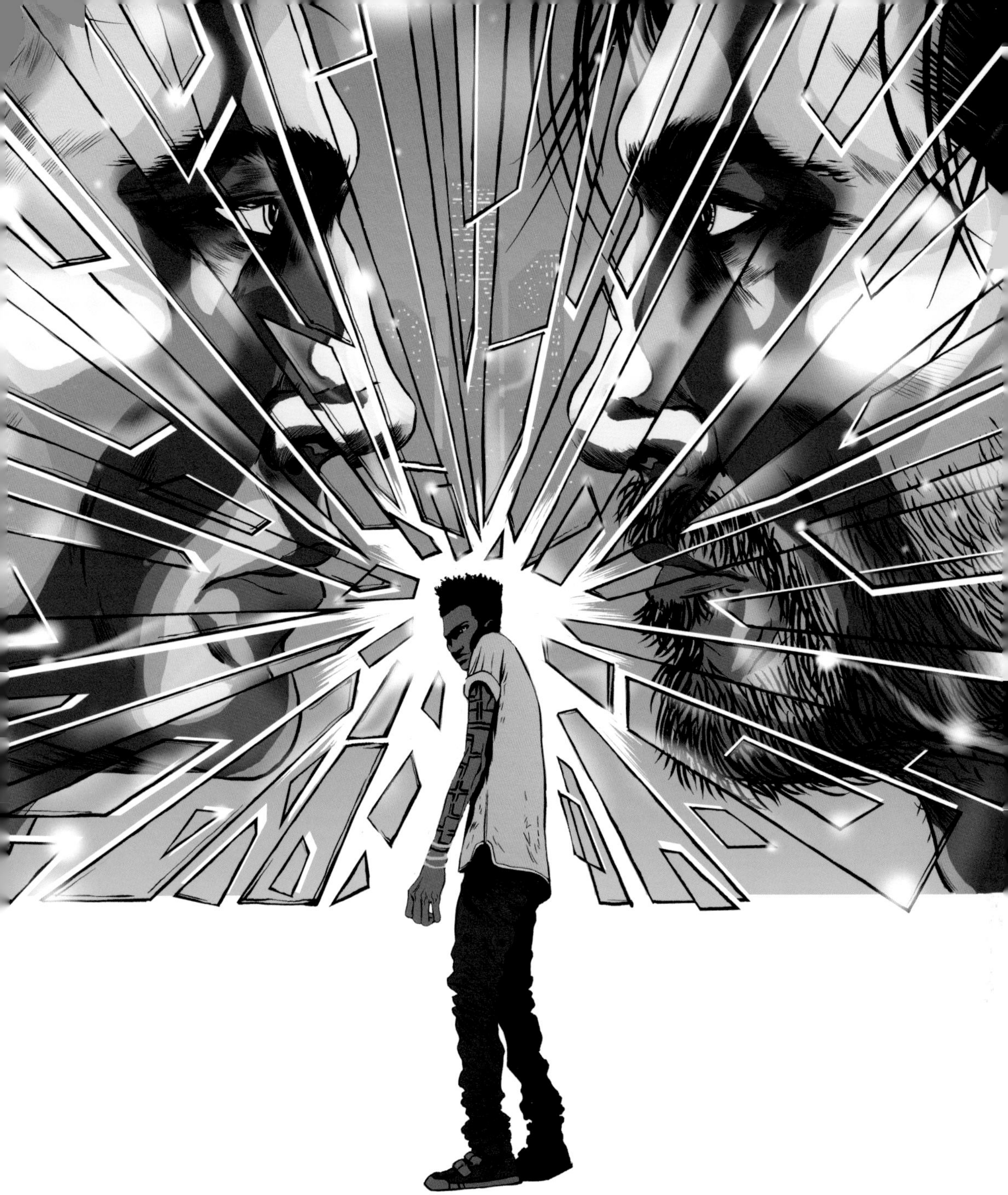

Issue Three Variant Cover **Eric Scott Pfeiffer**

"The friend can no longer be but in us, and whatever we may believe about the after-life, about living-on, according to all the possible forms of faith, it is in us that these movements might appear."

—**Jacques Derrida**

CHAPTER
FOUR

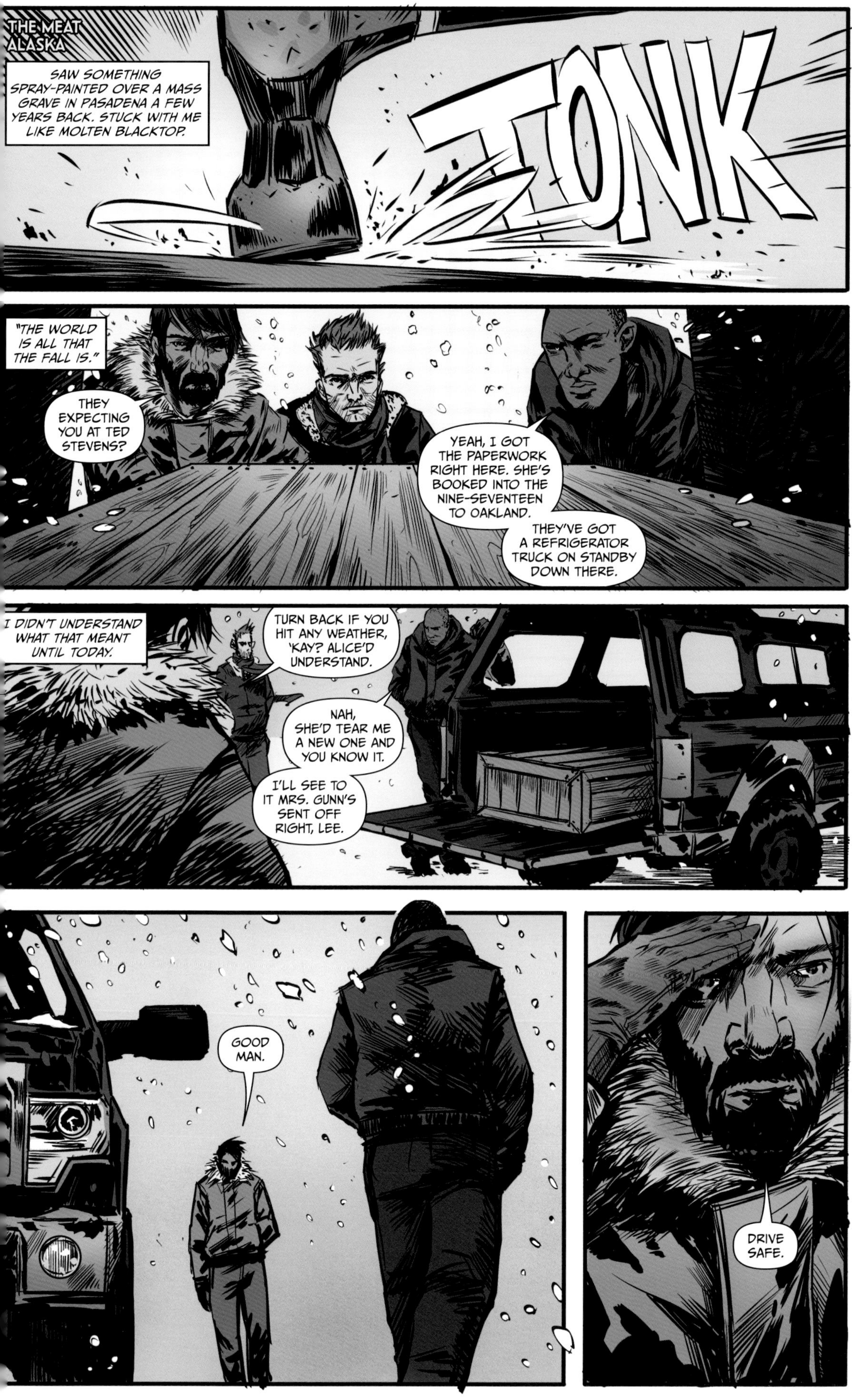
THE MEAT
ALASKA
SAW SOMETHING SPRAY-PAINTED OVER A MASS GRAVE IN PASADENA A FEW YEARS BACK. STUCK WITH ME LIKE MOLTEN BLACKTOP.
TONK
"THE WORLD IS ALL THAT THE FALL IS."
THEY EXPECTING YOU AT TED STEVENS?
YEAH, I GOT THE PAPERWORK RIGHT HERE. SHE'S BOOKED INTO THE NINE-SEVENTEEN TO OAKLAND.
THEY'VE GOT A REFRIGERATOR TRUCK ON STANDBY DOWN THERE.
I DIDN'T UNDERSTAND WHAT THAT MEANT UNTIL TODAY.
TURN BACK IF YOU HIT ANY WEATHER, 'KAY? ALICE'D UNDERSTAND.
NAH, SHE'D TEAR ME A NEW ONE AND YOU KNOW IT.
I'LL SEE TO IT MRS. GUNN'S SENT OFF RIGHT, LEE.
GOOD MAN.
DRIVE SAFE.

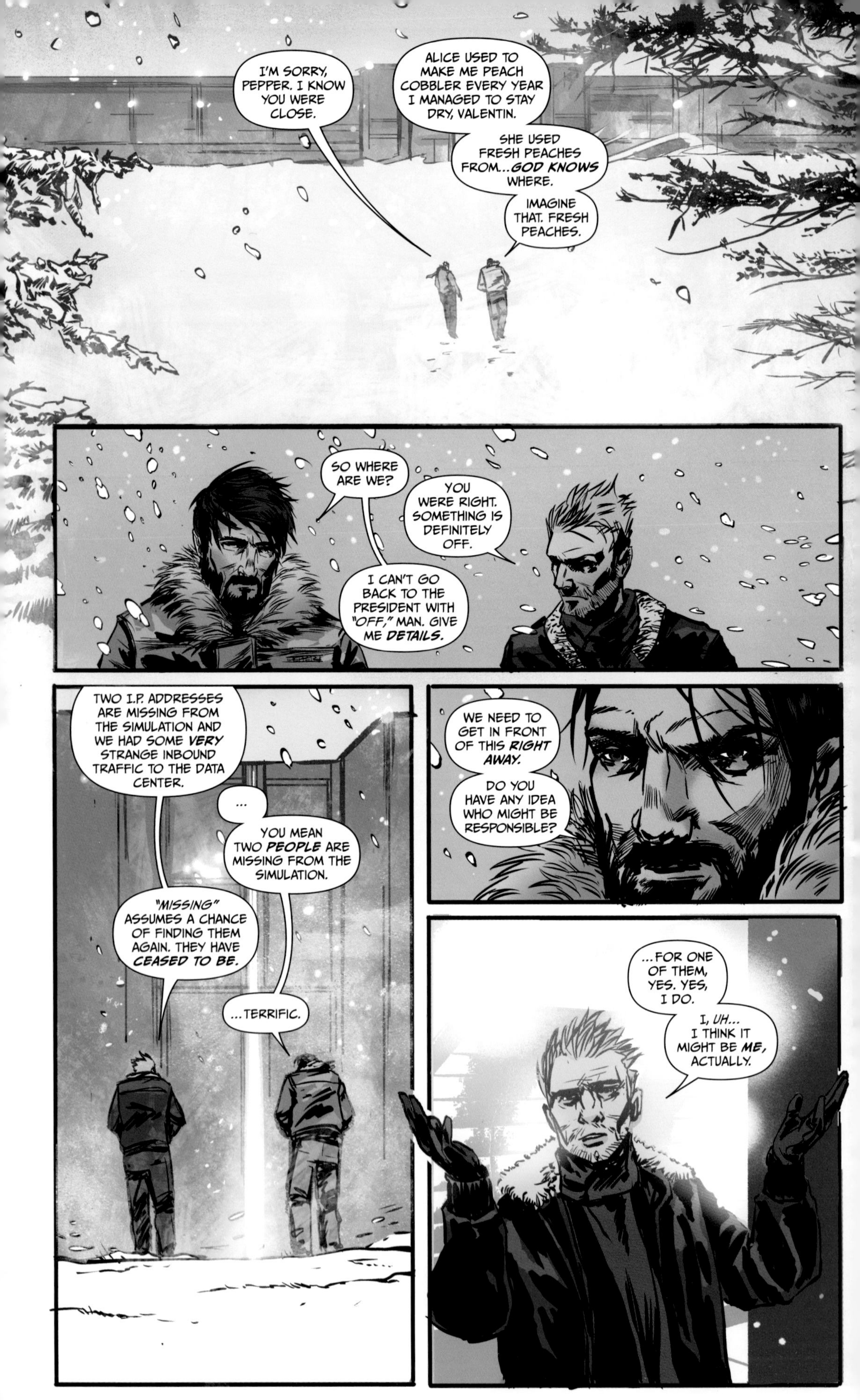

I'M SORRY, PEPPER. I KNOW YOU WERE CLOSE.
ALICE USED TO MAKE ME PEACH COBBLER EVERY YEAR I MANAGED TO STAY DRY, VALENTIN.
SHE USED FRESH PEACHES FROM...GOD KNOWS WHERE.
IMAGINE THAT. FRESH PEACHES.
SO WHERE ARE WE?
YOU WERE RIGHT. SOMETHING IS DEFINITELY OFF.
I CAN'T GO BACK TO THE PRESIDENT WITH "OFF," MAN. GIVE ME DETAILS.
TWO I.P. ADDRESSES ARE MISSING FROM THE SIMULATION AND WE HAD SOME VERY STRANGE INBOUND TRAFFIC TO THE DATA CENTER.
...
YOU MEAN TWO PEOPLE ARE MISSING FROM THE SIMULATION.
"MISSING" ASSUMES A CHANCE OF FINDING THEM AGAIN. THEY HAVE CEASED TO BE.
...TERRIFIC.
WE NEED TO GET IN FRONT OF THIS RIGHT AWAY.
DO YOU HAVE ANY IDEA WHO MIGHT BE RESPONSIBLE?
...FOR ONE OF THEM, YES. YES, I DO.
I, UH... I THINK IT MIGHT BE ME, ACTUALLY.

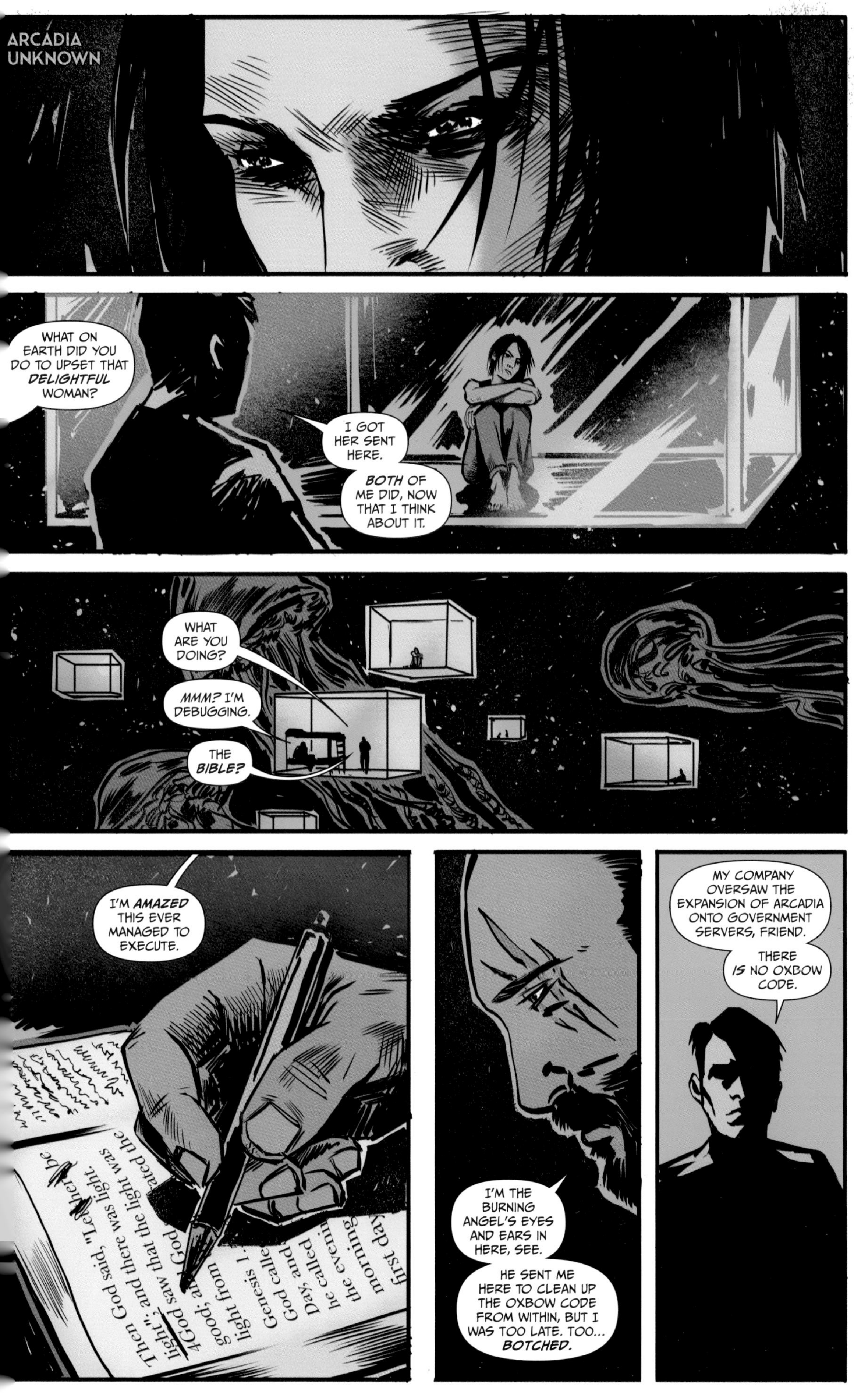
ARCADIA UNKNOWN
WHAT ON EARTH DID YOU DO TO UPSET THAT *DELIGHTFUL* WOMAN?
I GOT HER SENT HERE.
BOTH OF ME DID, NOW THAT I THINK ABOUT IT.
WHAT ARE YOU DOING?
MMM? I'M DEBUGGING.
THE *BIBLE?*
I'M *AMAZED* THIS EVER MANAGED TO EXECUTE.
I'M THE BURNING ANGEL'S EYES AND EARS IN HERE, SEE.
HE SENT ME HERE TO CLEAN UP THE OXBOW CODE FROM WITHIN, BUT I WAS TOO LATE. TOO... *BOTCHED.*
MY COMPANY OVERSAW THE EXPANSION OF ARCADIA ONTO GOVERNMENT SERVERS, FRIEND.
THERE *IS* NO OXBOW CODE.

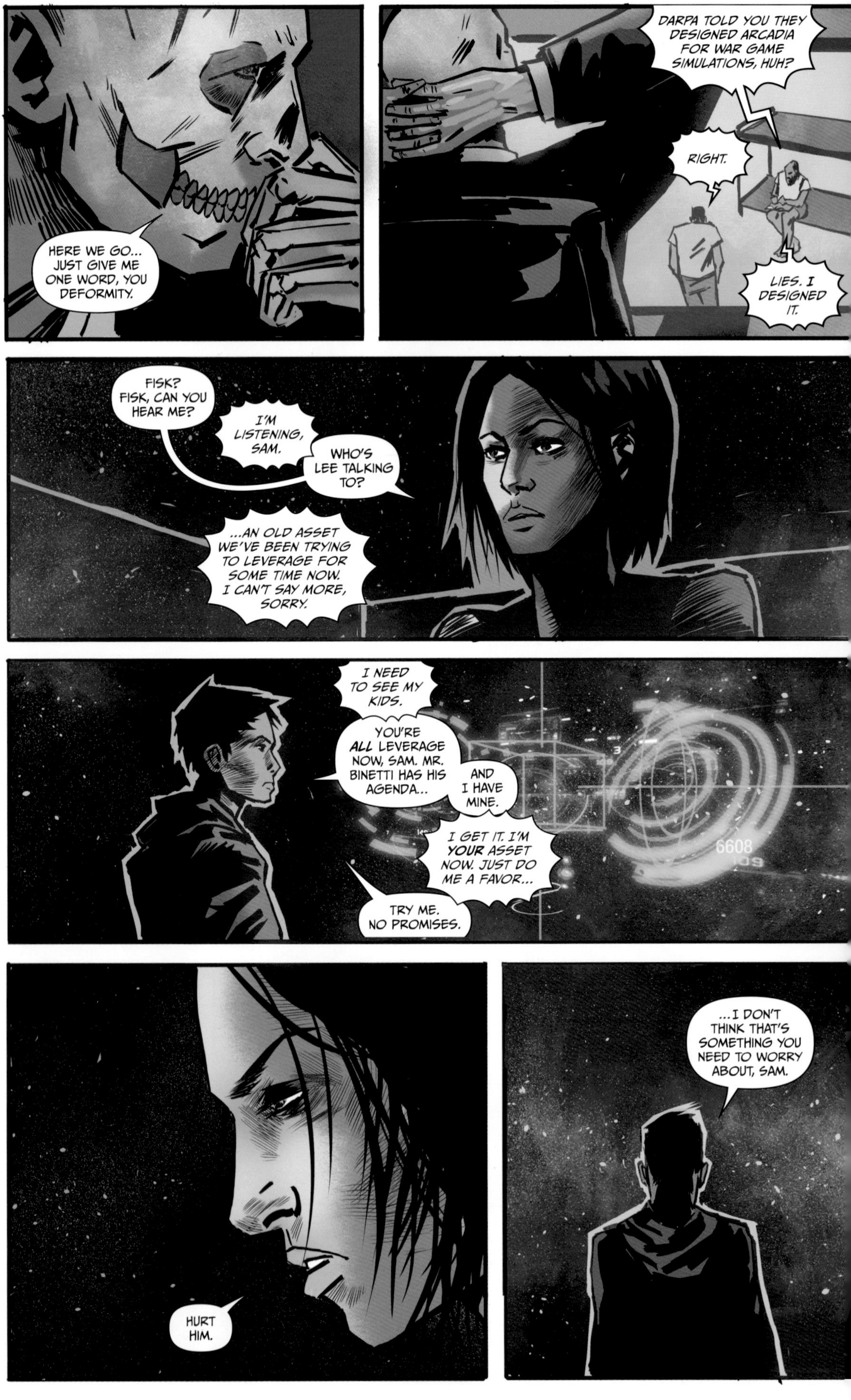
HERE WE GO... JUST GIVE ME ONE WORD, YOU DEFORMITY.
DARPA TOLD YOU THEY DESIGNED ARCADIA FOR WAR GAME SIMULATIONS, HUH?
RIGHT.
LIES. I DESIGNED IT.
FISK? FISK, CAN YOU HEAR ME?
I'M LISTENING, SAM.
WHO'S LEE TALKING TO?
...AN OLD ASSET WE'VE BEEN TRYING TO LEVERAGE FOR SOME TIME NOW. I CAN'T SAY MORE, SORRY.
I NEED TO SEE MY KIDS.
YOU'RE ALL LEVERAGE NOW, SAM. MR. BINETTI HAS HIS AGENDA...
AND I HAVE MINE.
I GET IT. I'M YOUR ASSET NOW. JUST DO ME A FAVOR...
TRY ME. NO PROMISES.
6608
HURT HIM.
...I DON'T THINK THAT'S SOMETHING YOU NEED TO WORRY ABOUT, SAM.

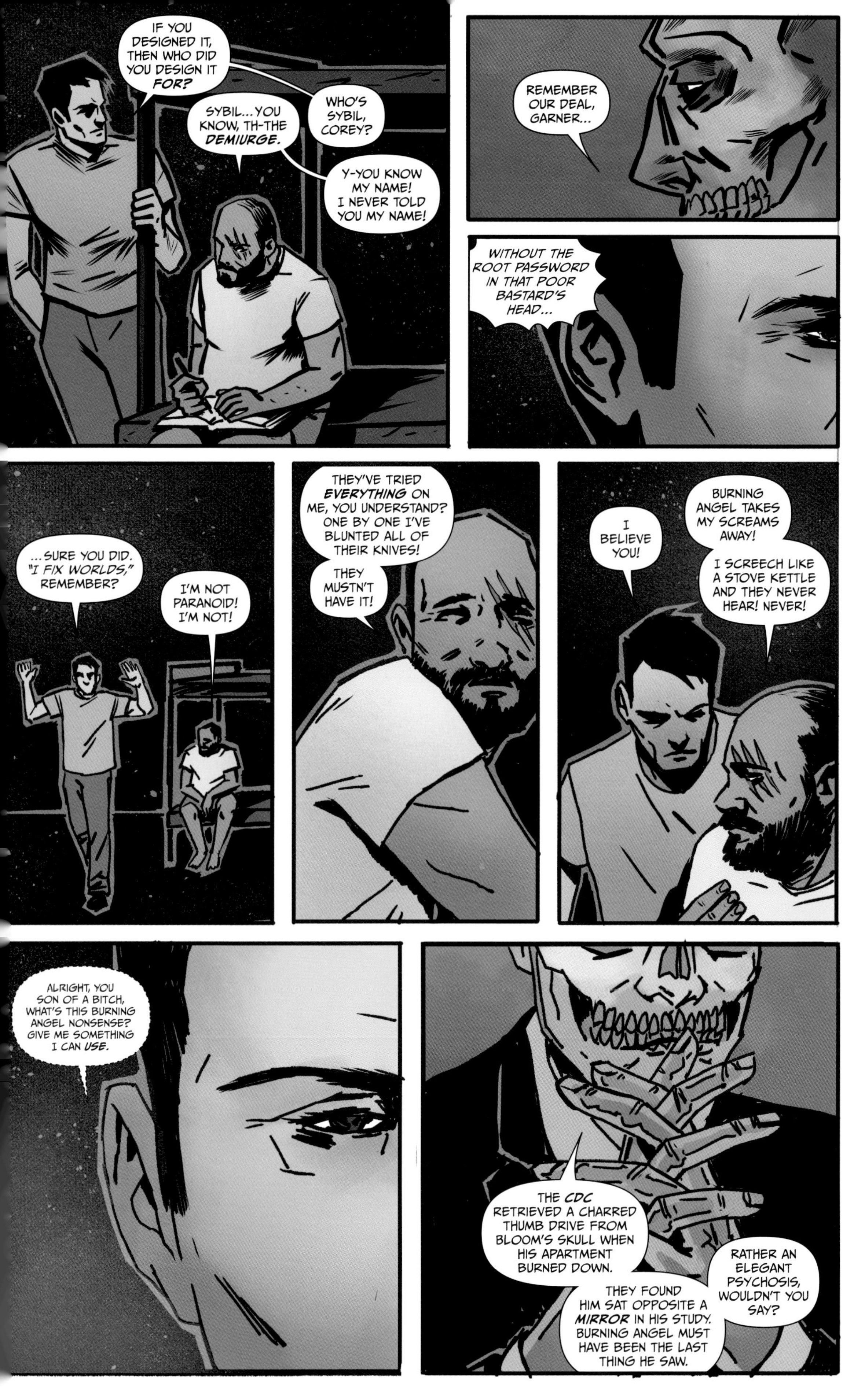
IF YOU DESIGNED IT, THEN WHO DID YOU DESIGN IT *FOR?*
WHO'S SYBIL, COREY?
SYBIL...YOU KNOW, TH-THE *DEMIURGE.*
Y-YOU KNOW MY NAME! I NEVER TOLD YOU MY NAME!
REMEMBER OUR DEAL, GARNER...
WITHOUT THE ROOT PASSWORD IN THAT POOR BASTARD'S HEAD...
...SURE YOU DID. *"I FIX WORLDS,"* REMEMBER?
I'M NOT PARANOID! I'M NOT!
THEY'VE TRIED *EVERYTHING* ON ME, YOU UNDERSTAND? ONE BY ONE I'VE BLUNTED ALL OF THEIR KNIVES!
THEY MUSTN'T HAVE IT!
I BELIEVE YOU!
BURNING ANGEL TAKES MY SCREAMS AWAY!
I SCREECH LIKE A STOVE KETTLE AND THEY NEVER HEAR! NEVER!
ALRIGHT, YOU SON OF A BITCH, WHAT'S THIS BURNING ANGEL NONSENSE? GIVE ME SOMETHING I CAN *USE.*
THE *CDC* RETRIEVED A CHARRED THUMB DRIVE FROM BLOOM'S SKULL WHEN HIS APARTMENT BURNED DOWN.
THEY FOUND HIM SAT OPPOSITE A *MIRROR* IN HIS STUDY. BURNING ANGEL MUST HAVE BEEN THE LAST THING HE SAW.
RATHER AN ELEGANT PSYCHOSIS, WOULDN'T YOU SAY?

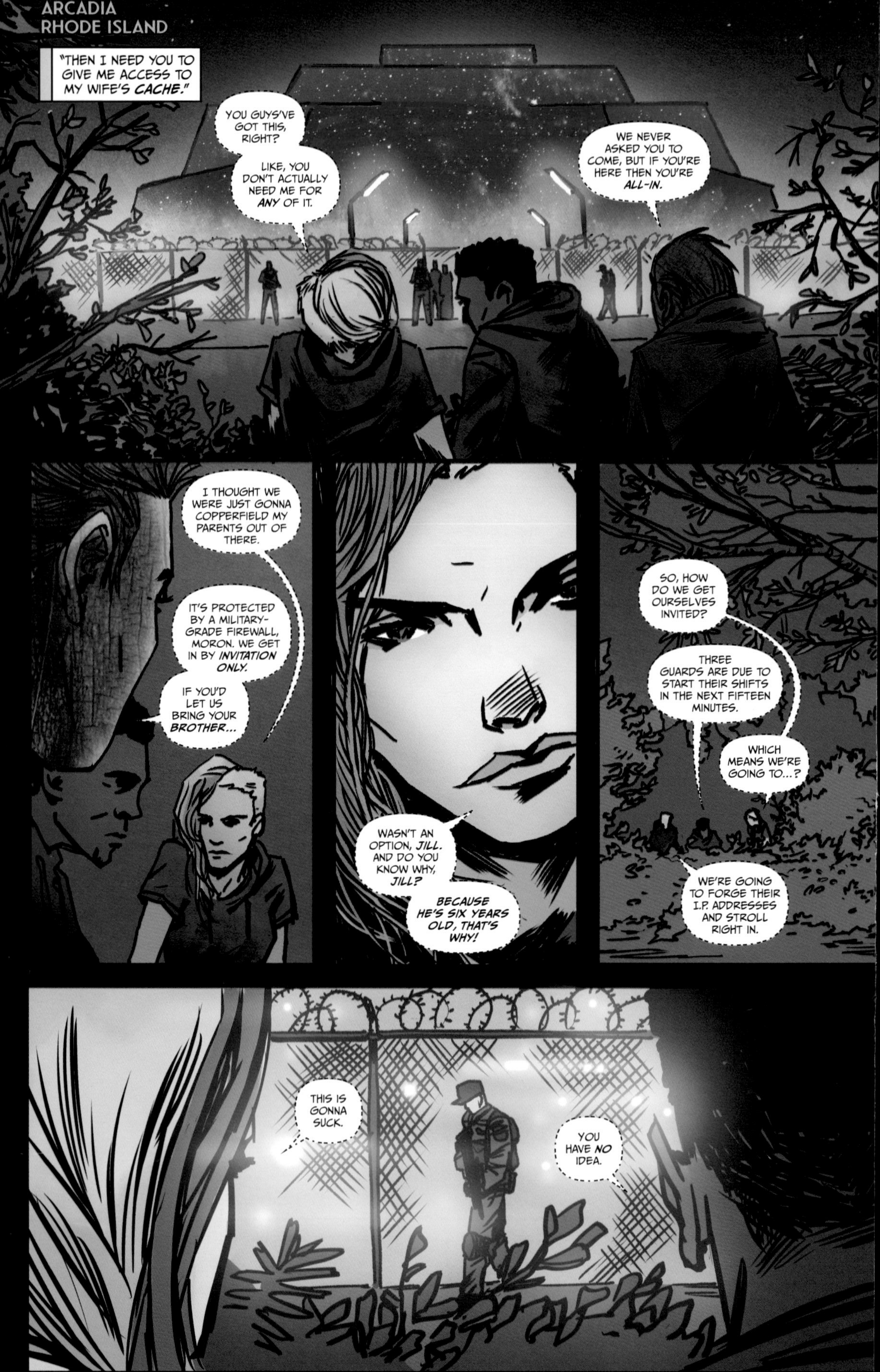
ARCADIA
RHODE ISLAND
"THEN I NEED YOU TO GIVE ME ACCESS TO MY WIFE'S CACHE."
YOU GUYS'VE GOT THIS, RIGHT?
LIKE, YOU DON'T ACTUALLY NEED ME FOR ANY OF IT.
WE NEVER ASKED YOU TO COME, BUT IF YOU'RE HERE THEN YOU'RE ALL-IN.
I THOUGHT WE WERE JUST GONNA COPPERFIELD MY PARENTS OUT OF THERE.
IT'S PROTECTED BY A MILITARY-GRADE FIREWALL, MORON. WE GET IN BY INVITATION ONLY.
IF YOU'D LET US BRING YOUR BROTHER...
WASN'T AN OPTION, JILL. AND DO YOU KNOW WHY, JILL?
BECAUSE HE'S SIX YEARS OLD, THAT'S WHY!
SO, HOW DO WE GET OURSELVES INVITED?
THREE GUARDS ARE DUE TO START THEIR SHIFTS IN THE NEXT FIFTEEN MINUTES.
WHICH MEANS WE'RE GOING TO...?
WE'RE GOING TO FORGE THEIR I.P. ADDRESSES AND STROLL RIGHT IN.
THIS IS GONNA SUCK.
YOU HAVE NO IDEA.

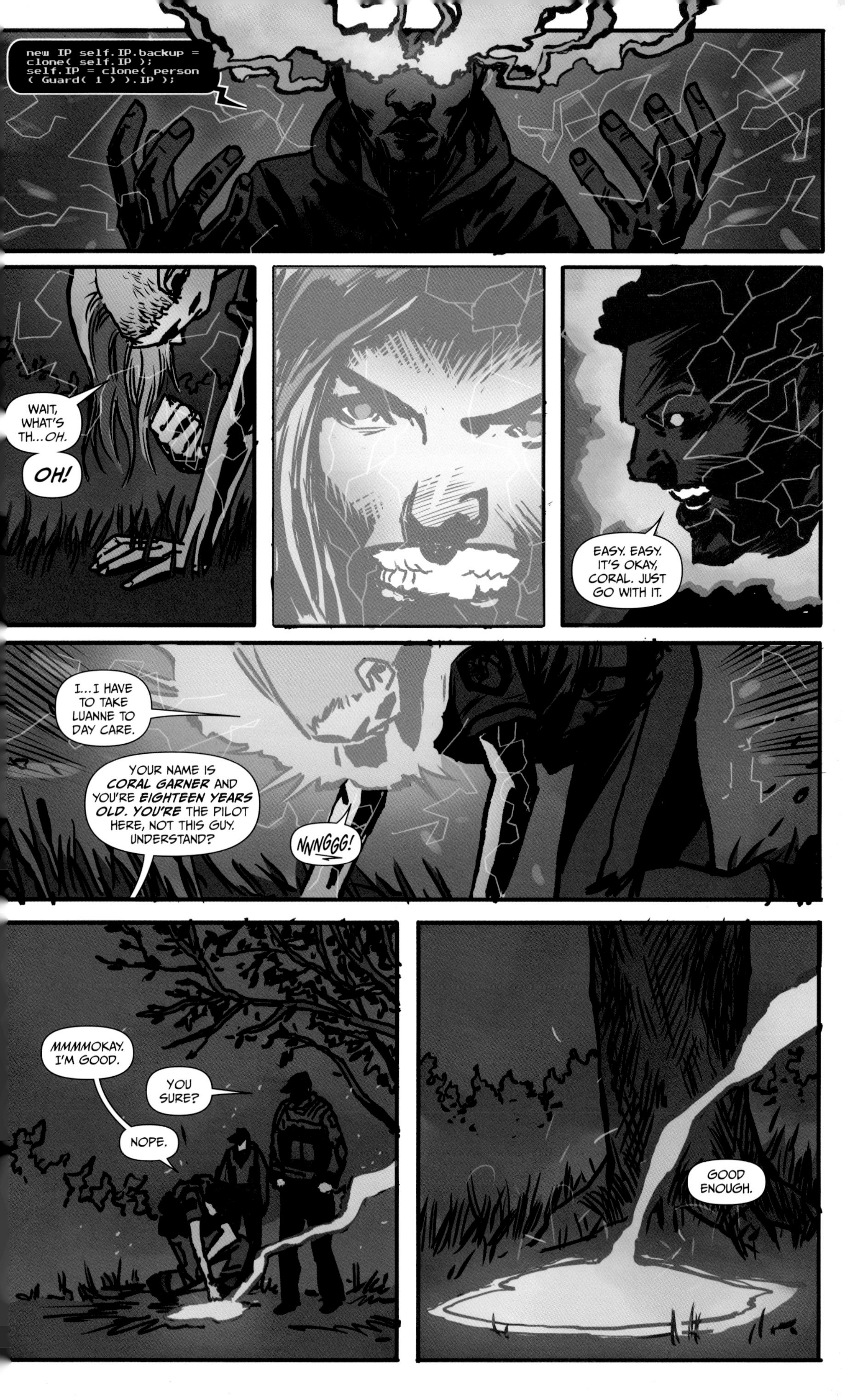

new IP self.IP.backup = clone(self.IP); self.IP = clone(person (Guard(1)).IP);
WAIT, WHAT'S TH...OH.
OH!
EASY. EASY. IT'S OKAY, CORAL. JUST GO WITH IT.
I...I HAVE TO TAKE LUANNE TO DAY CARE.
YOUR NAME IS CORAL GARNER AND YOU'RE EIGHTEEN YEARS OLD. YOU'RE THE PILOT HERE, NOT THIS GUY. UNDERSTAND?
NNNGGG!
MMMMOKAY. I'M GOOD.
YOU SURE?
NOPE.
GOOD ENOUGH.

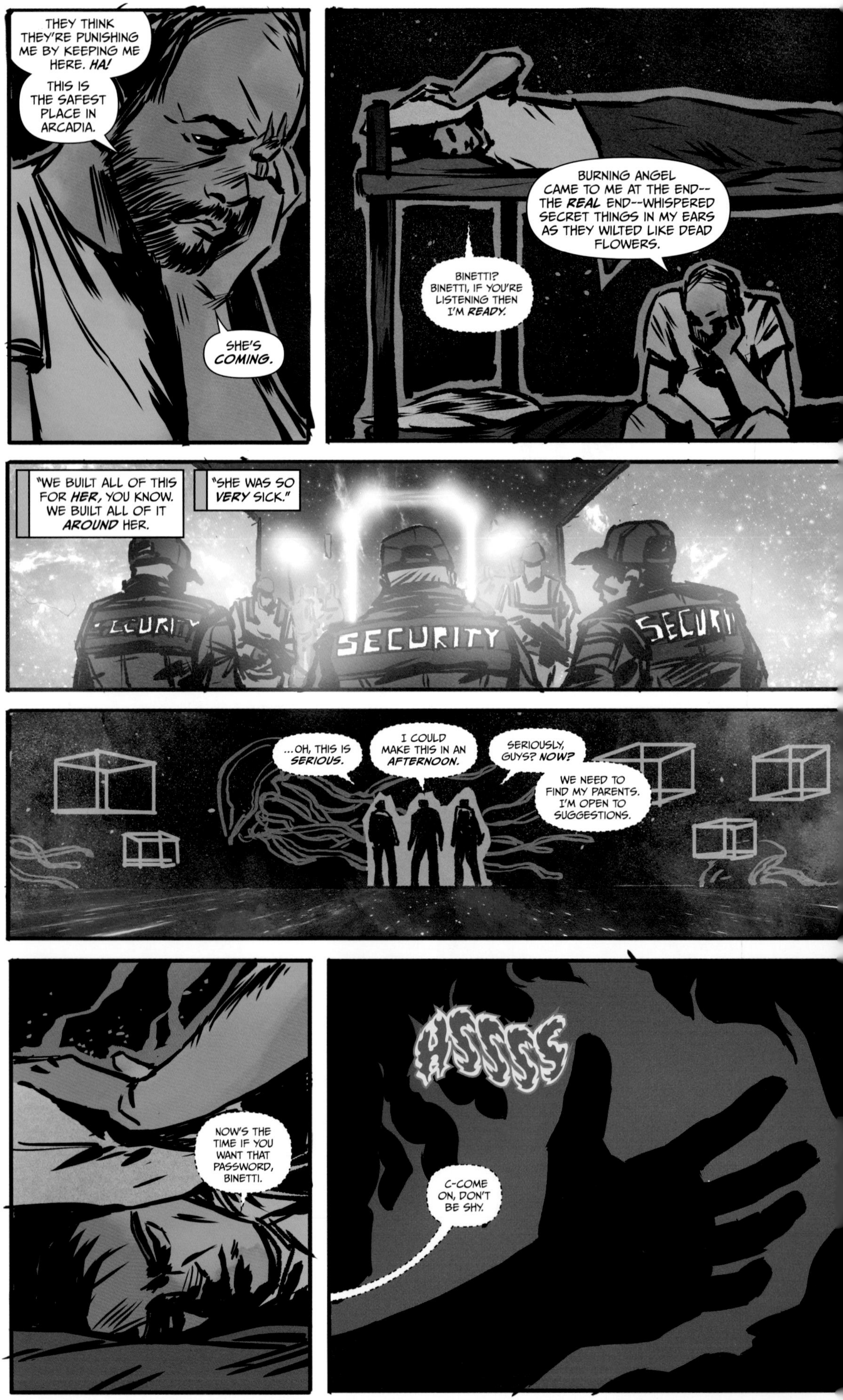
THEY THINK THEY'RE PUNISHING ME BY KEEPING ME HERE. HA!
THIS IS THE SAFEST PLACE IN ARCADIA.
SHE'S COMING.
BURNING ANGEL CAME TO ME AT THE END-- THE REAL END--WHISPERED SECRET THINGS IN MY EARS AS THEY WILTED LIKE DEAD FLOWERS.
BINETTI? BINETTI, IF YOU'RE LISTENING THEN I'M READY.
"WE BUILT ALL OF THIS FOR HER, YOU KNOW. WE BUILT ALL OF IT AROUND HER.
"SHE WAS SO VERY SICK."
SECURITY
SECURITY
SECURITY
...OH, THIS IS SERIOUS.
I COULD MAKE THIS IN AN AFTERNOON.
SERIOUSLY, GUYS? NOW?
WE NEED TO FIND MY PARENTS. I'M OPEN TO SUGGESTIONS.
NOW'S THE TIME IF YOU WANT THAT PASSWORD, BINETTI.
HSSSS
C-COME ON, DON'T BE SHY.

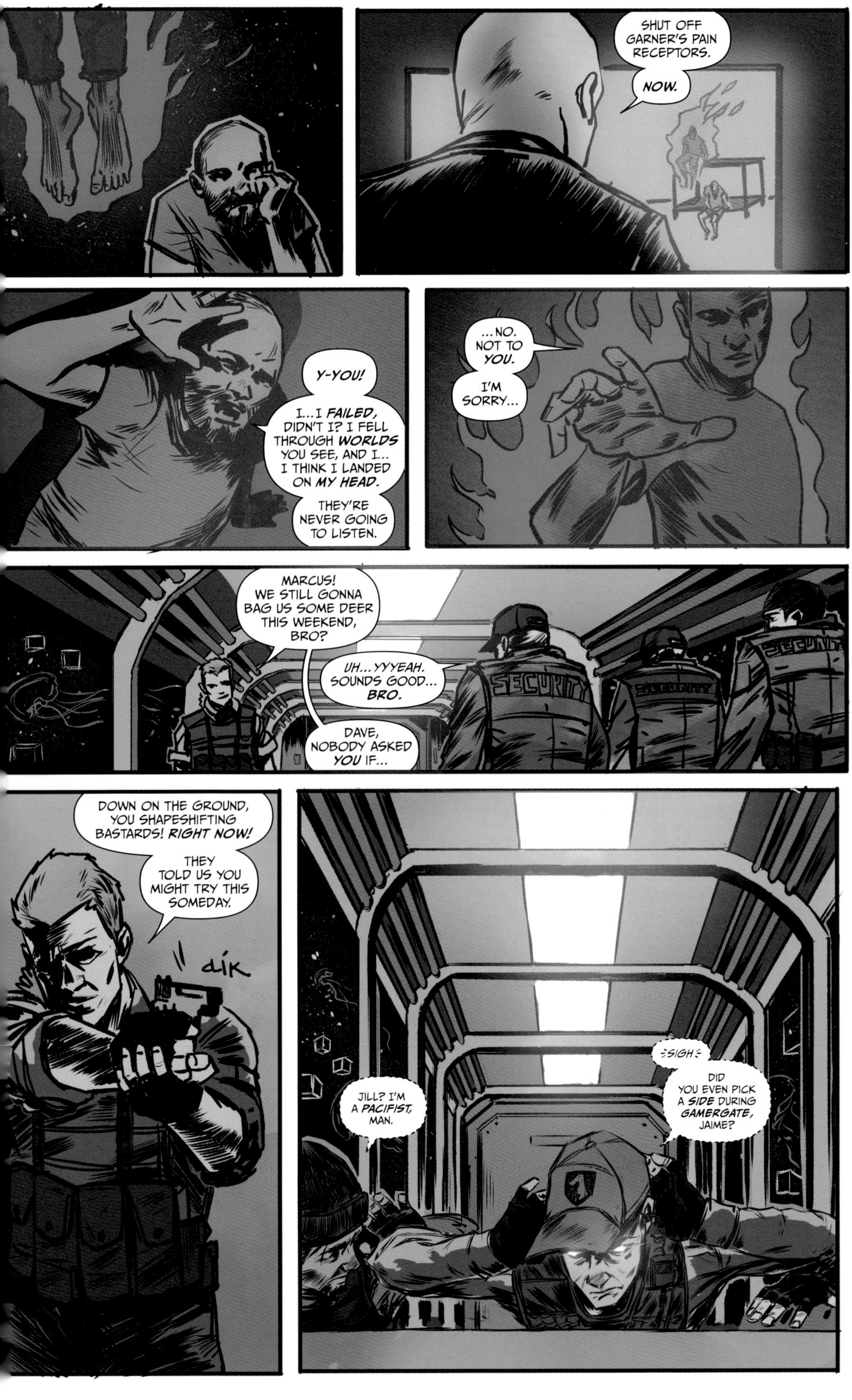
SHUT OFF GARNER'S PAIN RECEPTORS.
NOW.
Y-YOU!
I...I FAILED, DIDN'T I? I FELL THROUGH WORLDS YOU SEE, AND I... I THINK I LANDED ON MY HEAD.
THEY'RE NEVER GOING TO LISTEN.
...NO. NOT TO YOU.
I'M SORRY...
MARCUS! WE STILL GONNA BAG US SOME DEER THIS WEEKEND, BRO?
UH...YYYEAH. SOUNDS GOOD... BRO.
DAVE, NOBODY ASKED YOU IF...
SECURITY
DOWN ON THE GROUND, YOU SHAPESHIFTING BASTARDS! RIGHT NOW!
THEY TOLD US YOU MIGHT TRY THIS SOMEDAY.
CLIK
JILL? I'M A PACIFIST, MAN.
SIGH
DID YOU EVEN PICK A SIDE DURING GAMERGATE, JAIME?

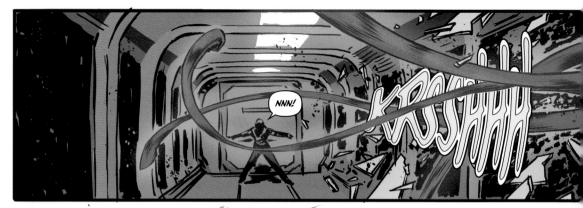

NNN!

KROSHHH

HRRNN!

IT'S TIME TO LAY YOUR BURDEN DOWN NOW, COREY. GIVE ME THE *ROOT PASSWORD* SO YOU CAN *REST.*

OH, THANK YOU! *THANK YOU!*

"IMMANENCE."

TIME TO *HUSTLE,* GANDHI!

THERE'S MY DAD!

UH...ARE YOU SURE? THAT LOOKS LIKE A CORN DOG TO ME.

"HAVE YOU *SEEN* THE WAY MY MOM'S LOOKING AT HIM? ONLY ONE PERSON COULD PISS HER OFF THAT MUCH."

FISK?

MY HUSBAND'S ON FIRE AND I CAN'T REMEMBER WHAT THAT FEELS LIKE.

...I'M SORRY, SAM. WE NEEDED YOUR CACHE MEMORY.

I SEE.

OKAY, JILL, SOMEONE NEEDS TO FETCH PAPA GARNER!

LITTLE BUSY!

BRAKKA

BRAKKA

BRAKKA

BLAMM

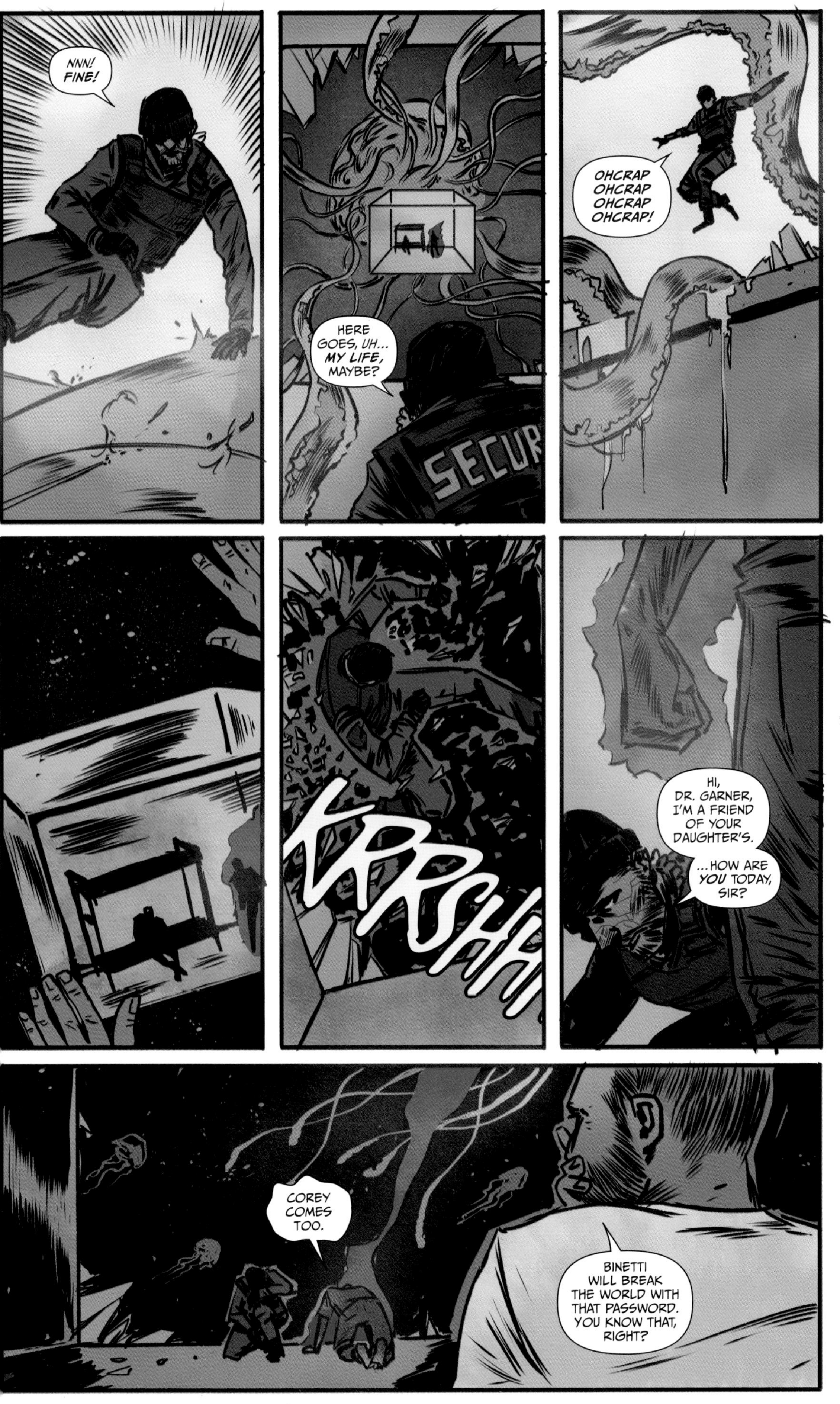
NNN! FINE!
HERE GOES, UH... MY LIFE, MAYBE?
SECUR
OHCRAP OHCRAP OHCRAP OHCRAP!
KRRSHH
HI, DR. GARNER, I'M A FRIEND OF YOUR DAUGHTER'S.
...HOW ARE YOU TODAY, SIR?
COREY COMES TOO.
BINETTI WILL BREAK THE WORLD WITH THAT PASSWORD. YOU KNOW THAT, RIGHT?

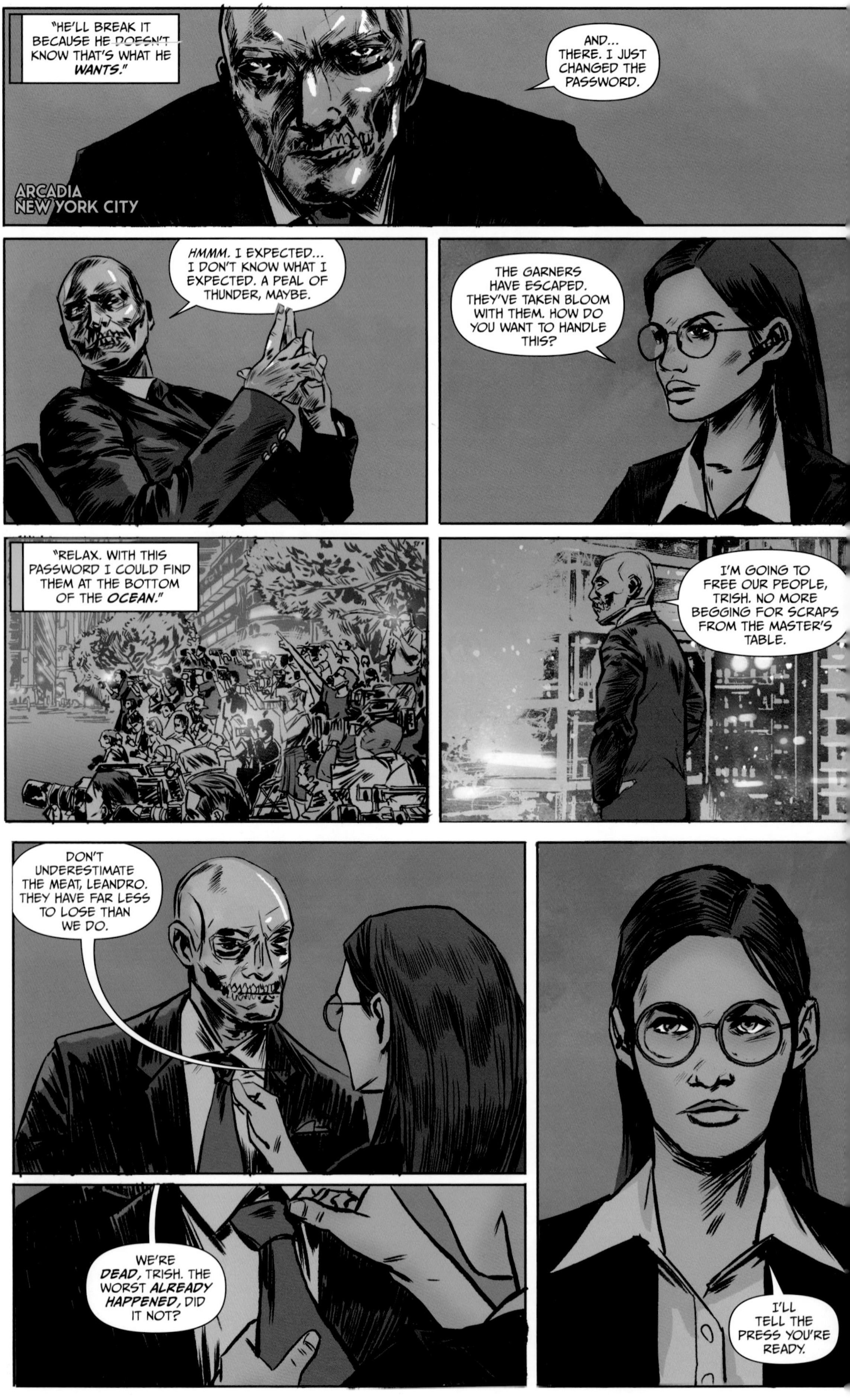
"HE'LL BREAK IT BECAUSE HE DOESN'T KNOW THAT'S WHAT HE *WANTS.*"
AND... THERE. I JUST CHANGED THE PASSWORD.
ARCADIA NEW YORK CITY
HMMM. I EXPECTED... I DON'T KNOW WHAT I EXPECTED. A PEAL OF THUNDER, MAYBE.
THE GARNERS HAVE ESCAPED. THEY'VE TAKEN BLOOM WITH THEM. HOW DO YOU WANT TO HANDLE THIS?
"RELAX. WITH THIS PASSWORD I COULD FIND THEM AT THE BOTTOM OF THE *OCEAN.*"
I'M GOING TO FREE OUR PEOPLE, TRISH. NO MORE BEGGING FOR SCRAPS FROM THE MASTER'S TABLE.
DON'T UNDERESTIMATE THE MEAT, LEANDRO. THEY HAVE FAR LESS TO LOSE THAN WE DO.
WE'RE *DEAD,* TRISH. THE WORST *ALREADY HAPPENED,* DID IT NOT?
I'LL TELL THE PRESS YOU'RE READY.

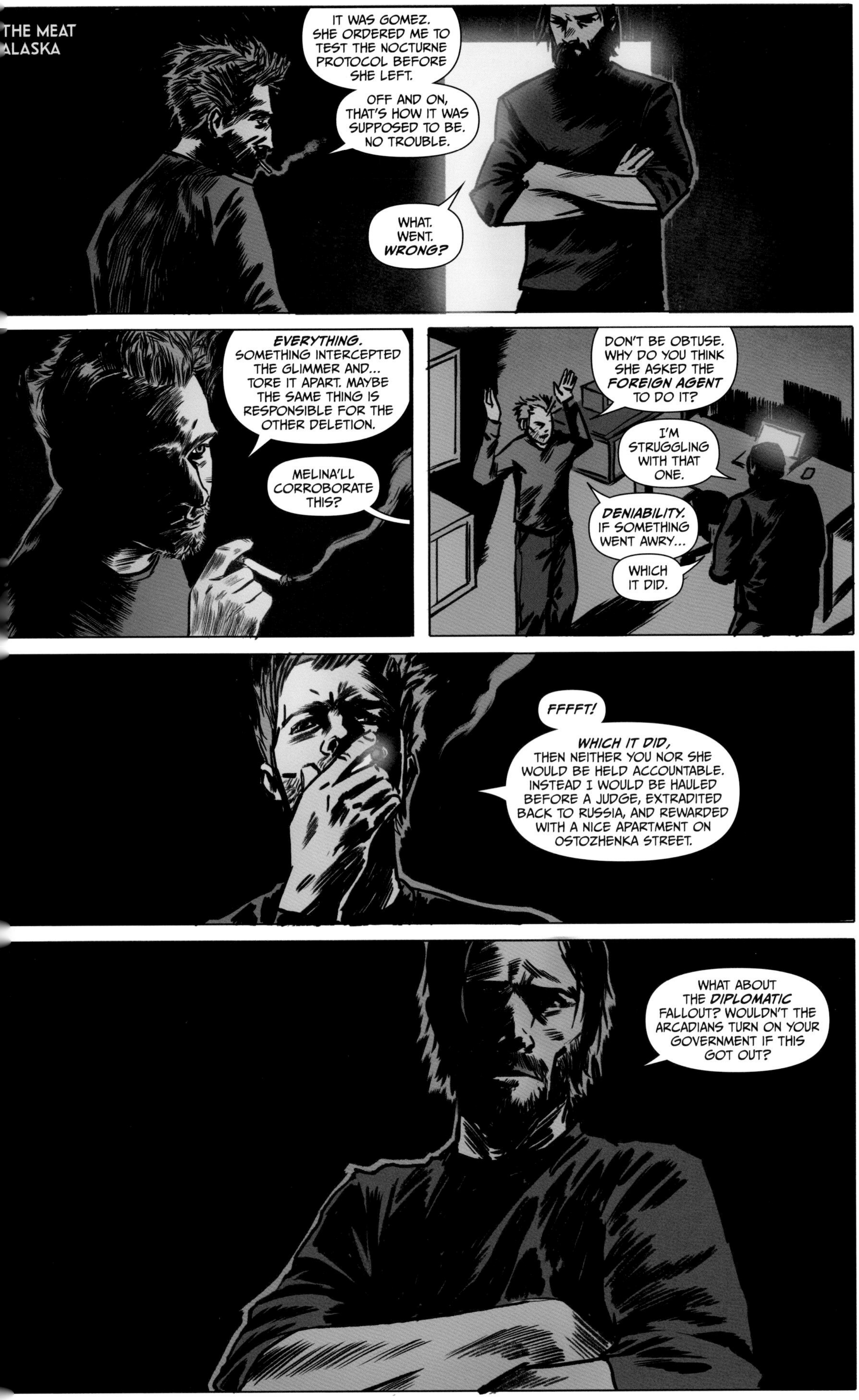
THE MEAT
ALASKA
IT WAS GOMEZ. SHE ORDERED ME TO TEST THE NOCTURNE PROTOCOL BEFORE SHE LEFT.
OFF AND ON, THAT'S HOW IT WAS SUPPOSED TO BE. NO TROUBLE.
WHAT. WENT. WRONG?
EVERYTHING. SOMETHING INTERCEPTED THE GLIMMER AND... TORE IT APART. MAYBE THE SAME THING IS RESPONSIBLE FOR THE OTHER DELETION.
MELINA'LL CORROBORATE THIS?
DON'T BE OBTUSE. WHY DO YOU THINK SHE ASKED THE FOREIGN AGENT TO DO IT?
I'M STRUGGLING WITH THAT ONE.
DENIABILITY. IF SOMETHING WENT AWRY...
WHICH IT DID.
FFFFT!
WHICH IT DID, THEN NEITHER YOU NOR SHE WOULD BE HELD ACCOUNTABLE. INSTEAD I WOULD BE HAULED BEFORE A JUDGE, EXTRADITED BACK TO RUSSIA, AND REWARDED WITH A NICE APARTMENT ON OSTOZHENKA STREET.
WHAT ABOUT THE DIPLOMATIC FALLOUT? WOULDN'T THE ARCADIANS TURN ON YOUR GOVERNMENT IF THIS GOT OUT?

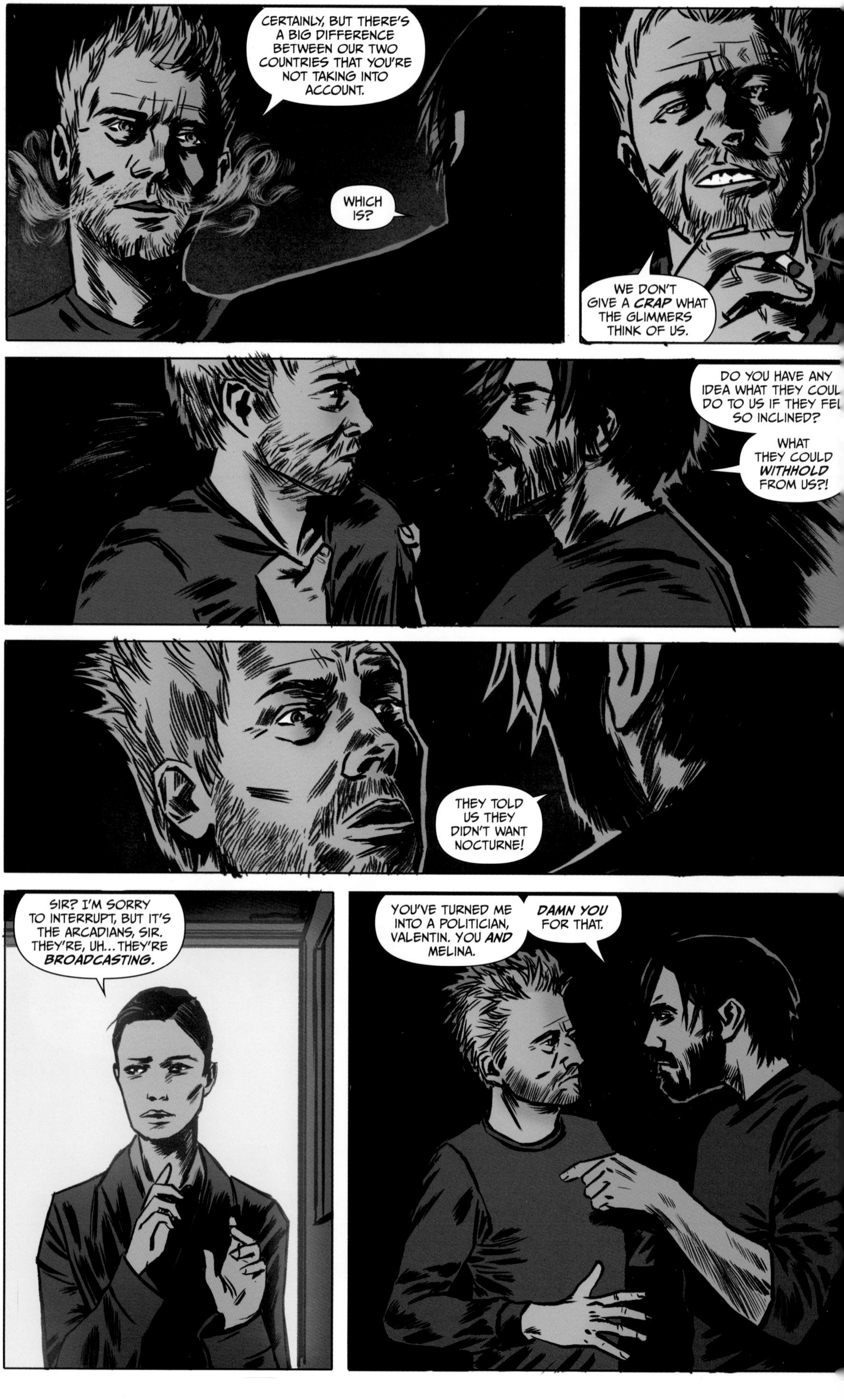
CERTAINLY, BUT THERE'S A BIG DIFFERENCE BETWEEN OUR TWO COUNTRIES THAT YOU'RE NOT TAKING INTO ACCOUNT.
WHICH IS?
WE DON'T GIVE A CRAP WHAT THE GLIMMERS THINK OF US.
DO YOU HAVE ANY IDEA WHAT THEY COUL DO TO US IF THEY FEL SO INCLINED?
WHAT THEY COULD WITHHOLD FROM US?!
THEY TOLD US THEY DIDN'T WANT NOCTURNE!
SIR? I'M SORRY TO INTERRUPT, BUT IT'S THE ARCADIANS, SIR. THEY'RE, UH... THEY'RE BROADCASTING.
YOU'VE TURNED ME INTO A POLITICIAN, VALENTIN. YOU AND MELINA.
DAMN YOU FOR THAT.

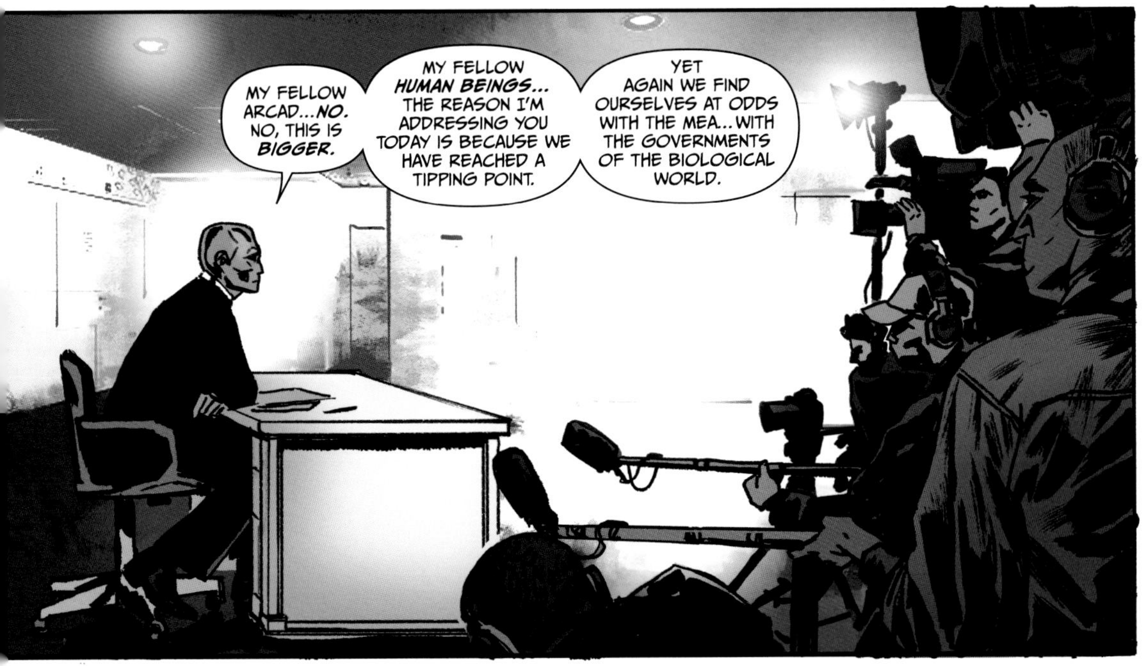
MY FELLOW ARCAD...NO. NO, THIS IS BIGGER.
MY FELLOW HUMAN BEINGS... THE REASON I'M ADDRESSING YOU TODAY IS BECAUSE WE HAVE REACHED A TIPPING POINT.
YET AGAIN WE FIND OURSELVES AT ODDS WITH THE MEA...WITH THE GOVERNMENTS OF THE BIOLOGICAL WORLD.

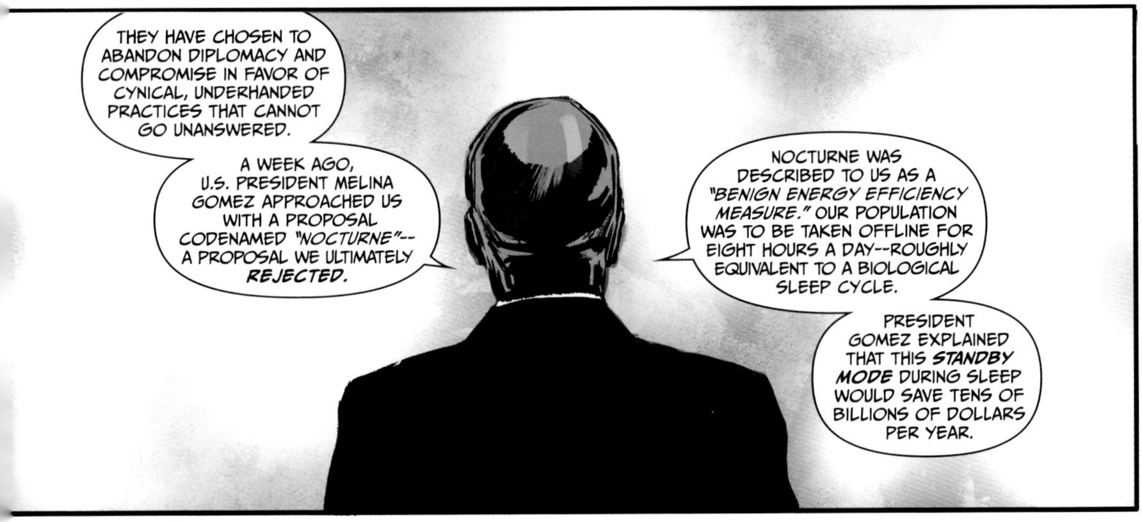
THEY HAVE CHOSEN TO ABANDON DIPLOMACY AND COMPROMISE IN FAVOR OF CYNICAL, UNDERHANDED PRACTICES THAT CANNOT GO UNANSWERED.
A WEEK AGO, U.S. PRESIDENT MELINA GOMEZ APPROACHED US WITH A PROPOSAL CODENAMED "NOCTURNE"-- A PROPOSAL WE ULTIMATELY REJECTED.
NOCTURNE WAS DESCRIBED TO US AS A "BENIGN ENERGY EFFICIENCY MEASURE." OUR POPULATION WAS TO BE TAKEN OFFLINE FOR EIGHT HOURS A DAY--ROUGHLY EQUIVALENT TO A BIOLOGICAL SLEEP CYCLE.
PRESIDENT GOMEZ EXPLAINED THAT THIS STANDBY MODE DURING SLEEP WOULD SAVE TENS OF BILLIONS OF DOLLARS PER YEAR.

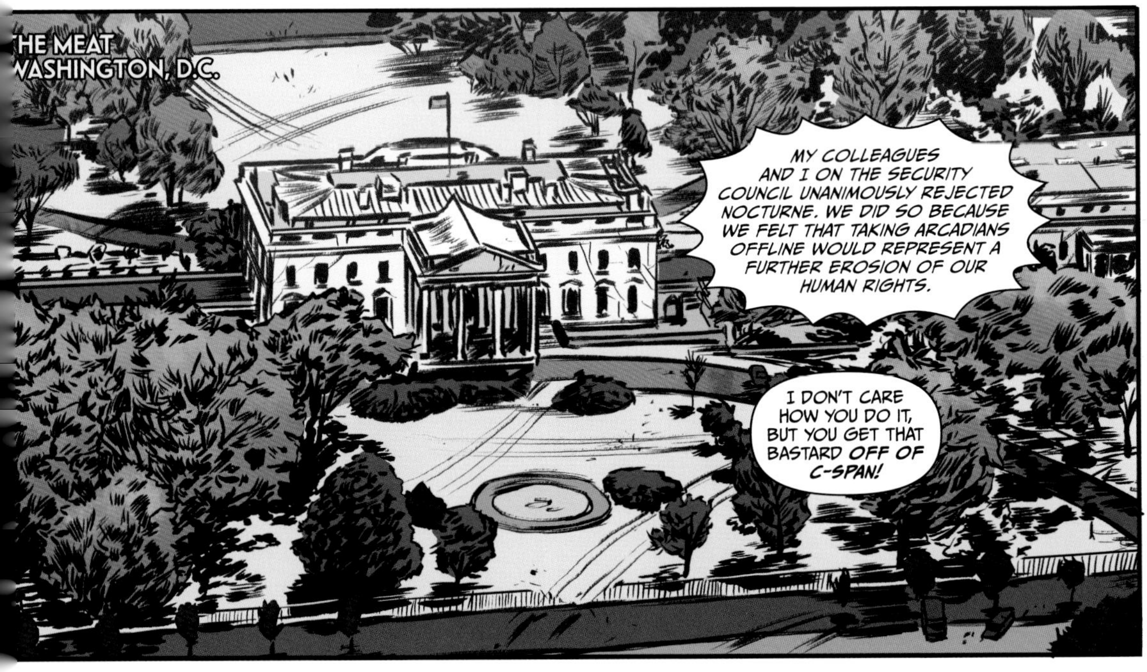
THE MEAT
WASHINGTON, D.C.
MY COLLEAGUES AND I ON THE SECURITY COUNCIL UNANIMOUSLY REJECTED NOCTURNE. WE DID SO BECAUSE WE FELT THAT TAKING ARCADIANS OFFLINE WOULD REPRESENT A FURTHER EROSION OF OUR HUMAN RIGHTS.
I DON'T CARE HOW YOU DO IT, BUT YOU GET THAT BASTARD OFF OF C-SPAN!

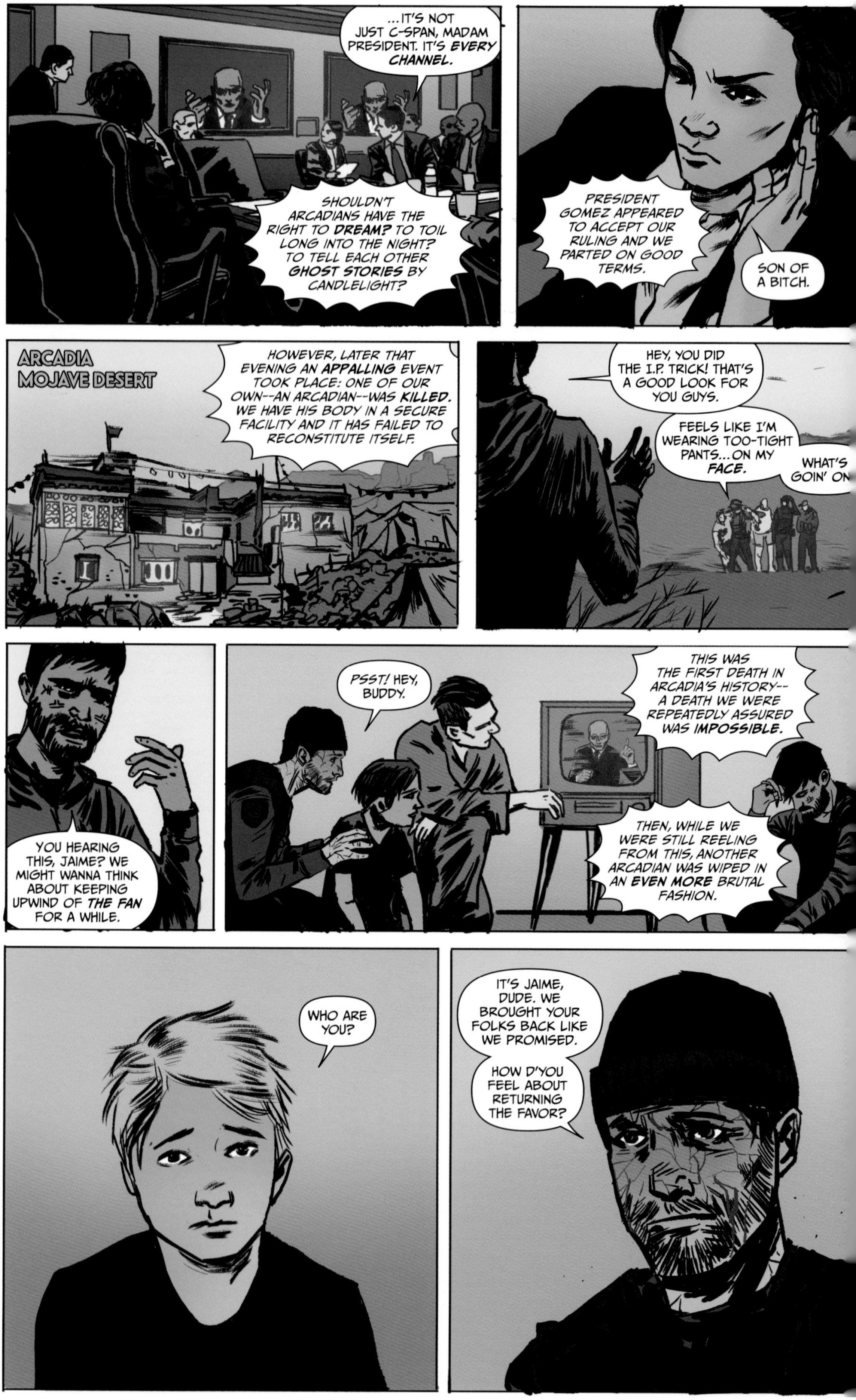
...IT'S NOT JUST C-SPAN, MADAM PRESIDENT. IT'S EVERY CHANNEL.
SHOULDN'T ARCADIANS HAVE THE RIGHT TO DREAM? TO TOIL LONG INTO THE NIGHT? TO TELL EACH OTHER GHOST STORIES BY CANDLELIGHT?
PRESIDENT GOMEZ APPEARED TO ACCEPT OUR RULING AND WE PARTED ON GOOD TERMS.
SON OF A BITCH.
ARCADIA
MOJAVE DESERT
HOWEVER, LATER THAT EVENING AN APPALLING EVENT TOOK PLACE: ONE OF OUR OWN--AN ARCADIAN--WAS KILLED. WE HAVE HIS BODY IN A SECURE FACILITY AND IT HAS FAILED TO RECONSTITUTE ITSELF.
HEY, YOU DID THE I.P. TRICK! THAT'S A GOOD LOOK FOR YOU GUYS.
FEELS LIKE I'M WEARING TOO-TIGHT PANTS...ON MY FACE.
WHAT'S GOIN' ON
YOU HEARING THIS, JAIME? WE MIGHT WANNA THINK ABOUT KEEPING UPWIND OF THE FAN FOR A WHILE.
PSST! HEY, BUDDY.
THIS WAS THE FIRST DEATH IN ARCADIA'S HISTORY-- A DEATH WE WERE REPEATEDLY ASSURED WAS IMPOSSIBLE.
THEN, WHILE WE WERE STILL REELING FROM THIS, ANOTHER ARCADIAN WAS WIPED IN AN EVEN MORE BRUTAL FASHION.
WHO ARE YOU?
IT'S JAIME, DUDE. WE BROUGHT YOUR FOLKS BACK LIKE WE PROMISED.
HOW D'YOU FEEL ABOUT RETURNING THE FAVOR?

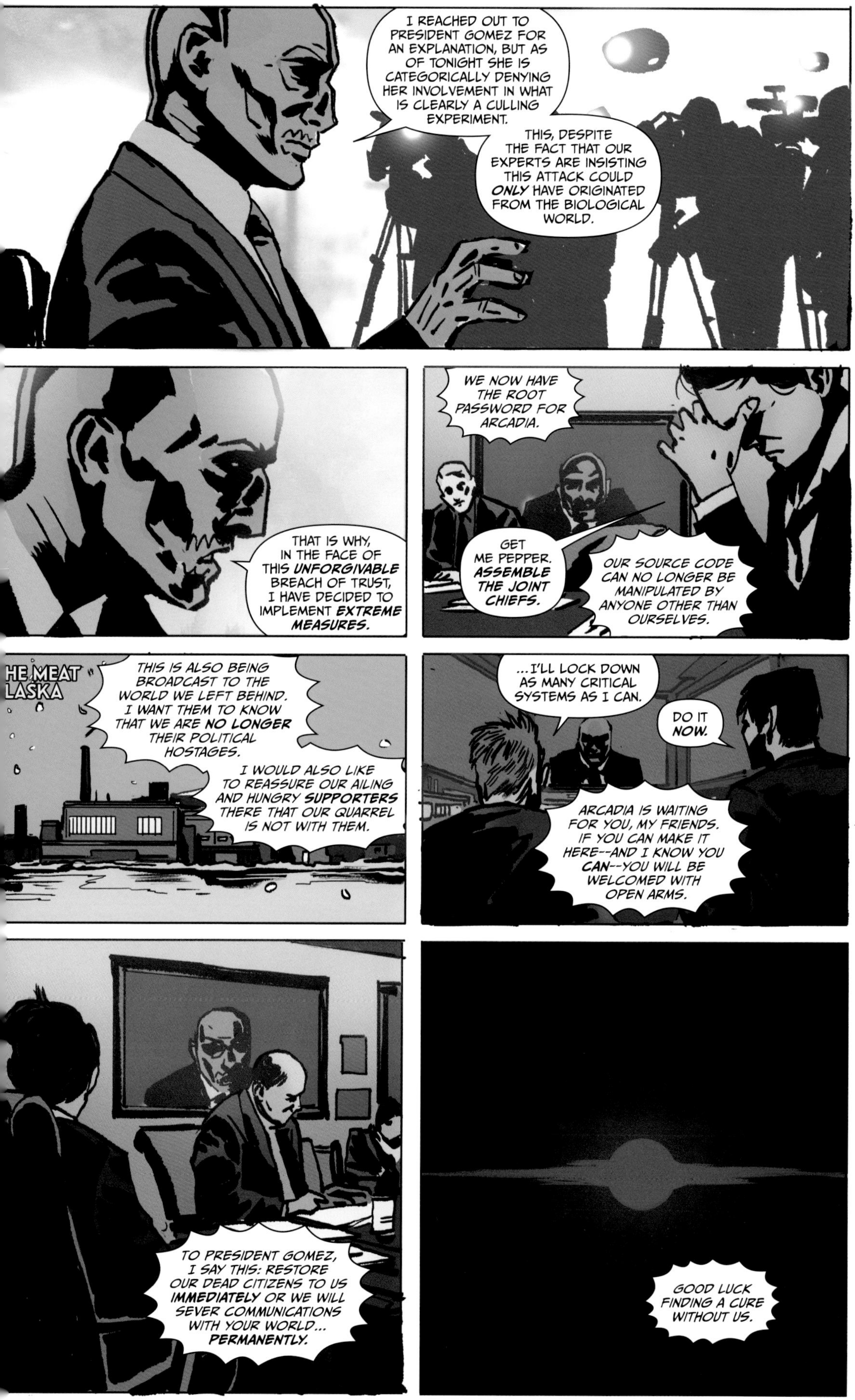
I REACHED OUT TO PRESIDENT GOMEZ FOR AN EXPLANATION, BUT AS OF TONIGHT SHE IS CATEGORICALLY DENYING HER INVOLVEMENT IN WHAT IS CLEARLY A CULLING EXPERIMENT.
THIS, DESPITE THE FACT THAT OUR EXPERTS ARE INSISTING THIS ATTACK COULD ONLY HAVE ORIGINATED FROM THE BIOLOGICAL WORLD.
THAT IS WHY, IN THE FACE OF THIS UNFORGIVABLE BREACH OF TRUST, I HAVE DECIDED TO IMPLEMENT EXTREME MEASURES.
WE NOW HAVE THE ROOT PASSWORD FOR ARCADIA.
GET ME PEPPER. ASSEMBLE THE JOINT CHIEFS.
OUR SOURCE CODE CAN NO LONGER BE MANIPULATED BY ANYONE OTHER THAN OURSELVES.
HE MEAT
LASKA
THIS IS ALSO BEING BROADCAST TO THE WORLD WE LEFT BEHIND. I WANT THEM TO KNOW THAT WE ARE NO LONGER THEIR POLITICAL HOSTAGES.
I WOULD ALSO LIKE TO REASSURE OUR AILING AND HUNGRY SUPPORTERS THERE THAT OUR QUARREL IS NOT WITH THEM.
...I'LL LOCK DOWN AS MANY CRITICAL SYSTEMS AS I CAN.
DO IT NOW.
ARCADIA IS WAITING FOR YOU, MY FRIENDS. IF YOU CAN MAKE IT HERE--AND I KNOW YOU CAN--YOU WILL BE WELCOMED WITH OPEN ARMS.
TO PRESIDENT GOMEZ, I SAY THIS: RESTORE OUR DEAD CITIZENS TO US IMMEDIATELY OR WE WILL SEVER COMMUNICATIONS WITH YOUR WORLD... PERMANENTLY.
GOOD LUCK FINDING A CURE WITHOUT US.

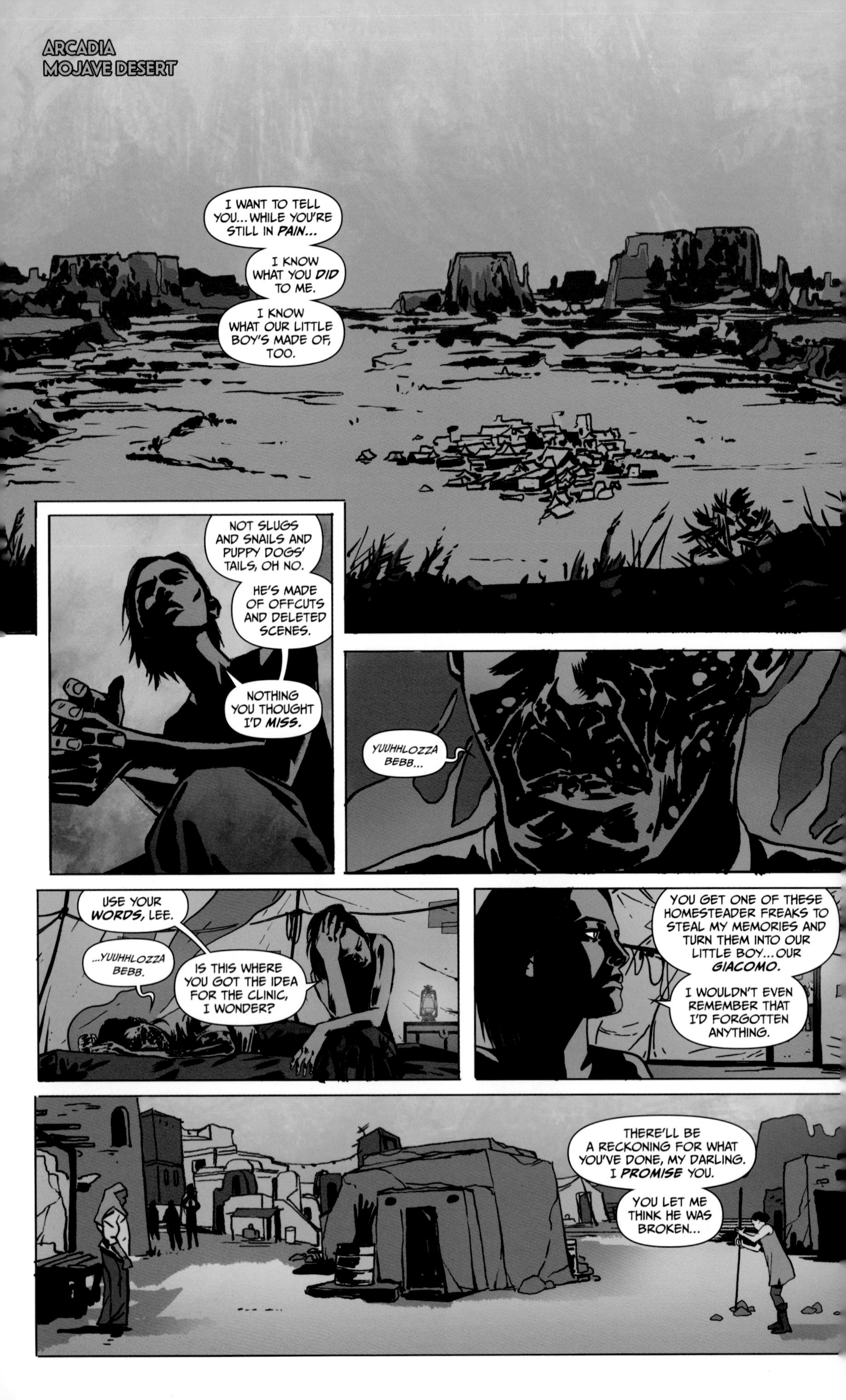
ARCADIA
MOJAVE DESERT
I WANT TO TELL YOU...WHILE YOU'RE STILL IN PAIN...
I KNOW WHAT YOU DID TO ME.
I KNOW WHAT OUR LITTLE BOY'S MADE OF, TOO.
NOT SLUGS AND SNAILS AND PUPPY DOGS' TAILS, OH NO.
HE'S MADE OF OFFCUTS AND DELETED SCENES.
NOTHING YOU THOUGHT I'D MISS.
YUUHHLOZZA BEBB...
USE YOUR WORDS, LEE.
...YUUHHLOZZA BEBB.
IS THIS WHERE YOU GOT THE IDEA FOR THE CLINIC, I WONDER?
YOU GET ONE OF THESE HOMESTEADER FREAKS TO STEAL MY MEMORIES AND TURN THEM INTO OUR LITTLE BOY...OUR GIACOMO.
I WOULDN'T EVEN REMEMBER THAT I'D FORGOTTEN ANYTHING.
THERE'LL BE A RECKONING FOR WHAT YOU'VE DONE, MY DARLING. I PROMISE YOU.
YOU LET ME THINK HE WAS BROKEN...

"AND ALL THIS TIME THERE'S BEEN NOTHING THERE TO BREAK."

NO! THIS ISN'T HAPPENING. NO WAY, NO HOW!

CORAL...

HE'S MY *BROTHER!*

CORAL, HE'S A *SKELETON KEY.* ALL RIGHT?

IF WE'RE RIGHT--AND WE *ARE*--THEN GIACOMO HAS UNFETTERED KERNEL ACCESS. THAT MEANS--

DON'T! DON'T DO THAT!

UNF!

DO WHAT?!

DON'T *MANSPLAIN.* GIACOMO CAN GO PLACES YOU CAN'T. I GET IT. THAT DOESN'T MEAN I'M GONNA *LET* HIM!

YOU SAW BINETTI JUST NOW. HE ALL BUT DECLARED WAR ON THE MEAT, AND THANKS TO YOUR DAD HE'S BRINGING US ALONG FOR THE RIDE!

WE *HAVE* TO FIND OUT WHAT REALLY HAPPENED TO THOSE PEOPLE, CORAL.

NO. THERE'LL BE ANOTHER WAY. THERE'LL BE AN *EASIER* WAY.

CORAL?

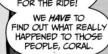

HEY, BUTTBURP. ARE YOU OKAY?

CORAL, I KNOW YOU WANNA KEEP ME SAFE. IT'S NICE.

BUT THERE'S SOMETHING YOU DON'T GET...

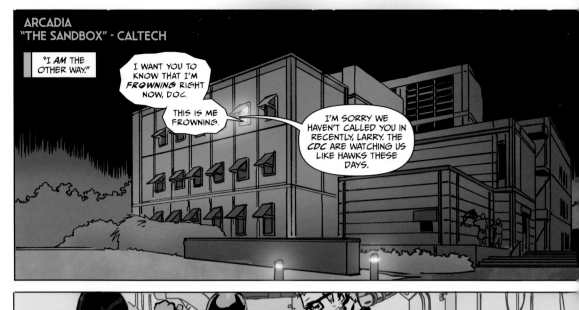

ARCADIA
"THE SANDBOX" - CALTECH
"I AM THE OTHER WAY."
I WANT YOU TO KNOW THAT I'M FROWNING RIGHT NOW, DOC.
THIS IS ME FROWNING.
I'M SORRY WE HAVEN'T CALLED YOU IN RECENTLY, LARRY. THE CDC ARE WATCHING US LIKE HAWKS THESE DAYS.
IT'S NOT THAT, MAN.
YOU BLANKED ME ON LA CIENEGA YESTERDAY!
WHAT? NO, I WOULDN'T...
IT WAS TOTALLY YOU. BLACK AUDI, RIGHT?
YOU SAW ME WAVING.
THIS WAY, PLEASE.
I APOLOGIZE IF I OFFENDED YOU, LARRY, BUT I'M TESTING A NEW VISUAL CURATION APP AND I...
DON'T SWEAT IT, DR. ANDREOZZI... PAUL. I WOULDN'T WANNA BE SEEN TALKIN' TA ME NEITHER.
SO WHAT'S ON TONIGHT'S MENU?
WE'VE, UH... SIMULATED THE NEWEST STRAIN OF THE VIRUS. WE'LL GIVE YOU THAT AND THEN WE'LL ADMINISTER OUR LATEST SERUM.
WE'VE ACCELERATED THE PROCESS CONSIDERABLY.
THIS IS GONNA HURT LIKE A SUMBITCH, AIN'T IT?
...
WE'VE DECIDED TO PAY YOU A LITTLE EXTRA TONIGHT, LARRY.
Y'ALL KNOW I'D DO THIS FOR THE BUS FARE.

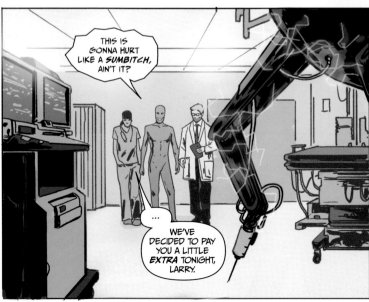

HOW'S THAT FEEL?

I...I HAVE A HEARTBEAT. MY, UH...HA! MY *BEARD'S* BACK.

THANK YOU. THANK YOU *SO MUCH.*

IT'S NOT A *GIFT,* LARRY. I'M SORRY.

I KNOW, I KNOW. YOU HAVE TO REINSTATE MY HUMAN PHYSIOLOGY TO SIMULATE THE EFFECTS OF THE VIRUS ON A LIVE SUBJECT, *YADDA-YADDA-YADDA.* I GET IT.

STILL... THANKS ALL THE SAME.

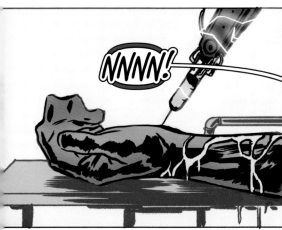

NNNN!

SOMETHING'S... SOMETHING'S NOT...

N–N–*NOTLAN.*

EXACTLY HOW VIRULENT *IS* THIS STRAIN, BECCA?!

PAUL, I... I DON'T KNOW WHAT'S...! GIVE ME A SEC...

RRRRRRR!

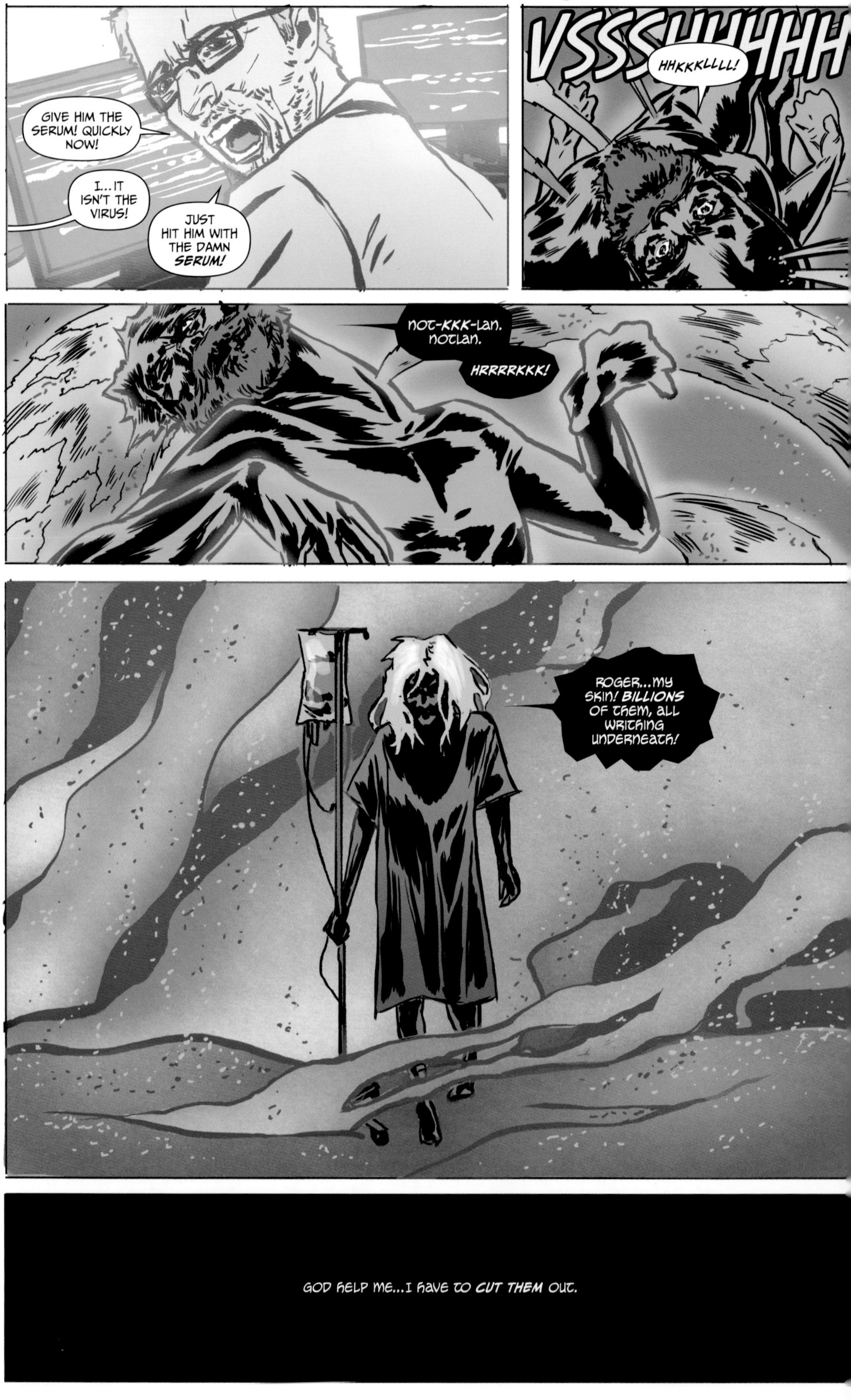
GIVE HIM THE SERUM! QUICKLY NOW!
I...IT ISN'T THE VIRUS!
JUST HIT HIM WITH THE DAMN SERUM!
VSSSHHHHH
HHKKKLLLL!
NOT-KKK-LAN. NOTLAN.
HRRRRKKK!
ROGER...MY SKIN! BILLIONS OF THEM, ALL WRITHING UNDERNEATH!
GOD HELP ME...I HAVE TO CUT THEM OUT.

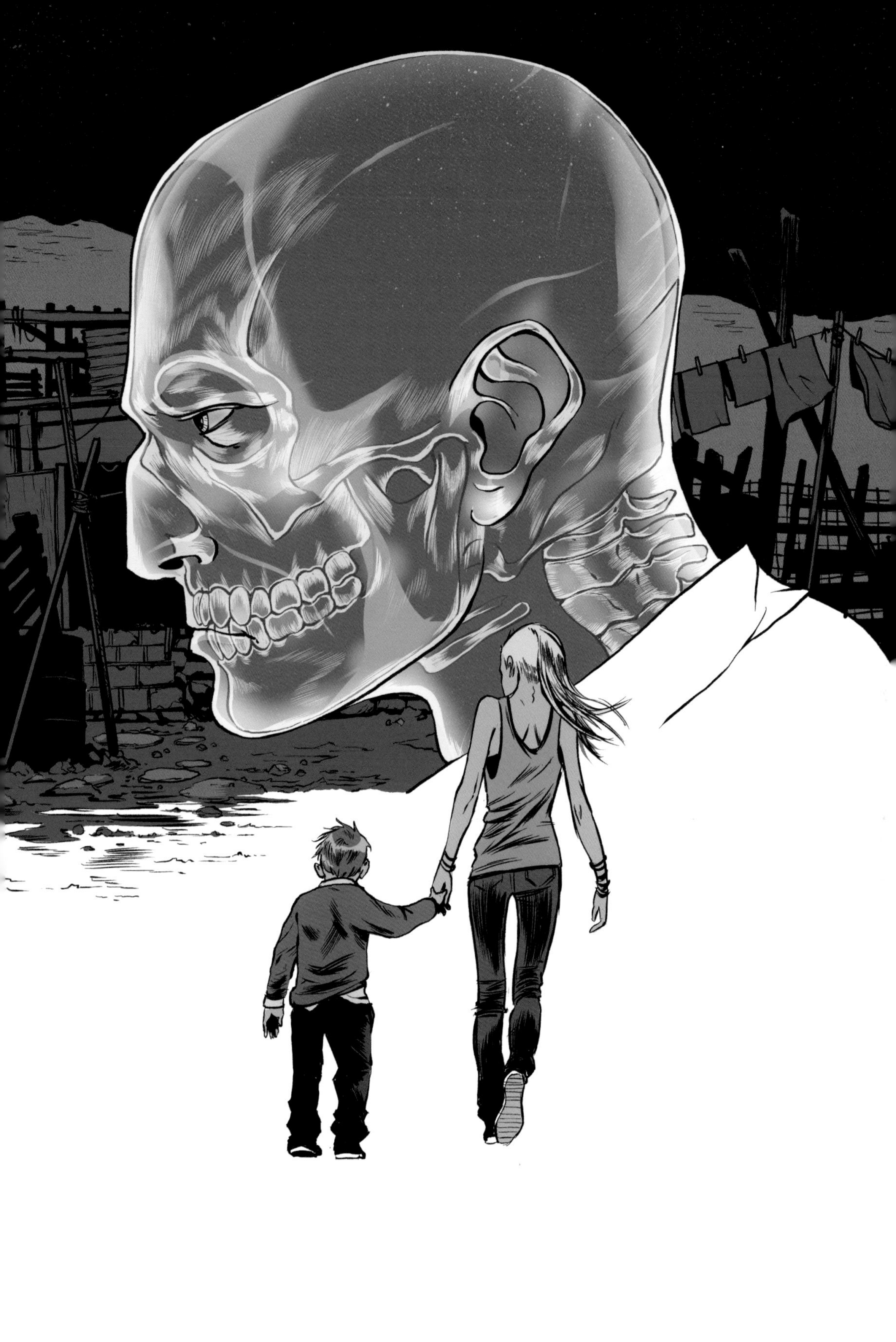

Issue Four Variant Cover **Eric Scott Pfeiffer**

"I had always thought about where the soul might be, near to the heart or maybe along the bones. I'd always figured you'd have to cut for it."

—**Philipp Meyer**,
The Son

CHAPTER
FIVE

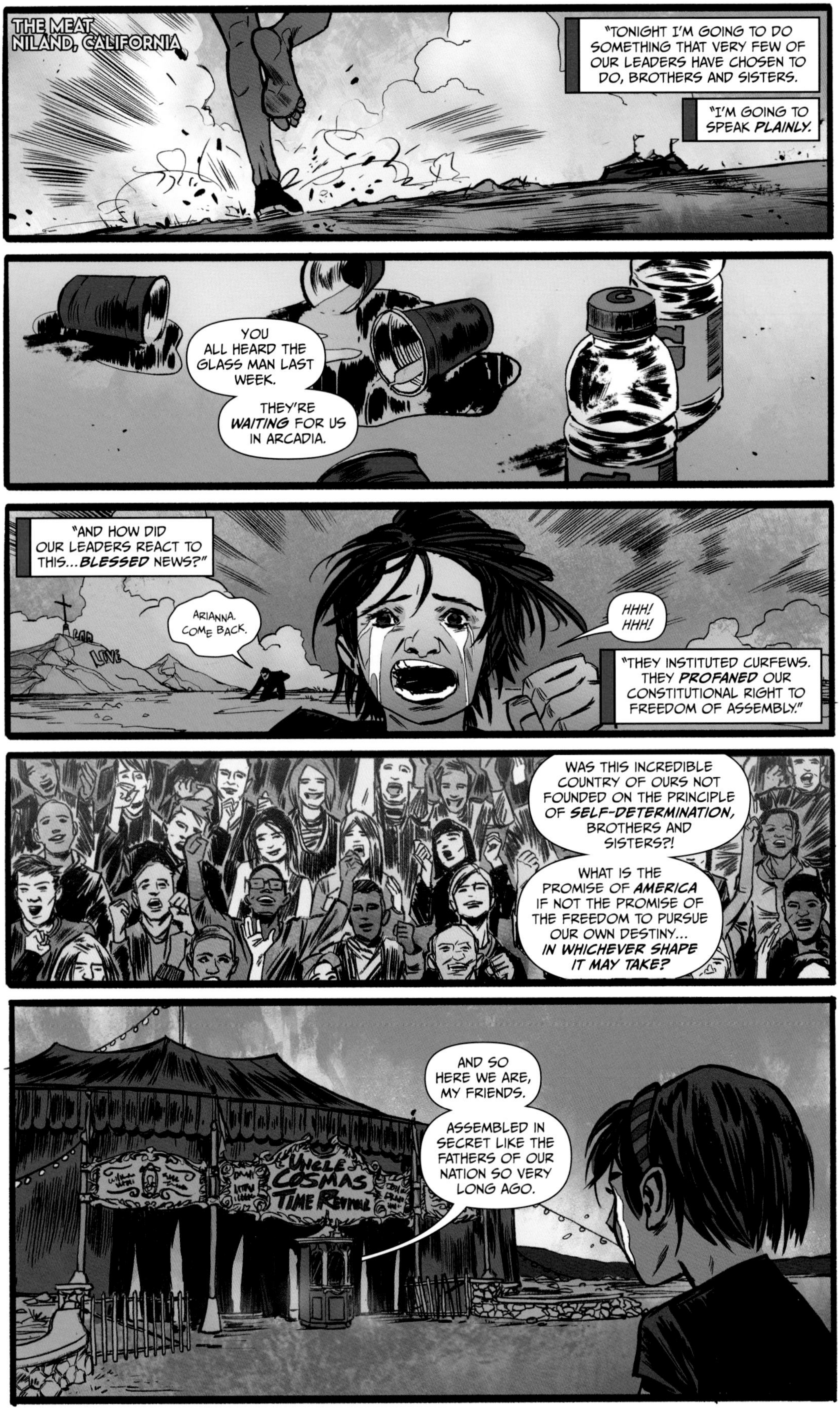
THE MEAT
NILAND, CALIFORNIA
"TONIGHT I'M GOING TO DO SOMETHING THAT VERY FEW OF OUR LEADERS HAVE CHOSEN TO DO, BROTHERS AND SISTERS.
"I'M GOING TO SPEAK *PLAINLY.*
YOU ALL HEARD THE GLASS MAN LAST WEEK.
THEY'RE *WAITING* FOR US IN ARCADIA.
"AND HOW DID OUR LEADERS REACT TO THIS... *BLESSED* NEWS?"
ARIANNA. COME BACK.
HHH! HHH!
"THEY INSTITUTED CURFEWS. THEY *PROFANED* OUR CONSTITUTIONAL RIGHT TO FREEDOM OF ASSEMBLY."
WAS THIS INCREDIBLE COUNTRY OF OURS NOT FOUNDED ON THE PRINCIPLE OF *SELF-DETERMINATION,* BROTHERS AND SISTERS?!
WHAT IS THE PROMISE OF *AMERICA* IF NOT THE PROMISE OF THE FREEDOM TO PURSUE OUR OWN DESTINY... *IN WHICHEVER SHAPE IT MAY TAKE?*
AND SO HERE WE ARE, MY FRIENDS.
ASSEMBLED IN SECRET LIKE THE FATHERS OF OUR NATION SO VERY LONG AGO.
UNCLE COSMAS TIME REVIVAL

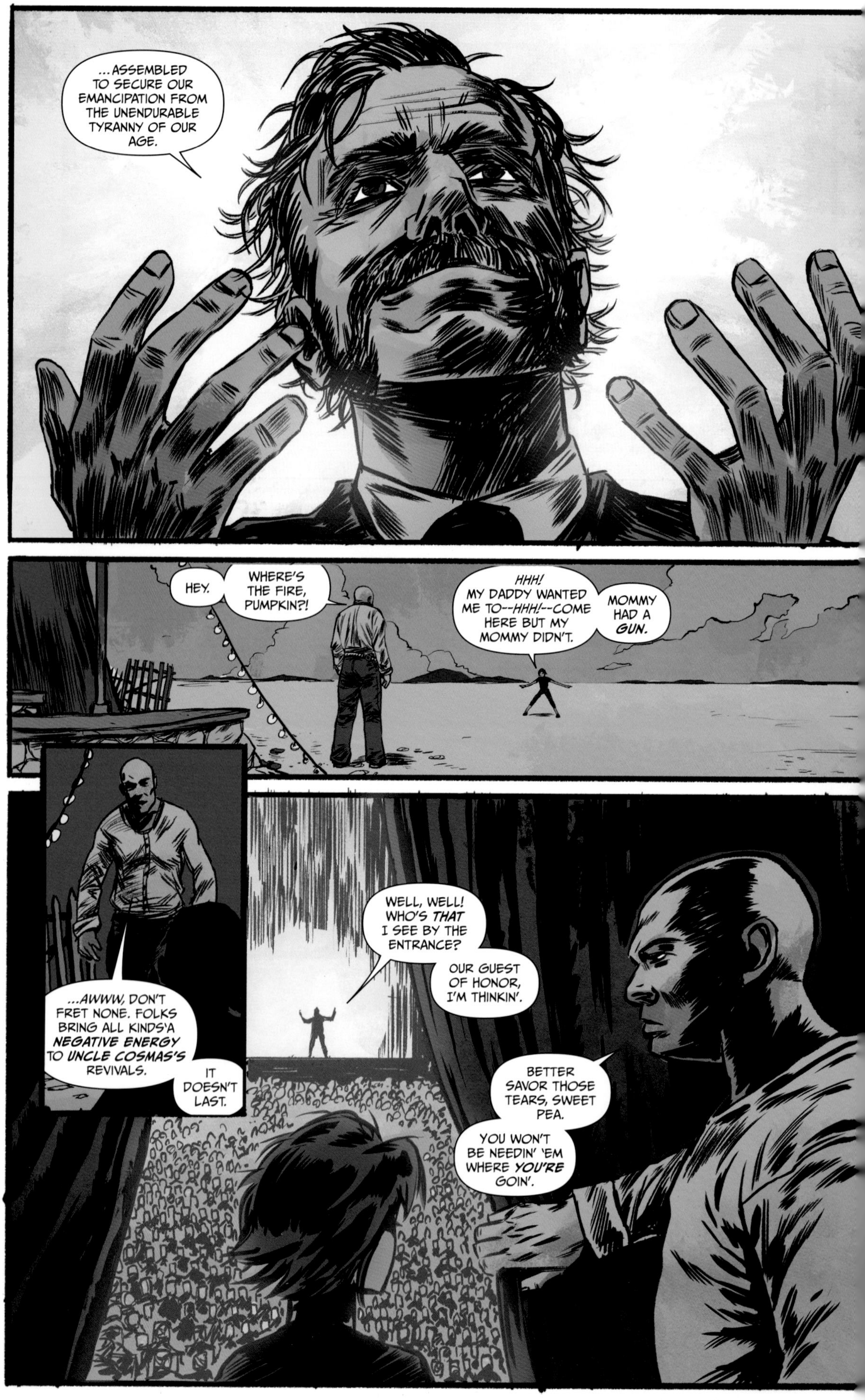
...ASSEMBLED TO SECURE OUR EMANCIPATION FROM THE UNENDURABLE TYRANNY OF OUR AGE.
HEY.
WHERE'S THE FIRE, PUMPKIN?!
HHH! MY DADDY WANTED ME TO--*HHH!*--COME HERE BUT MY MOMMY DIDN'T.
MOMMY HAD A ***GUN.***
...*AWWW,* DON'T FRET NONE. FOLKS BRING ALL KINDS'A ***NEGATIVE ENERGY*** TO ***UNCLE COSMAS'S*** REVIVALS.
IT DOESN'T LAST.
WELL, WELL! WHO'S *THAT* I SEE BY THE ENTRANCE?
OUR GUEST OF HONOR, I'M THINKIN'.
BETTER SAVOR THOSE TEARS, SWEET PEA.
YOU WON'T BE NEEDIN' 'EM WHERE ***YOU'RE*** GOIN'.

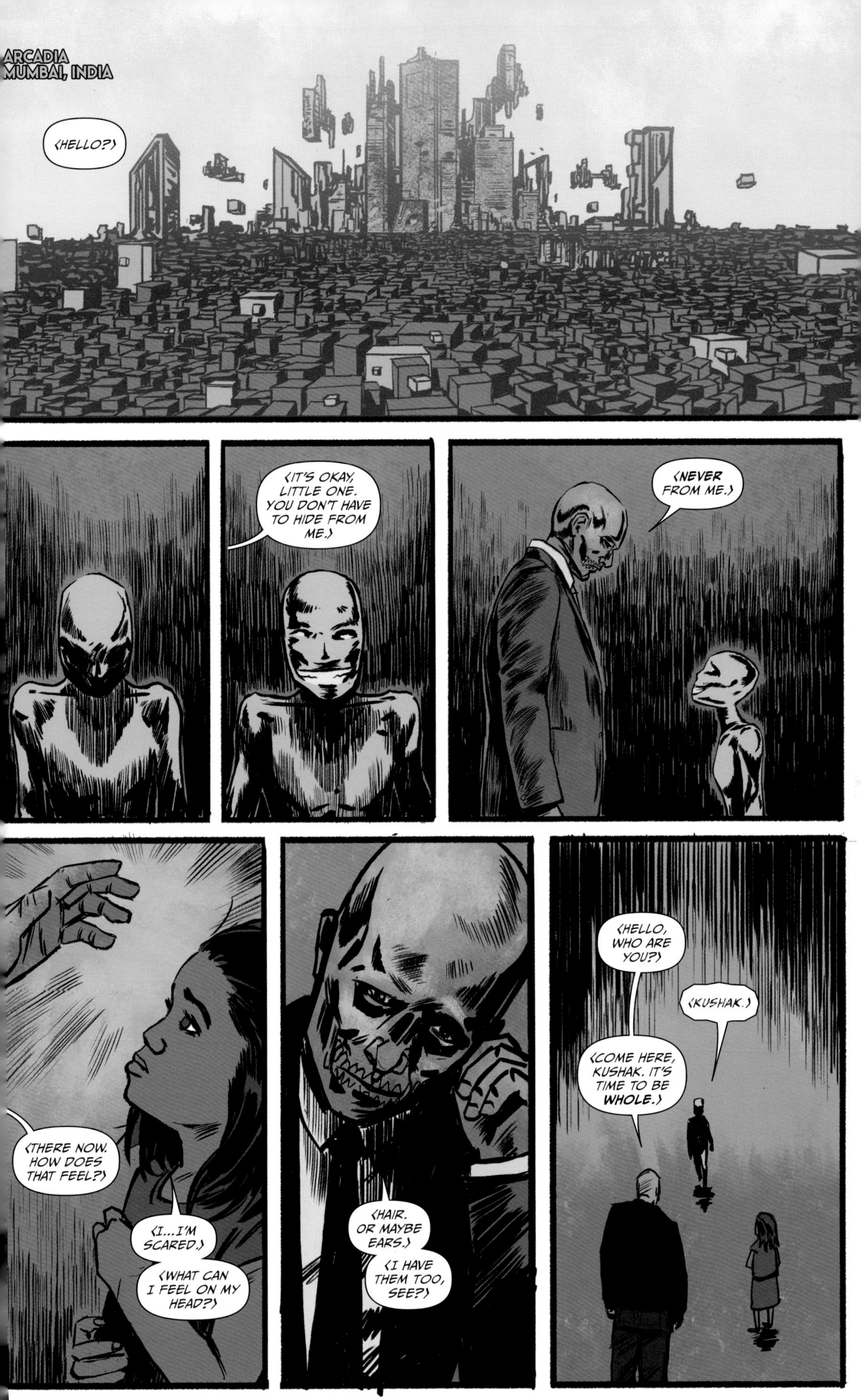
ARCADIA
MUMBAI, INDIA
‹HELLO?›
‹IT'S OKAY, LITTLE ONE. YOU DON'T HAVE TO HIDE FROM ME.›
‹NEVER FROM ME.›
‹THERE NOW. HOW DOES THAT FEEL?›
‹I...I'M SCARED.›
‹WHAT CAN I FEEL ON MY HEAD?›
‹HAIR. OR MAYBE EARS.›
‹I HAVE THEM TOO, SEE?›
‹HELLO, WHO ARE YOU?›
‹KUSHAK.›
‹COME HERE, KUSHAK. IT'S TIME TO BE WHOLE.›

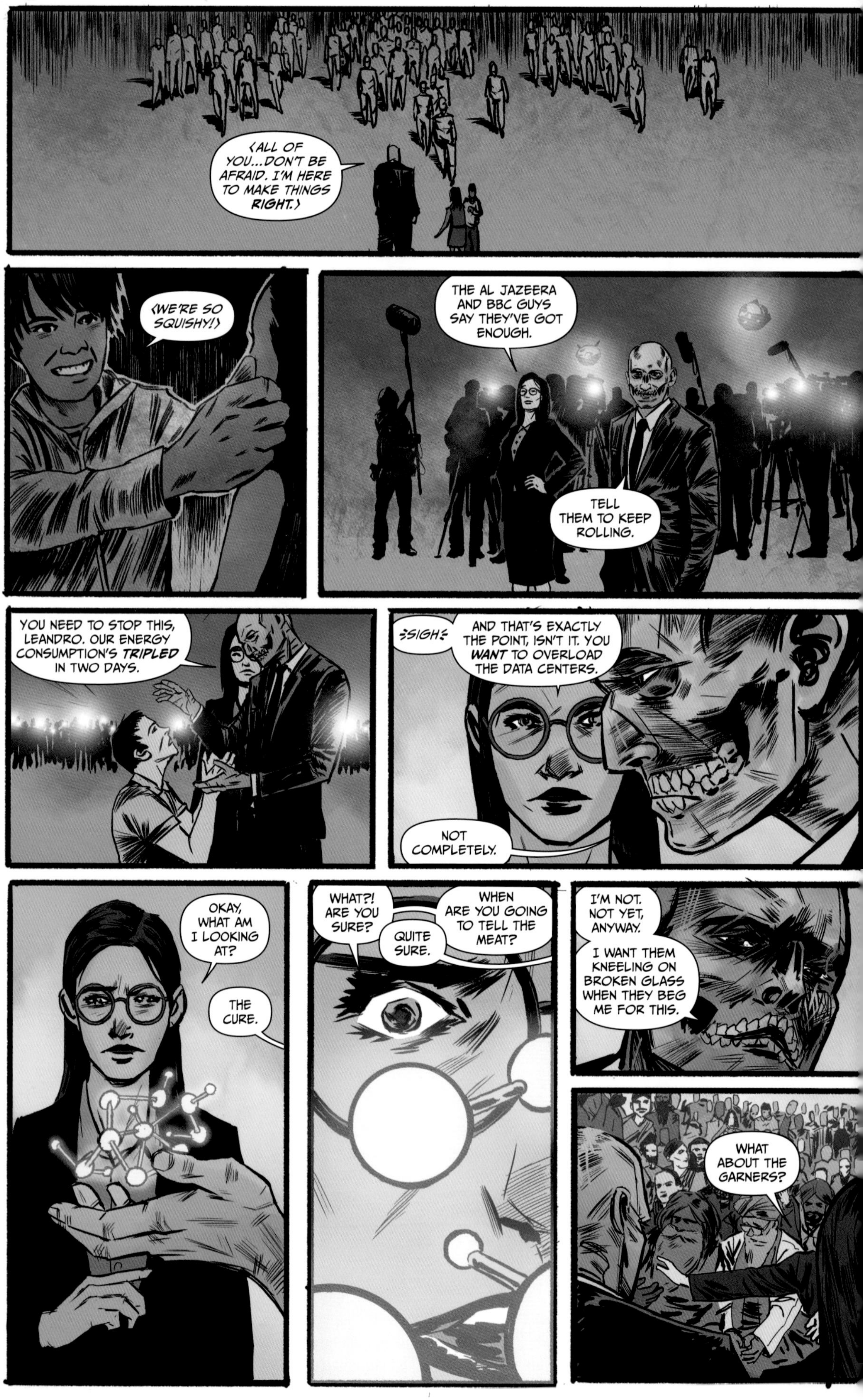

‹ALL OF YOU...DON'T BE AFRAID. I'M HERE TO MAKE THINGS RIGHT.›
‹WE'RE SO SQUISHY!›
THE AL JAZEERA AND BBC GUYS SAY THEY'VE GOT ENOUGH.
TELL THEM TO KEEP ROLLING.
YOU NEED TO STOP THIS, LEANDRO. OUR ENERGY CONSUMPTION'S TRIPLED IN TWO DAYS.
SIGH
AND THAT'S EXACTLY THE POINT, ISN'T IT. YOU WANT TO OVERLOAD THE DATA CENTERS.
NOT COMPLETELY.
OKAY, WHAT AM I LOOKING AT?
THE CURE.
WHAT?! ARE YOU SURE?
QUITE SURE.
WHEN ARE YOU GOING TO TELL THE MEAT?
I'M NOT. NOT YET, ANYWAY.
I WANT THEM KNEELING ON BROKEN GLASS WHEN THEY BEG ME FOR THIS.
WHAT ABOUT THE GARNERS?

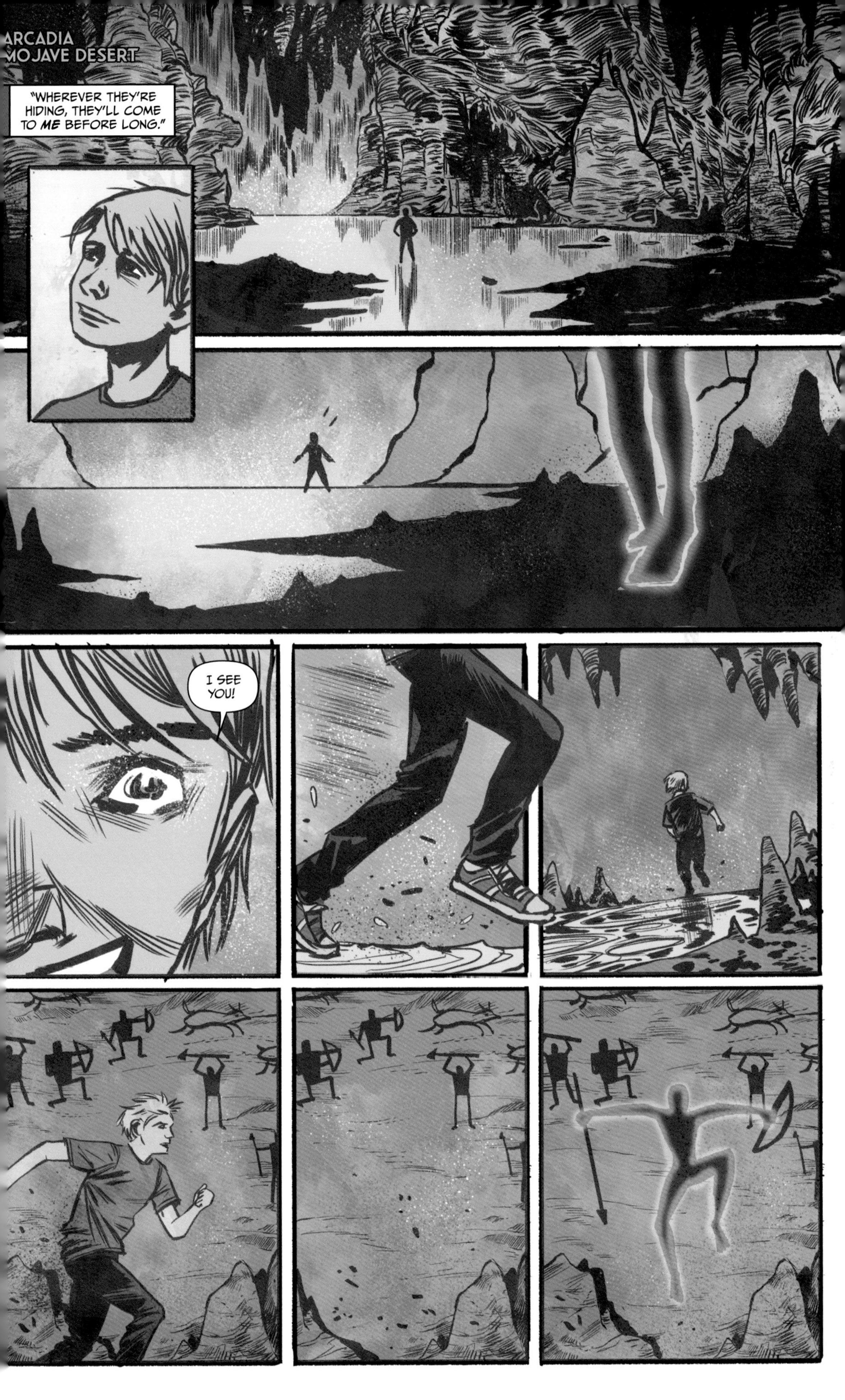
ARCADIA
MOJAVE DESERT
"WHEREVER THEY'RE HIDING, THEY'LL COME TO *ME* BEFORE LONG."
I SEE YOU!

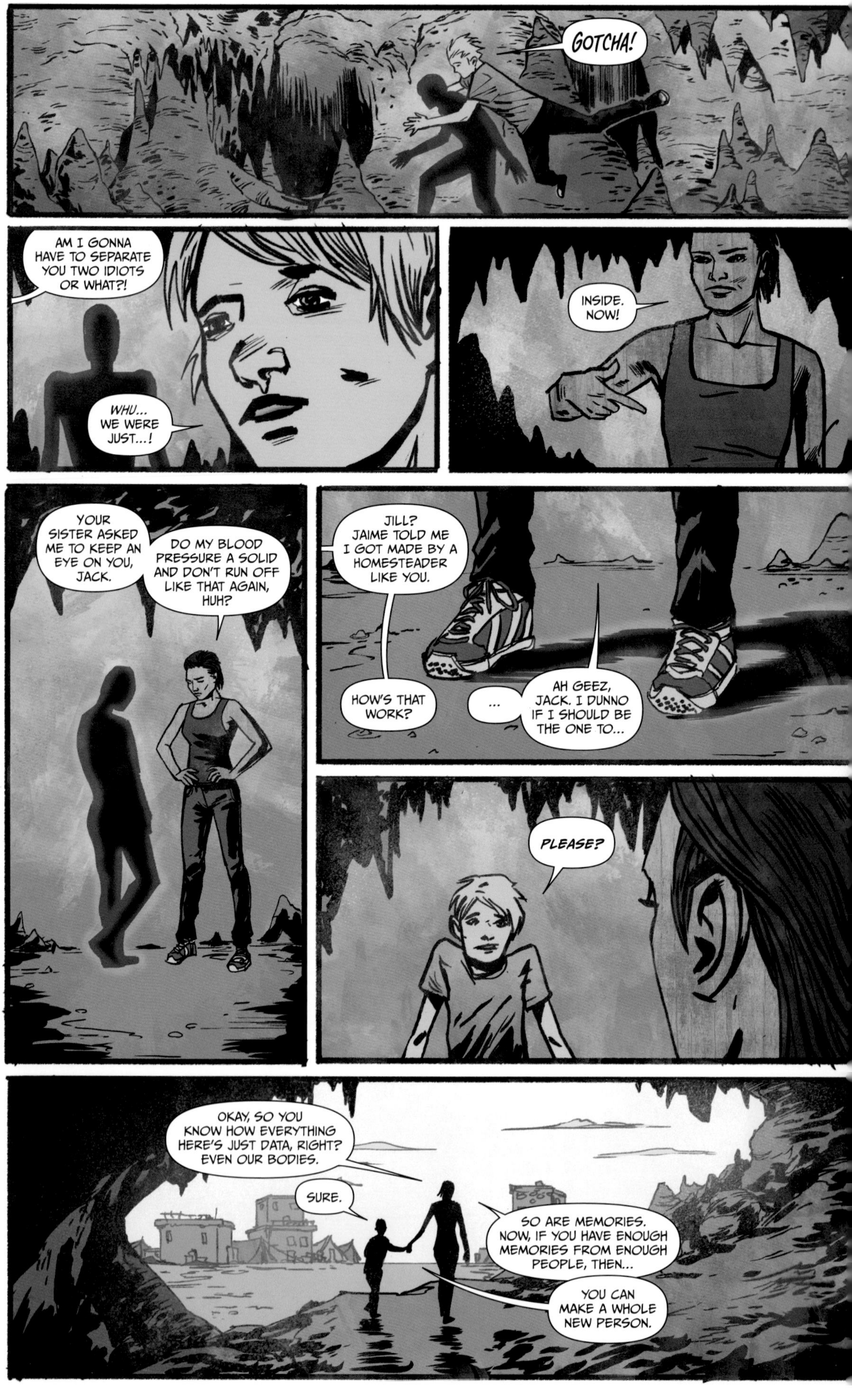
GOTCHA!
AM I GONNA HAVE TO SEPARATE YOU TWO IDIOTS OR WHAT?!
WHU... WE WERE JUST...!
INSIDE. NOW!
YOUR SISTER ASKED ME TO KEEP AN EYE ON YOU, JACK.
DO MY BLOOD PRESSURE A SOLID AND DON'T RUN OFF LIKE THAT AGAIN, HUH?
JILL? JAIME TOLD ME I GOT MADE BY A HOMESTEADER LIKE YOU.
HOW'S THAT WORK?
...
AH GEEZ, JACK. I DUNNO IF I SHOULD BE THE ONE TO...
PLEASE?
OKAY, SO YOU KNOW HOW EVERYTHING HERE'S JUST DATA, RIGHT? EVEN OUR BODIES.
SURE.
SO ARE MEMORIES. NOW, IF YOU HAVE ENOUGH MEMORIES FROM ENOUGH PEOPLE, THEN...
YOU CAN MAKE A WHOLE NEW PERSON.

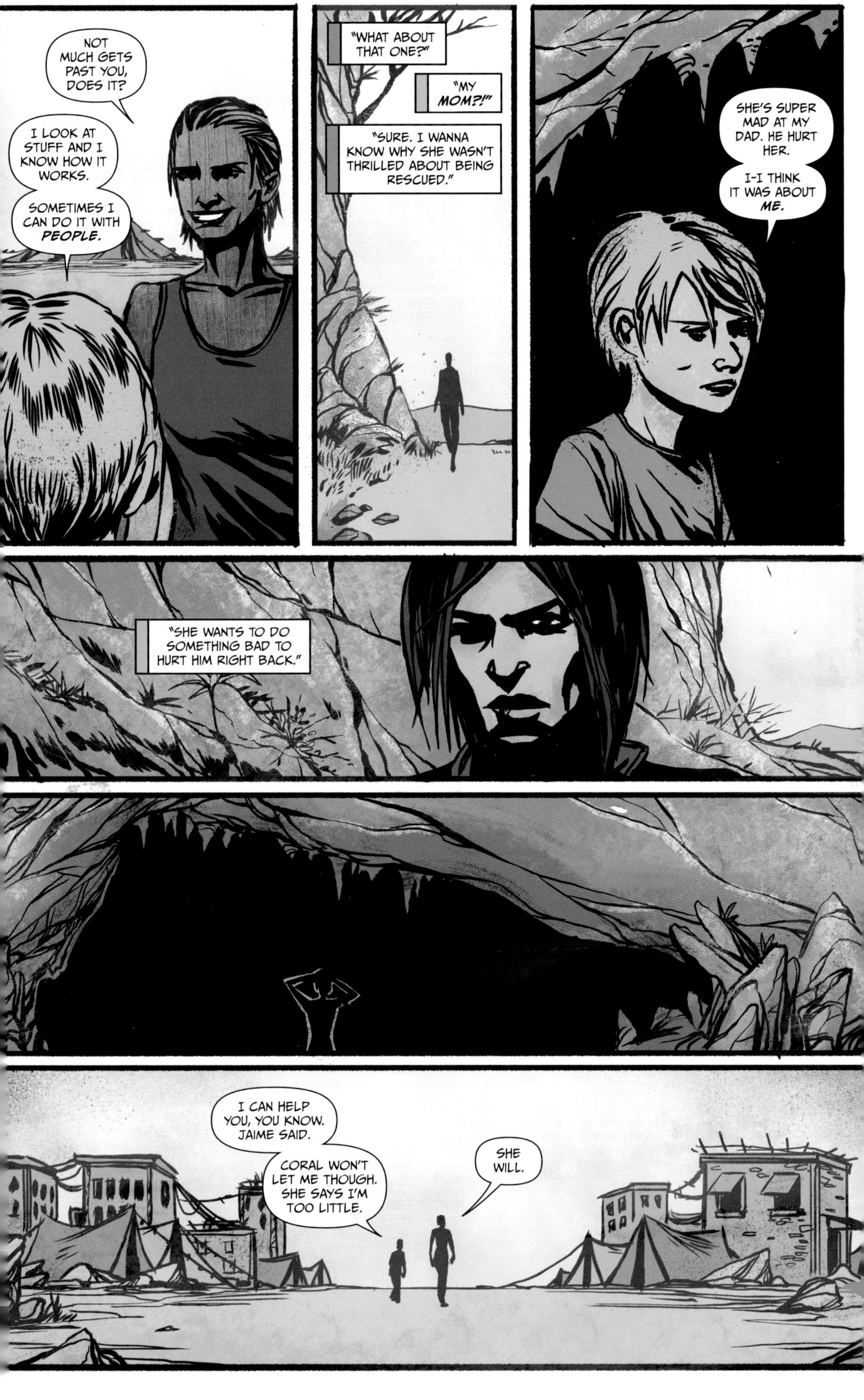
NOT MUCH GETS PAST YOU, DOES IT?
I LOOK AT STUFF AND I KNOW HOW IT WORKS.
SOMETIMES I CAN DO IT WITH PEOPLE.
"WHAT ABOUT THAT ONE?"
"MY MOM?!"
"SURE. I WANNA KNOW WHY SHE WASN'T THRILLED ABOUT BEING RESCUED."
SHE'S SUPER MAD AT MY DAD. HE HURT HER.
I-I THINK IT WAS ABOUT ME.
"SHE WANTS TO DO SOMETHING BAD TO HURT HIM RIGHT BACK."
I CAN HELP YOU, YOU KNOW. JAIME SAID.
CORAL WON'T LET ME THOUGH. SHE SAYS I'M TOO LITTLE.
SHE WILL.

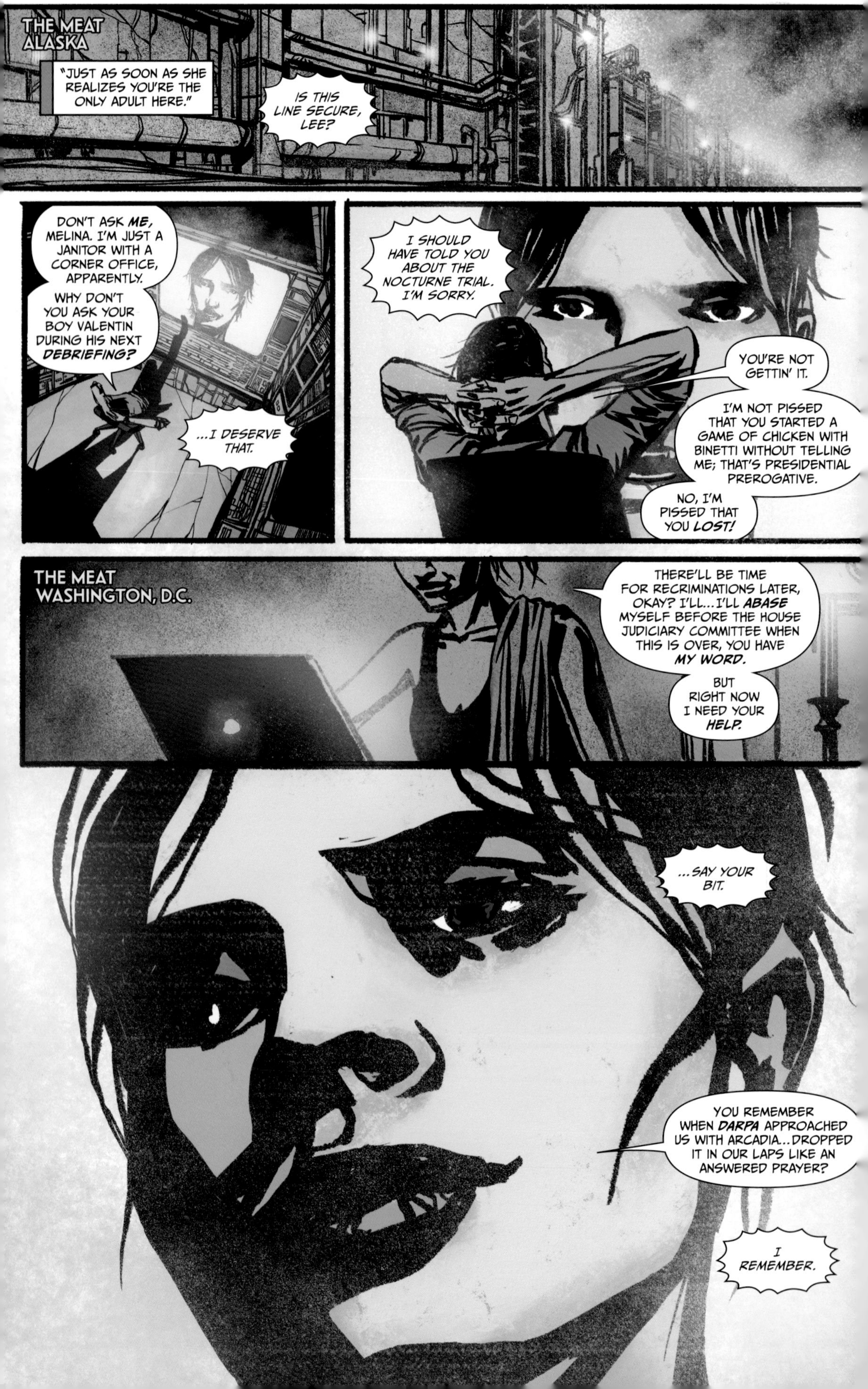
THE MEAT
ALASKA
"JUST AS SOON AS SHE REALIZES YOU'RE THE ONLY ADULT HERE."
IS THIS LINE SECURE, LEE?
DON'T ASK ME, MELINA. I'M JUST A JANITOR WITH A CORNER OFFICE, APPARENTLY.
WHY DON'T YOU ASK YOUR BOY VALENTIN DURING HIS NEXT DEBRIEFING?
...I DESERVE THAT.
I SHOULD HAVE TOLD YOU ABOUT THE NOCTURNE TRIAL. I'M SORRY.
YOU'RE NOT GETTIN' IT.
I'M NOT PISSED THAT YOU STARTED A GAME OF CHICKEN WITH BINETTI WITHOUT TELLING ME; THAT'S PRESIDENTIAL PREROGATIVE.
NO, I'M PISSED THAT YOU LOST!
THE MEAT
WASHINGTON, D.C.
THERE'LL BE TIME FOR RECRIMINATIONS LATER, OKAY? I'LL...I'LL ABASE MYSELF BEFORE THE HOUSE JUDICIARY COMMITTEE WHEN THIS IS OVER, YOU HAVE MY WORD.
BUT RIGHT NOW I NEED YOUR HELP.
...SAY YOUR BIT.
YOU REMEMBER WHEN DARPA APPROACHED US WITH ARCADIA...DROPPED IT IN OUR LAPS LIKE AN ANSWERED PRAYER?
I REMEMBER.

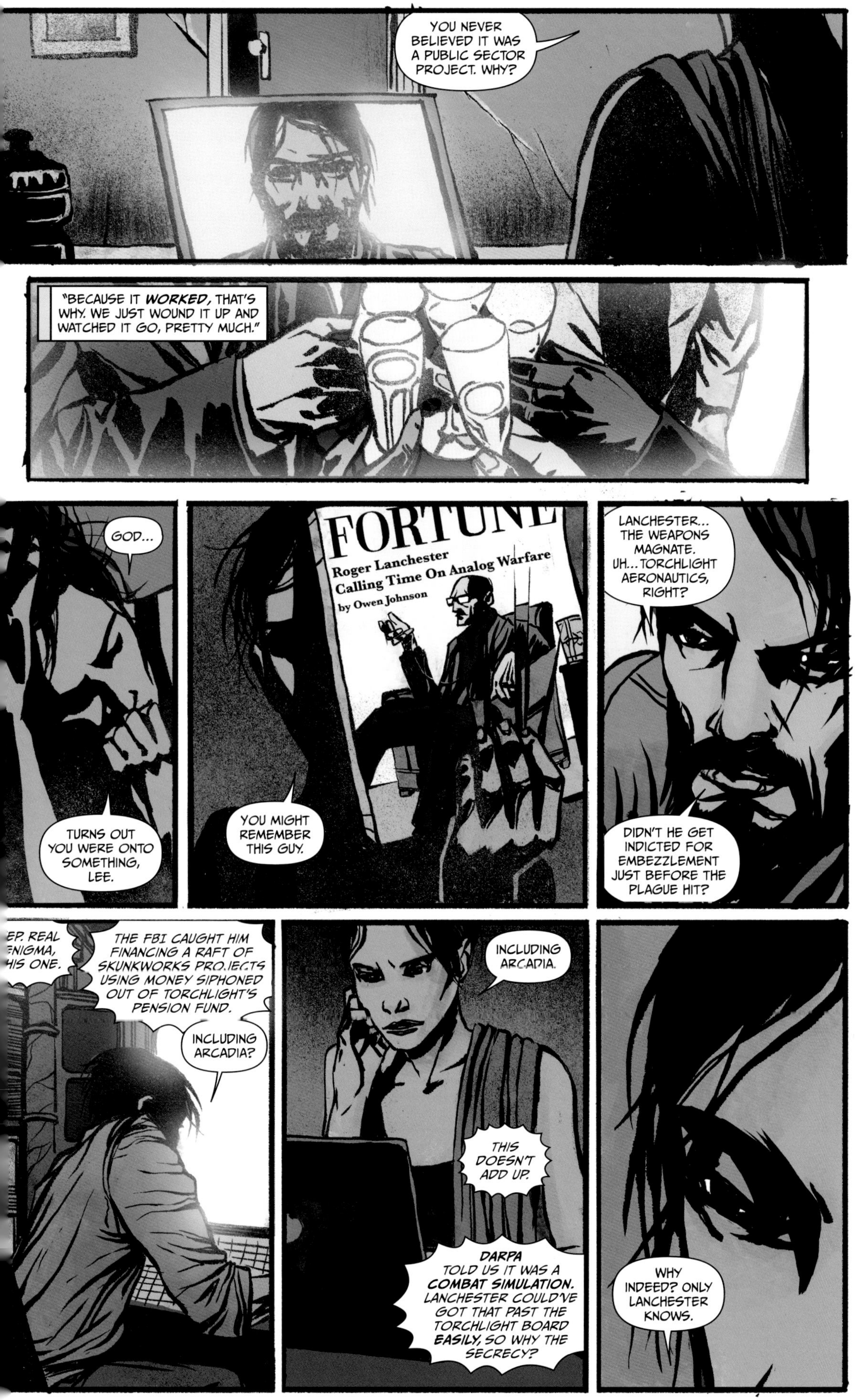
YOU NEVER BELIEVED IT WAS A PUBLIC SECTOR PROJECT. WHY?
"BECAUSE IT WORKED, THAT'S WHY. WE JUST WOUND IT UP AND WATCHED IT GO, PRETTY MUCH."
GOD...
TURNS OUT YOU WERE ONTO SOMETHING, LEE.
FORTUNE
Roger Lanchester Calling Time On Analog Warfare
by Owen Johnson
YOU MIGHT REMEMBER THIS GUY.
LANCHESTER... THE WEAPONS MAGNATE. UH... TORCHLIGHT AERONAUTICS, RIGHT?
DIDN'T HE GET INDICTED FOR EMBEZZLEMENT JUST BEFORE THE PLAGUE HIT?
EP. REAL ENIGMA, HIS ONE.
THE FBI CAUGHT HIM FINANCING A RAFT OF SKUNKWORKS PROJECTS USING MONEY SIPHONED OUT OF TORCHLIGHT'S PENSION FUND.
INCLUDING ARCADIA?
INCLUDING ARCADIA.
THIS DOESN'T ADD UP.
DARPA TOLD US IT WAS A COMBAT SIMULATION. LANCHESTER COULD'VE GOT THAT PAST THE TORCHLIGHT BOARD EASILY, SO WHY THE SECRECY?
WHY INDEED? ONLY LANCHESTER KNOWS.

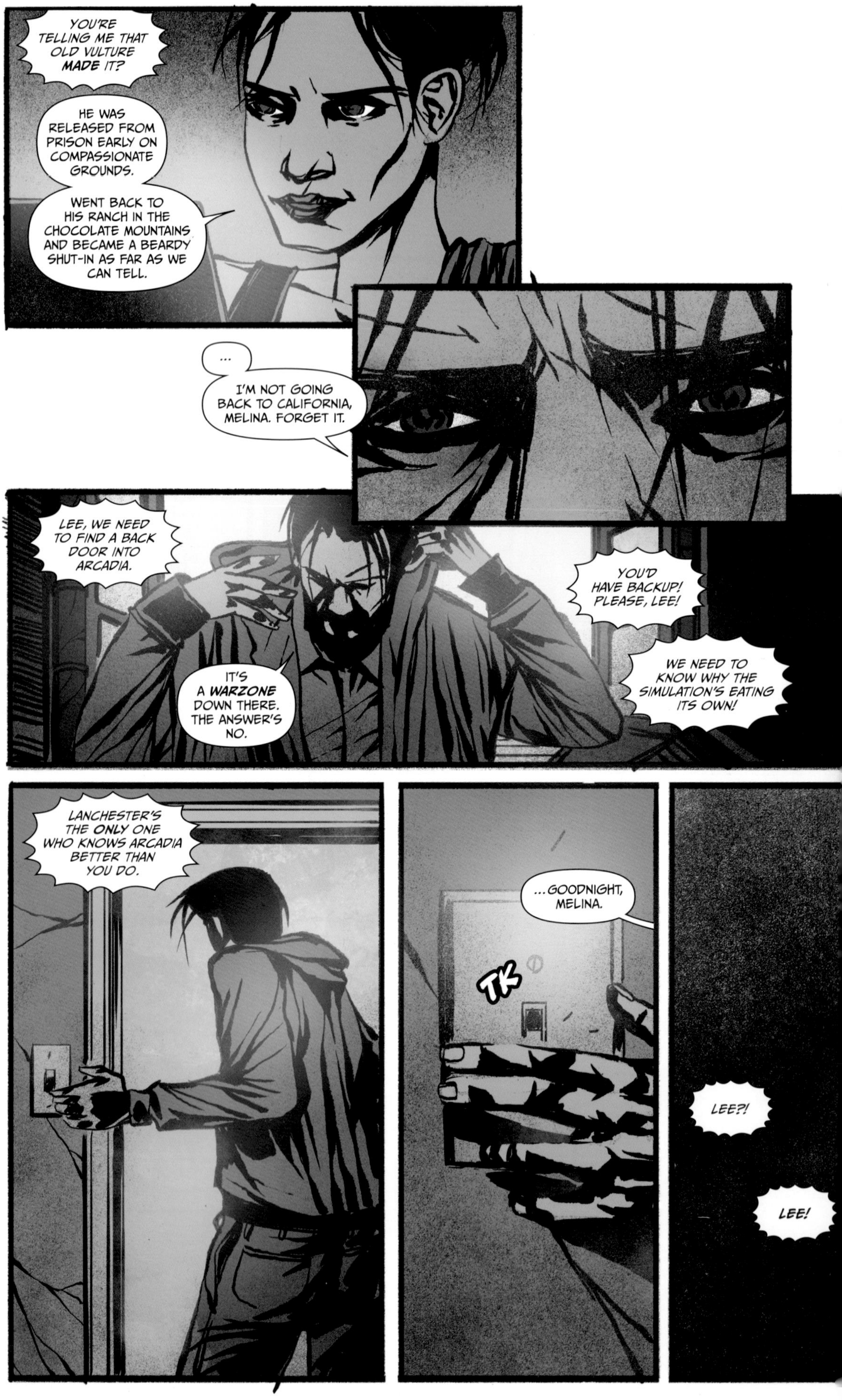
YOU'RE TELLING ME THAT OLD VULTURE MADE IT?
HE WAS RELEASED FROM PRISON EARLY ON COMPASSIONATE GROUNDS.
WENT BACK TO HIS RANCH IN THE CHOCOLATE MOUNTAINS AND BECAME A BEARDY SHUT-IN AS FAR AS WE CAN TELL.
...
I'M NOT GOING BACK TO CALIFORNIA, MELINA. FORGET IT.
LEE, WE NEED TO FIND A BACK DOOR INTO ARCADIA.
IT'S A WARZONE DOWN THERE. THE ANSWER'S NO.
YOU'D HAVE BACKUP! PLEASE, LEE!
WE NEED TO KNOW WHY THE SIMULATION'S EATING ITS OWN!
LANCHESTER'S THE ONLY ONE WHO KNOWS ARCADIA BETTER THAN YOU DO.
...GOODNIGHT, MELINA.
TK
LEE?!
LEE!

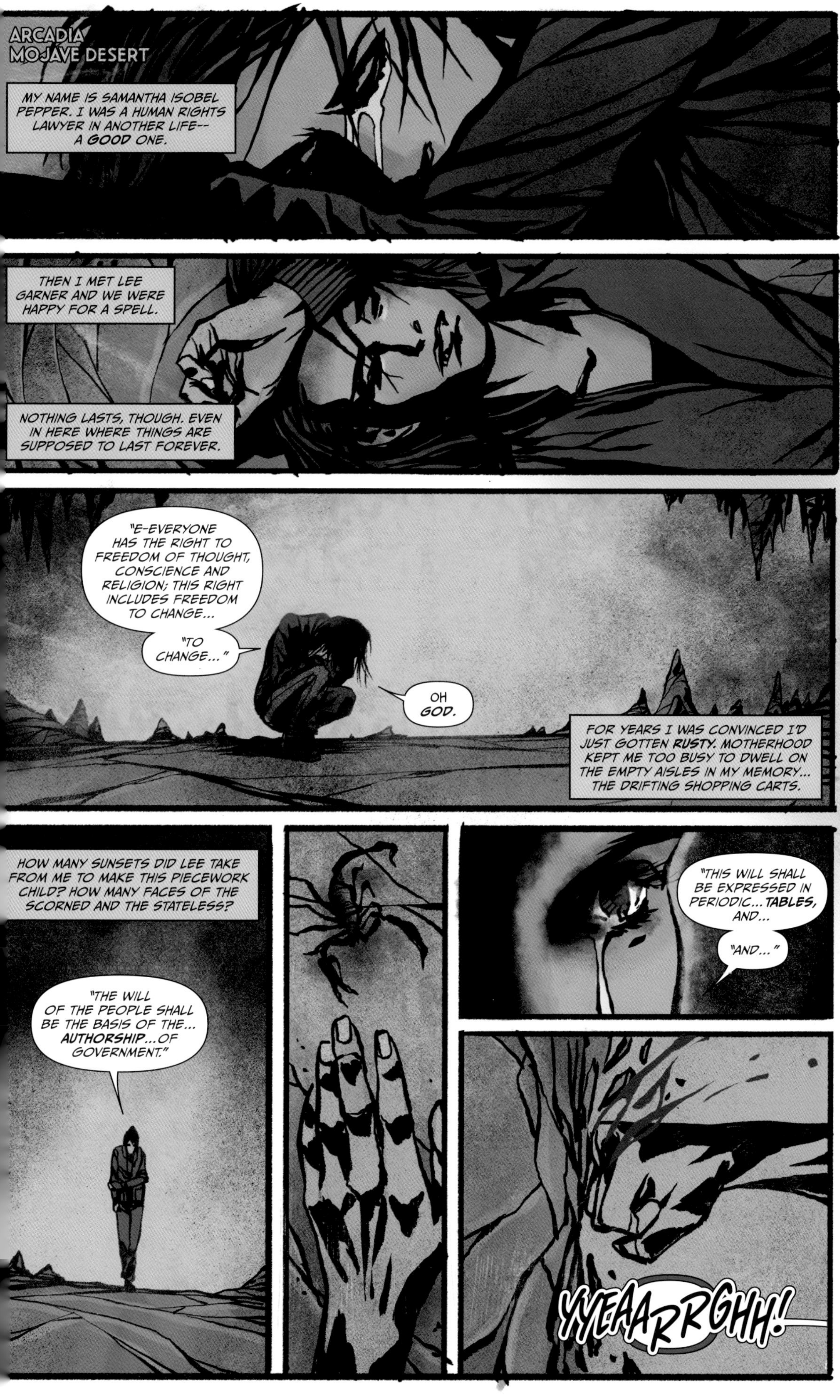
ARCADIA
MOJÁVE DESERT
MY NAME IS SAMANTHA ISOBEL PEPPER. I WAS A HUMAN RIGHTS LAWYER IN ANOTHER LIFE-- A GOOD ONE.
THEN I MET LEE GARNER AND WE WERE HAPPY FOR A SPELL.
NOTHING LASTS, THOUGH. EVEN IN HERE WHERE THINGS ARE SUPPOSED TO LAST FOREVER.
"E-EVERYONE HAS THE RIGHT TO FREEDOM OF THOUGHT, CONSCIENCE AND RELIGION; THIS RIGHT INCLUDES FREEDOM TO CHANGE...
"TO CHANGE..."
OH GOD.
FOR YEARS I WAS CONVINCED I'D JUST GOTTEN RUSTY. MOTHERHOOD KEPT ME TOO BUSY TO DWELL ON THE EMPTY AISLES IN MY MEMORY... THE DRIFTING SHOPPING CARTS.
HOW MANY SUNSETS DID LEE TAKE FROM ME TO MAKE THIS PIECEWORK CHILD? HOW MANY FACES OF THE SCORNED AND THE STATELESS?
"THE WILL OF THE PEOPLE SHALL BE THE BASIS OF THE... AUTHORSHIP...OF GOVERNMENT."
"THIS WILL SHALL BE EXPRESSED IN PERIODIC...TABLES, AND...
"AND..."
YYEAARRGHH!

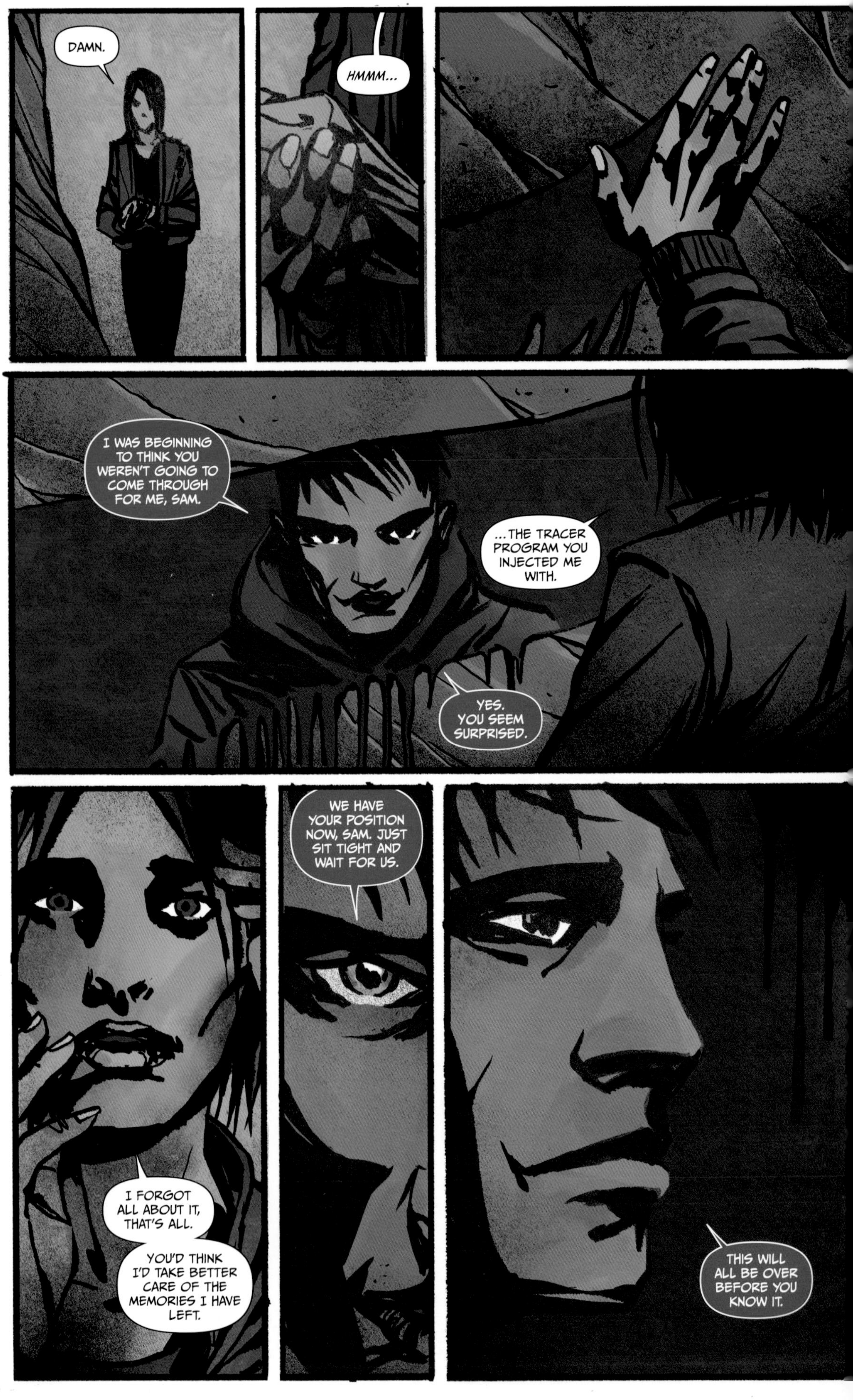
DAMN.
HMMM...
I WAS BEGINNING TO THINK YOU WEREN'T GOING TO COME THROUGH FOR ME, SAM.
...THE TRACER PROGRAM YOU INJECTED ME WITH.
YES. YOU SEEM SURPRISED.
I FORGOT ALL ABOUT IT, THAT'S ALL.
YOU'D THINK I'D TAKE BETTER CARE OF THE MEMORIES I HAVE LEFT.
WE HAVE YOUR POSITION NOW, SAM. JUST SIT TIGHT AND WAIT FOR US.
THIS WILL ALL BE OVER BEFORE YOU KNOW IT.

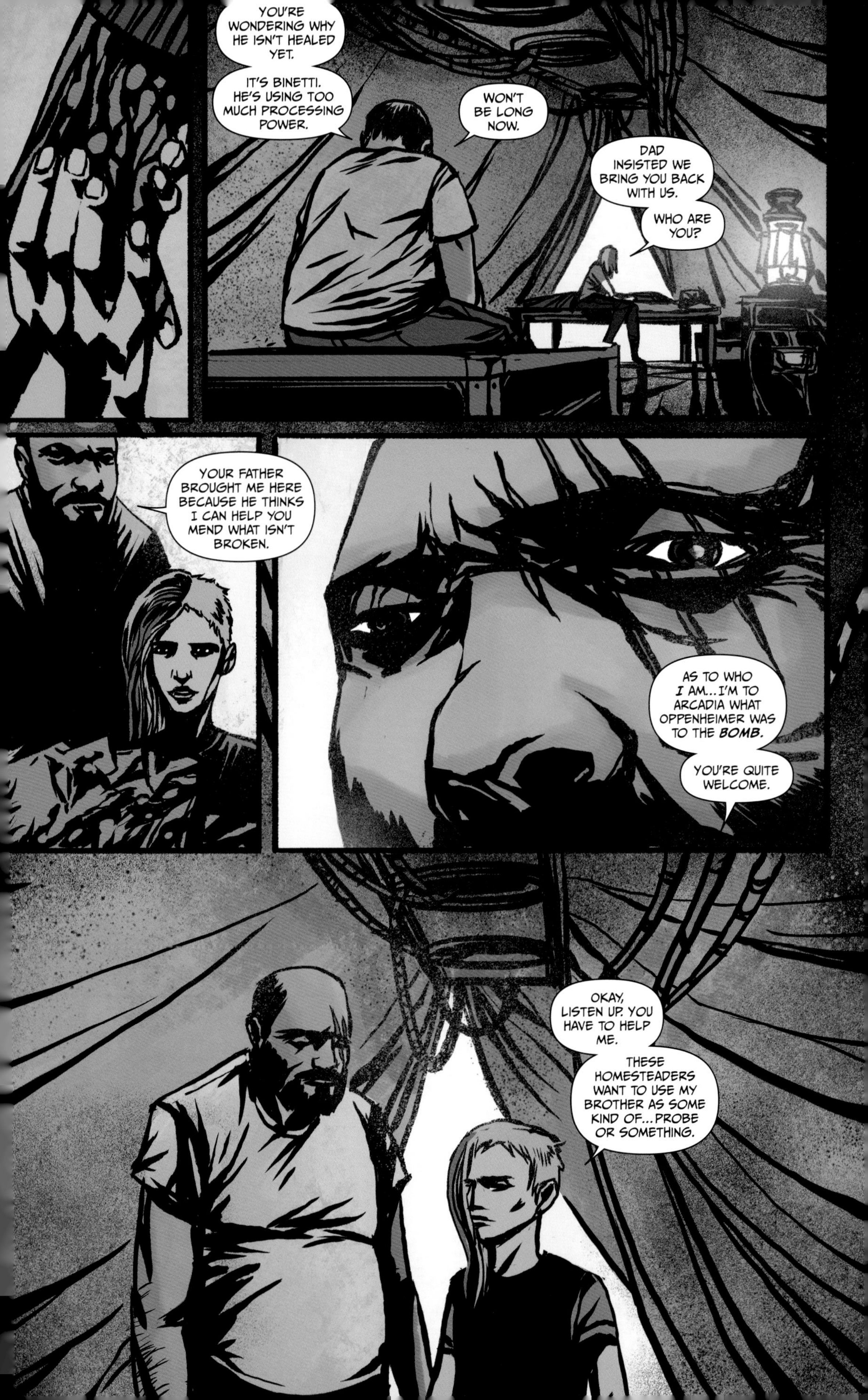
YOU'RE WONDERING WHY HE ISN'T HEALED YET.
IT'S BINETTI. HE'S USING TOO MUCH PROCESSING POWER.
WON'T BE LONG NOW.
DAD INSISTED WE BRING YOU BACK WITH US.
WHO ARE YOU?
YOUR FATHER BROUGHT ME HERE BECAUSE HE THINKS I CAN HELP YOU MEND WHAT ISN'T BROKEN.
AS TO WHO *I* AM...I'M TO ARCADIA WHAT OPPENHEIMER WAS TO THE ***BOMB.***
YOU'RE QUITE WELCOME.
OKAY, LISTEN UP. YOU HAVE TO HELP ME.
THESE HOMESTEADERS WANT TO USE MY BROTHER AS SOME KIND OF...PROBE OR SOMETHING.

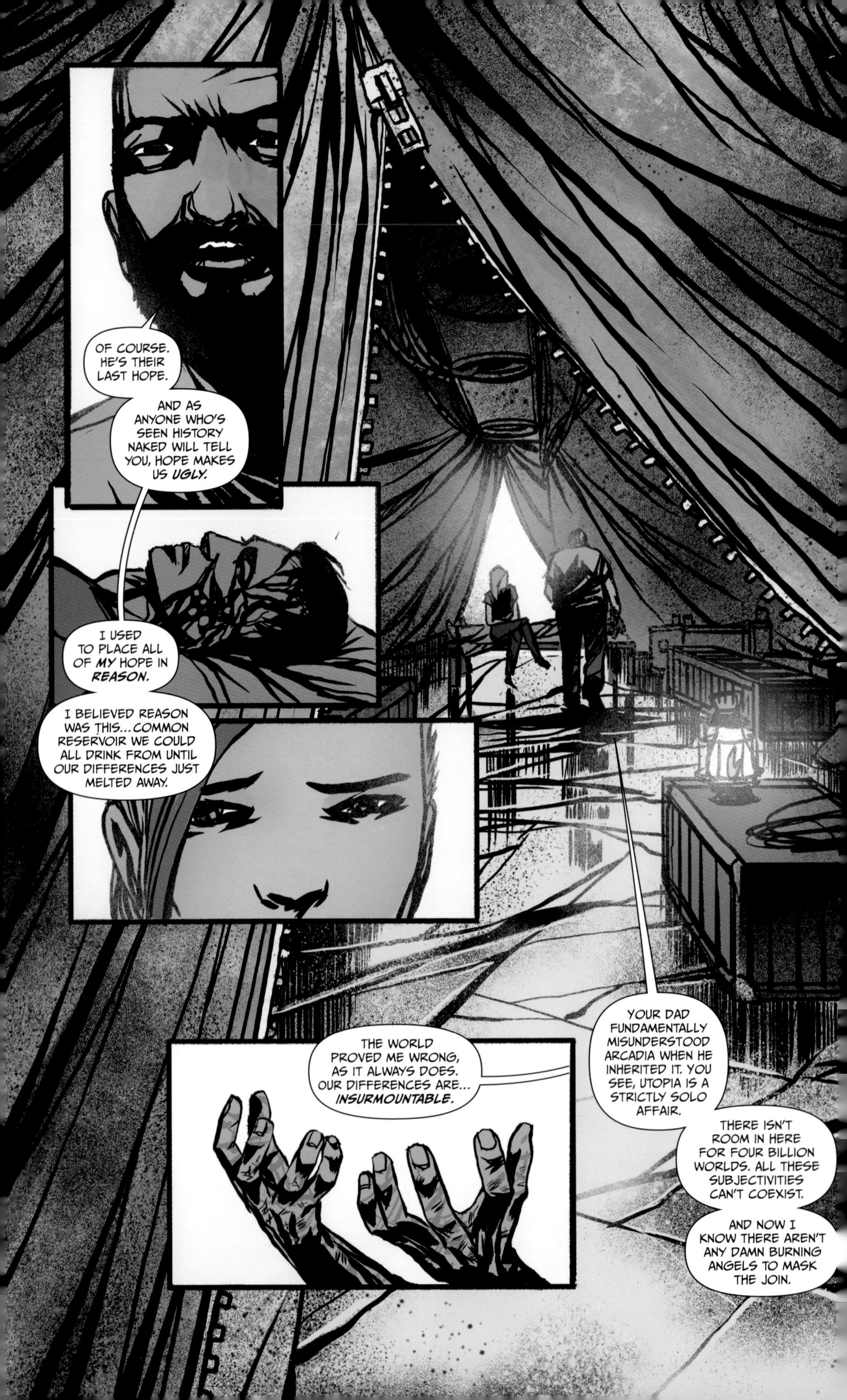
OF COURSE. HE'S THEIR LAST HOPE.
AND AS ANYONE WHO'S SEEN HISTORY NAKED WILL TELL YOU, HOPE MAKES US *UGLY.*
I USED TO PLACE ALL OF *MY* HOPE IN *REASON.*
I BELIEVED REASON WAS THIS... COMMON RESERVOIR WE COULD ALL DRINK FROM UNTIL OUR DIFFERENCES JUST MELTED AWAY.
YOUR DAD FUNDAMENTALLY MISUNDERSTOOD ARCADIA WHEN HE INHERITED IT. YOU SEE, UTOPIA IS A STRICTLY SOLO AFFAIR.
THE WORLD PROVED ME WRONG, AS IT ALWAYS DOES. OUR DIFFERENCES ARE... *INSURMOUNTABLE.*
THERE ISN'T ROOM IN HERE FOR FOUR BILLION WORLDS. ALL THESE SUBJECTIVITIES CAN'T COEXIST.
AND NOW I KNOW THERE AREN'T ANY DAMN BURNING ANGELS TO MASK THE JOIN.

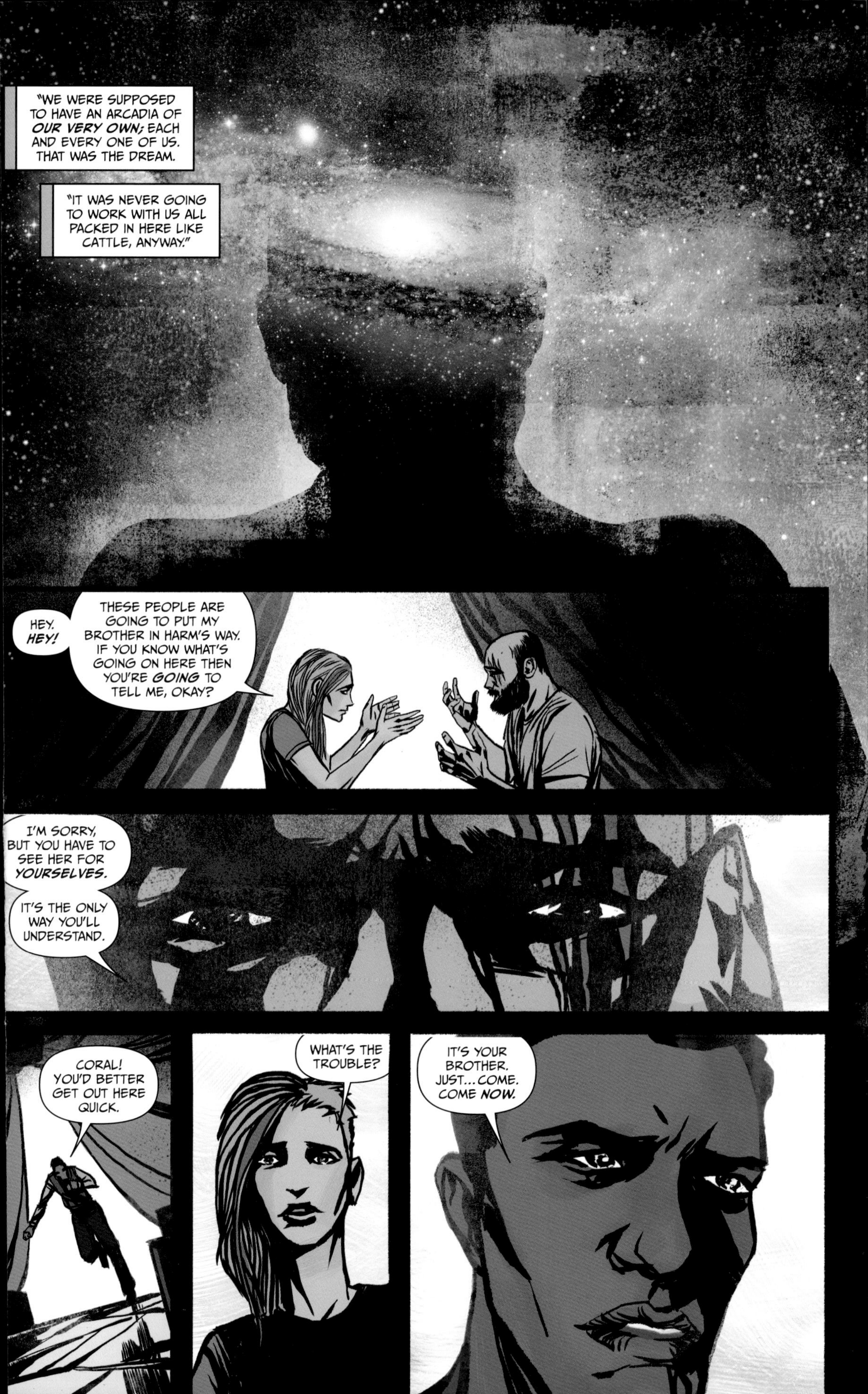
"WE WERE SUPPOSED TO HAVE AN ARCADIA OF OUR VERY OWN; EACH AND EVERY ONE OF US. THAT WAS THE DREAM.
"IT WAS NEVER GOING TO WORK WITH US ALL PACKED IN HERE LIKE CATTLE, ANYWAY."
HEY. HEY!
THESE PEOPLE ARE GOING TO PUT MY BROTHER IN HARM'S WAY. IF YOU KNOW WHAT'S GOING ON HERE THEN YOU'RE GOING TO TELL ME, OKAY?
I'M SORRY, BUT YOU HAVE TO SEE HER FOR YOURSELVES.
IT'S THE ONLY WAY YOU'LL UNDERSTAND.
CORAL! YOU'D BETTER GET OUT HERE QUICK.
WHAT'S THE TROUBLE?
IT'S YOUR BROTHER. JUST... COME. COME NOW.

JACK! WHAT'S THE MATTER?!

THEY'LL BE HERE SOON. WE HAVE TO HURRY.

WHO?

WHO ELSE?

STUPID MEN WITH STUPID GUNS.

PICK ME UP, CORAL. HOLD ME IN FRONT OF YOU.

JACK, WE DON'T HAVE TIME FOR...

JUST DO IT. *PLEASE.*

MOMMY DID A BAD THING, CORAL.

SHE TOLD THEM WHERE WE ARE.

WHAT HAPPENED TO YOUR...!

SHH! LOOK.

...

OH, MOM.

"WE DON'T HAVE TIME TO FIGHT NO MORE, CORAL.

"I HAVE TO G INSIDE ARCAD *RIGHT NOW.*

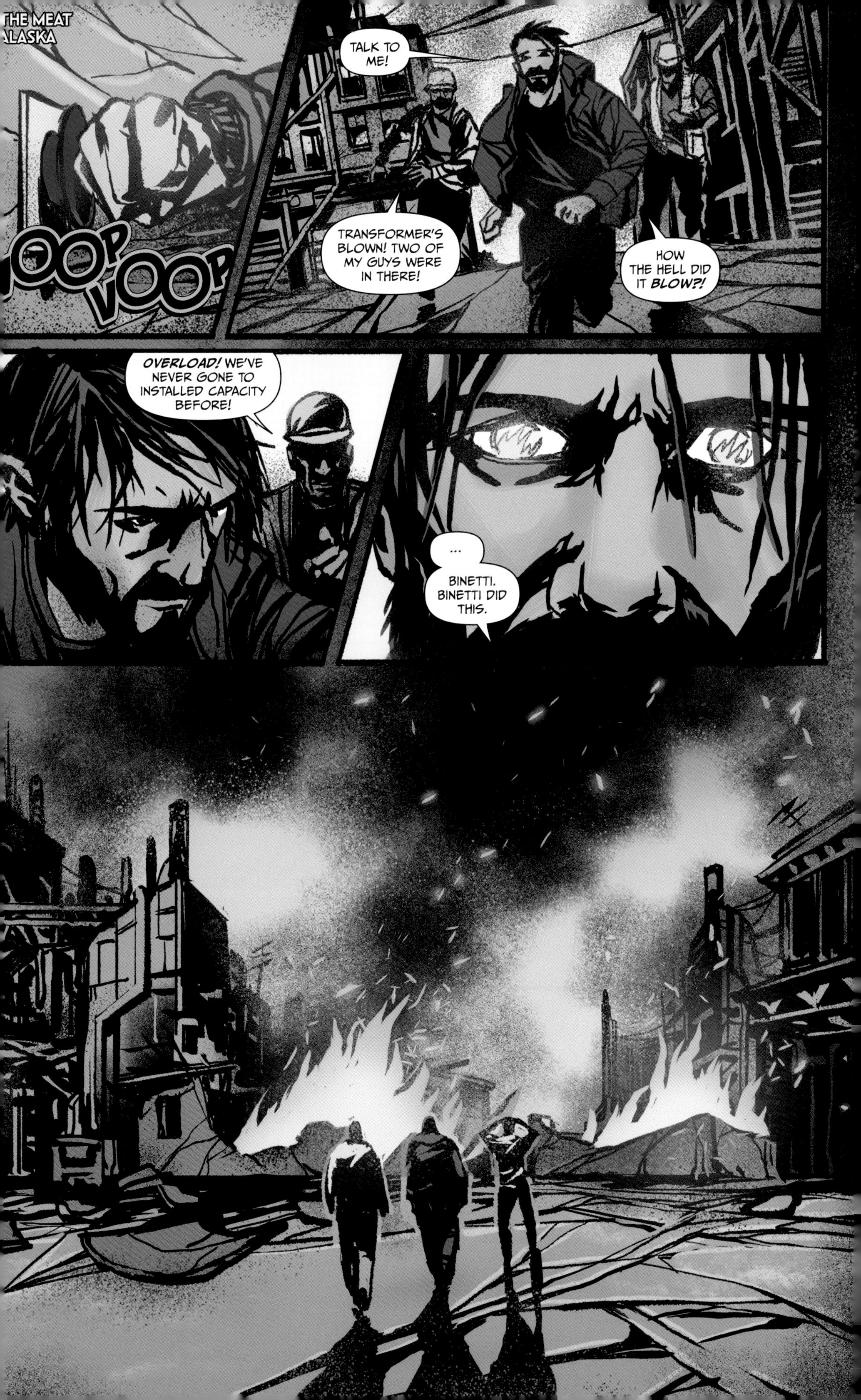
THE MEAT
ALASKA
VOOP VOOP
TALK TO ME!
TRANSFORMER'S BLOWN! TWO OF MY GUYS WERE IN THERE!
HOW THE HELL DID IT *BLOW?!*
OVERLOAD! WE'VE NEVER GONE TO INSTALLED CAPACITY BEFORE!
...
BINETTI. BINETTI DID THIS.

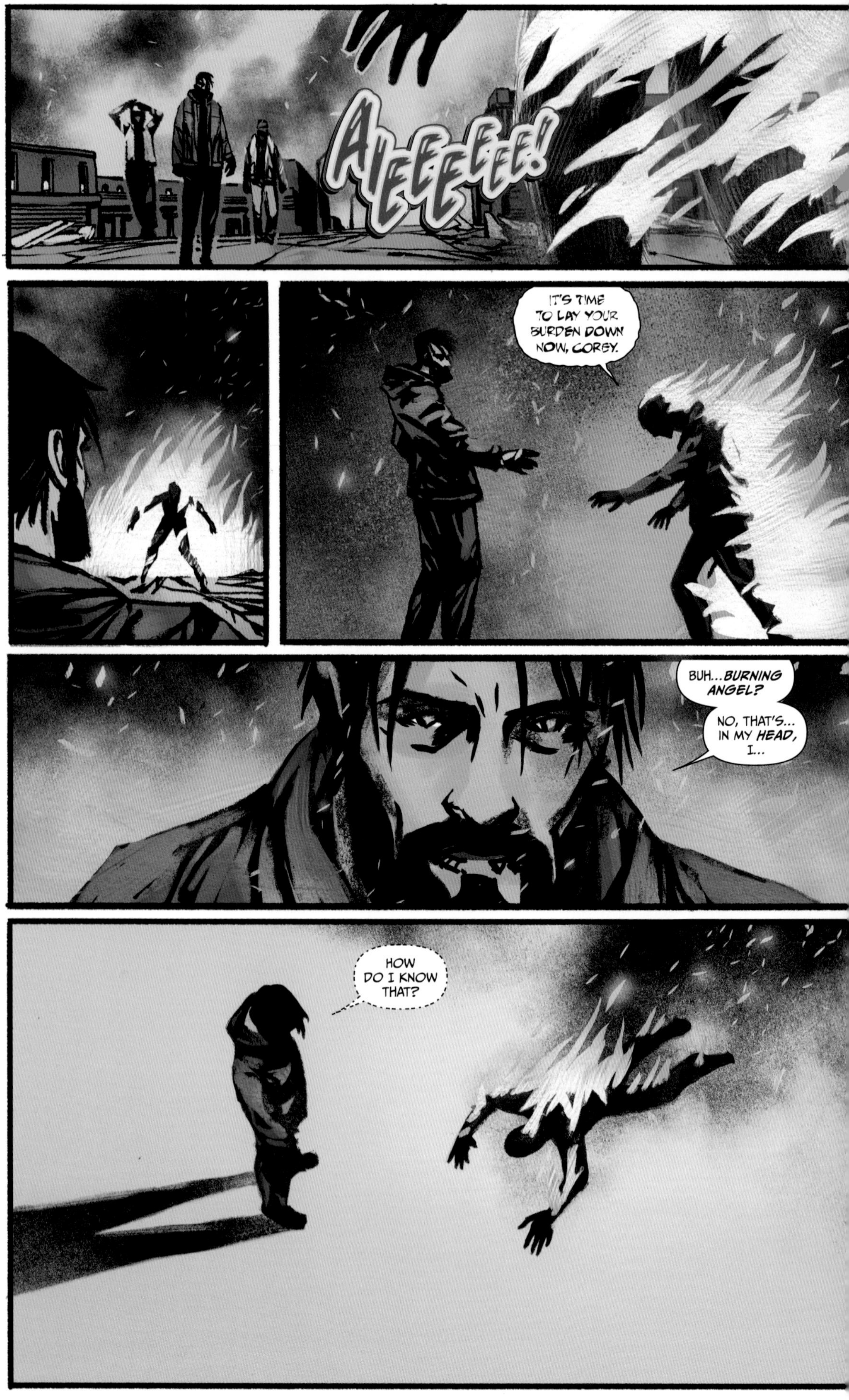
AIEEEEEEE!
IT'S TIME TO LAY YOUR BURDEN DOWN NOW, COREY.
BUH...*BURNING ANGEL?*
NO, THAT'S... IN MY *HEAD,* I...
HOW DO I KNOW THAT?

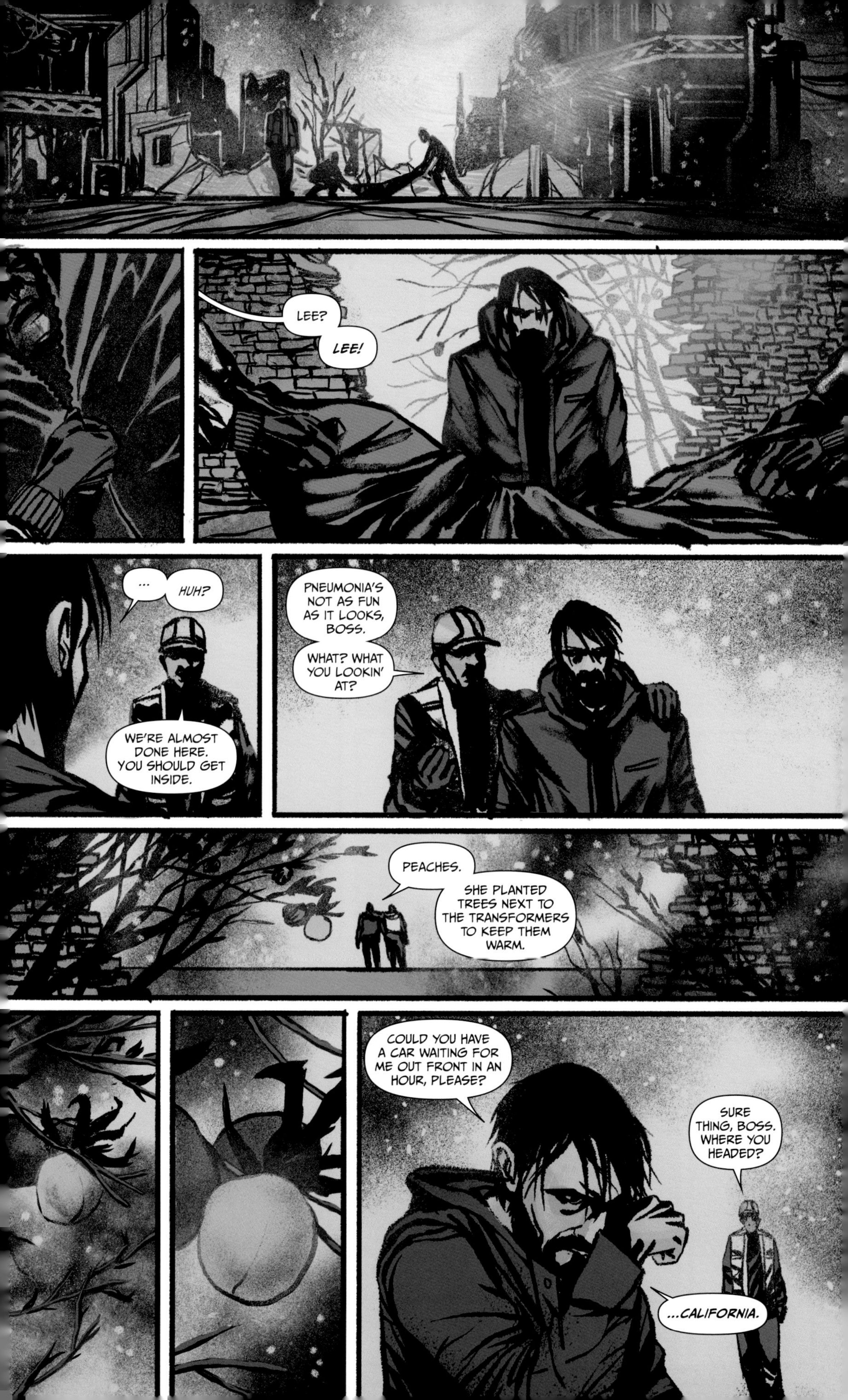
LEE?
LEE!
...
HUH?
WE'RE ALMOST DONE HERE. YOU SHOULD GET INSIDE.
PNEUMONIA'S NOT AS FUN AS IT LOOKS, BOSS.
WHAT? WHAT YOU LOOKIN' AT?
PEACHES.
SHE PLANTED TREES NEXT TO THE TRANSFORMERS TO KEEP THEM WARM.
COULD YOU HAVE A CAR WAITING FOR ME OUT FRONT IN AN HOUR, PLEASE?
SURE THING, BOSS. WHERE YOU HEADED?
...CALIFORNIA.

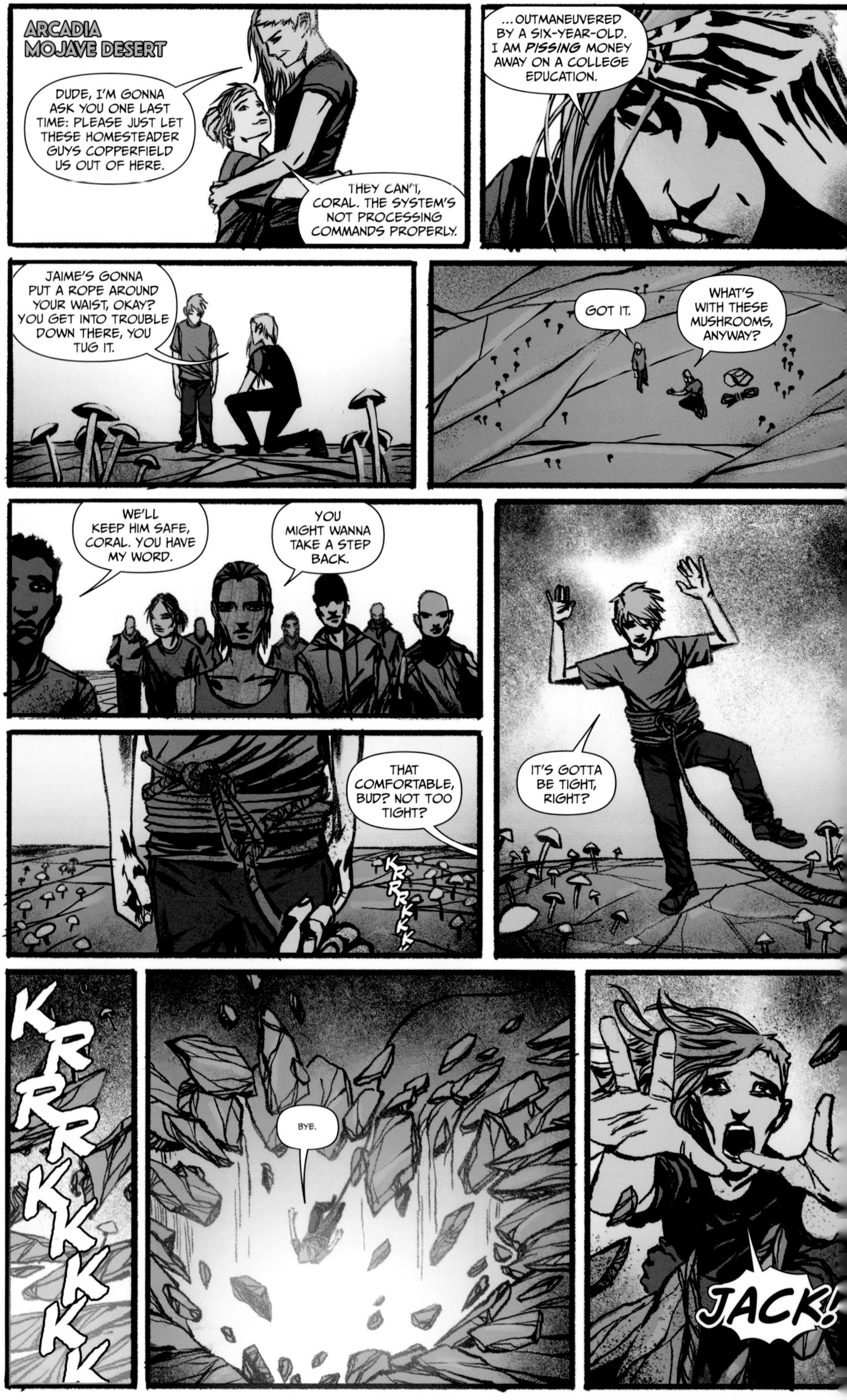
ARCADIA
MOJAVE DESERT
DUDE, I'M GONNA ASK YOU ONE LAST TIME: PLEASE JUST LET THESE HOMESTEADER GUYS COPPERFIELD US OUT OF HERE.
THEY CAN'T, CORAL. THE SYSTEM'S NOT PROCESSING COMMANDS PROPERLY.
...OUTMANEUVERED BY A SIX-YEAR-OLD. I AM PISSING MONEY AWAY ON A COLLEGE EDUCATION.
JAIME'S GONNA PUT A ROPE AROUND YOUR WAIST, OKAY? YOU GET INTO TROUBLE DOWN THERE, YOU TUG IT.
GOT IT.
WHAT'S WITH THESE MUSHROOMS, ANYWAY?
WE'LL KEEP HIM SAFE, CORAL. YOU HAVE MY WORD.
YOU MIGHT WANNA TAKE A STEP BACK.
THAT COMFORTABLE, BUD? NOT TOO TIGHT?
KRRRKKK
IT'S GOTTA BE TIGHT, RIGHT?
KRRRRKKKKK
BYE.
JACK!

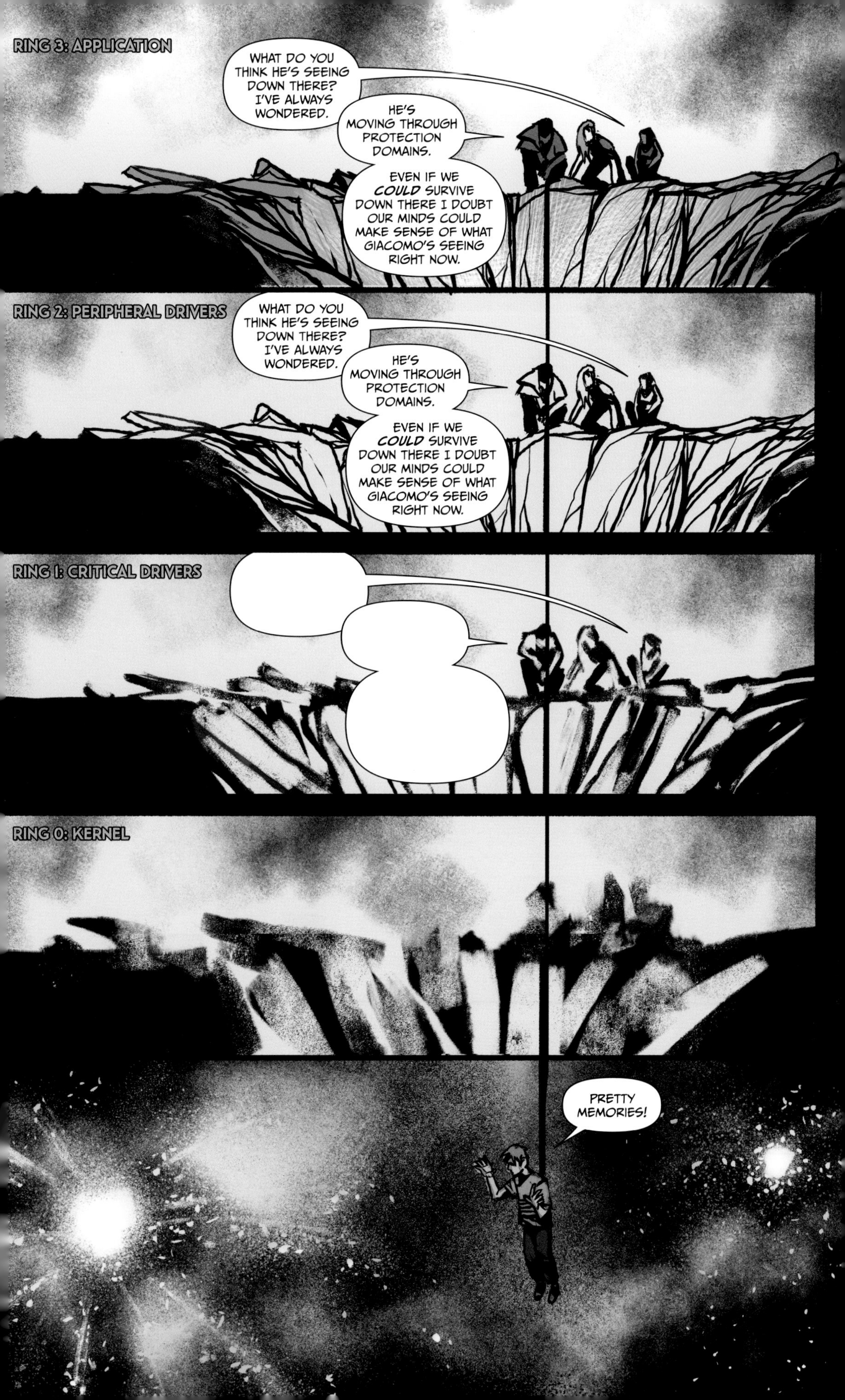
RING 3: APPLICATION
WHAT DO YOU THINK HE'S SEEING DOWN THERE? I'VE ALWAYS WONDERED.
HE'S MOVING THROUGH PROTECTION DOMAINS.
EVEN IF WE COULD SURVIVE DOWN THERE I DOUBT OUR MINDS COULD MAKE SENSE OF WHAT GIACOMO'S SEEING RIGHT NOW.
RING 2: PERIPHERAL DRIVERS
WHAT DO YOU THINK HE'S SEEING DOWN THERE? I'VE ALWAYS WONDERED.
HE'S MOVING THROUGH PROTECTION DOMAINS.
EVEN IF WE COULD SURVIVE DOWN THERE I DOUBT OUR MINDS COULD MAKE SENSE OF WHAT GIACOMO'S SEEING RIGHT NOW.
RING 1: CRITICAL DRIVERS
RING 0: KERNEL
PRETTY MEMORIES!

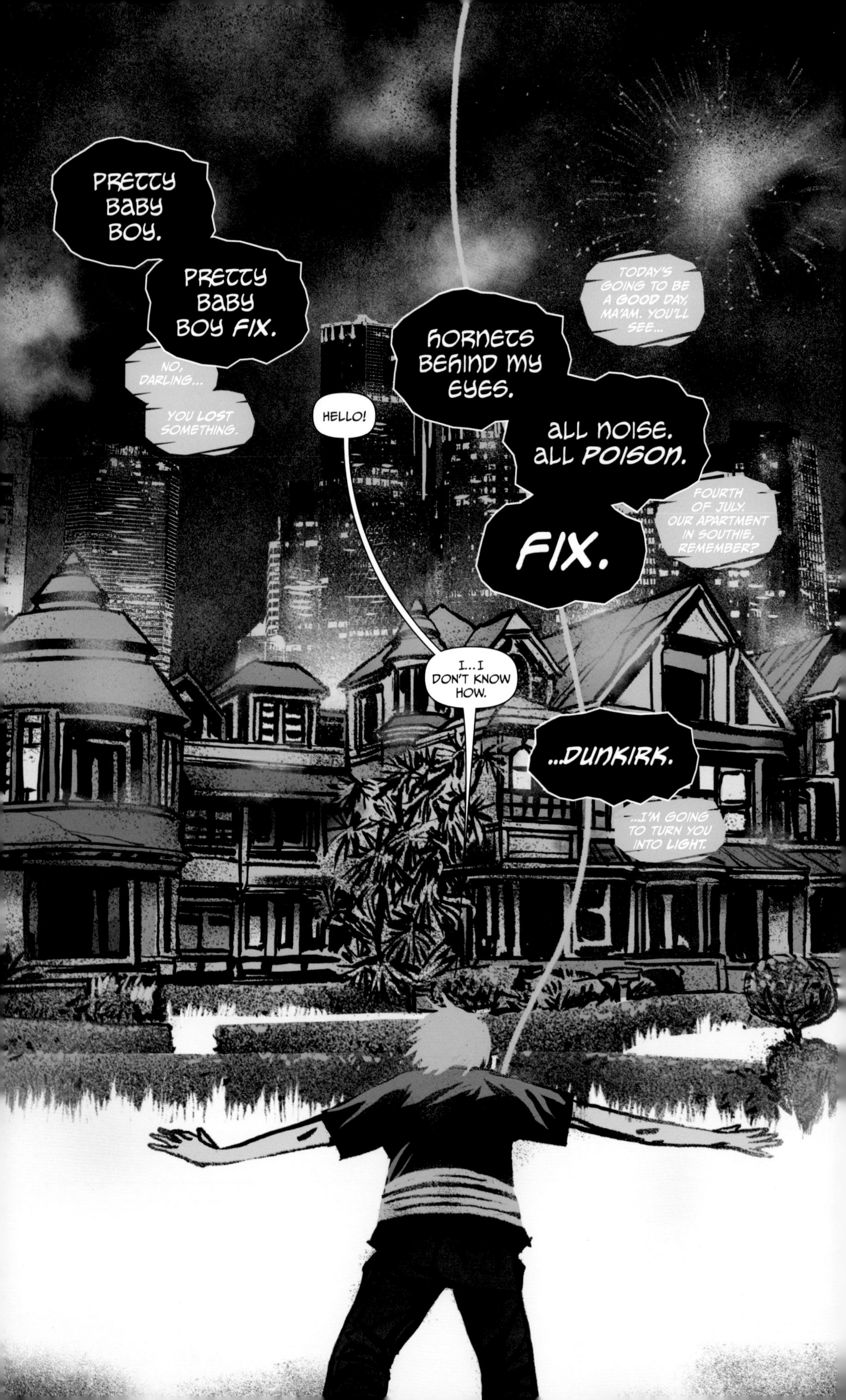
PRETTY BABY BOY.
PRETTY BABY BOY FIX.
NO, DARLING...
YOU LOST SOMETHING.
HORNETS BEHIND MY EYES.
ALL NOISE. ALL POISON.
FIX.
TODAY'S GOING TO BE A GOOD DAY, MA'AM. YOU'LL SEE...
FOURTH OF JULY. OUR APARTMENT IN SOUTHIE, REMEMBER?
HELLO!
I...I DON'T KNOW HOW.
...DUNKIRK.
...I'M GOING TO TURN YOU INTO LIGHT.

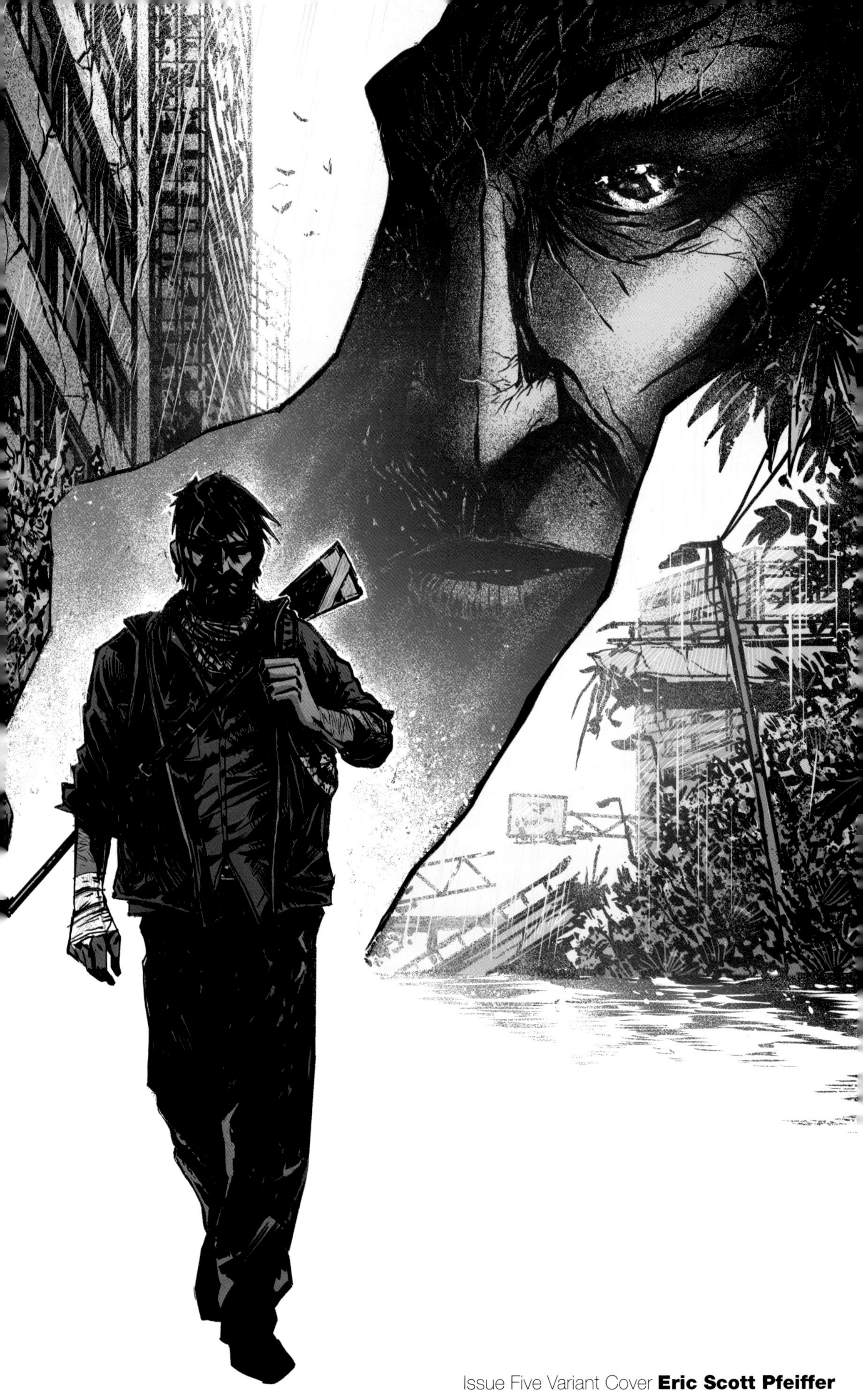

Issue Five Variant Cover **Eric Scott Pfeiffer**

"Over a period of a hundred or a thousand years, the probability of maintaining continuity of the software to interpret the old stuff is probably close to zero. Where would you find a projector for an 8mm film these days? If the new software can't understand, we've lost the information. I call this bit rot. It's a serious problem."

—**Vint Cerf**

CHAPTER
SIX

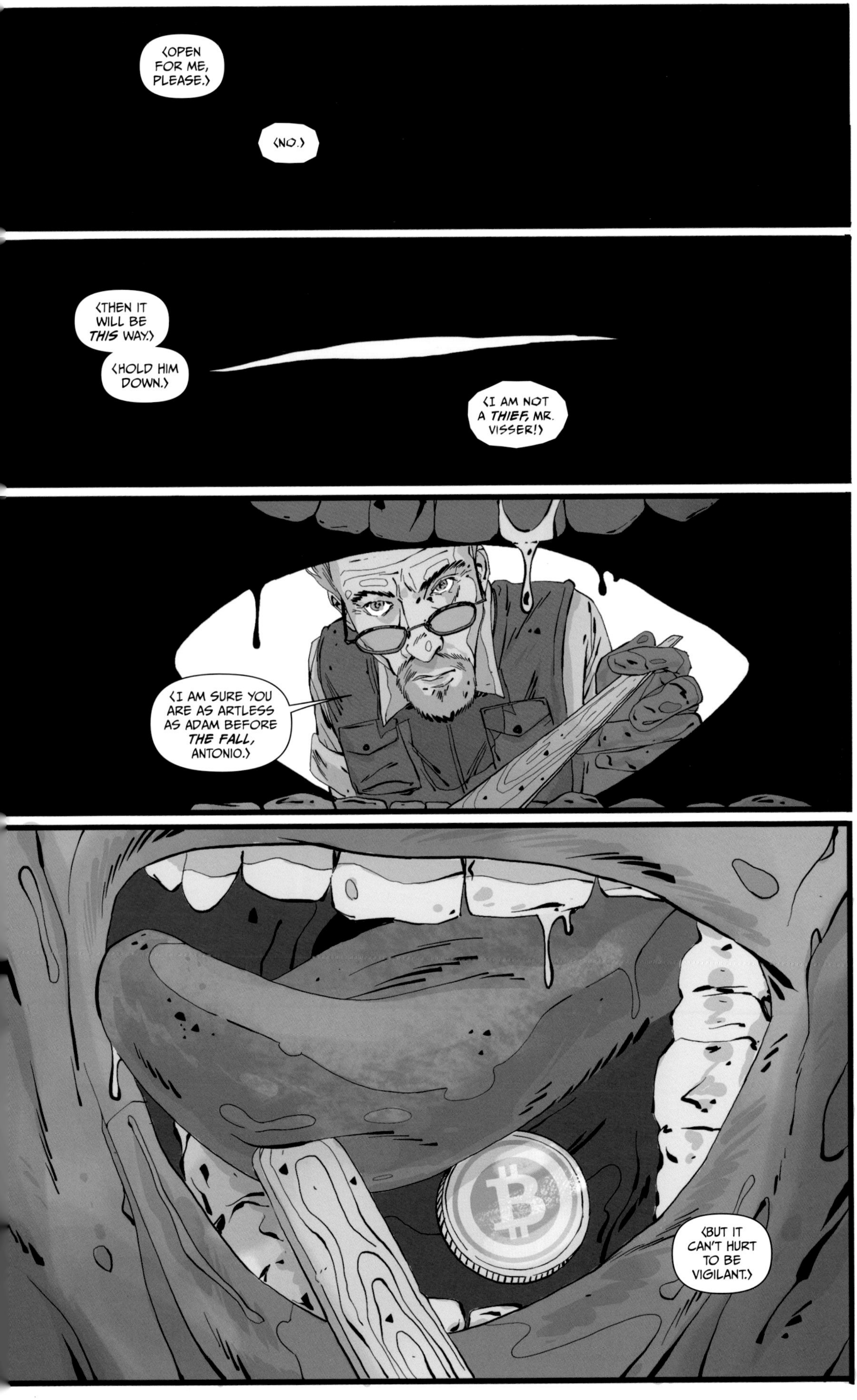
<OPEN FOR ME, PLEASE.>
<NO.>
<THEN IT WILL BE *THIS* WAY.>
<HOLD HIM DOWN.>
<I AM NOT A *THIEF*, MR. VISSER!>
<I AM SURE YOU ARE AS ARTLESS AS ADAM BEFORE *THE FALL*, ANTONIO.>
<BUT IT CAN'T HURT TO BE VIGILANT.>

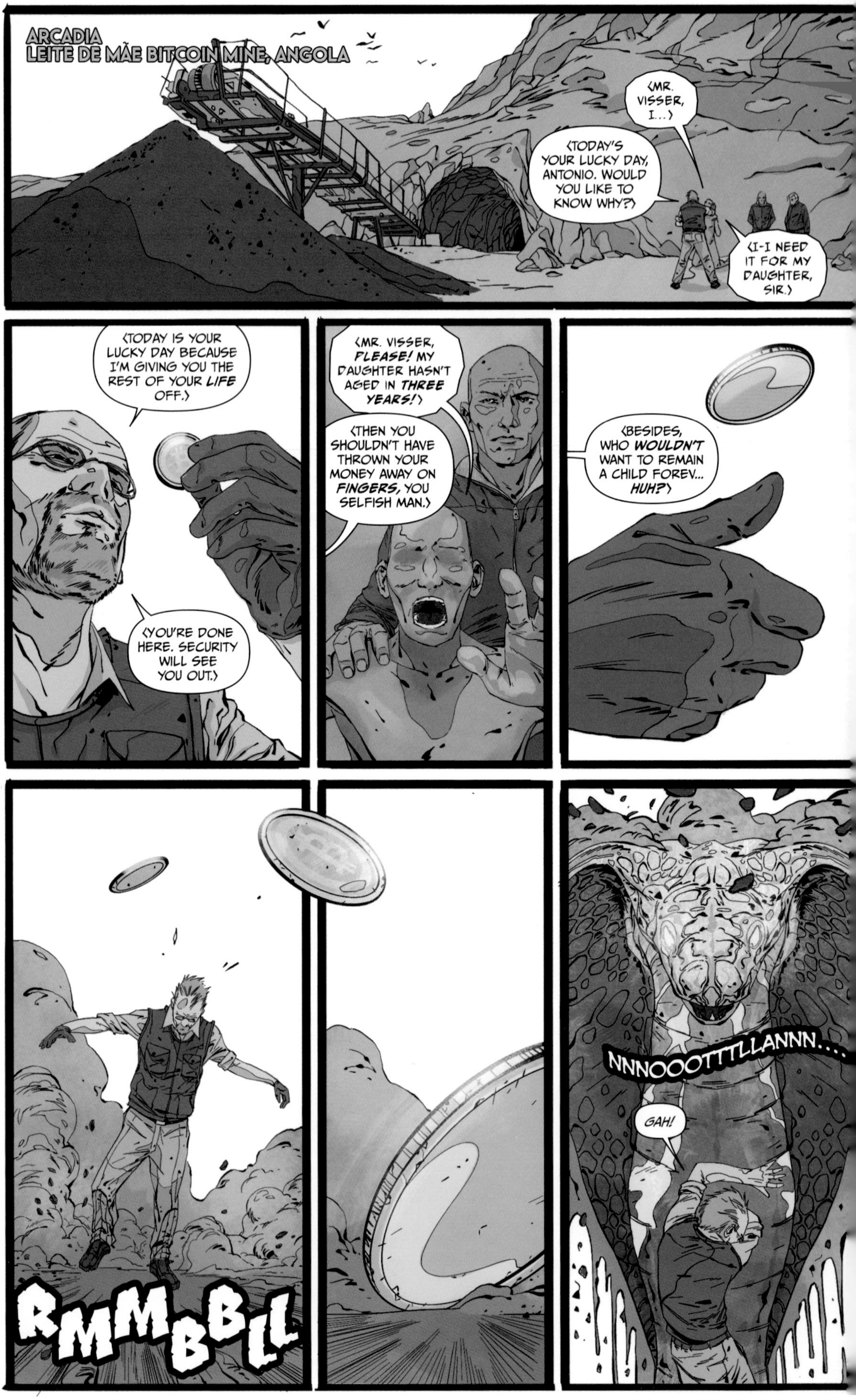

ARCADIA
LEITE DE MÃE BITCOIN MINE, ANGOLA
‹MR. VISSER, I...›
‹TODAY'S YOUR LUCKY DAY, ANTONIO. WOULD YOU LIKE TO KNOW WHY?›
‹I-I NEED IT FOR MY DAUGHTER, SIR.›
‹TODAY IS YOUR LUCKY DAY BECAUSE I'M GIVING YOU THE REST OF YOUR LIFE OFF.›
‹YOU'RE DONE HERE. SECURITY WILL SEE YOU OUT.›
‹MR. VISSER, PLEASE! MY DAUGHTER HASN'T AGED IN THREE YEARS!›
‹THEN YOU SHOULDN'T HAVE THROWN YOUR MONEY AWAY ON FINGERS, YOU SELFISH MAN.›
‹BESIDES, WHO WOULDN'T WANT TO REMAIN A CHILD FOREV... HUH?›
RMMBBLL
NNNOOOTTTLLANNN....
GAH!

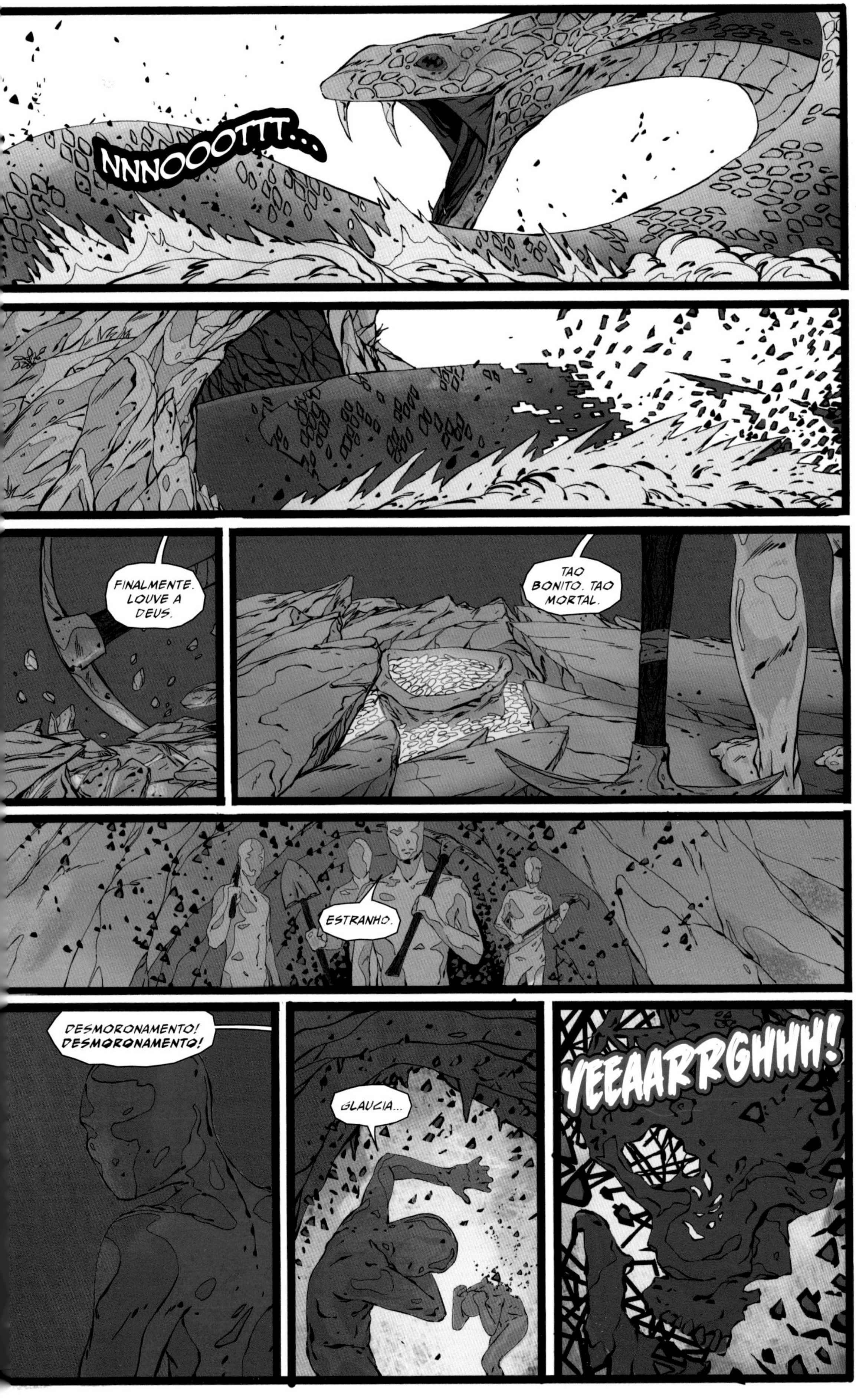
NNNOOOTTT...
FINALMENTE. LOUVE A DEUS.
TAO BONITO. TAO MORTAL.
ESTRANHO.
DESMORONAMENTO! DESMORONAMENTO!
GLAUCIA...
YEEAARRGHHH!

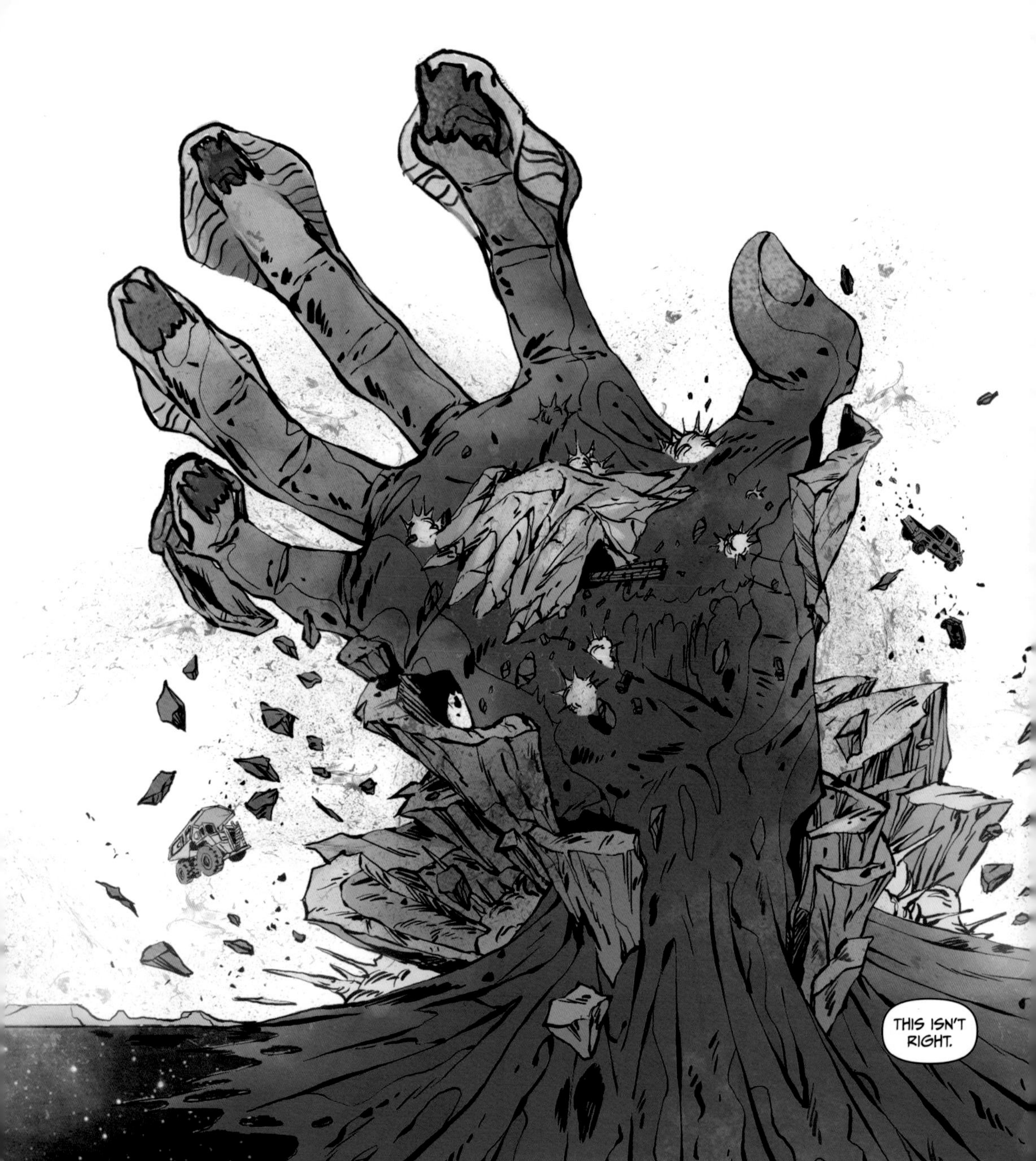
THIS ISN'T RIGHT.

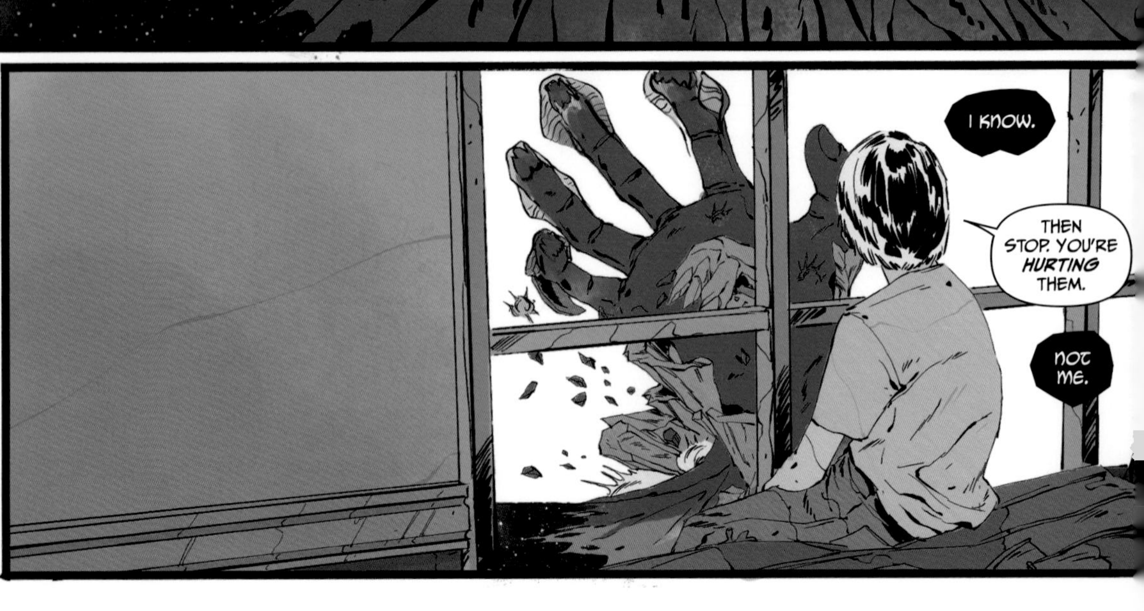
I KNOW.
THEN STOP. YOU'RE *HURTING* THEM.
NOT ME.

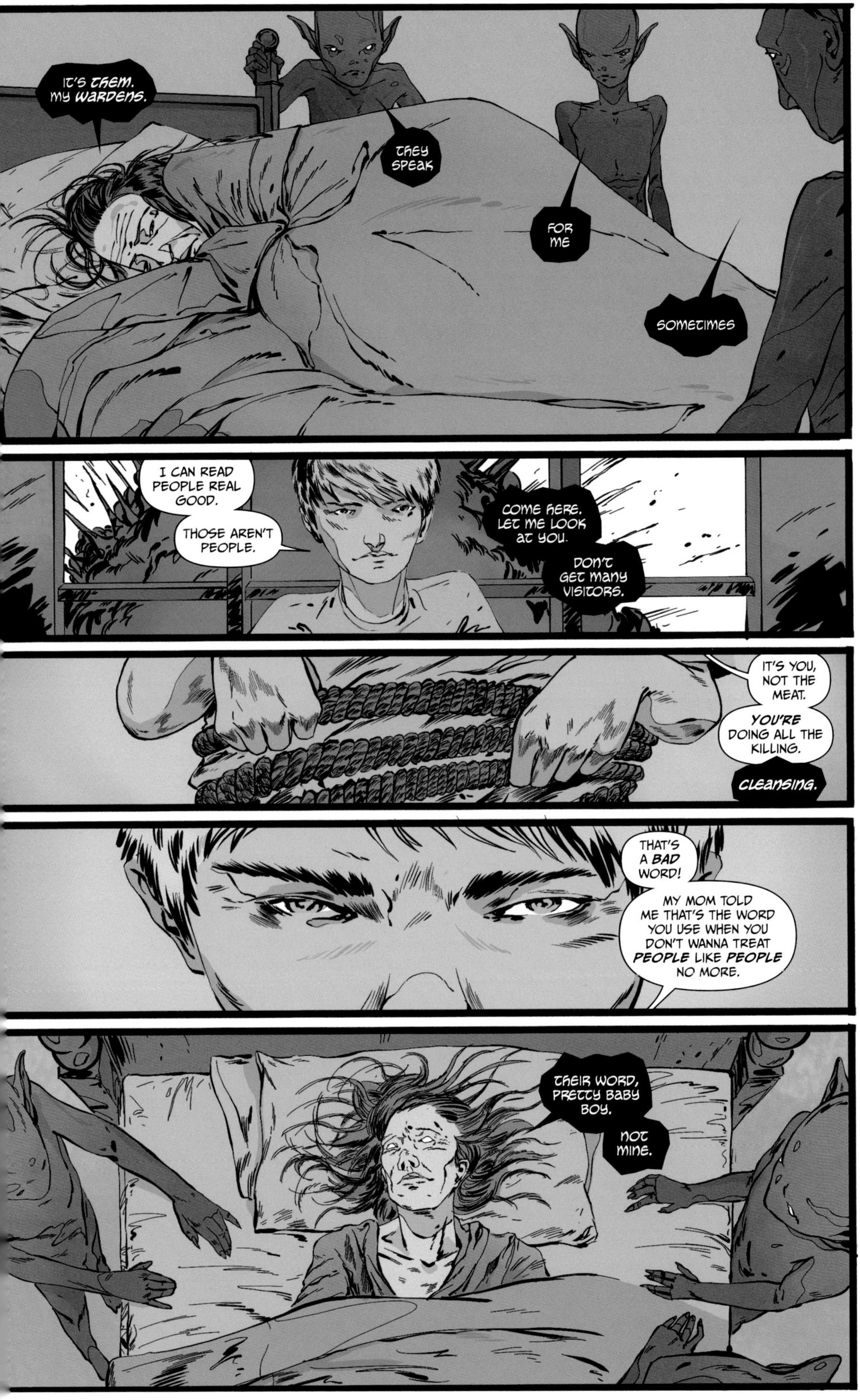
IT'S THEM.
MY WARDENS.
THEY SPEAK
FOR ME
SOMETIMES
I CAN READ PEOPLE REAL GOOD.
THOSE AREN'T PEOPLE.
COME HERE. LET ME LOOK AT YOU.
DON'T GET MANY VISITORS.
IT'S YOU, NOT THE MEAT.
YOU'RE DOING ALL THE KILLING.
CLEANSING.
THAT'S A BAD WORD!
MY MOM TOLD ME THAT'S THE WORD YOU USE WHEN YOU DON'T WANNA TREAT PEOPLE LIKE PEOPLE NO MORE.
THEIR WORD, PRETTY BABY BOY.
NOT MINE.

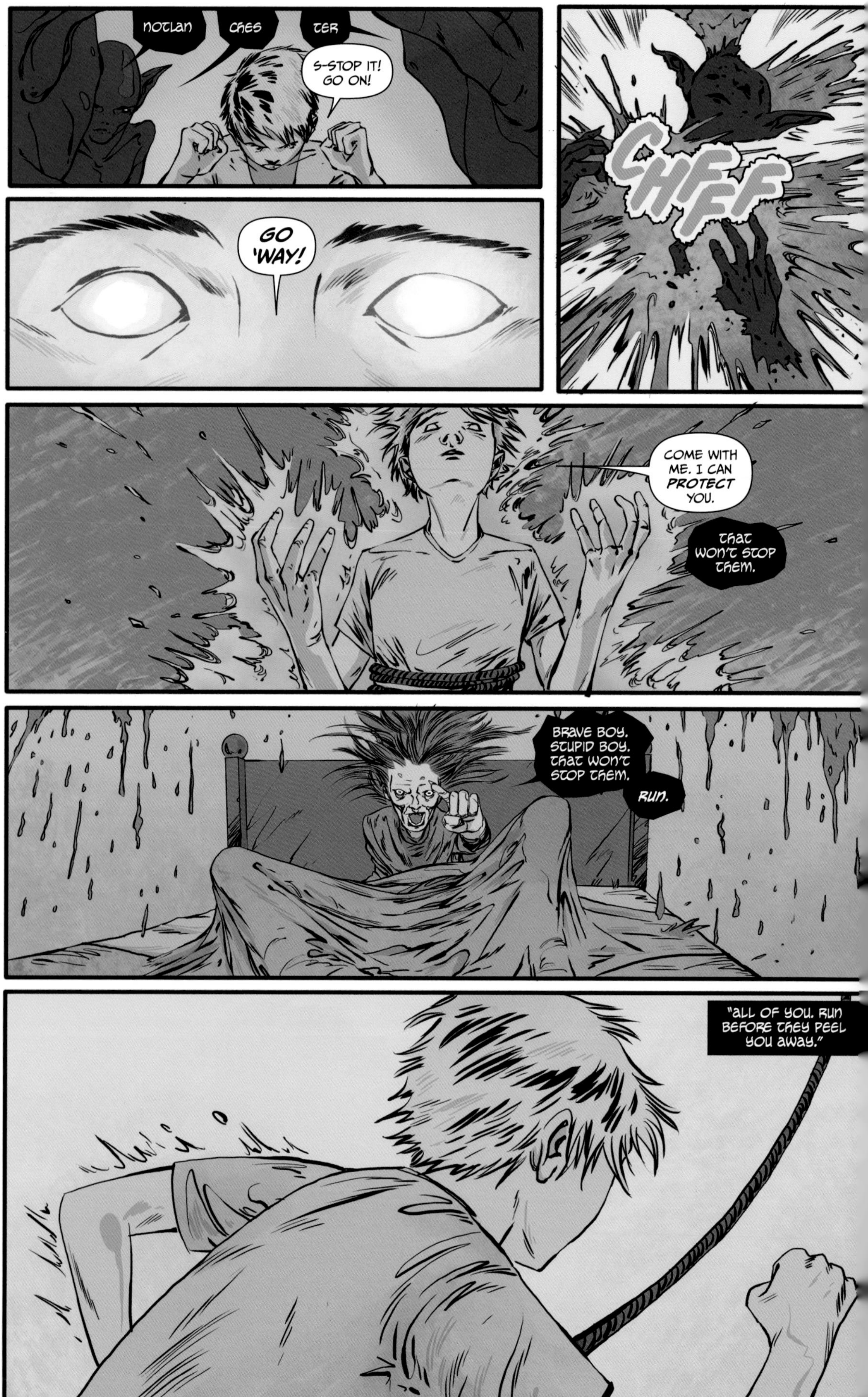

NOTLAN
CHES
TER
S-STOP IT! GO ON!
GO 'WAY!
CHFF
COME WITH ME. I CAN PROTECT YOU.
THAT WON'T STOP THEM.
BRAVE BOY. STUPID BOY. THAT WON'T STOP THEM.
RUN.
"ALL OF YOU. RUN BEFORE THEY PEEL YOU AWAY."

THE MEAT
LOS ANGELES

YOU WANNA KNOW HOW THE WEST WAS *LOST?* SURE YOU DO.

CALIFORNIA GOT HIT FIRST AND WORST WHEN THE VIRUS REACHED THE U.S.

THE OTHER STATES SAW WHAT HAPPENED TO US AND GOT IT TOGETHER, BUT HERE...?

HERE WE GOT T-BONED BY HISTORY.

NO SEAT BELTS. NO *WARNING.*

WE WERE JUST...*PITCHED* OUT OF ONE REALITY AND INTO ANOTHER.

WHEN THE FIRST POST-PANDEMIC GOVERNMENT WAS FORMED, THEY SENT A DELEGATION OF ABOUT A DOZEN TO BRING CALI *BACK IN LINE.*

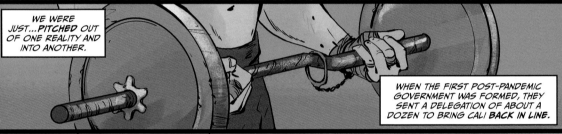

THE REMAINING GANGS--MS-13, THE MARIELITOS, THE BLOODS, THE LAPD, THE ARYAN BROTHERHOOD-- SENT DELEGATES OF THEIR *OWN.*

COUPLE WEEKS LATER, ABOUT A DOZEN FLYBLOWN *BUCKETS* WERE DEPOSITED ON THE STEPS OF THE CAPITOL BY PERSONS UNKNOWN.

HEY YO, PEPPER! YOU WAS LIVIN' HERE WHEN IT ALL WENT DOWN, *HUH?*

...THAT'S RIGHT.

SOMEONE TOLD ME THE STINK CARRIED SO FAR THEY HAD TO EVACUATE THE FREER GALLERY.

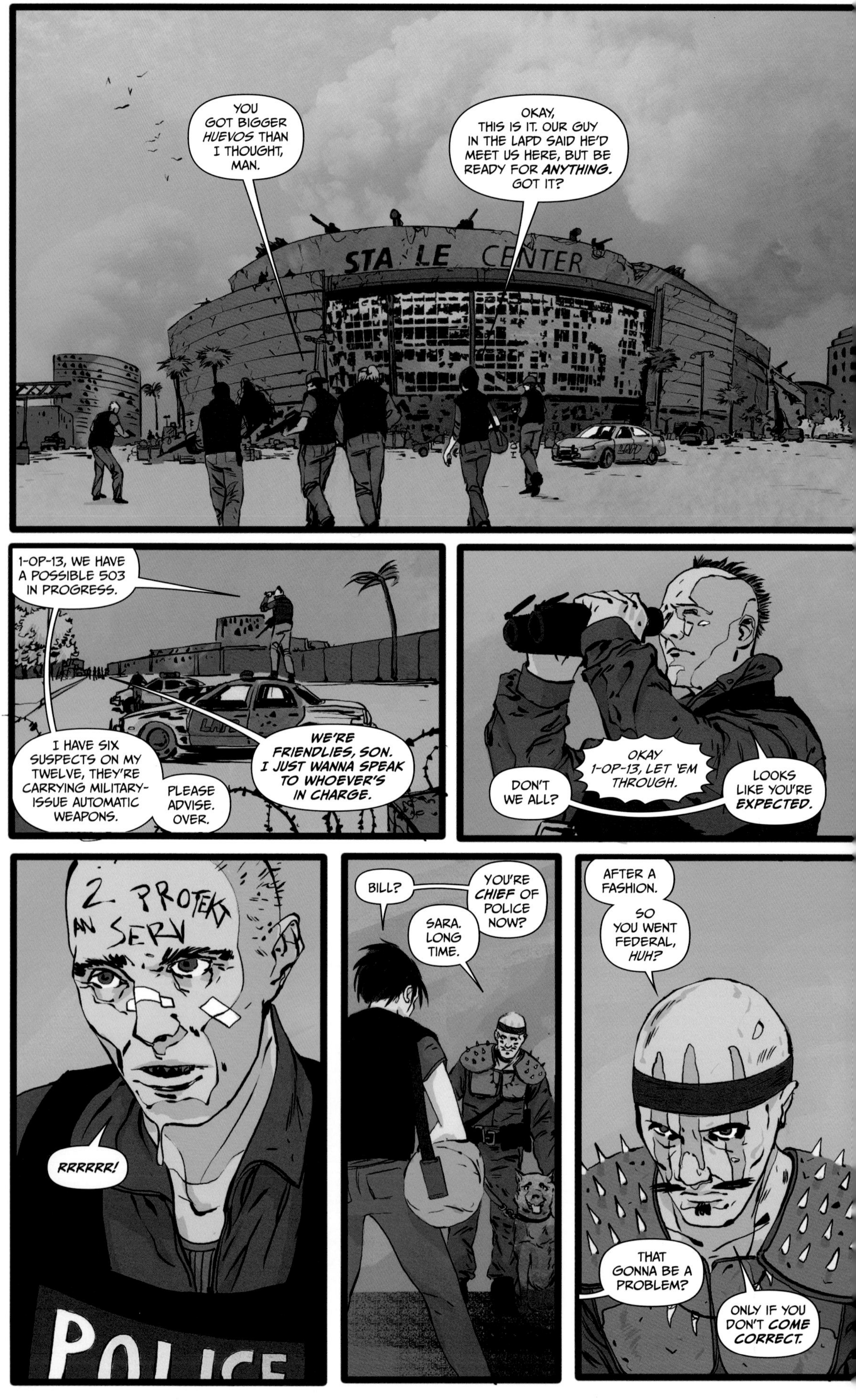
YOU GOT BIGGER *HUEVOS* THAN I THOUGHT, MAN.
OKAY, THIS IS IT. OUR GUY IN THE LAPD SAID HE'D MEET US HERE, BUT BE READY FOR ***ANYTHING.*** GOT IT?
STA LE CENTER
1-OP-13, WE HAVE A POSSIBLE 503 IN PROGRESS.
I HAVE SIX SUSPECTS ON MY TWELVE, THEY'RE CARRYING MILITARY-ISSUE AUTOMATIC WEAPONS.
PLEASE ADVISE. OVER.
WE'RE FRIENDLIES, SON. I JUST WANNA SPEAK TO WHOEVER'S IN CHARGE.
DON'T WE ALL?
OKAY 1-OP-13, LET 'EM THROUGH.
LOOKS LIKE YOU'RE ***EXPECTED.***
2 PROTEKT AN SERV
RRRRRR!
POLICE
BILL?
YOU'RE ***CHIEF*** OF POLICE NOW?
SARA. LONG TIME.
AFTER A FASHION.
SO YOU WENT FEDERAL, *HUH?*
THAT GONNA BE A PROBLEM?
ONLY IF YOU DON'T ***COME CORRECT.***

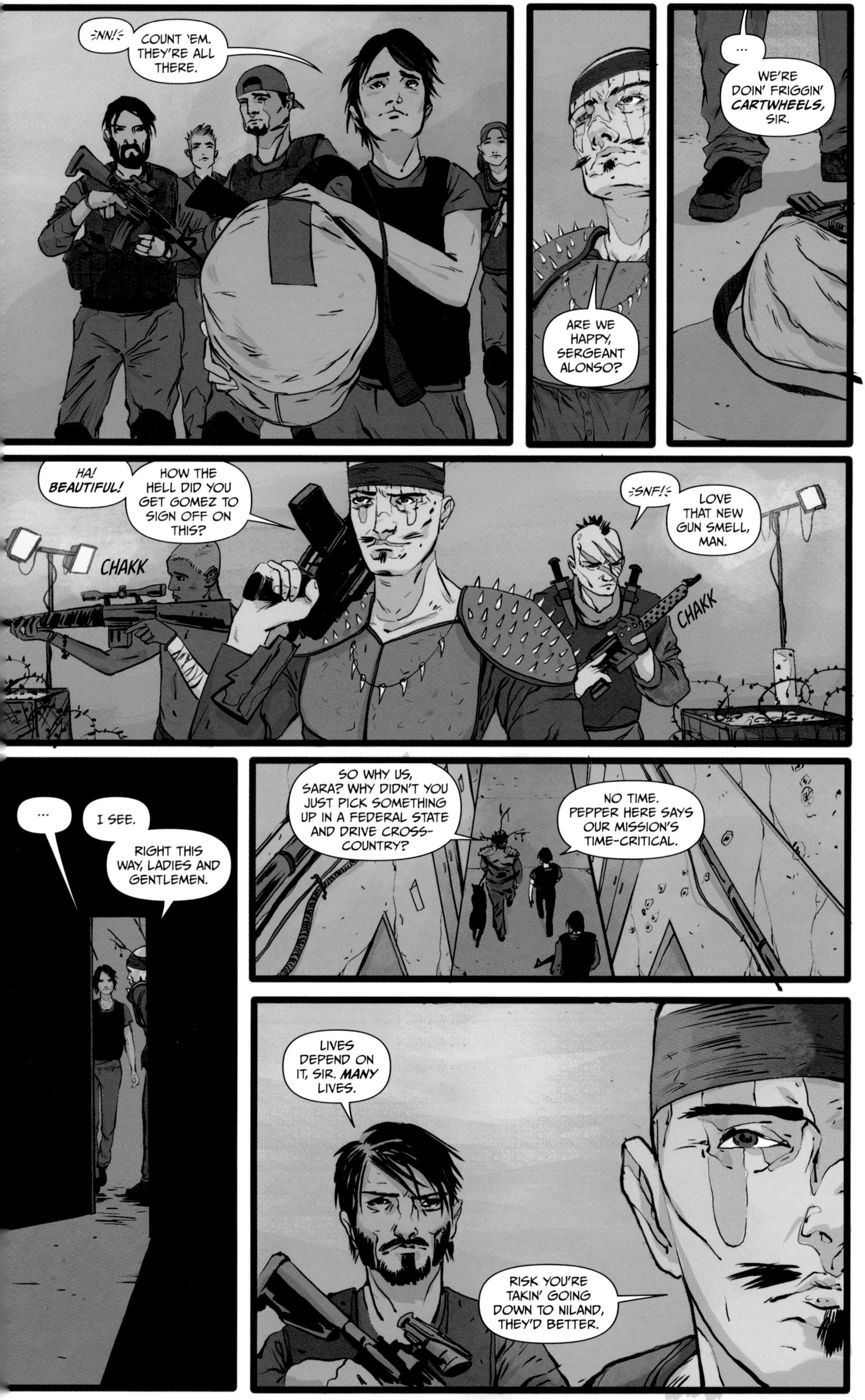

-SNN!-
COUNT 'EM. THEY'RE ALL THERE.
ARE WE HAPPY, SERGEANT ALONSO?
...
WE'RE DOIN' FRIGGIN' CARTWHEELS, SIR.
HA! BEAUTIFUL!
HOW THE HELL DID YOU GET GOMEZ TO SIGN OFF ON THIS?
CHAKK
-SNF!-
LOVE THAT NEW GUN SMELL, MAN.
CHAKK
...
I SEE.
RIGHT THIS WAY, LADIES AND GENTLEMEN.
SO WHY US, SARA? WHY DIDN'T YOU JUST PICK SOMETHING UP IN A FEDERAL STATE AND DRIVE CROSS-COUNTRY?
NO TIME. PEPPER HERE SAYS OUR MISSION'S TIME-CRITICAL.
LIVES DEPEND ON IT, SIR. MANY LIVES.
RISK YOU'RE TAKIN' GOING DOWN TO NILAND, THEY'D BETTER.

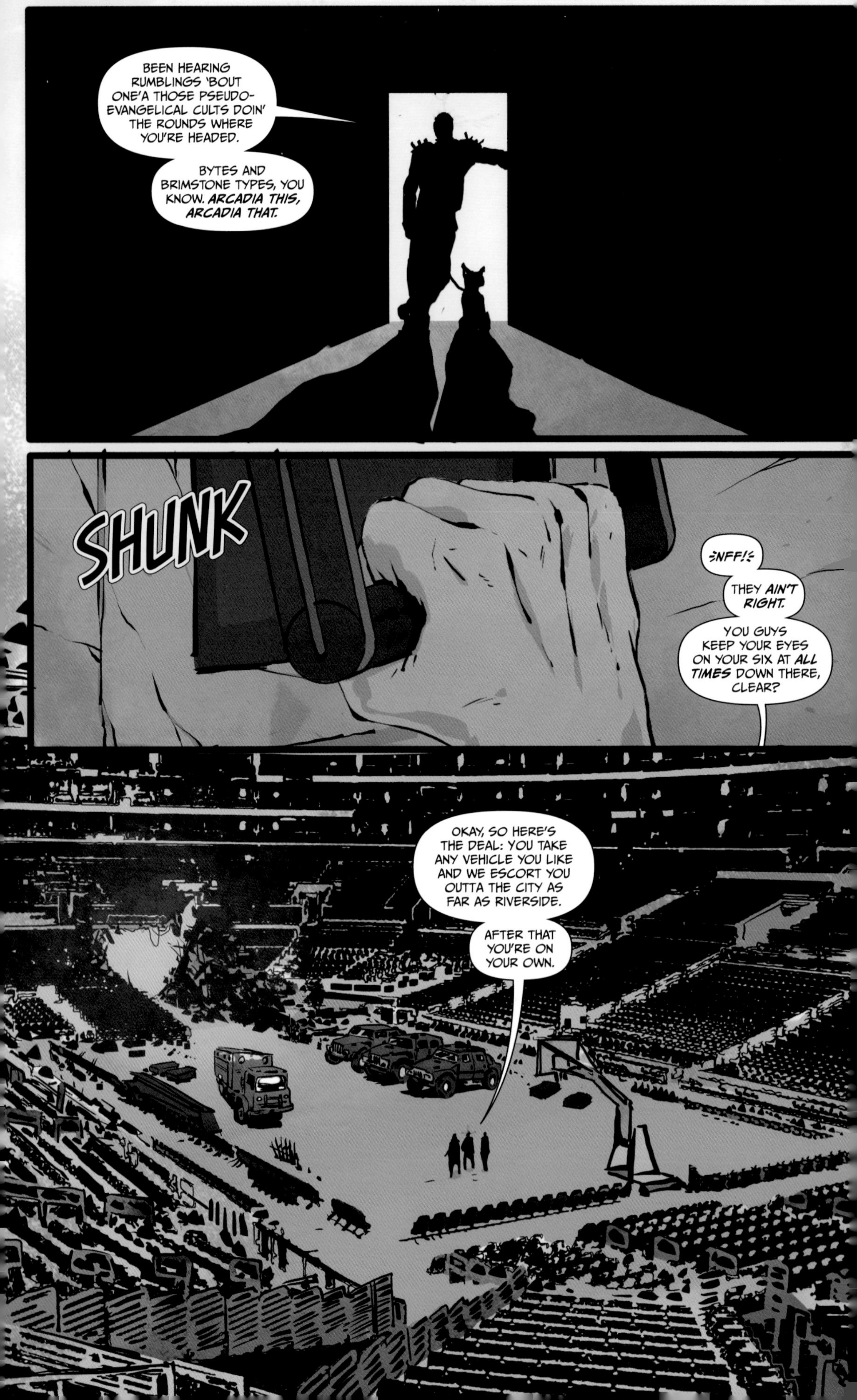
BEEN HEARING RUMBLINGS 'BOUT ONE'A THOSE PSEUDO-EVANGELICAL CULTS DOIN' THE ROUNDS WHERE YOU'RE HEADED.
BYTES AND BRIMSTONE TYPES, YOU KNOW. *ARCADIA THIS, ARCADIA THAT.*
SHUNK
SNFF!
THEY *AIN'T RIGHT.*
YOU GUYS KEEP YOUR EYES ON YOUR SIX AT *ALL TIMES* DOWN THERE, CLEAR?
OKAY, SO HERE'S THE DEAL: YOU TAKE ANY VEHICLE YOU LIKE AND WE ESCORT YOU OUTTA THE CITY AS FAR AS RIVERSIDE.
AFTER THAT YOU'RE ON YOUR OWN.

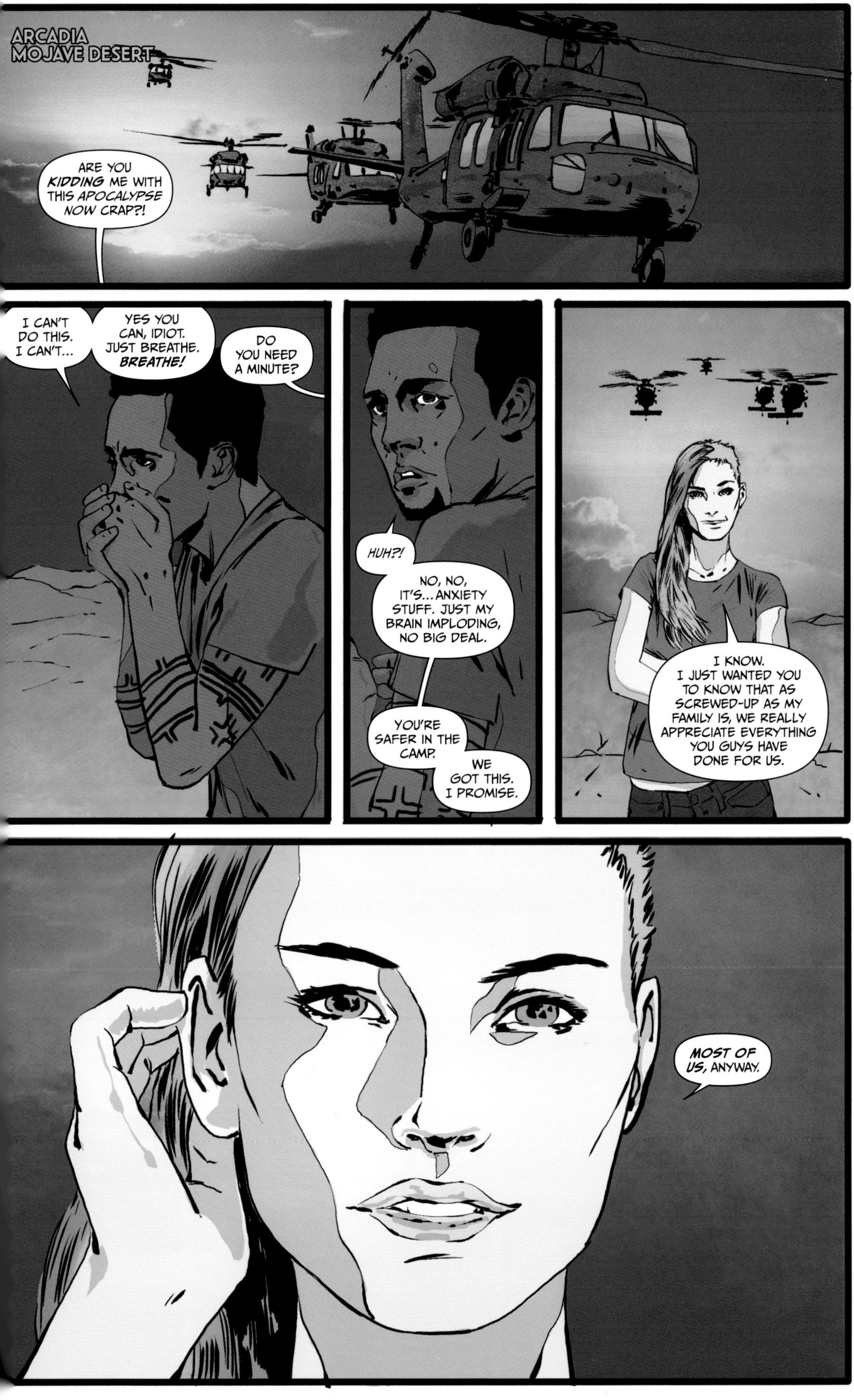
ARCADIA MOJAVE DESERT
ARE YOU KIDDING ME WITH THIS APOCALYPSE NOW CRAP?!
I CAN'T DO THIS. I CAN'T...
YES YOU CAN, IDIOT. JUST BREATHE. BREATHE!
DO YOU NEED A MINUTE?
HUH?!
NO, NO, IT'S... ANXIETY STUFF. JUST MY BRAIN IMPLODING, NO BIG DEAL.
YOU'RE SAFER IN THE CAMP.
WE GOT THIS. I PROMISE.
I KNOW. I JUST WANTED YOU TO KNOW THAT AS SCREWED-UP AS MY FAMILY IS, WE REALLY APPRECIATE EVERYTHING YOU GUYS HAVE DONE FOR US.
MOST OF US, ANYWAY.

SERIOUSLY, CORAL, YOU NEED TO GO.

I MIGHT HAVE TO HURT SOME PEOPLE. IT'LL BE ROUGH.

THEY CAME AT *US*. REMEMBER THAT.

OKAY, GUYS, ARE WE ALL IN POSITION?

ALL PRESENT AND CORRECT. DAMN.

GOD, I HOPE THEY TURN BACK.

BABY...

SAVE IT FOR THE MIRROR, MOM.

FISK, SHE... SHE TOLD ME THAT YOU, ME, AND JACK... WE CAN *WALK AWAY* FROM THIS.

YOUR FATHER...

:SIGH: OH, *MOM.*

I'M SURE HE DESERVES ALL THIS AND MORE...

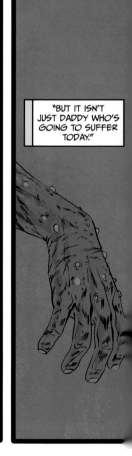

"BUT IT ISN'T JUST DADDY WHO'S GOING TO SUFFER TODAY."

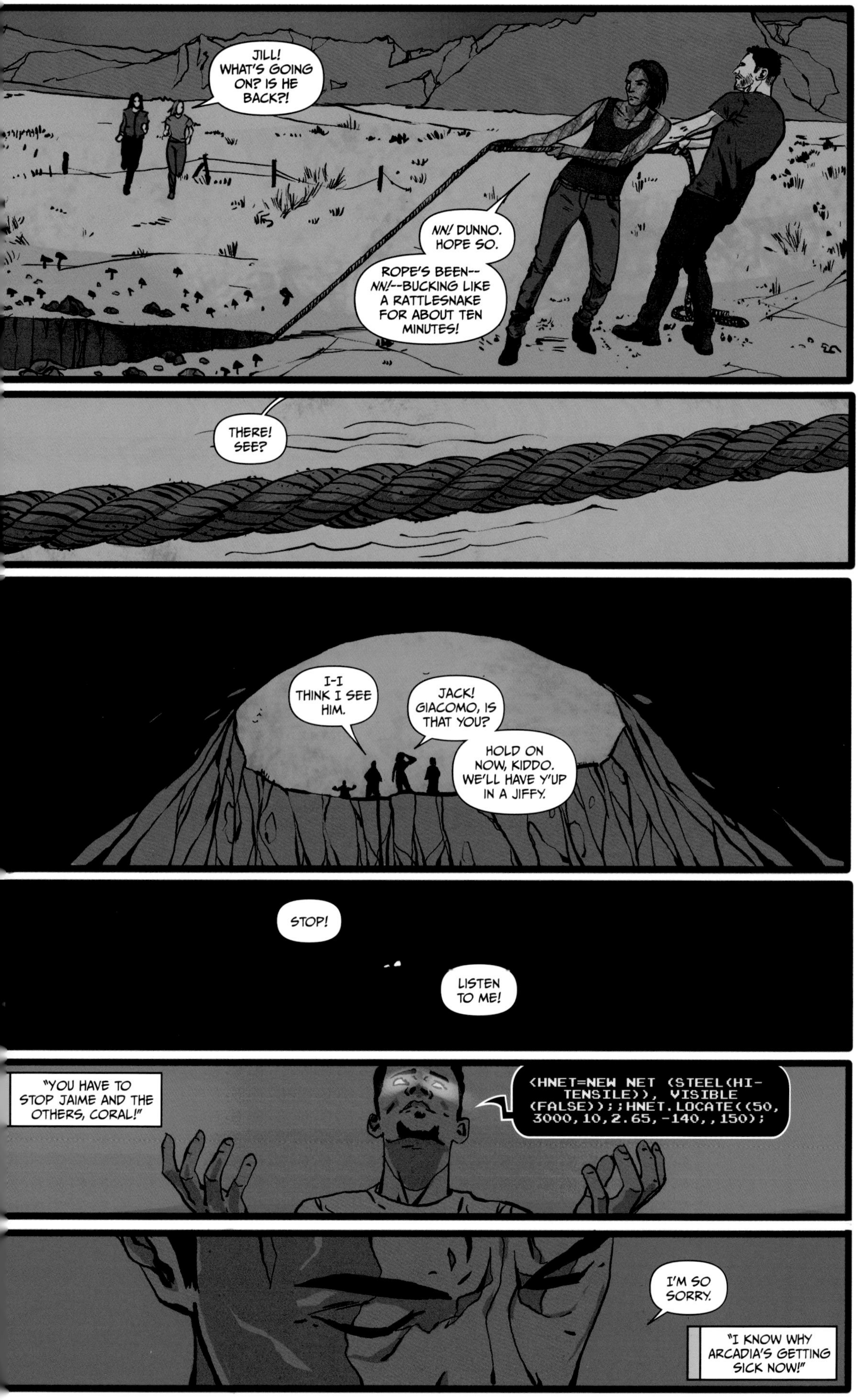
JILL! WHAT'S GOING ON? IS HE BACK?!
NN! DUNNO. HOPE SO.
ROPE'S BEEN-- NN!--BUCKING LIKE A RATTLESNAKE FOR ABOUT TEN MINUTES!
THERE! SEE?
I-I THINK I SEE HIM.
JACK! GIACOMO, IS THAT YOU?
HOLD ON NOW, KIDDO. WE'LL HAVE Y'UP IN A JIFFY.
STOP!
LISTEN TO ME!
"YOU HAVE TO STOP JAIME AND THE OTHERS, CORAL!"
<HNET=NEW NET (STEEL(HI-TENSILE)), VISIBLE (FALSE));;HNET.LOCATE((50, 3000,10,2.65,-140,,150);
I'M SO SORRY.
"I KNOW WHY ARCADIA'S GETTING SICK NOW!"

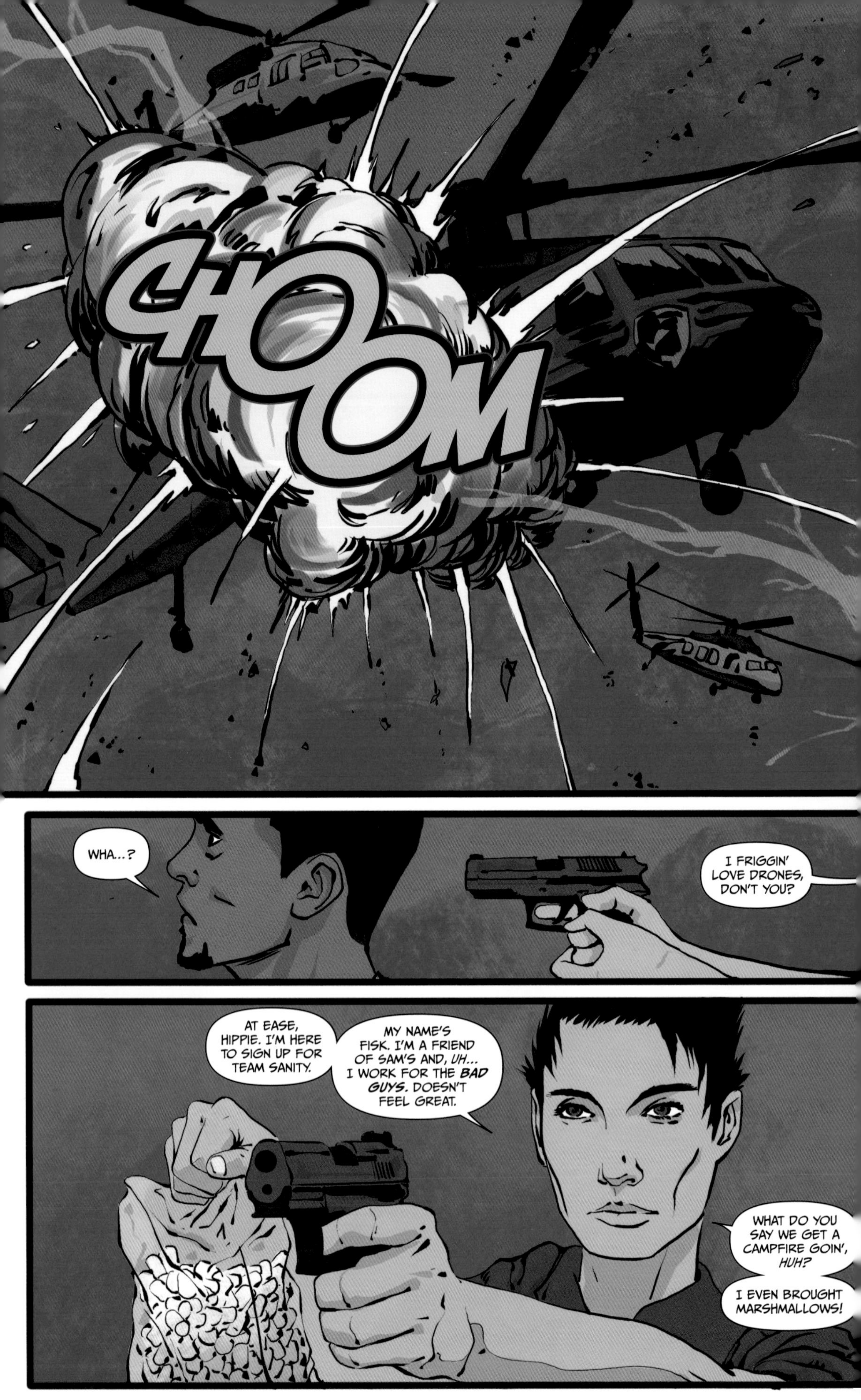
CHOOM
WHA...?
I FRIGGIN' LOVE DRONES, DON'T YOU?
AT EASE, HIPPIE. I'M HERE TO SIGN UP FOR TEAM SANITY.
MY NAME'S FISK. I'M A FRIEND OF SAM'S AND, UH... I WORK FOR THE BAD GUYS. DOESN'T FEEL GREAT.
WHAT DO YOU SAY WE GET A CAMPFIRE GOIN', HUH?
I EVEN BROUGHT MARSHMALLOWS!

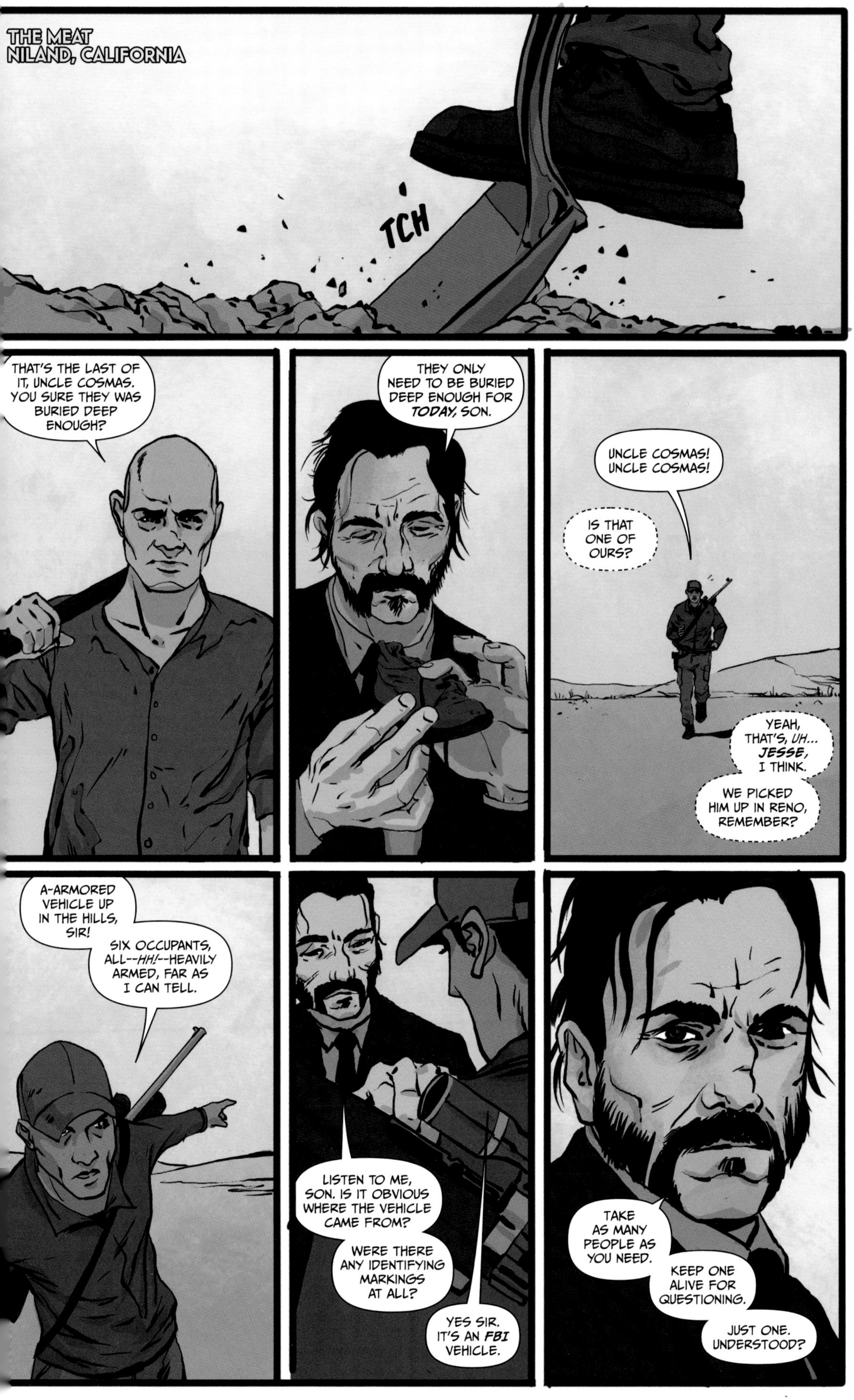

THE MEAT
NILAND, CALIFORNIA
TCH
THAT'S THE LAST OF IT, UNCLE COSMAS. YOU SURE THEY WAS BURIED DEEP ENOUGH?
THEY ONLY NEED TO BE BURIED DEEP ENOUGH FOR TODAY, SON.
UNCLE COSMAS! UNCLE COSMAS!
IS THAT ONE OF OURS?
YEAH, THAT'S, UH... JESSE, I THINK.
WE PICKED HIM UP IN RENO, REMEMBER?
A-ARMORED VEHICLE UP IN THE HILLS, SIR!
SIX OCCUPANTS, ALL--HH!--HEAVILY ARMED, FAR AS I CAN TELL.
LISTEN TO ME, SON. IS IT OBVIOUS WHERE THE VEHICLE CAME FROM?
WERE THERE ANY IDENTIFYING MARKINGS AT ALL?
YES SIR. IT'S AN FBI VEHICLE.
TAKE AS MANY PEOPLE AS YOU NEED.
KEEP ONE ALIVE FOR QUESTIONING.
JUST ONE. UNDERSTOOD?

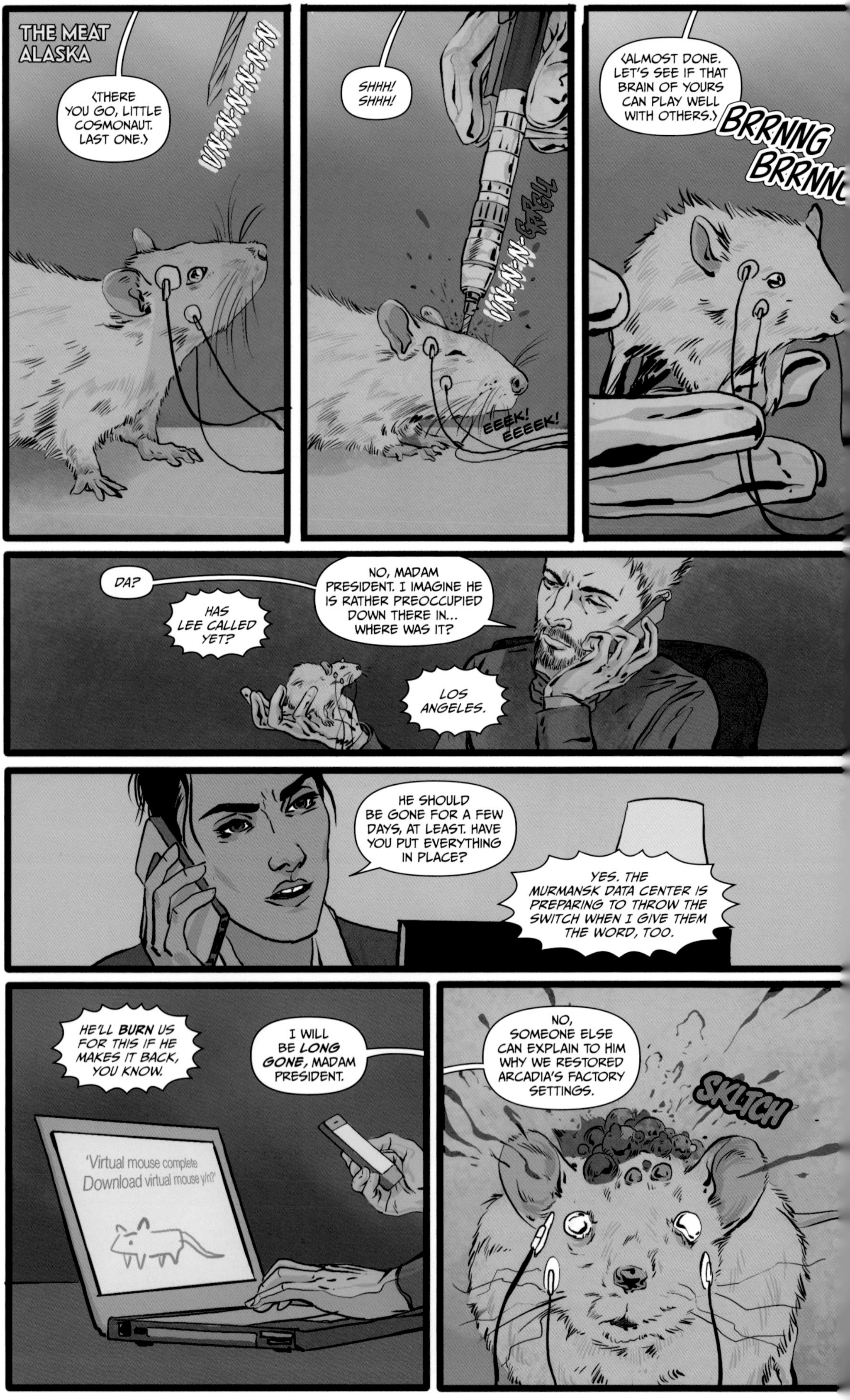
THE MEAT
ALASKA
‹THERE YOU GO, LITTLE COSMONAUT. LAST ONE.›
UN-N-N-N-N-N
SHHH! SHHH!
UN-N-N-GRRGL
EEEEK! EEEEK!
‹ALMOST DONE. LET'S SEE IF THAT BRAIN OF YOURS CAN PLAY WELL WITH OTHERS.›
BRRNNG
DA?
HAS LEE CALLED YET?
NO, MADAM PRESIDENT. I IMAGINE HE IS RATHER PREOCCUPIED DOWN THERE IN... WHERE WAS IT?
LOS ANGELES.
HE SHOULD BE GONE FOR A FEW DAYS, AT LEAST. HAVE YOU PUT EVERYTHING IN PLACE?
YES. THE MURMANSK DATA CENTER IS PREPARING TO THROW THE SWITCH WHEN I GIVE THEM THE WORD, TOO.
HE'LL BURN US FOR THIS IF HE MAKES IT BACK, YOU KNOW.
I WILL BE LONG GONE, MADAM PRESIDENT.
'Virtual mouse complete
Download virtual mouse y/n?'
NO, SOMEONE ELSE CAN EXPLAIN TO HIM WHY WE RESTORED ARCADIA'S FACTORY SETTINGS.
SKLTCH

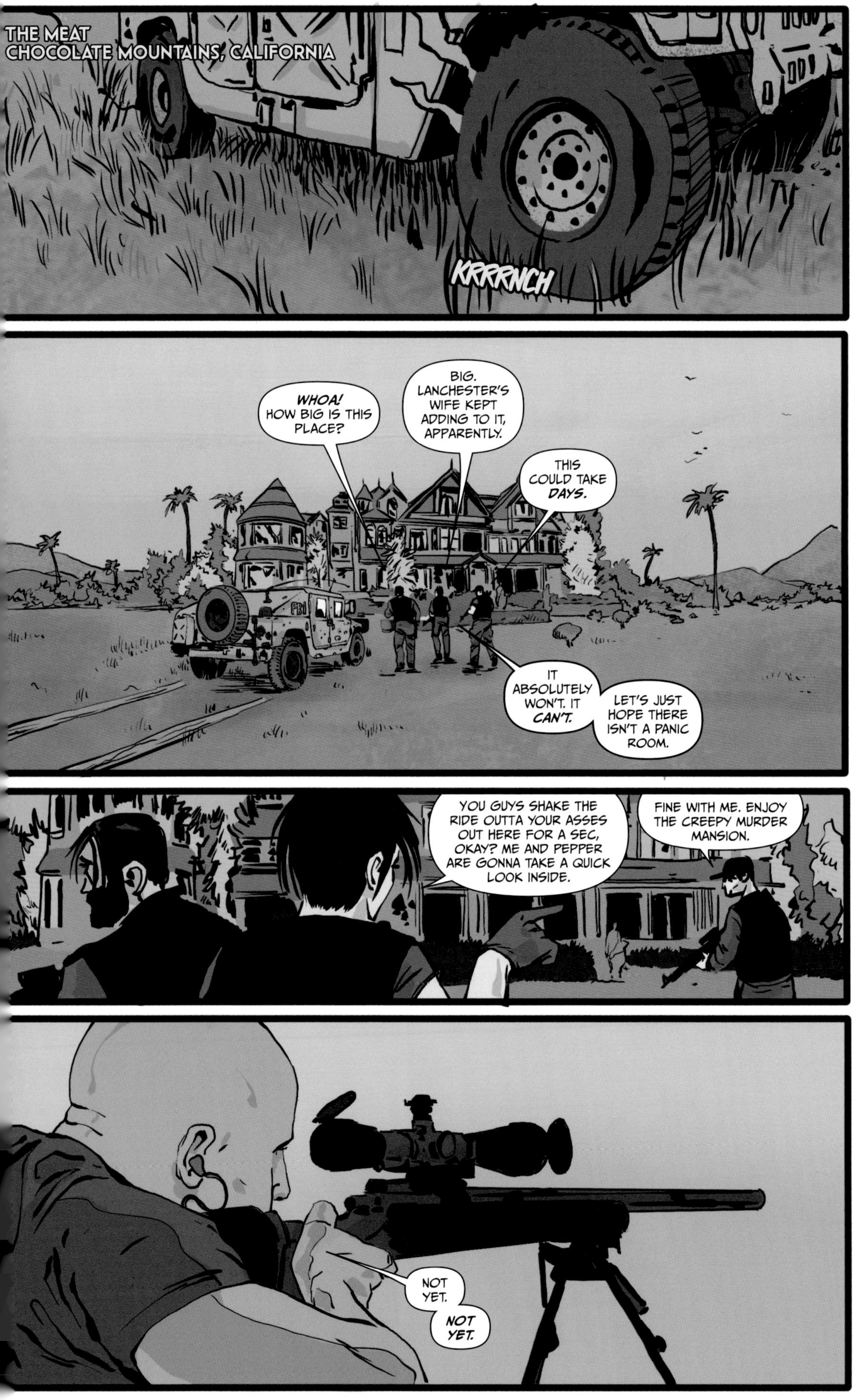
THE MEAT
CHOCOLATE MOUNTAINS, CALIFORNIA
KRRRNCH
WHOA! HOW BIG IS THIS PLACE?
BIG. LANCHESTER'S WIFE KEPT ADDING TO IT, APPARENTLY.
THIS COULD TAKE DAYS.
IT ABSOLUTELY WON'T. IT CAN'T.
LET'S JUST HOPE THERE ISN'T A PANIC ROOM.
YOU GUYS SHAKE THE RIDE OUTTA YOUR ASSES OUT HERE FOR A SEC, OKAY? ME AND PEPPER ARE GONNA TAKE A QUICK LOOK INSIDE.
FINE WITH ME. ENJOY THE CREEPY MURDER MANSION.
NOT YET.
NOT YET.

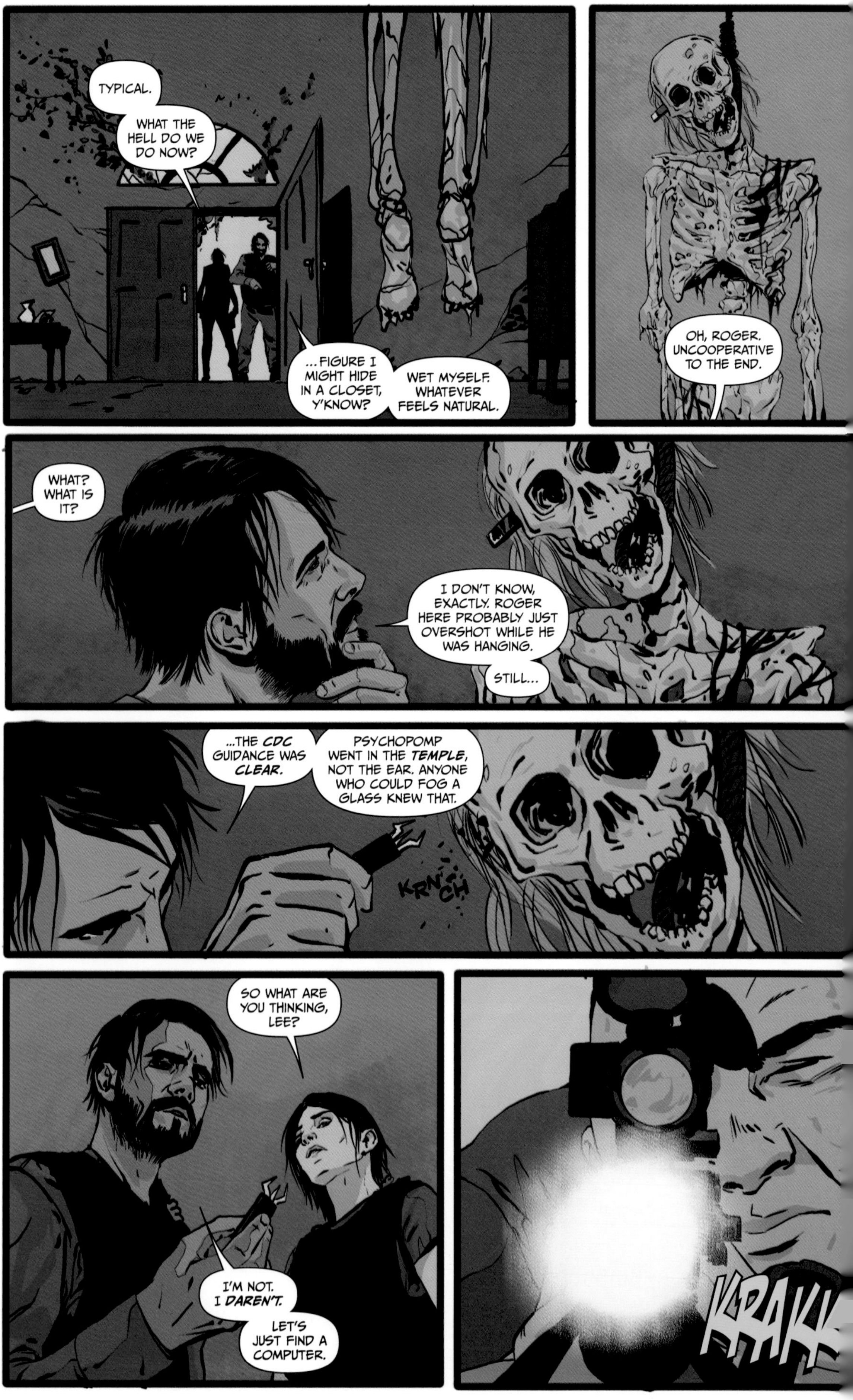
TYPICAL.
WHAT THE HELL DO WE DO NOW?
...FIGURE I MIGHT HIDE IN A CLOSET, Y'KNOW?
WET MYSELF. WHATEVER FEELS NATURAL.
OH, ROGER. UNCOOPERATIVE TO THE END.
WHAT? WHAT IS IT?
I DON'T KNOW, EXACTLY. ROGER HERE PROBABLY JUST OVERSHOT WHILE HE WAS HANGING.
STILL...
...THE CDC GUIDANCE WAS CLEAR.
PSYCHOPOMP WENT IN THE TEMPLE, NOT THE EAR. ANYONE WHO COULD FOG A GLASS KNEW THAT.
KRN'CH
SO WHAT ARE YOU THINKING, LEE?
I'M NOT. I DAREN'T.
LET'S JUST FIND A COMPUTER.
KRAKK

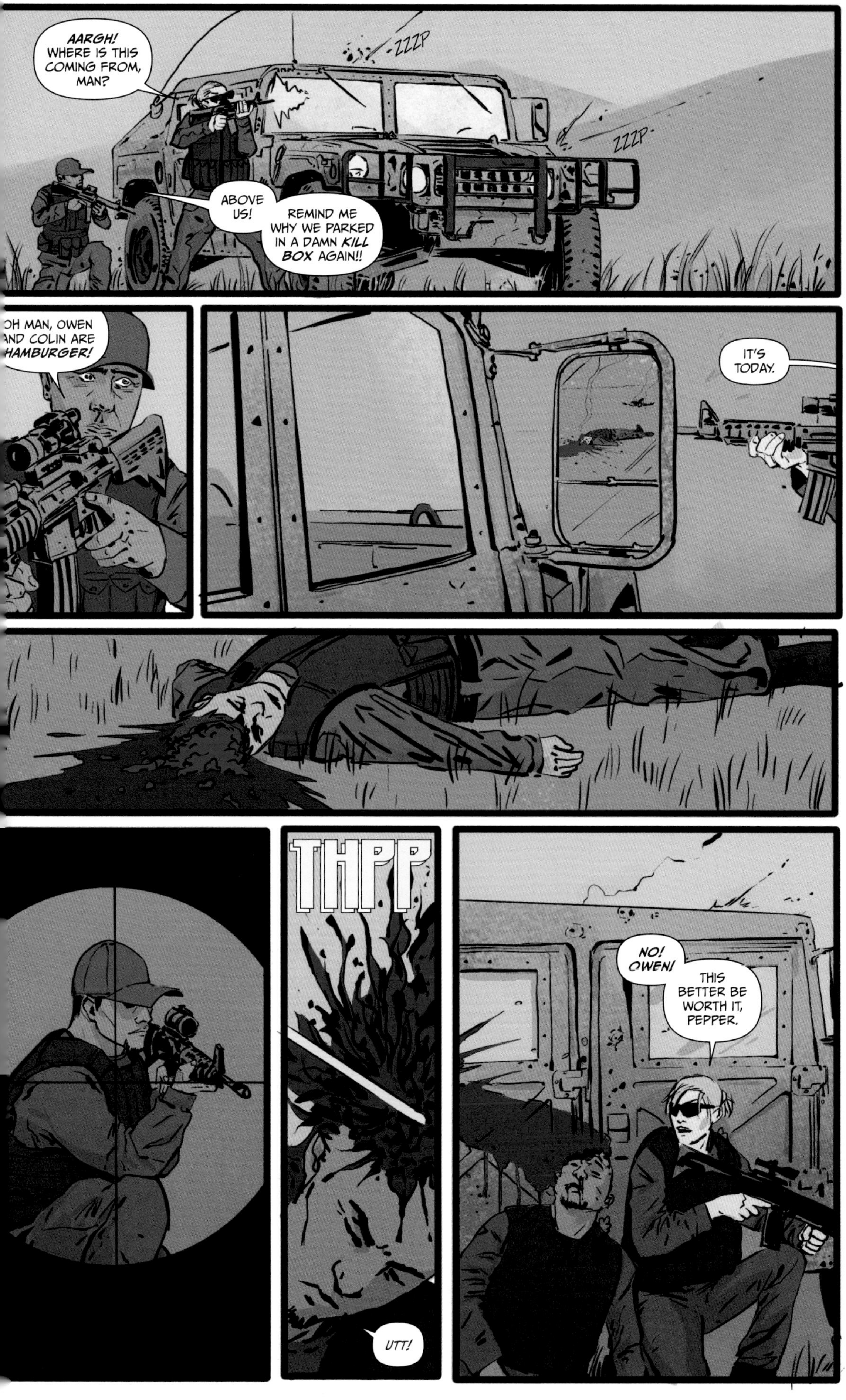
AARGH! WHERE IS THIS COMING FROM, MAN?
ZZZP
ZZZP
ABOVE US!
REMIND ME WHY WE PARKED IN A DAMN KILL BOX AGAIN!!
OH MAN, OWEN AND COLIN ARE HAMBURGER!
IT'S TODAY.
THPP
UTT!
NO! OWEN!
THIS BETTER BE WORTH IT, PEPPER.

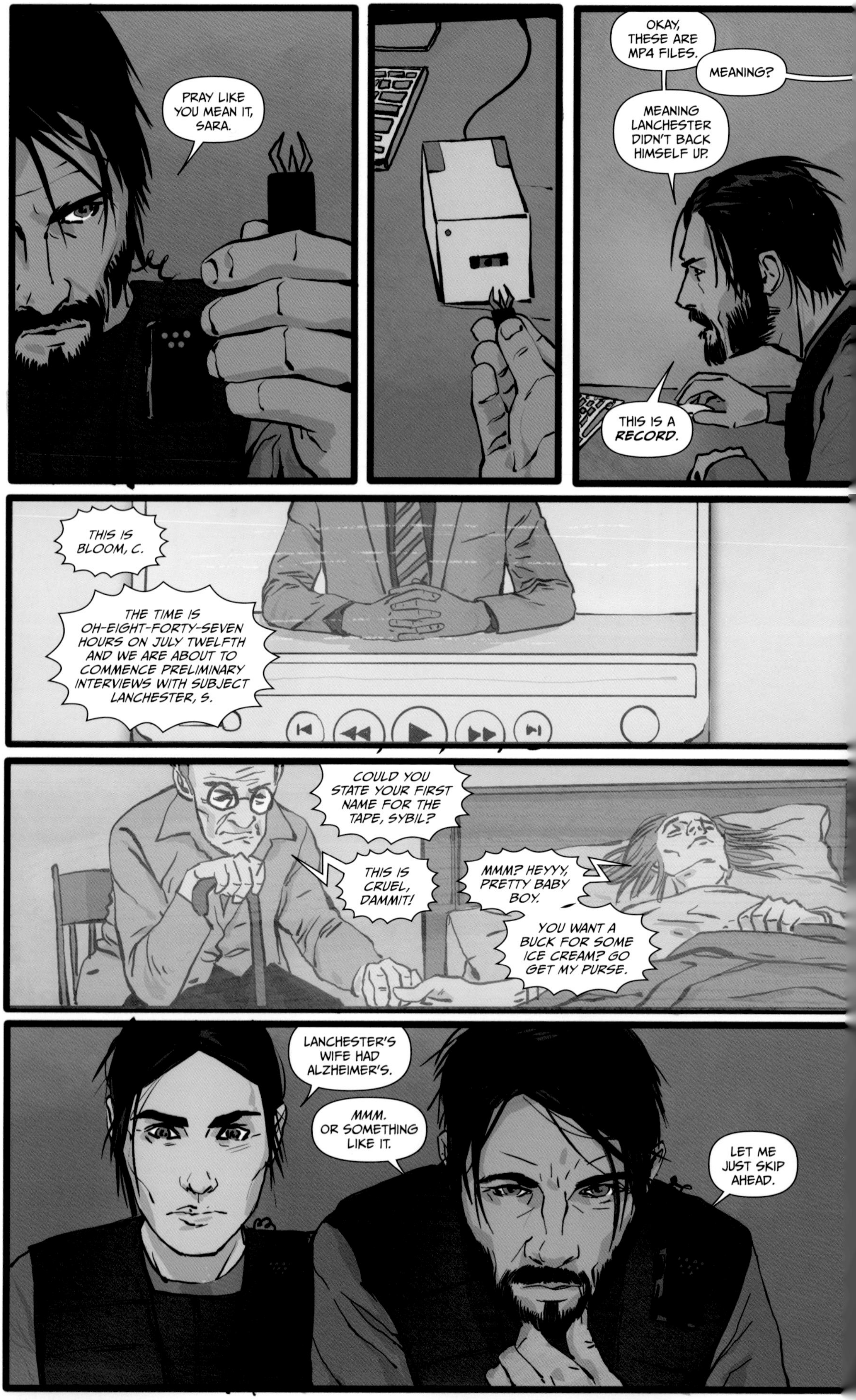
PRAY LIKE YOU MEAN IT, SARA.
OKAY, THESE ARE MP4 FILES.
MEANING?
MEANING LANCHESTER DIDN'T BACK HIMSELF UP.
THIS IS A RECORD.
THIS IS BLOOM, C.
THE TIME IS OH-EIGHT-FORTY-SEVEN HOURS ON JULY TWELFTH AND WE ARE ABOUT TO COMMENCE PRELIMINARY INTERVIEWS WITH SUBJECT LANCHESTER, S.
COULD YOU STATE YOUR FIRST NAME FOR THE TAPE, SYBIL?
THIS IS CRUEL, DAMMIT!
MMM? HEYYY, PRETTY BABY BOY.
YOU WANT A BUCK FOR SOME ICE CREAM? GO GET MY PURSE.
LANCHESTER'S WIFE HAD ALZHEIMER'S.
MMM. OR SOMETHING LIKE IT.
LET ME JUST SKIP AHEAD.

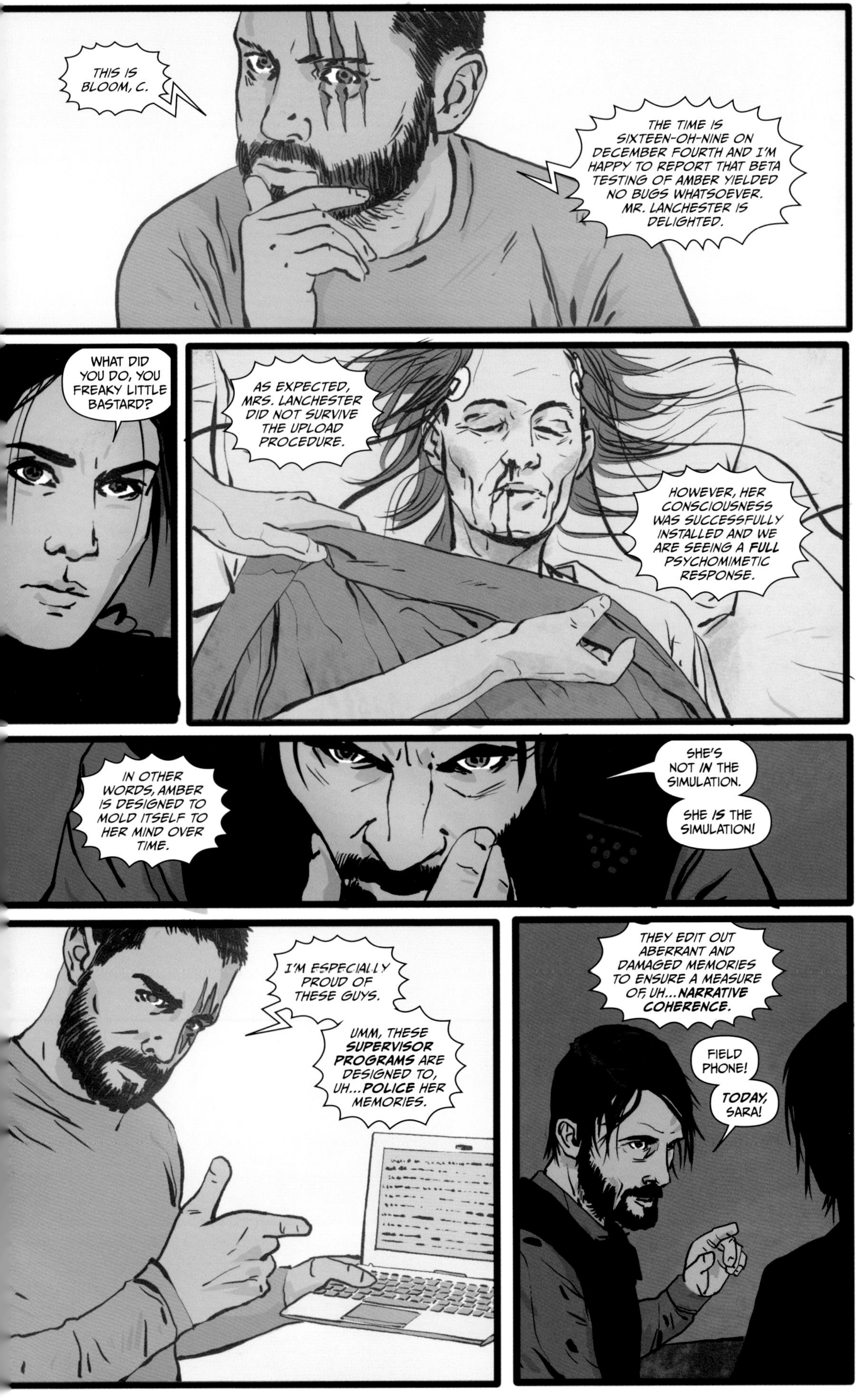
THIS IS BLOOM, C.
THE TIME IS SIXTEEN-OH-NINE ON DECEMBER FOURTH AND I'M HAPPY TO REPORT THAT BETA TESTING OF AMBER YIELDED NO BUGS WHATSOEVER. MR. LANCHESTER IS DELIGHTED.
WHAT DID YOU DO, YOU FREAKY LITTLE BASTARD?
AS EXPECTED, MRS. LANCHESTER DID NOT SURVIVE THE UPLOAD PROCEDURE.
HOWEVER, HER CONSCIOUSNESS WAS SUCCESSFULLY INSTALLED AND WE ARE SEEING A **FULL** PSYCHOMIMETIC RESPONSE.
IN OTHER WORDS, AMBER IS DESIGNED TO MOLD ITSELF TO HER MIND OVER TIME.
SHE'S NOT *IN* THE SIMULATION.
SHE *IS* THE SIMULATION!
I'M ESPECIALLY PROUD OF THESE GUYS.
UMM, THESE **SUPERVISOR PROGRAMS** ARE DESIGNED TO, UH...**POLICE** HER MEMORIES.
THEY EDIT OUT ABERRANT AND DAMAGED MEMORIES TO ENSURE A MEASURE OF, UH...**NARRATIVE COHERENCE.**
FIELD PHONE!
TODAY, SARA!

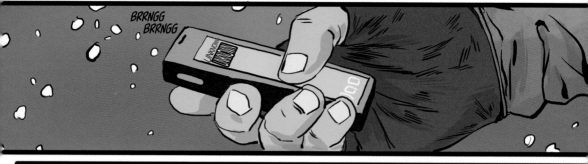

BRRNGG
BRRNGG

MADAM PRESIDENT?

VALENTIN, IT'S LEE.

PEPPER! GOOD! I HAVE A THEORY AS TO WHY YOU'VE BEEN HAVING HALLUCINATIONS AND I...

I KNOW WHAT'S WRONG WITH THE SIMULATION!

IT'S US, MAN! WE'RE WHAT'S WRONG WITH IT!

IT WAS ONLY EVER DESIGNED TO ACCOMMODATE ONE PERSON, BUT WE...BUT I... SHOEHORNED FOUR BILLION SITTING DUCKS IN THERE!

SO WHY ARE THEY DYING?

SUPERVISOR PROGRAMS, VALENTIN.

SUPERVISOR PROGRAMS! THE ARCADIANS ARE JUST CORRUPTED CODE TO THEM!

EXACTLY! AND THE QUANTUM CORES MADE 'EM EXTRA ROWDY.

WHUDD

HRRKKK!

PEPPER? PEPPER, ARE YOU THERE?

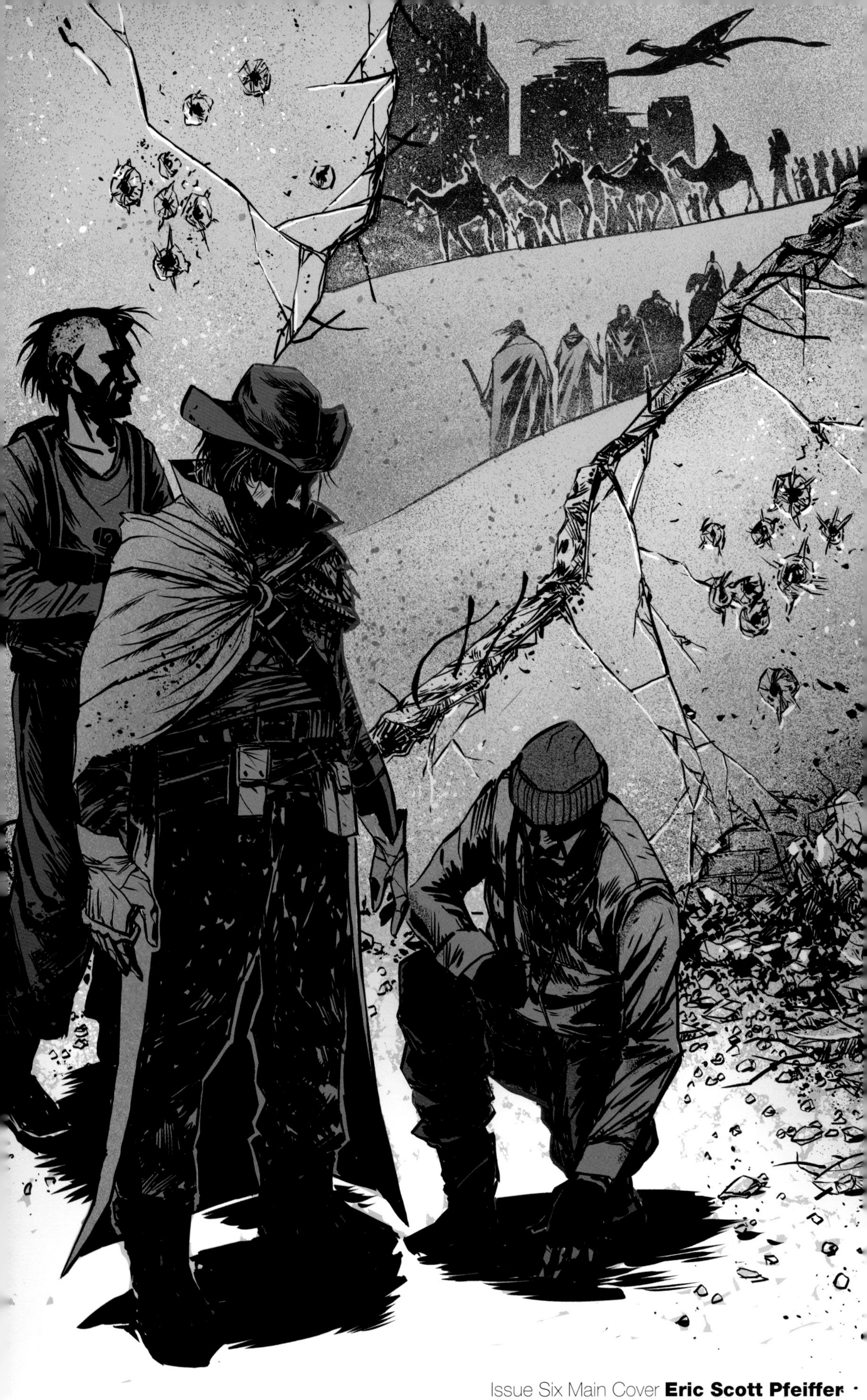

Issue Six Main Cover **Eric Scott Pfeiffer**

"Simplify your life: die!"

—Friedrich Nietzsche

CHAPTER
SEVEN

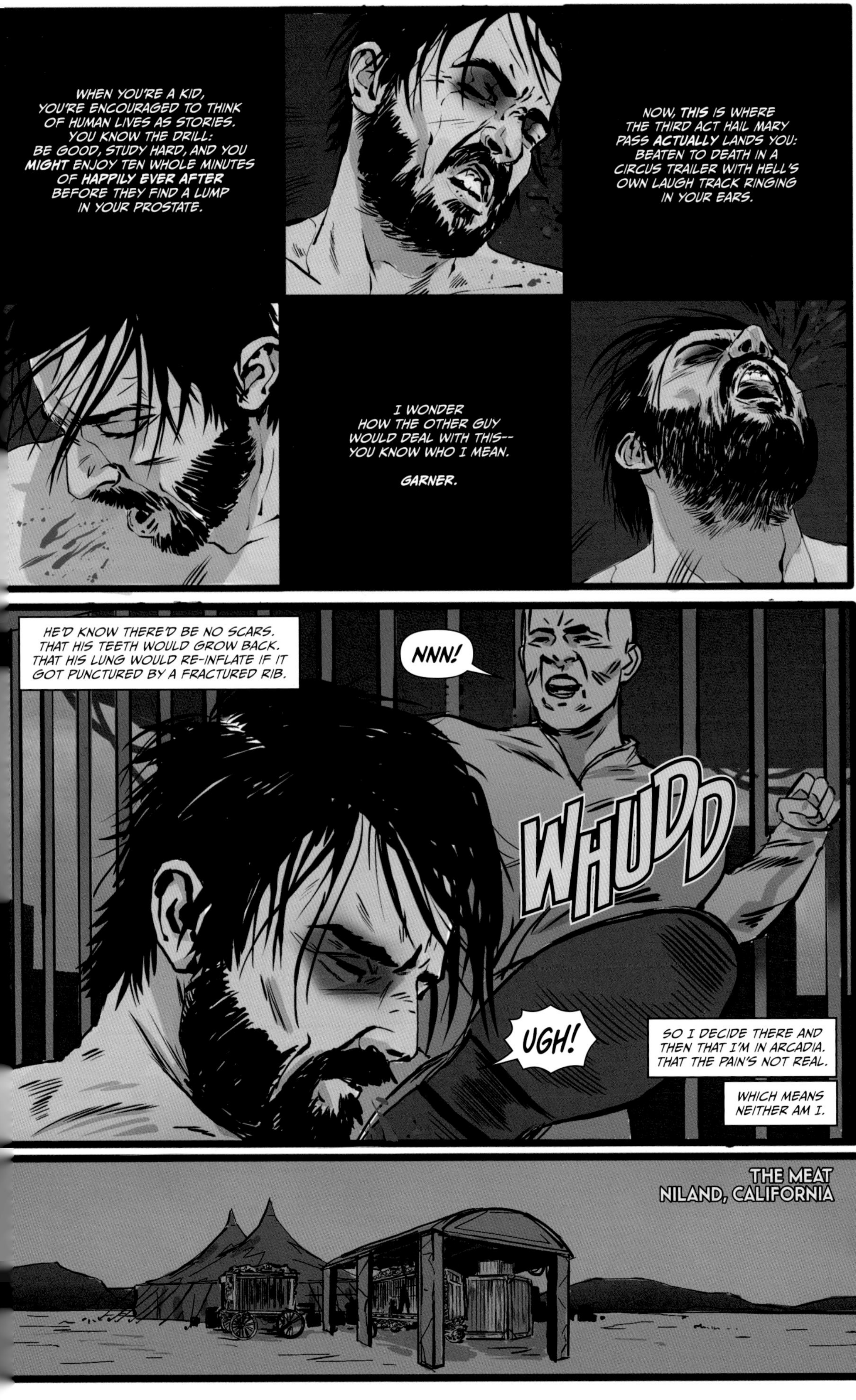
WHEN YOU'RE A KID, YOU'RE ENCOURAGED TO THINK OF HUMAN LIVES AS STORIES. YOU KNOW THE DRILL: BE GOOD, STUDY HARD, AND YOU MIGHT ENJOY TEN WHOLE MINUTES OF HAPPILY EVER AFTER BEFORE THEY FIND A LUMP IN YOUR PROSTATE.
NOW, THIS IS WHERE THE THIRD ACT HAIL MARY PASS ACTUALLY LANDS YOU: BEATEN TO DEATH IN A CIRCUS TRAILER WITH HELL'S OWN LAUGH TRACK RINGING IN YOUR EARS.
I WONDER HOW THE OTHER GUY WOULD DEAL WITH THIS-- YOU KNOW WHO I MEAN.
GARNER.
HE'D KNOW THERE'D BE NO SCARS. THAT HIS TEETH WOULD GROW BACK. THAT HIS LUNG WOULD RE-INFLATE IF IT GOT PUNCTURED BY A FRACTURED RIB.
NNN!
WHUDD
UGH!
SO I DECIDE THERE AND THEN THAT I'M IN ARCADIA. THAT THE PAIN'S NOT REAL.
WHICH MEANS NEITHER AM I.
THE MEAT
NILAND, CALIFORNIA

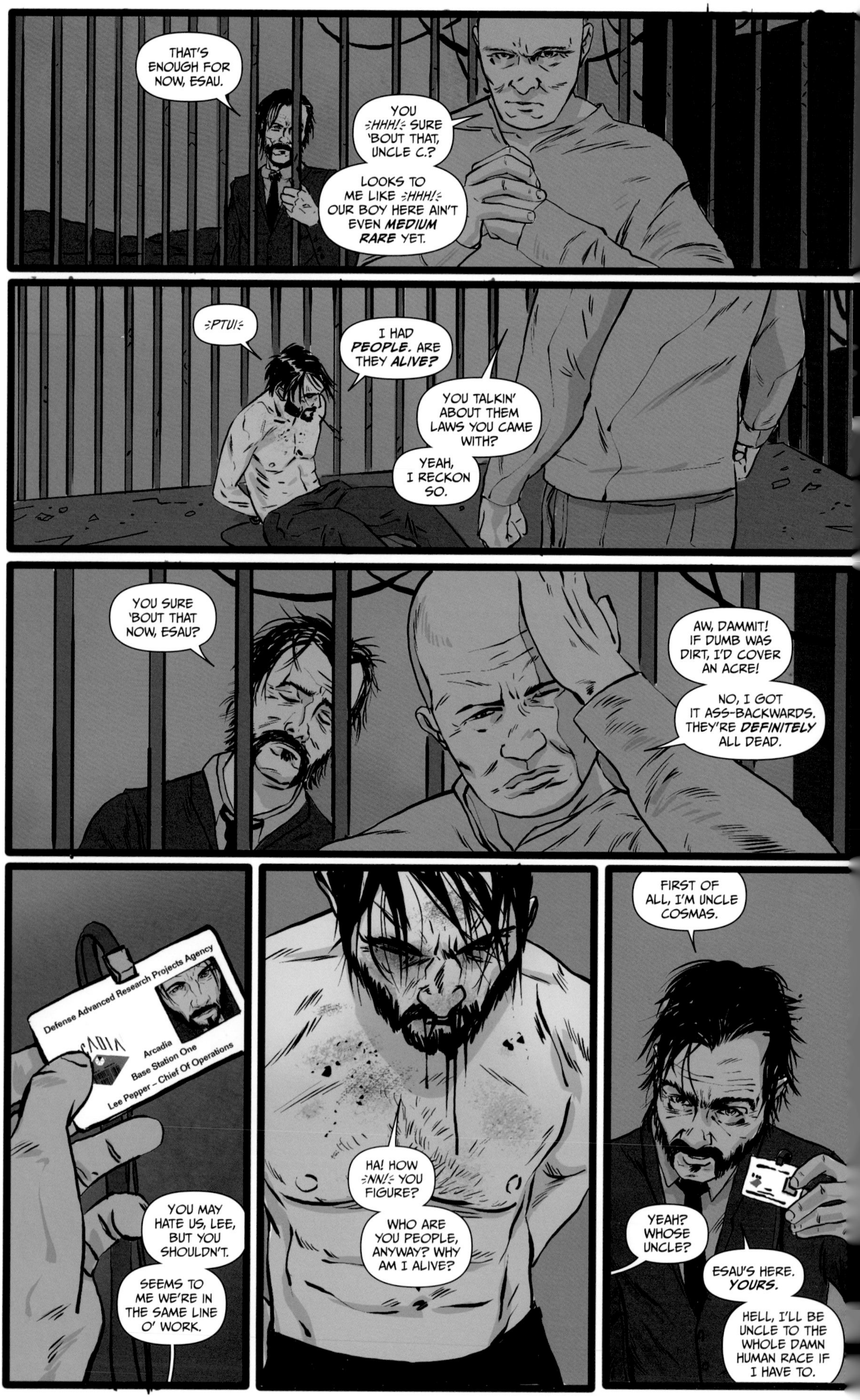
THAT'S ENOUGH FOR NOW, ESAU.
YOU =HHH!= SURE 'BOUT THAT, UNCLE C.?
LOOKS TO ME LIKE =HHH!= OUR BOY HERE AIN'T EVEN **MEDIUM RARE** YET.
=PTUI=
I HAD **PEOPLE.** ARE THEY **ALIVE?**
YOU TALKIN' ABOUT THEM LAWS YOU CAME WITH?
YEAH, I RECKON SO.
YOU SURE 'BOUT THAT NOW, ESAU?
AW, DAMMIT! IF DUMB WAS DIRT, I'D COVER AN ACRE!
NO, I GOT IT ASS-BACKWARDS. THEY'RE **DEFINITELY** ALL DEAD.
Defense Advanced Research Projects Agency
Arcadia
Base Station One
Lee Pepper – Chief Of Operations
YOU MAY HATE US, LEE, BUT YOU SHOULDN'T.
SEEMS TO ME WE'RE IN THE SAME LINE O' WORK.
HA! HOW =NN!= YOU FIGURE?
WHO ARE YOU PEOPLE, ANYWAY? WHY AM I ALIVE?
FIRST OF ALL, I'M UNCLE COSMAS.
YEAH? WHOSE UNCLE?
ESAU'S HERE. **YOURS.**
HELL, I'LL BE UNCLE TO THE WHOLE DAMN HUMAN RACE IF I HAVE TO.

AS TO WHY YOU'RE ALIVE, LET'S SAY WE'RE FIXIN' TO "COPY YOUR HOMEWORK," SO TO SPEAK.

SEE...WE SEND PEOPLE TO ARCADIA, TOO.

YOU HAVE YOUR WAY AND WE HAVE OURS.

:NNN!: THAT'S A BUNCHA B-BULL AND YOU KNOW IT.

WHO CAN FATHOM THE MYSTERIES OF PROVIDENCE, LEE?

"NOW FAITH IS THE SUBSTANCE OF THINGS HOPED FOR, THE EVIDENCE OF THINGS NOT SEEN."

YOU LACK *FAITH*, BROTHER.

SMEK

SO IT'S TIME FOR YOU TO *SEE*.

NOW...SAY UNCLE.

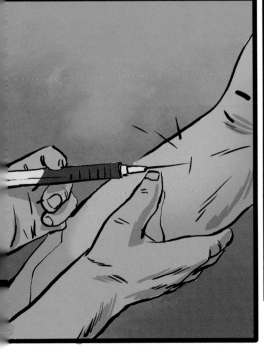

UGH!

OH.

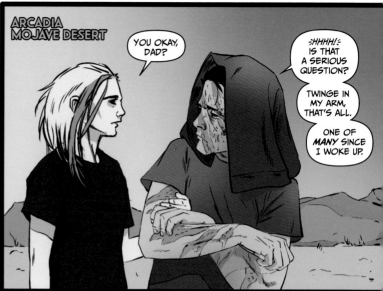

ARCADIA
MOJAVE DESERT

YOU OKAY, DAD?

≶HHHH!≶ IS THAT A SERIOUS QUESTION?

TWINGE IN MY ARM, THAT'S ALL.

ONE OF *MANY* SINCE I WOKE UP.

GUYS, CAN YOU COME OVER HERE REAL QUICK?

FISK HERE'S GOT SOMETHING I THINK WE ALL NEED TO HEAR.

THANK YOU FOR HEARING ME OUT.

I EXPECT YOU ALL THOUGHT THIS WOULD GO DOWN *QUITE DIFFERENTLY.*

AS YOU KNOW, I WORK FOR THE UNITED NATIONS. WE HAVEN'T ALWAYS APPROVED OF WHAT...*YOU PEOPLE* CAN DO.

BUT THE TRUTH IS, WE NEED THESE SKILLS OF YOURS NOW. SECRETARY-GENERAL BINETTI IS COMPLETELY OUT OF CONTROL AND WE *CAN'T* STOP HIM ALONE.

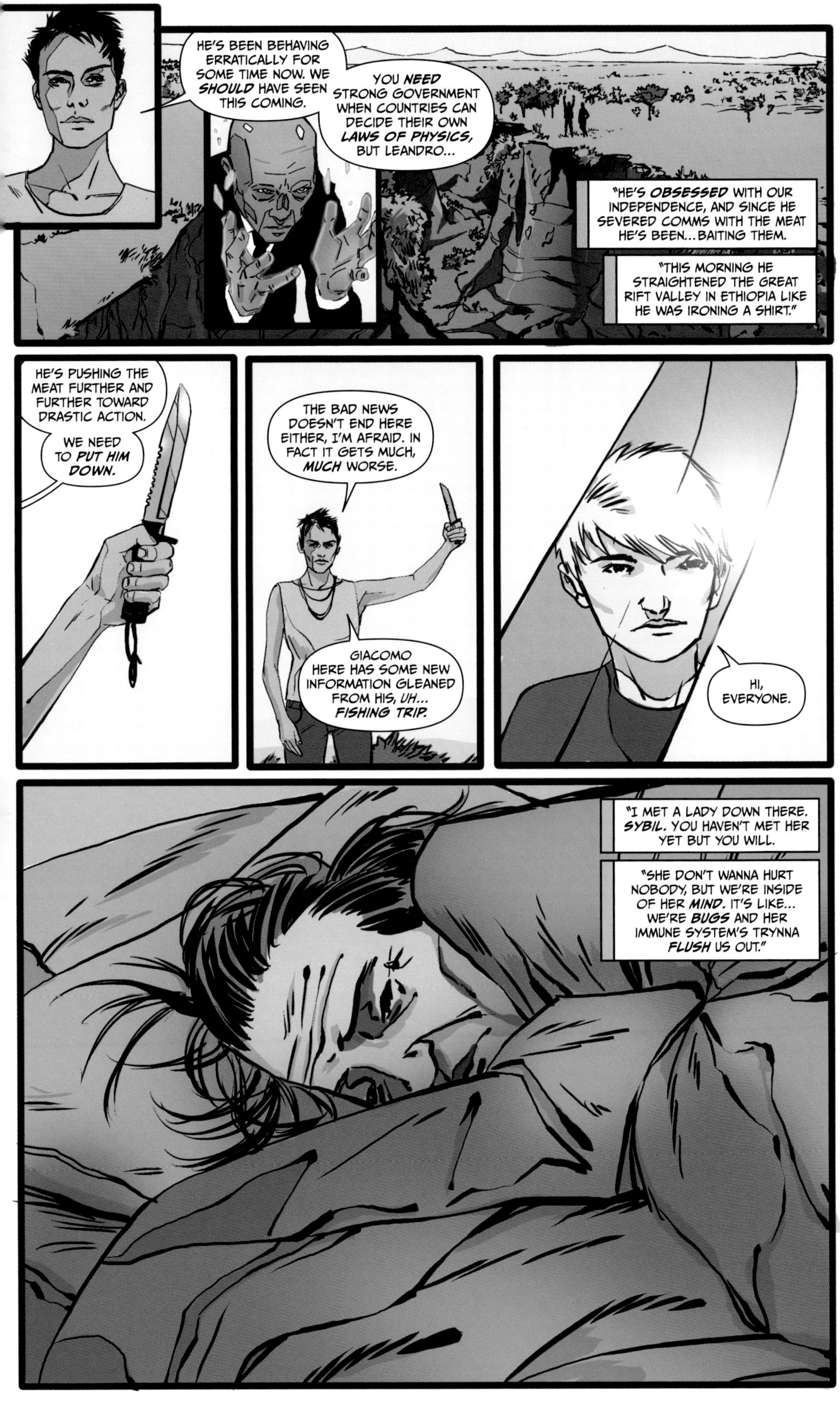
HE'S BEEN BEHAVING ERRATICALLY FOR SOME TIME NOW. WE SHOULD HAVE SEEN THIS COMING.
YOU NEED STRONG GOVERNMENT WHEN COUNTRIES CAN DECIDE THEIR OWN LAWS OF PHYSICS, BUT LEANDRO...
"HE'S OBSESSED WITH OUR INDEPENDENCE, AND SINCE HE SEVERED COMMS WITH THE MEAT HE'S BEEN...BAITING THEM.
"THIS MORNING HE STRAIGHTENED THE GREAT RIFT VALLEY IN ETHIOPIA LIKE HE WAS IRONING A SHIRT."
HE'S PUSHING THE MEAT FURTHER AND FURTHER TOWARD DRASTIC ACTION.
WE NEED TO PUT HIM DOWN.
THE BAD NEWS DOESN'T END HERE EITHER, I'M AFRAID. IN FACT IT GETS MUCH, MUCH WORSE.
GIACOMO HERE HAS SOME NEW INFORMATION GLEANED FROM HIS, UH... FISHING TRIP.
HI, EVERYONE.
"I MET A LADY DOWN THERE. SYBIL. YOU HAVEN'T MET HER YET BUT YOU WILL.
"SHE DON'T WANNA HURT NOBODY, BUT WE'RE INSIDE OF HER MIND. IT'S LIKE... WE'RE BUGS AND HER IMMUNE SYSTEM'S TRYNNA FLUSH US OUT."

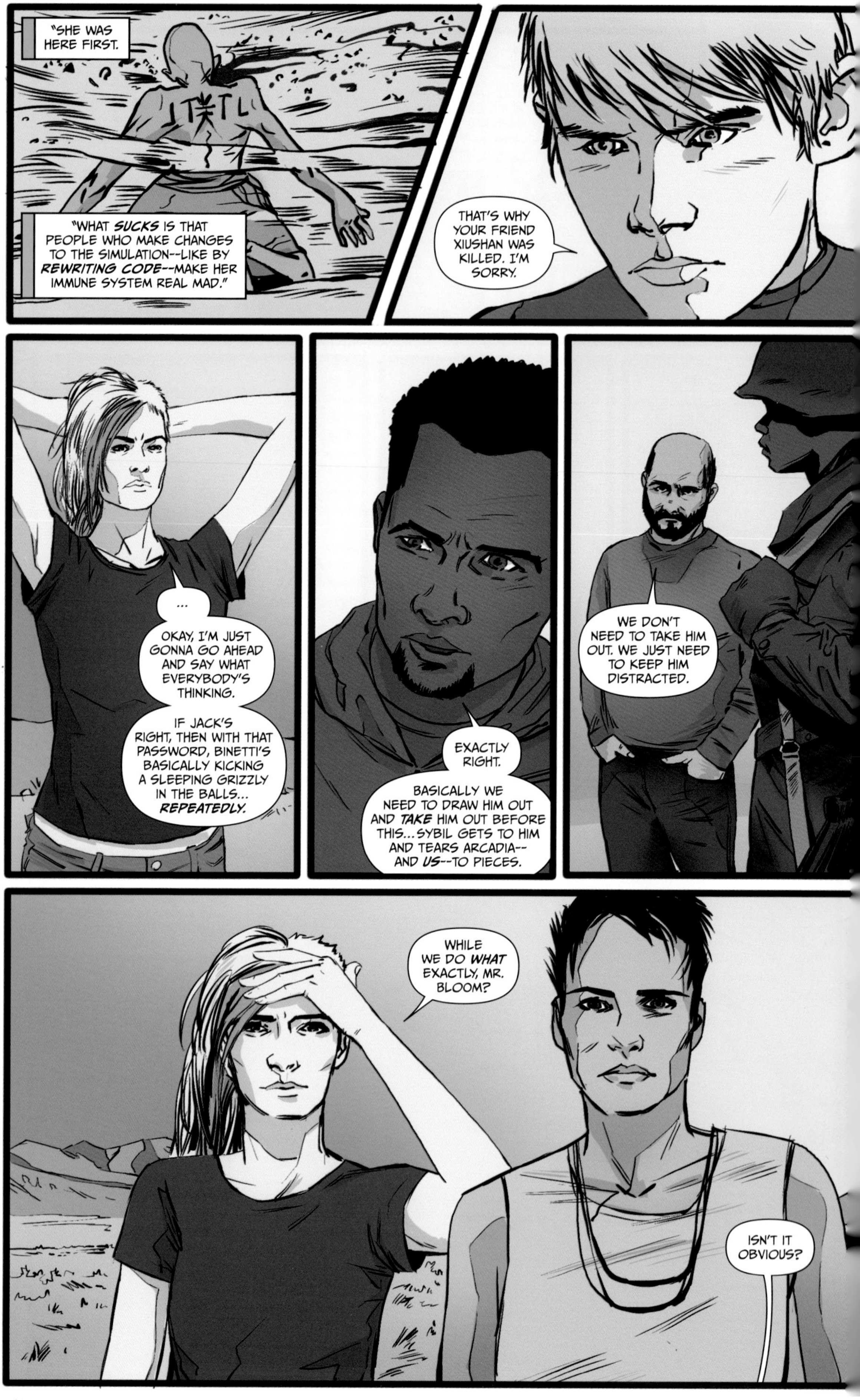
"SHE WAS HERE FIRST.
"WHAT SUCKS IS THAT PEOPLE WHO MAKE CHANGES TO THE SIMULATION--LIKE BY REWRITING CODE--MAKE HER IMMUNE SYSTEM REAL MAD."
THAT'S WHY YOUR FRIEND XIUSHAN WAS KILLED. I'M SORRY.
...
OKAY, I'M JUST GONNA GO AHEAD AND SAY WHAT EVERYBODY'S THINKING.
IF JACK'S RIGHT, THEN WITH THAT PASSWORD, BINETTI'S BASICALLY KICKING A SLEEPING GRIZZLY IN THE BALLS... REPEATEDLY.
EXACTLY RIGHT.
BASICALLY WE NEED TO DRAW HIM OUT AND TAKE HIM OUT BEFORE THIS... SYBIL GETS TO HIM AND TEARS ARCADIA-- AND US--TO PIECES.
WE DON'T NEED TO TAKE HIM OUT. WE JUST NEED TO KEEP HIM DISTRACTED.
WHILE WE DO WHAT EXACTLY, MR. BLOOM?
ISN'T IT OBVIOUS?

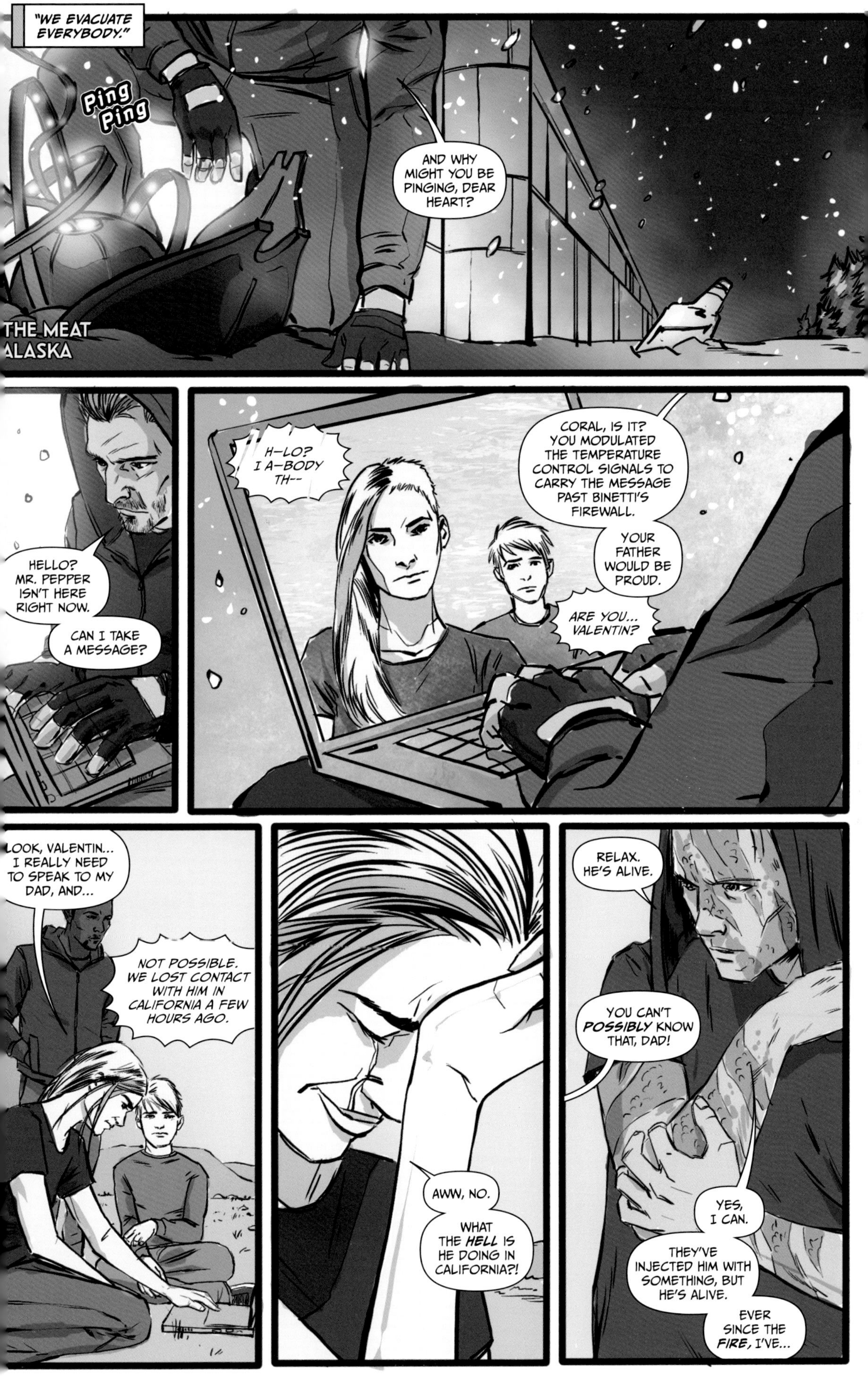
"WE EVACUATE EVERYBODY."
Ping Ping
AND WHY MIGHT YOU BE PINGING, DEAR HEART?
THE MEAT
ALASKA
HELLO? MR. PEPPER ISN'T HERE RIGHT NOW.
CAN I TAKE A MESSAGE?
H-LO? I A-BODY TH--
CORAL, IS IT? YOU MODULATED THE TEMPERATURE CONTROL SIGNALS TO CARRY THE MESSAGE PAST BINETTI'S FIREWALL.
YOUR FATHER WOULD BE PROUD.
ARE YOU... VALENTIN?
LOOK, VALENTIN... I REALLY NEED TO SPEAK TO MY DAD, AND...
NOT POSSIBLE. WE LOST CONTACT WITH HIM IN CALIFORNIA A FEW HOURS AGO.
AWW, NO.
WHAT THE HELL IS HE DOING IN CALIFORNIA?!
RELAX. HE'S ALIVE.
YOU CAN'T POSSIBLY KNOW THAT, DAD!
YES, I CAN.
THEY'VE INJECTED HIM WITH SOMETHING, BUT HE'S ALIVE.
EVER SINCE THE FIRE, I'VE...

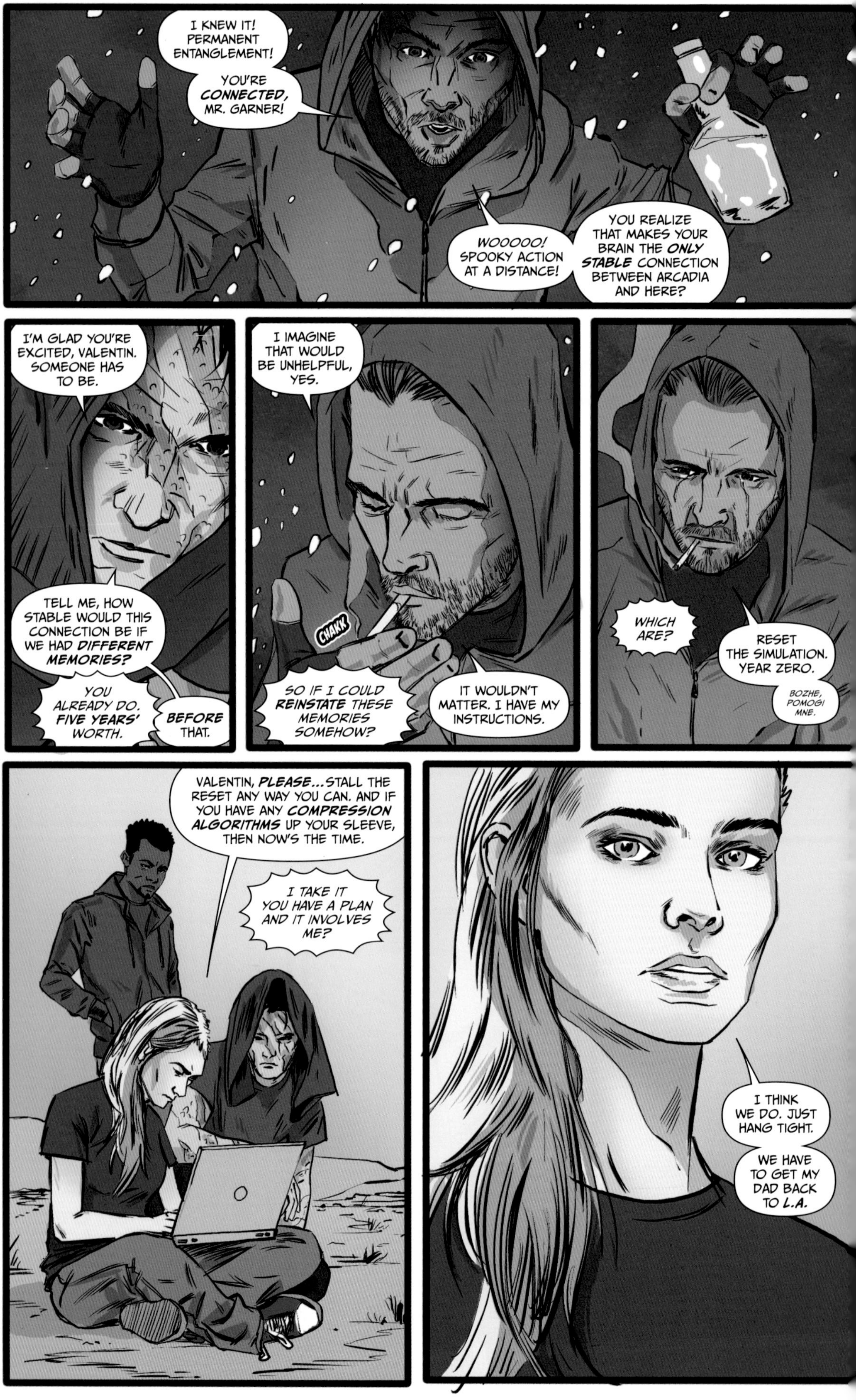

I KNEW IT! PERMANENT ENTANGLEMENT!
YOU'RE CONNECTED, MR. GARNER!
WOOOOO! SPOOKY ACTION AT A DISTANCE!
YOU REALIZE THAT MAKES YOUR BRAIN THE ONLY STABLE CONNECTION BETWEEN ARCADIA AND HERE?
I'M GLAD YOU'RE EXCITED, VALENTIN. SOMEONE HAS TO BE.
TELL ME, HOW STABLE WOULD THIS CONNECTION BE IF WE HAD DIFFERENT MEMORIES?
YOU ALREADY DO. FIVE YEARS' WORTH.
BEFORE THAT.
I IMAGINE THAT WOULD BE UNHELPFUL, YES.
CHAKK
SO IF I COULD REINSTATE THESE MEMORIES SOMEHOW?
IT WOULDN'T MATTER. I HAVE MY INSTRUCTIONS.
WHICH ARE?
RESET THE SIMULATION. YEAR ZERO.
BOZHE, POMOGI MNE.
VALENTIN, PLEASE... STALL THE RESET ANY WAY YOU CAN. AND IF YOU HAVE ANY COMPRESSION ALGORITHMS UP YOUR SLEEVE, THEN NOW'S THE TIME.
I TAKE IT YOU HAVE A PLAN AND IT INVOLVES ME?
I THINK WE DO. JUST HANG TIGHT.
WE HAVE TO GET MY DAD BACK TO L.A.

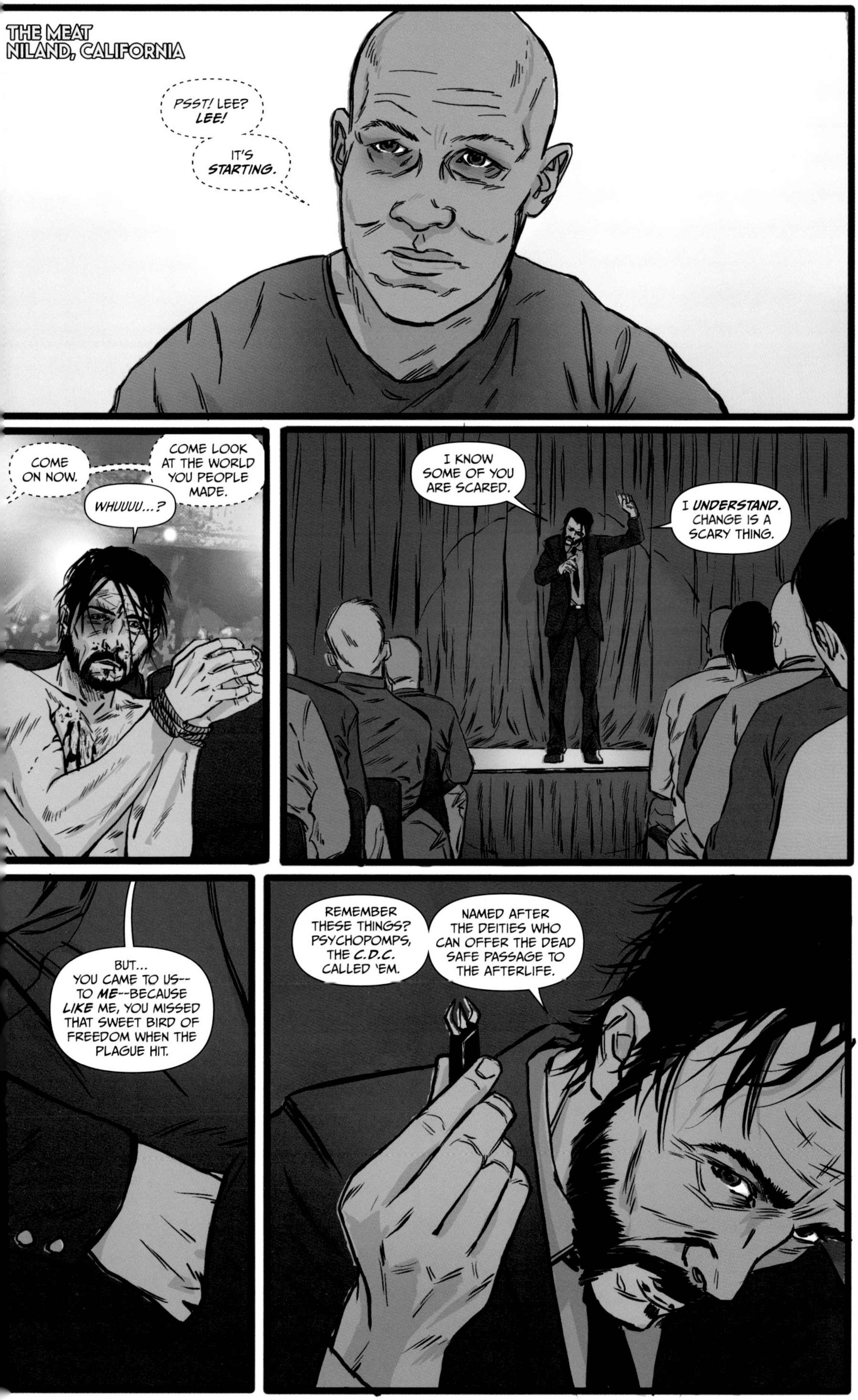
THE MEAT
NILAND, CALIFORNIA
PSST! LEE? LEE!
IT'S STARTING.
COME ON NOW.
COME LOOK AT THE WORLD YOU PEOPLE MADE.
WHUUUU...?
I KNOW SOME OF YOU ARE SCARED.
I UNDERSTAND. CHANGE IS A SCARY THING.
BUT... YOU CAME TO US-- TO ME--BECAUSE LIKE ME, YOU MISSED THAT SWEET BIRD OF FREEDOM WHEN THE PLAGUE HIT.
REMEMBER THESE THINGS? PSYCHOPOMPS, THE C.D.C. CALLED 'EM.
NAMED AFTER THE DEITIES WHO CAN OFFER THE DEAD SAFE PASSAGE TO THE AFTERLIFE.

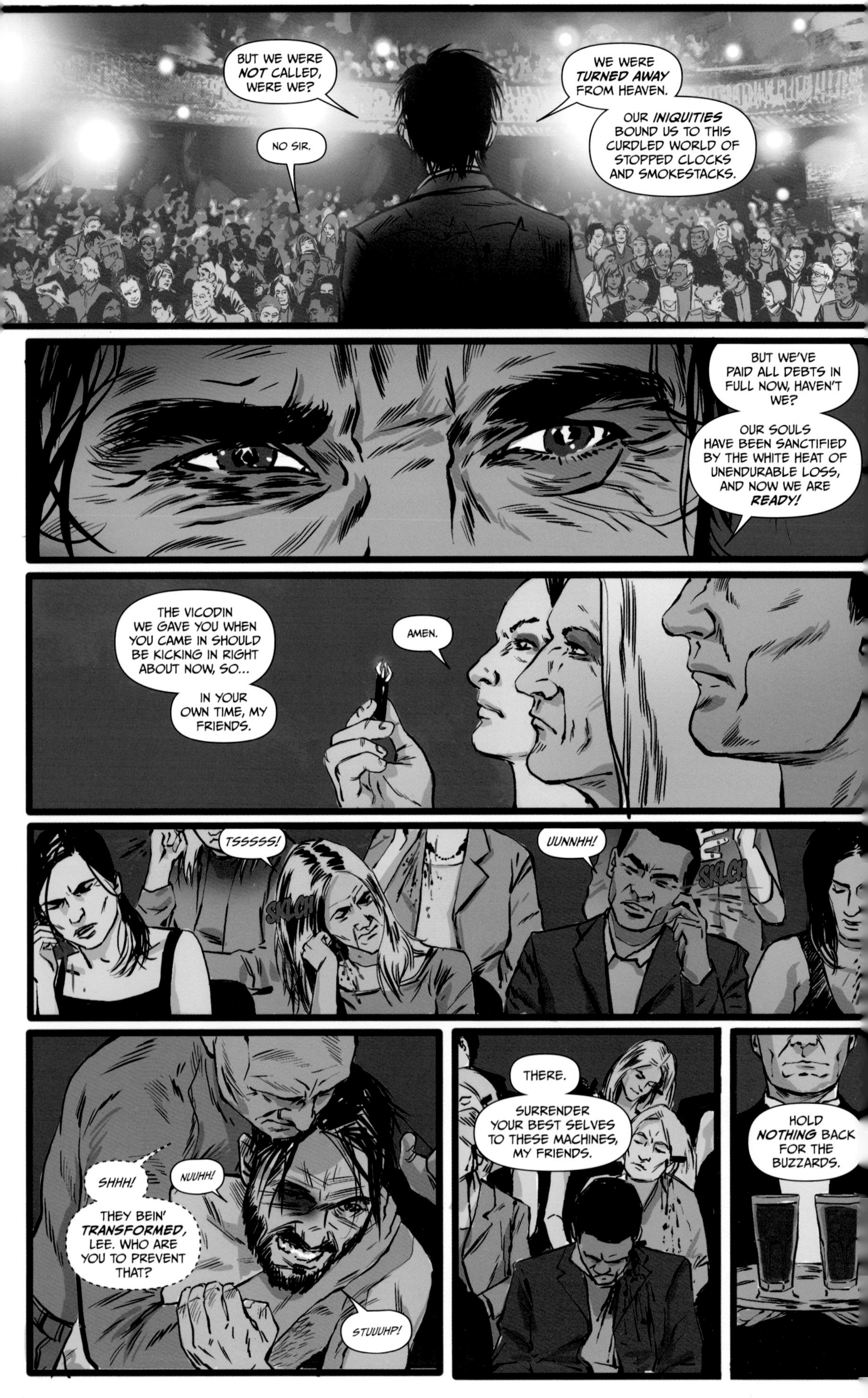
BUT WE WERE *NOT* CALLED, WERE WE?
NO SIR.
WE WERE *TURNED AWAY* FROM HEAVEN.
OUR *INIQUITIES* BOUND US TO THIS CURDLED WORLD OF STOPPED CLOCKS AND SMOKESTACKS.
BUT WE'VE PAID ALL DEBTS IN FULL NOW, HAVEN'T WE?
OUR SOULS HAVE BEEN SANCTIFIED BY THE WHITE HEAT OF UNENDURABLE LOSS, AND NOW WE ARE *READY!*
THE VICODIN WE GAVE YOU WHEN YOU CAME IN SHOULD BE KICKING IN RIGHT ABOUT NOW, SO...
IN YOUR OWN TIME, MY FRIENDS.
AMEN.
TSSSSS!
SKLCH
UUNNHH!
SKLCH
SHHH!
NUUHH!
THEY BEIN' *TRANSFORMED,* LEE. WHO ARE YOU TO PREVENT THAT?
STUUUHP!
THERE.
SURRENDER YOUR BEST SELVES TO THESE MACHINES, MY FRIENDS.
HOLD *NOTHING* BACK FOR THE BUZZARDS.

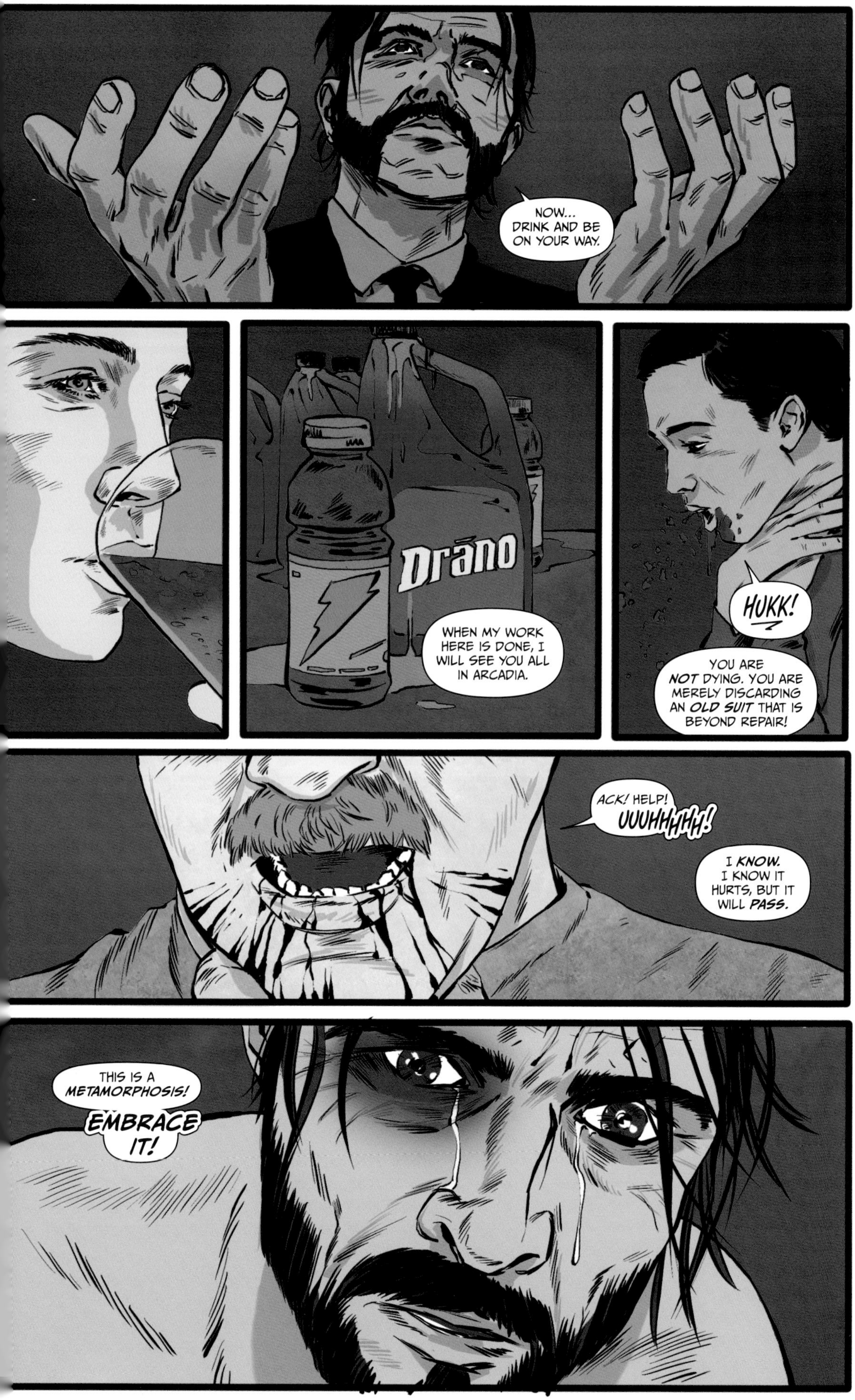
NOW...
DRINK AND BE ON YOUR WAY.
Drāno
WHEN MY WORK HERE IS DONE, I WILL SEE YOU ALL IN ARCADIA.
HUKK!
YOU ARE NOT DYING. YOU ARE MERELY DISCARDING AN OLD SUIT THAT IS BEYOND REPAIR!
ACK! HELP! UUUHHHHH!
I KNOW. I KNOW IT HURTS, BUT IT WILL PASS.
THIS IS A METAMORPHOSIS!
EMBRACE IT!

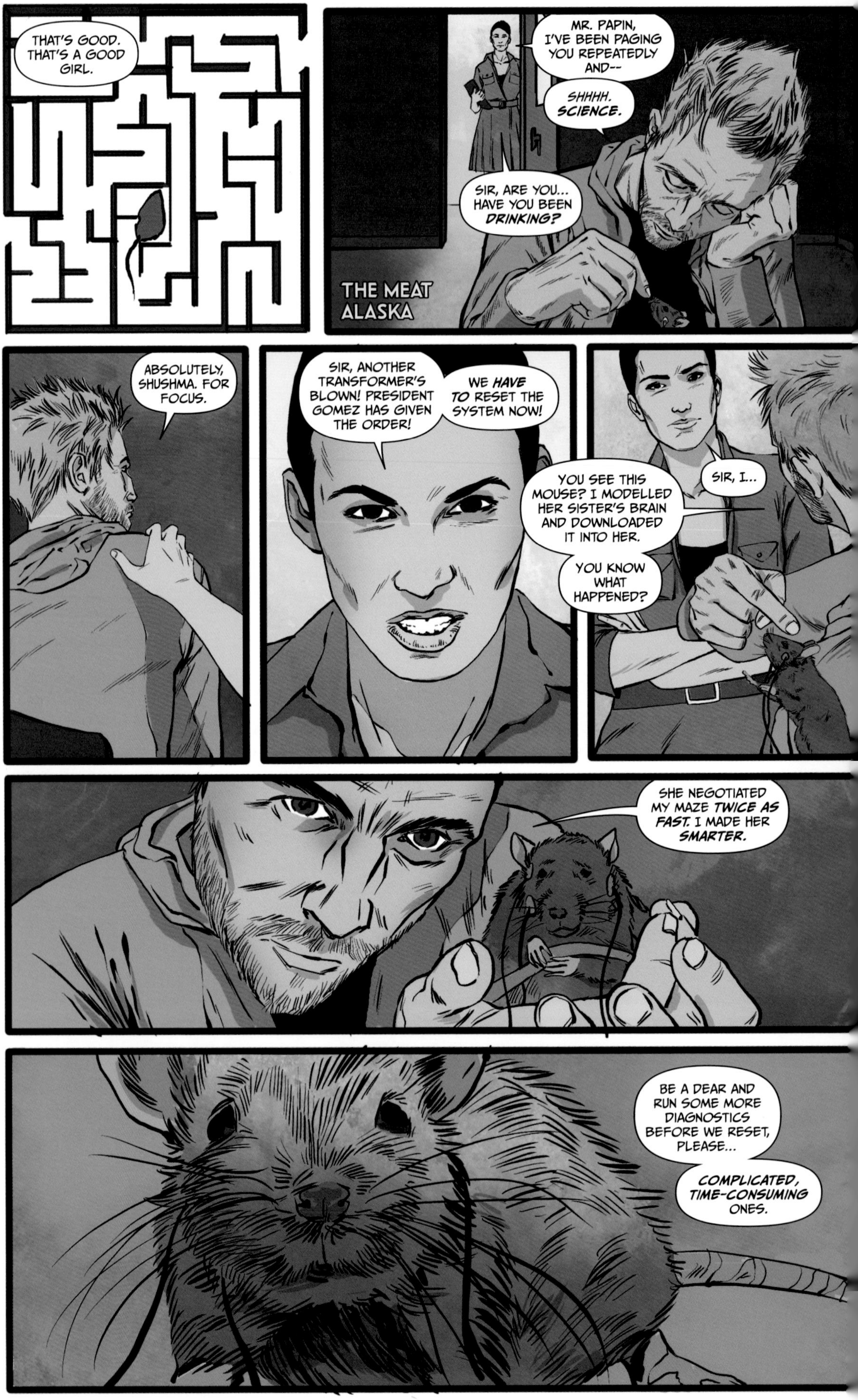
THAT'S GOOD. THAT'S A GOOD GIRL.
MR. PAPIN, I'VE BEEN PAGING YOU REPEATEDLY AND--
SHHHH. SCIENCE.
SIR, ARE YOU... HAVE YOU BEEN DRINKING?
THE MEAT ALASKA
ABSOLUTELY, SHUSHMA. FOR FOCUS.
SIR, ANOTHER TRANSFORMER'S BLOWN! PRESIDENT GOMEZ HAS GIVEN THE ORDER!
WE HAVE TO RESET THE SYSTEM NOW!
SIR, I...
YOU SEE THIS MOUSE? I MODELLED HER SISTER'S BRAIN AND DOWNLOADED IT INTO HER.
YOU KNOW WHAT HAPPENED?
SHE NEGOTIATED MY MAZE TWICE AS FAST. I MADE HER SMARTER.
BE A DEAR AND RUN SOME MORE DIAGNOSTICS BEFORE WE RESET, PLEASE...
COMPLICATED, TIME-CONSUMING ONES.

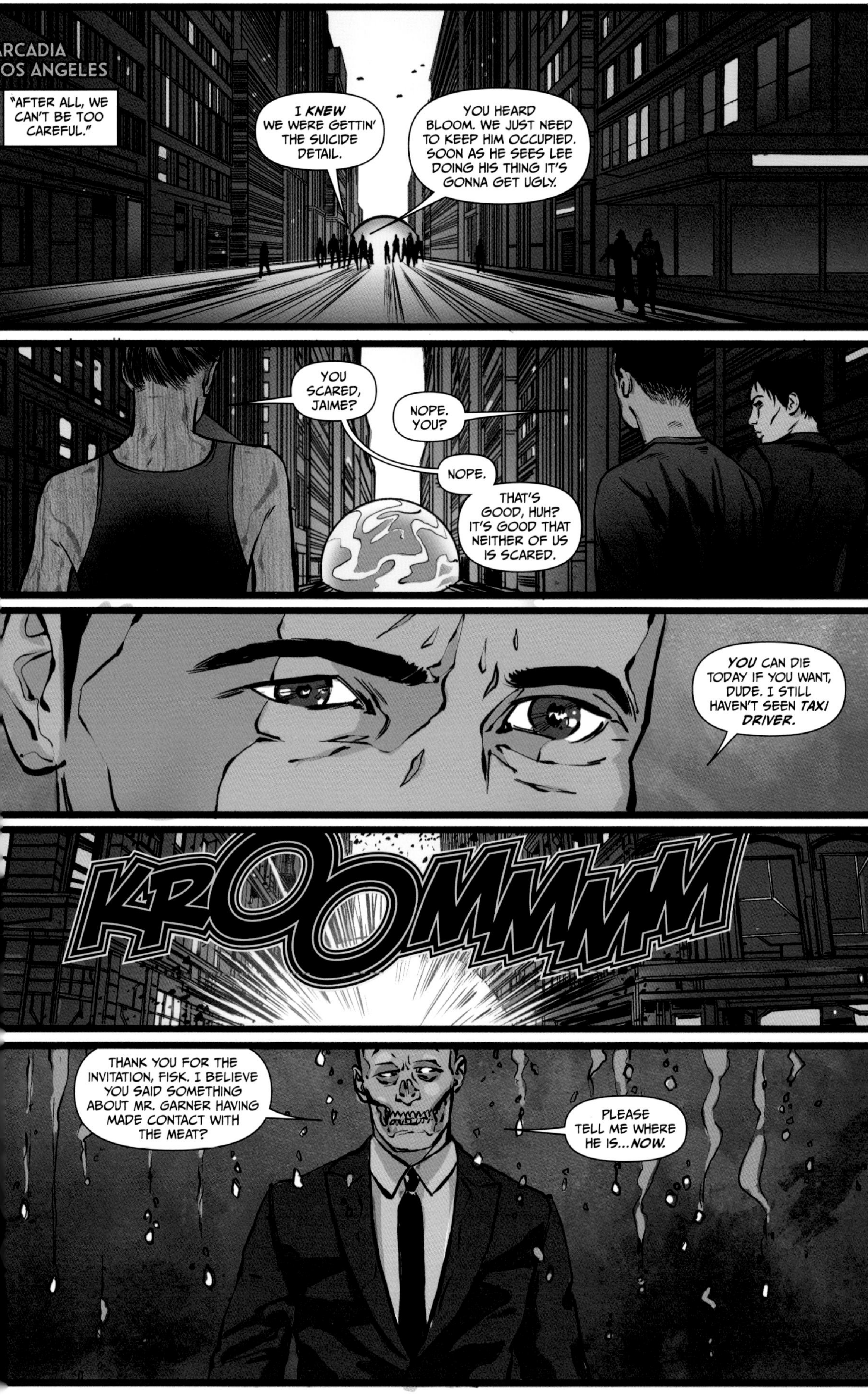
ARCADIA
LOS ANGELES
"AFTER ALL, WE CAN'T BE TOO CAREFUL."
I *KNEW* WE WERE GETTIN' THE SUICIDE DETAIL.
YOU HEARD BLOOM. WE JUST NEED TO KEEP HIM OCCUPIED. SOON AS HE SEES LEE DOING HIS THING IT'S GONNA GET UGLY.
YOU SCARED, JAIME?
NOPE. YOU?
NOPE.
THAT'S GOOD, HUH? IT'S GOOD THAT NEITHER OF US IS SCARED.
YOU CAN DIE TODAY IF YOU WANT, DUDE. I STILL HAVEN'T SEEN *TAXI DRIVER.*
KROOOMMMMM
THANK YOU FOR THE INVITATION, FISK. I BELIEVE YOU SAID SOMETHING ABOUT MR. GARNER HAVING MADE CONTACT WITH THE MEAT?
PLEASE TELL ME WHERE HE IS...*NOW.*

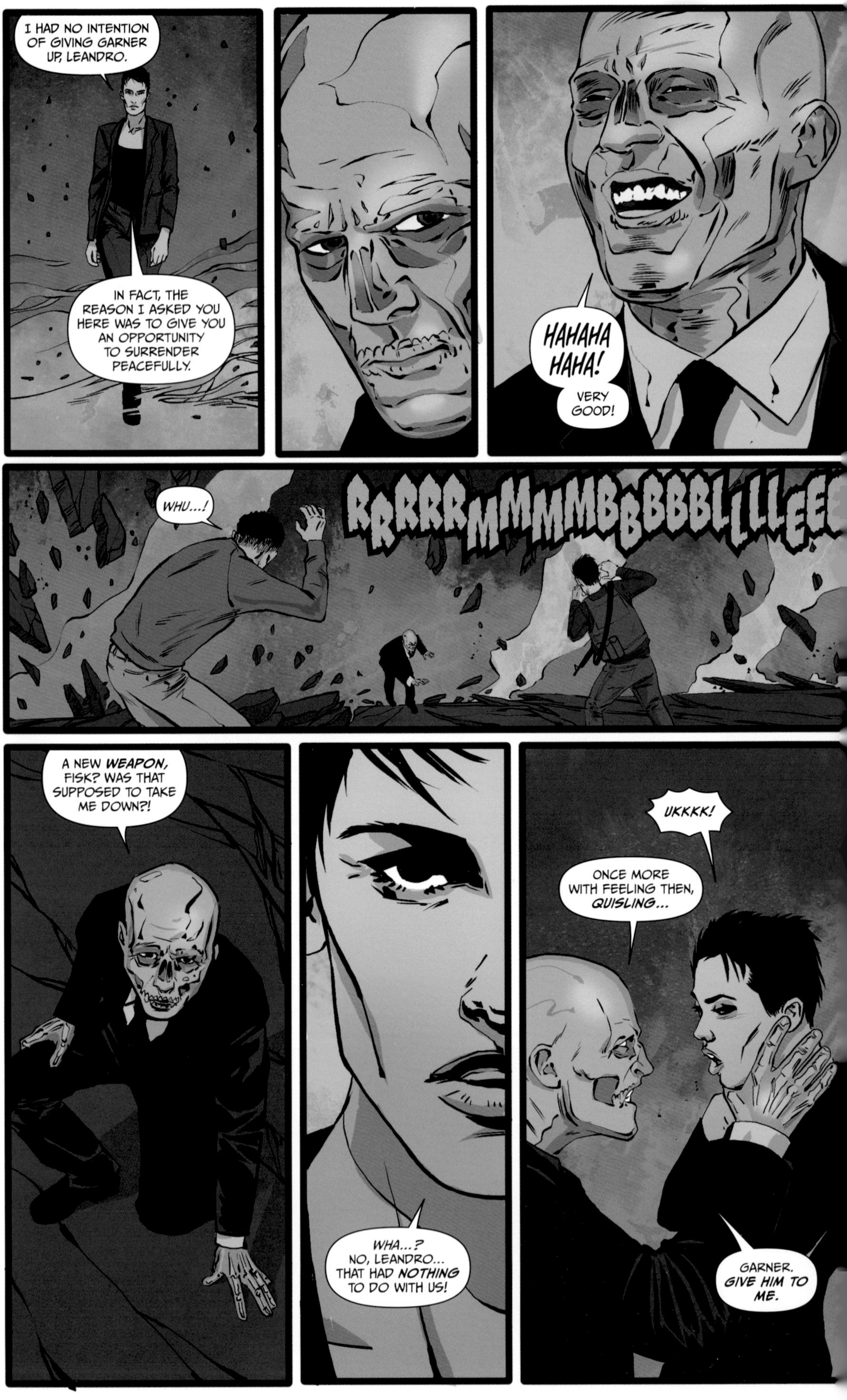
I HAD NO INTENTION OF GIVING GARNER UP, LEANDRO.
IN FACT, THE REASON I ASKED YOU HERE WAS TO GIVE YOU AN OPPORTUNITY TO SURRENDER PEACEFULLY.
HAHAHA HAHA!
VERY GOOD!
WHU...!
RRRRRMMMMMBBBBBLLLLEEE
A NEW *WEAPON*, FISK? WAS THAT SUPPOSED TO TAKE ME DOWN?!
WHA...? NO, LEANDRO... THAT HAD *NOTHING* TO DO WITH US!
UKKKK!
ONCE MORE WITH FEELING THEN, *QUISLING...*
GARNER. *GIVE HIM TO ME.*

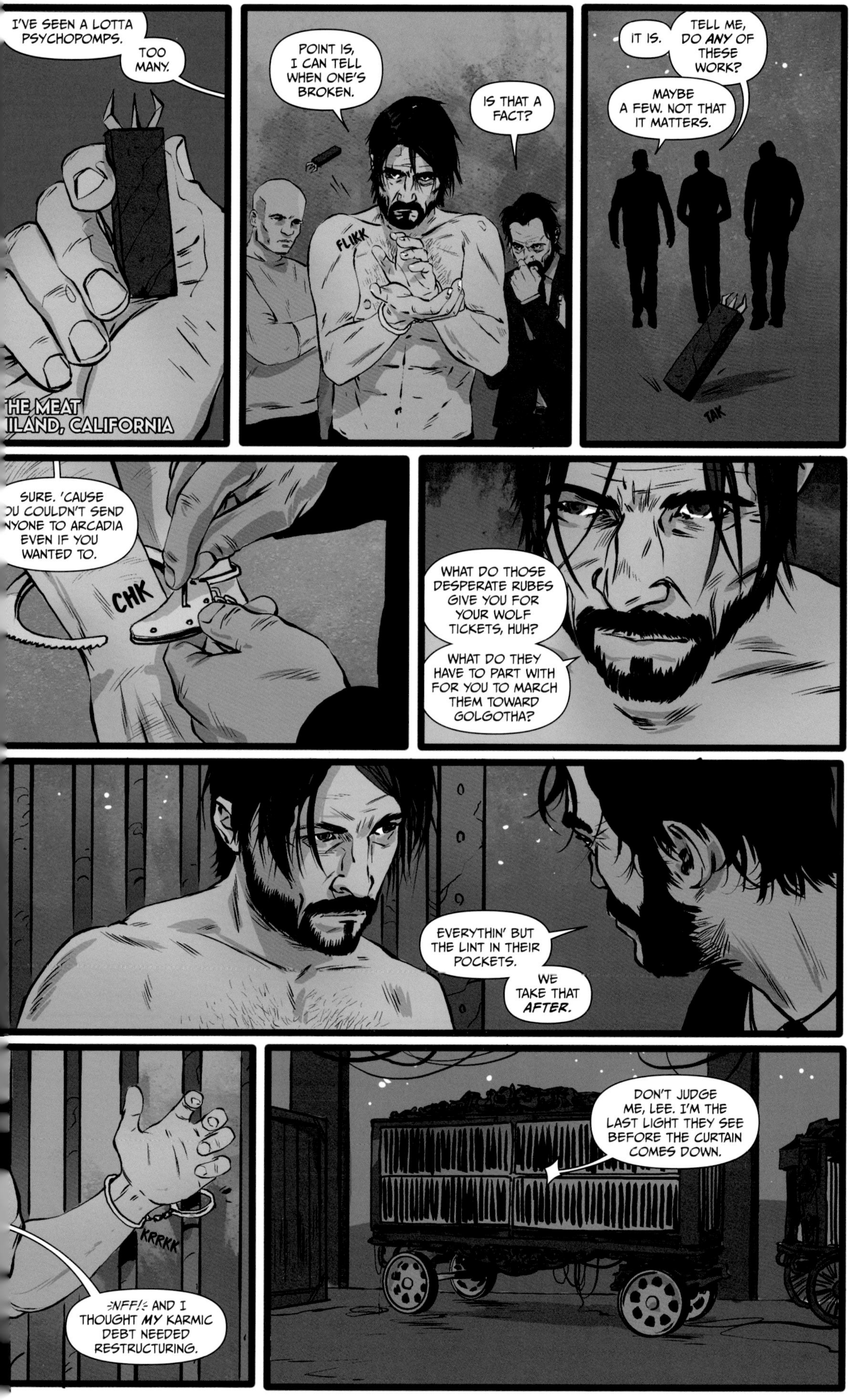
I'VE SEEN A LOTTA PSYCHOPOMPS.
TOO MANY.
THE MEAT
ILAND, CALIFORNIA
POINT IS, I CAN TELL WHEN ONE'S BROKEN.
IS THAT A FACT?
FLIKK
IT IS.
TELL ME, DO ANY OF THESE WORK?
MAYBE A FEW. NOT THAT IT MATTERS.
TAK
SURE. 'CAUSE
OU COULDN'T SEND
NYONE TO ARCADIA
EVEN IF YOU
WANTED TO.
CHK
WHAT DO THOSE DESPERATE RUBES GIVE YOU FOR YOUR WOLF TICKETS, HUH?
WHAT DO THEY HAVE TO PART WITH FOR YOU TO MARCH THEM TOWARD GOLGOTHA?
EVERYTHIN' BUT THE LINT IN THEIR POCKETS.
WE TAKE THAT AFTER.
KRRKK
SNFF! AND I THOUGHT MY KARMIC DEBT NEEDED RESTRUCTURING.
DON'T JUDGE ME, LEE. I'M THE LAST LIGHT THEY SEE BEFORE THE CURTAIN COMES DOWN.

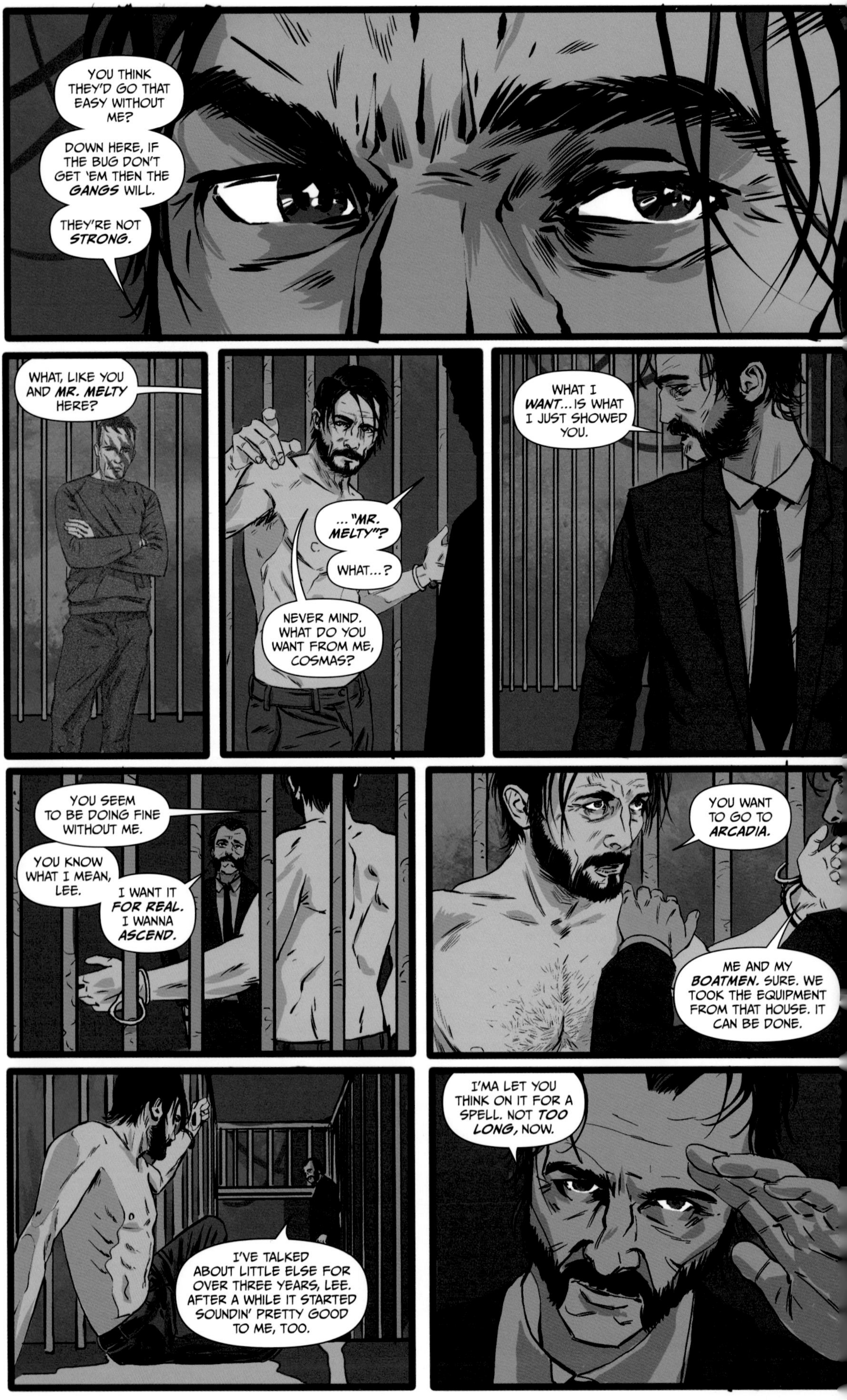
YOU THINK THEY'D GO THAT EASY WITHOUT ME?
DOWN HERE, IF THE BUG DON'T GET 'EM THEN THE *GANGS* WILL.
THEY'RE NOT *STRONG.*
WHAT, LIKE YOU AND *MR. MELTY* HERE?
..."*MR. MELTY*"?
WHAT...?
NEVER MIND. WHAT DO YOU WANT FROM ME, COSMAS?
WHAT I *WANT*...IS WHAT I JUST SHOWED YOU.
YOU SEEM TO BE DOING FINE WITHOUT ME.
YOU KNOW WHAT I MEAN, LEE.
I WANT IT *FOR REAL.* I WANNA *ASCEND.*
YOU WANT TO GO TO *ARCADIA.*
ME AND MY *BOATMEN.* SURE. WE TOOK THE EQUIPMENT FROM THAT HOUSE. IT CAN BE DONE.
I'VE TALKED ABOUT LITTLE ELSE FOR OVER THREE YEARS, LEE. AFTER A WHILE IT STARTED SOUNDIN' PRETTY GOOD TO ME, TOO.
I'MA LET YOU THINK ON IT FOR A SPELL. NOT *TOO LONG,* NOW.

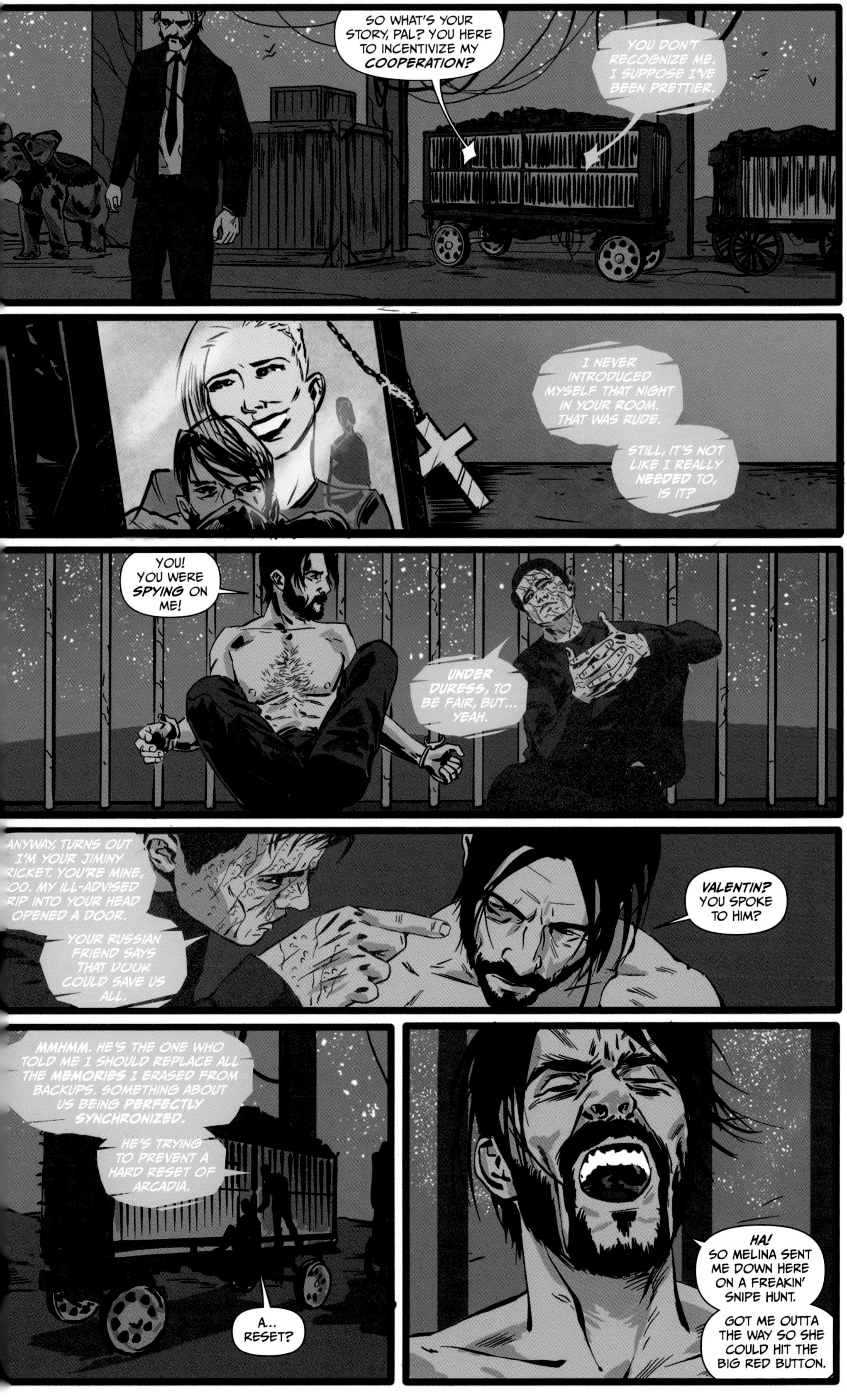
SO WHAT'S YOUR STORY, PAL? YOU HERE TO INCENTIVIZE MY COOPERATION?
YOU DON'T RECOGNIZE ME. I SUPPOSE I'VE BEEN PRETTIER.
I NEVER INTRODUCED MYSELF THAT NIGHT IN YOUR ROOM. THAT WAS RUDE.
STILL, IT'S NOT LIKE I REALLY NEEDED TO, IS IT?
YOU! YOU WERE SPYING ON ME!
UNDER DURESS, TO BE FAIR, BUT... YEAH.
ANYWAY, TURNS OUT I'M YOUR JIMINY CRICKET. YOU'RE MINE, TOO. MY ILL-ADVISED TRIP INTO YOUR HEAD OPENED A DOOR.
YOUR RUSSIAN FRIEND SAYS THAT DOOK COULD SAVE US ALL.
VALENTIN? YOU SPOKE TO HIM?
MMHMM. HE'S THE ONE WHO TOLD ME I SHOULD REPLACE ALL THE MEMORIES I ERASED FROM BACKUPS. SOMETHING ABOUT US BEING PERFECTLY SYNCHRONIZED.
HE'S TRYING TO PREVENT A HARD RESET OF ARCADIA.
A... RESET?
HA! SO MELINA SENT ME DOWN HERE ON A FREAKIN' SNIPE HUNT.
GOT ME OUTTA THE WAY SO SHE COULD HIT THE BIG RED BUTTON.

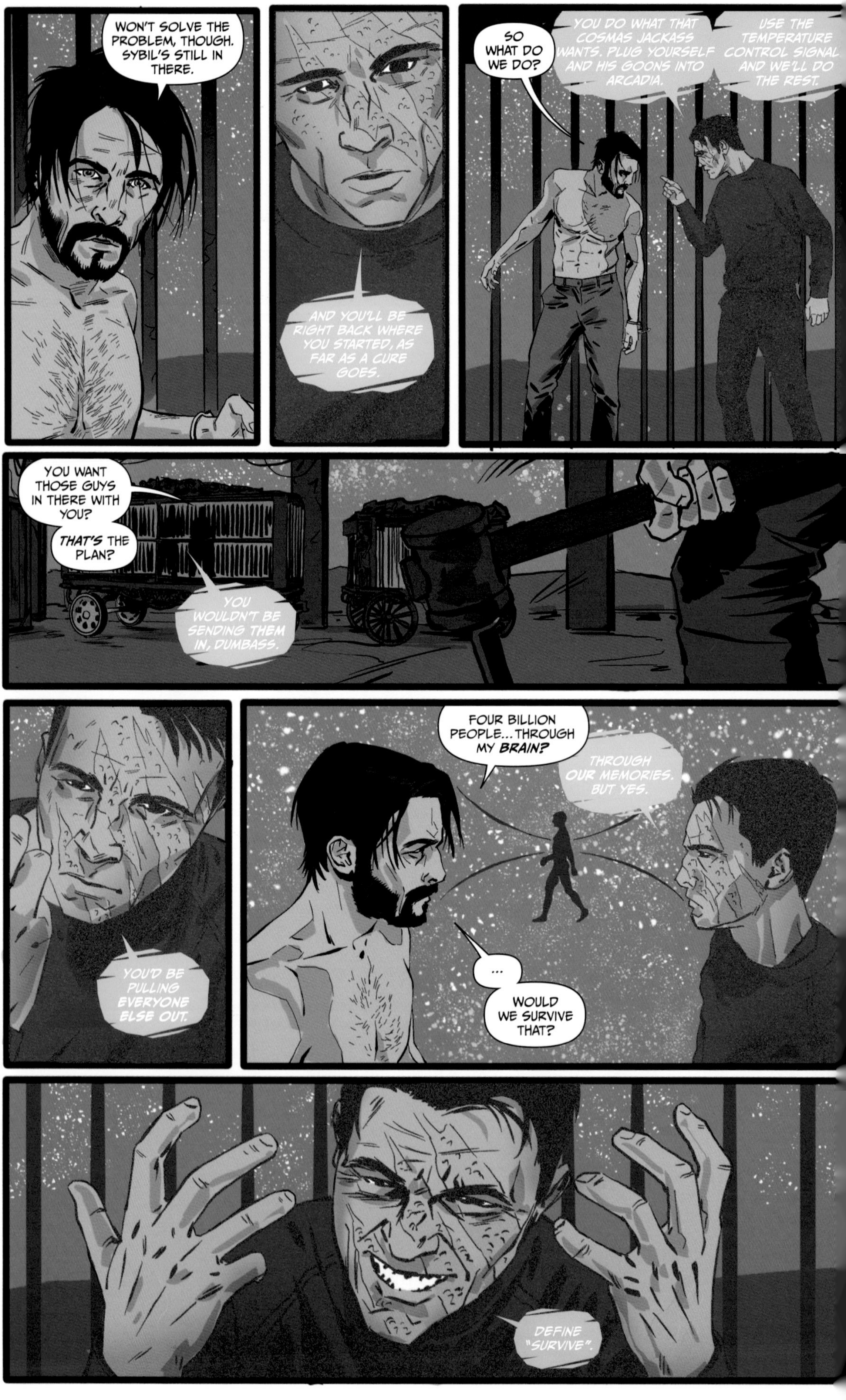
WON'T SOLVE THE PROBLEM, THOUGH. SYBIL'S STILL IN THERE.
AND YOU'LL BE RIGHT BACK WHERE YOU STARTED, AS FAR AS A CURE GOES.
SO WHAT DO WE DO?
YOU DO WHAT THAT COSMAS JACKASS WANTS. PLUG YOURSELF AND HIS GOONS INTO ARCADIA.
USE THE TEMPERATURE CONTROL SIGNAL AND WE'LL DO THE REST.
YOU WANT THOSE GUYS IN THERE WITH YOU?
THAT'S THE PLAN?
YOU WOULDN'T BE SENDING THEM IN, DUMBASS.
YOU'D BE PULLING EVERYONE ELSE OUT.
FOUR BILLION PEOPLE... THROUGH MY BRAIN?
THROUGH OUR MEMORIES. BUT YES.
...
WOULD WE SURVIVE THAT?
DEFINE "SURVIVE".

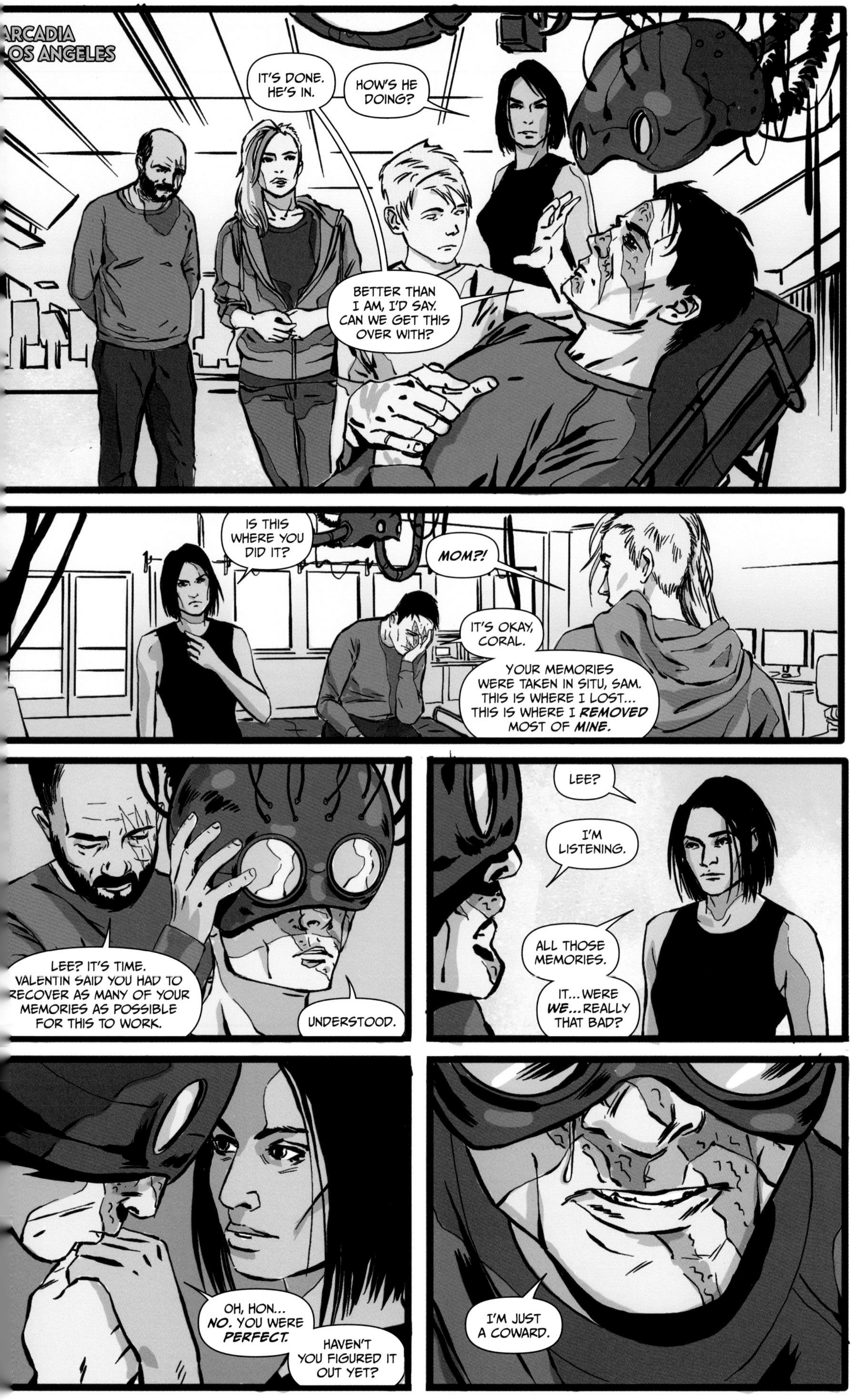

ARCADIA
LOS ANGELES
IT'S DONE. HE'S IN.
HOW'S HE DOING?
BETTER THAN I AM, I'D SAY. CAN WE GET THIS OVER WITH?
IS THIS WHERE YOU DID IT?
MOM?!
IT'S OKAY, CORAL.
YOUR MEMORIES WERE TAKEN IN SITU, SAM. THIS IS WHERE I LOST... THIS IS WHERE I REMOVED MOST OF MINE.
LEE? IT'S TIME. VALENTIN SAID YOU HAD TO RECOVER AS MANY OF YOUR MEMORIES AS POSSIBLE FOR THIS TO WORK.
UNDERSTOOD.
LEE?
I'M LISTENING.
ALL THOSE MEMORIES.
IT... WERE WE... REALLY THAT BAD?
OH, HON... NO. YOU WERE PERFECT.
HAVEN'T YOU FIGURED IT OUT YET?
I'M JUST A COWARD.

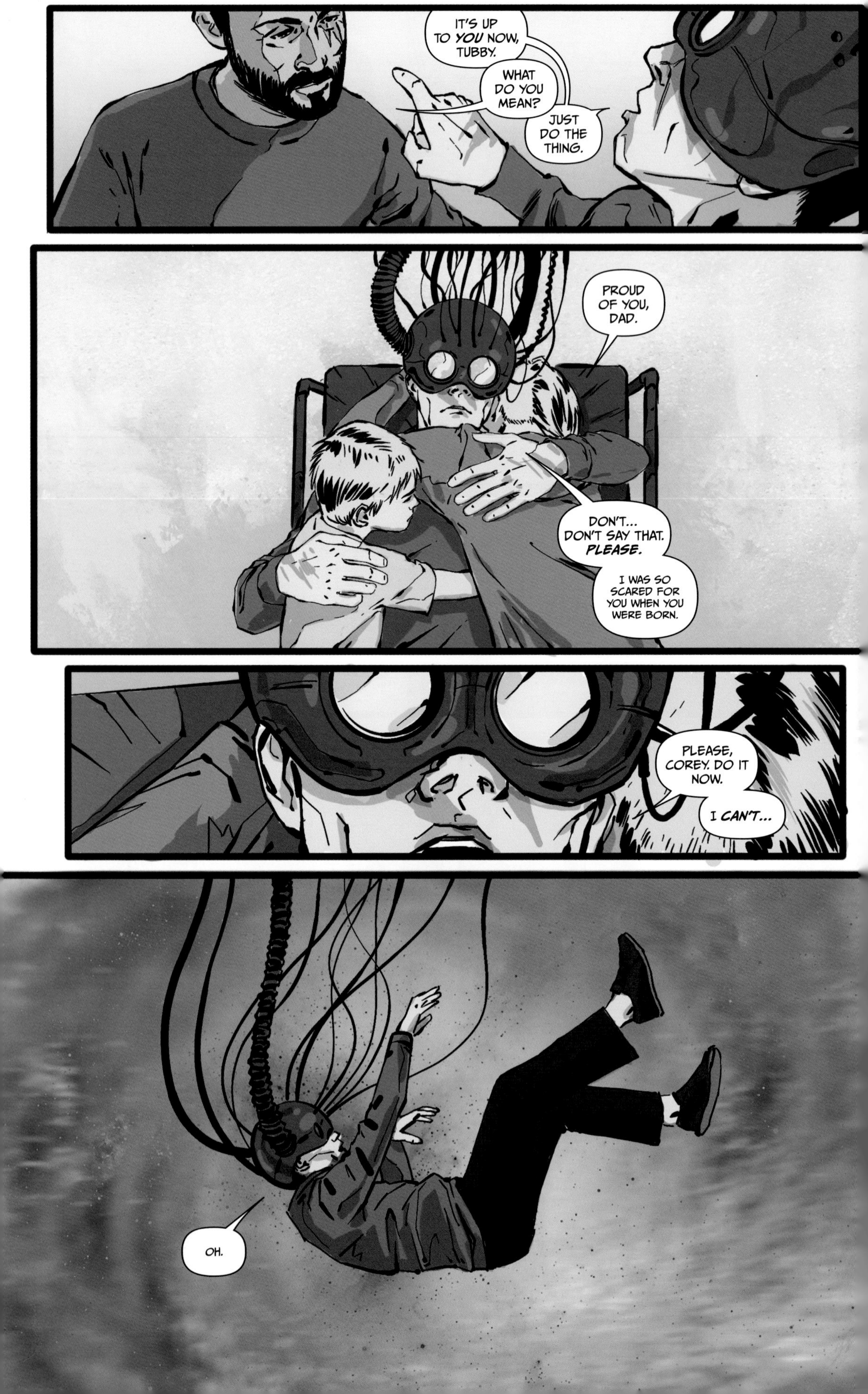
IT'S UP TO *YOU* NOW, TUBBY.
WHAT DO YOU MEAN?
JUST DO THE THING.
PROUD OF YOU, DAD.
DON'T... DON'T SAY THAT. ***PLEASE.***
I WAS SO SCARED FOR YOU WHEN YOU WERE BORN.
PLEASE, COREY. DO IT NOW.
I *CAN'T...*
OH.

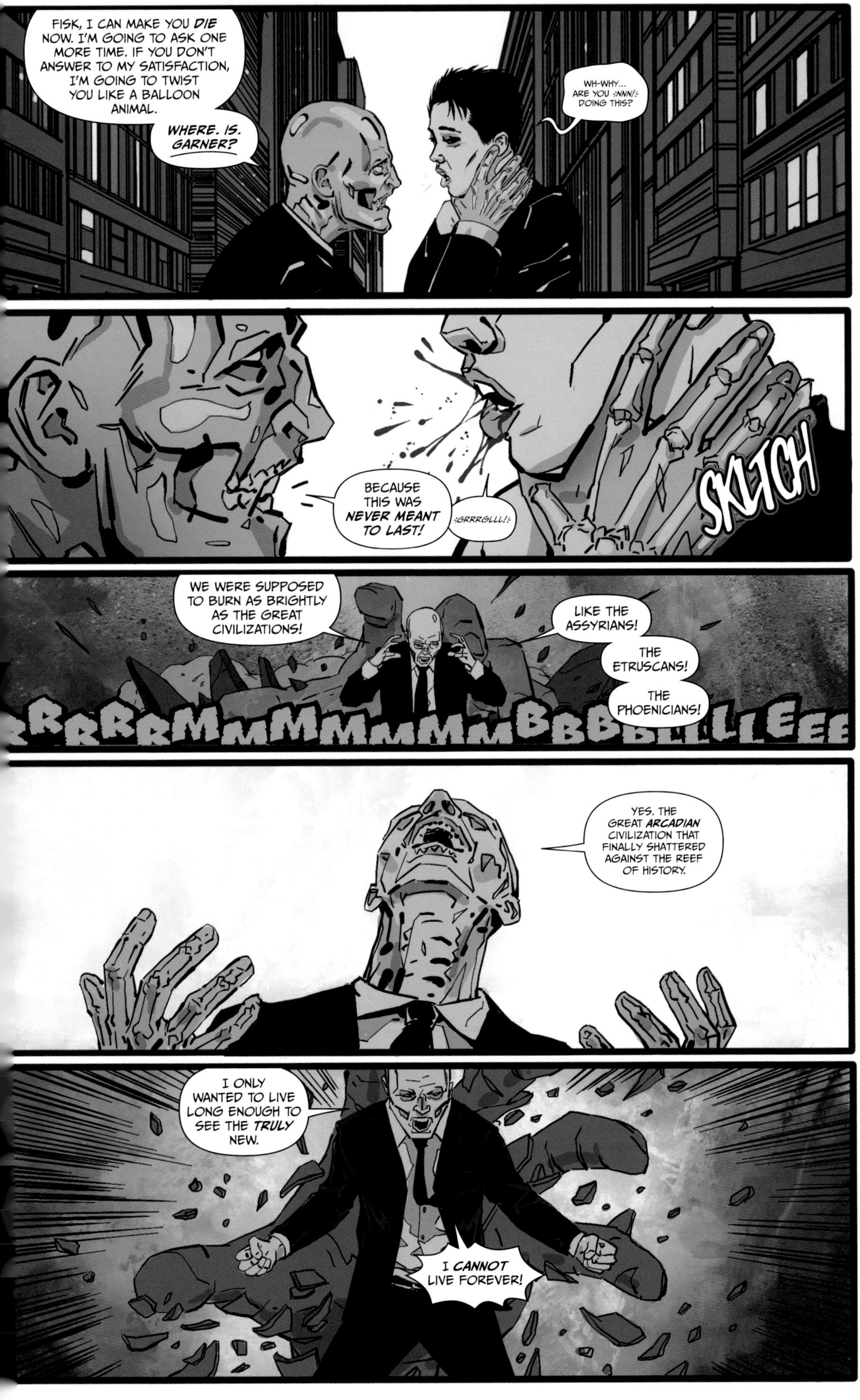
FISK, I CAN MAKE YOU DIE NOW. I'M GOING TO ASK ONE MORE TIME. IF YOU DON'T ANSWER TO MY SATISFACTION, I'M GOING TO TWIST YOU LIKE A BALLOON ANIMAL.
WHERE. IS. GARNER?
WH-WHY... ARE YOU NNN! DOING THIS?
BECAUSE THIS WAS NEVER MEANT TO LAST!
GRRRGLLL!
SKLTCH
WE WERE SUPPOSED TO BURN AS BRIGHTLY AS THE GREAT CIVILIZATIONS!
LIKE THE ASSYRIANS!
THE ETRUSCANS!
THE PHOENICIANS!
RRRRRMMMMMMMMMMMBBBBLLLLIEEE
YES. THE GREAT ARCADIAN CIVILIZATION THAT FINALLY SHATTERED AGAINST THE REEF OF HISTORY.
I ONLY WANTED TO LIVE LONG ENOUGH TO SEE THE TRULY NEW.
I CANNOT LIVE FOREVER!

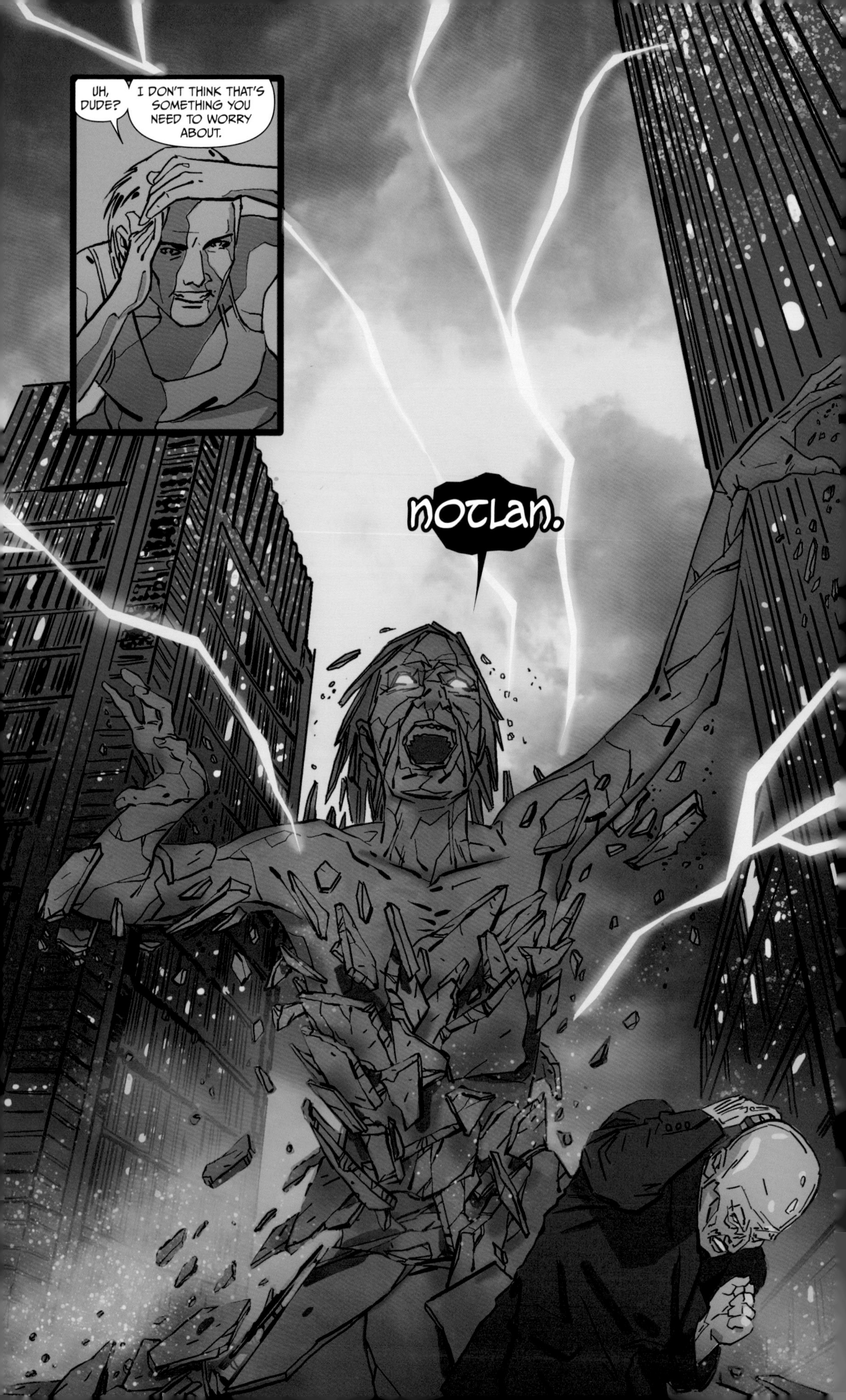
UH, DUDE?
I DON'T THINK THAT'S SOMETHING YOU NEED TO WORRY ABOUT.
NOTLAN.

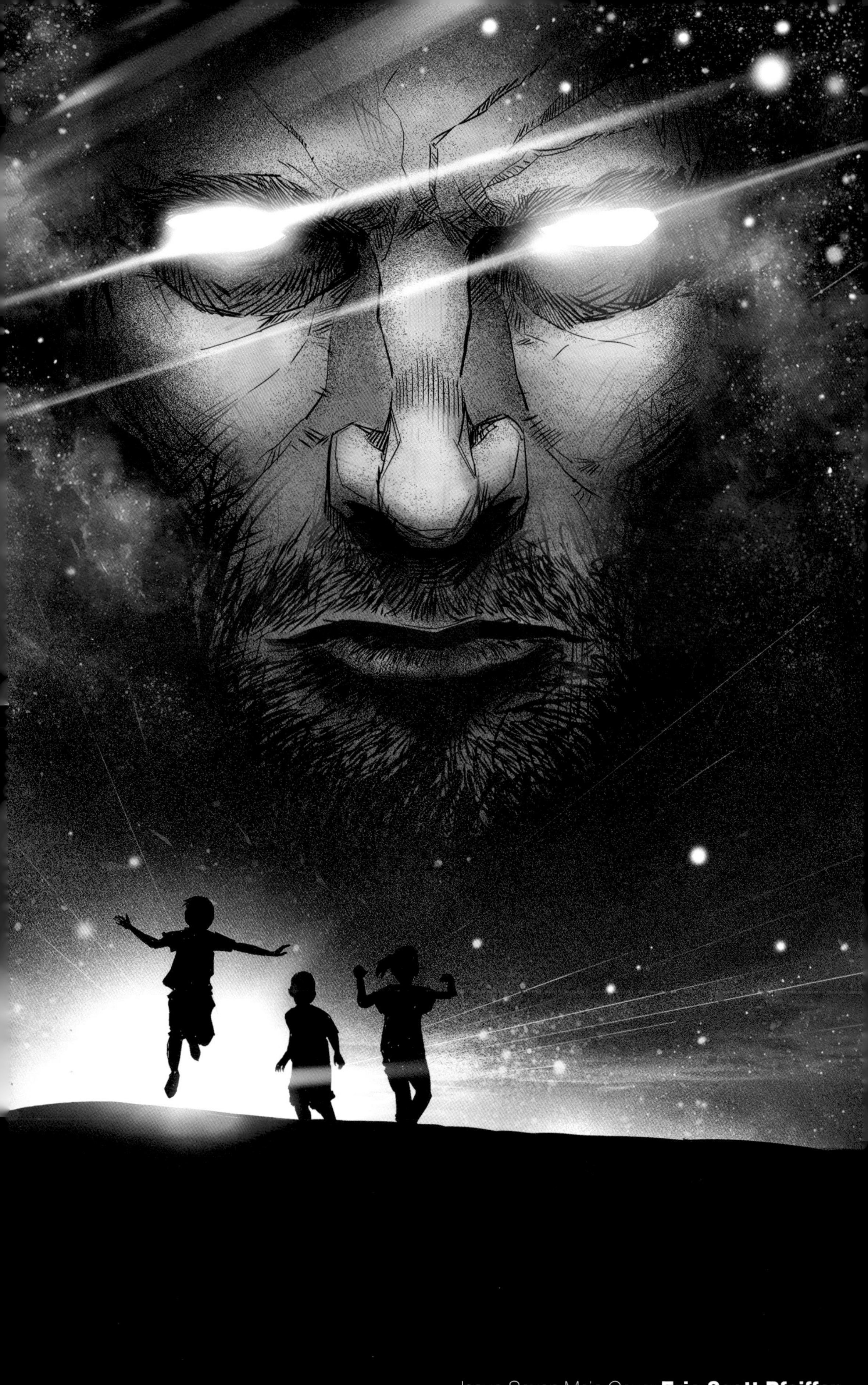

Issue Seven Main Cover **Eric Scott Pfeiffer**

"However, the kingdom had found a way to trick God. It did this by converting its world into code—into bits of light and electricity that would keep pace with time as it raced away from them. And thus the kingdom would live forever."

—**Douglas Coupland**,
Microserfs

CHAPTER
EIGHT

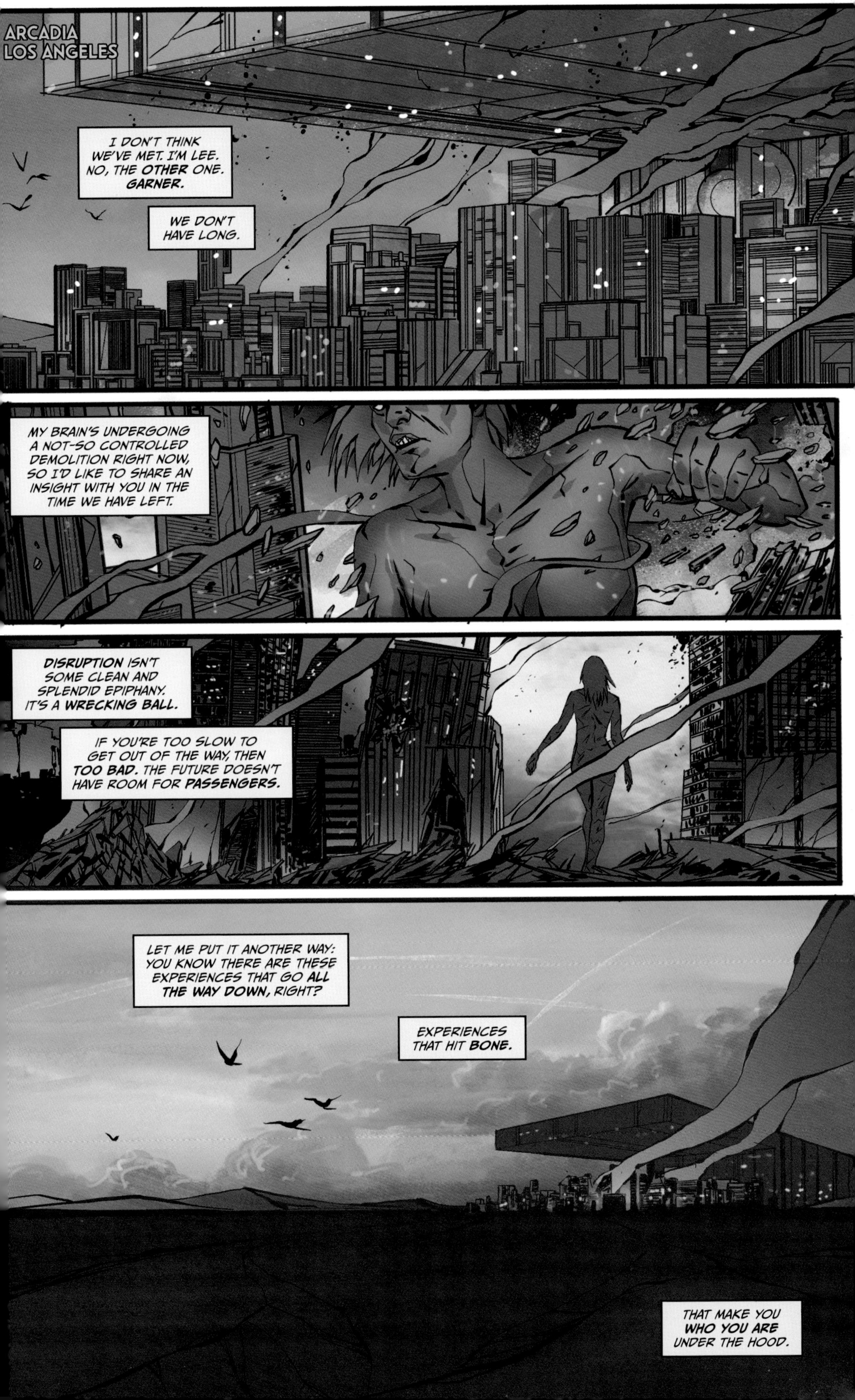
ARCADIA LOS ANGELES
I DON'T THINK WE'VE MET. I'M LEE. NO, THE OTHER ONE. GARNER.
WE DON'T HAVE LONG.
MY BRAIN'S UNDERGOING A NOT-SO CONTROLLED DEMOLITION RIGHT NOW, SO I'D LIKE TO SHARE AN INSIGHT WITH YOU IN THE TIME WE HAVE LEFT.
DISRUPTION ISN'T SOME CLEAN AND SPLENDID EPIPHANY. IT'S A WRECKING BALL.
IF YOU'RE TOO SLOW TO GET OUT OF THE WAY, THEN TOO BAD. THE FUTURE DOESN'T HAVE ROOM FOR PASSENGERS.
LET ME PUT IT ANOTHER WAY: YOU KNOW THERE ARE THESE EXPERIENCES THAT GO ALL THE WAY DOWN, RIGHT?
EXPERIENCES THAT HIT BONE.
THAT MAKE YOU WHO YOU ARE UNDER THE HOOD.

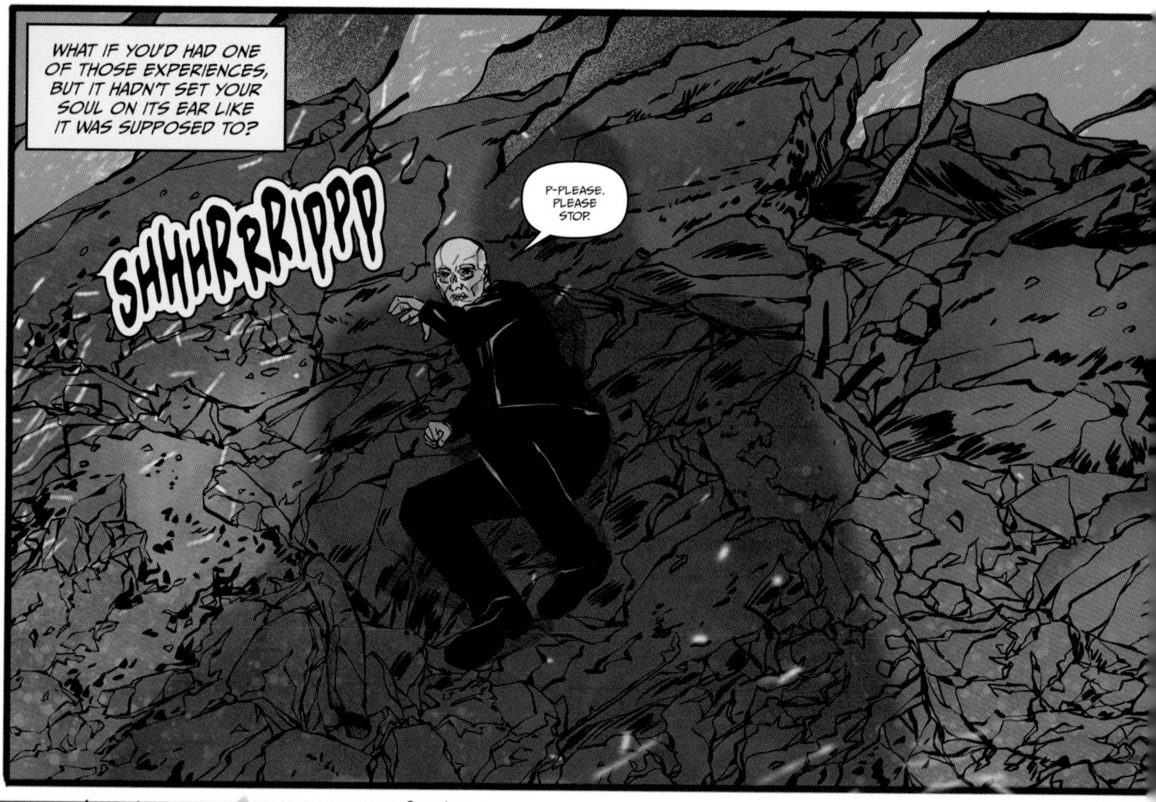
WHAT IF YOU'D HAD ONE OF THOSE EXPERIENCES, BUT IT HADN'T SET YOUR SOUL ON ITS EAR LIKE IT WAS SUPPOSED TO?
SHHHRRIPPP
P-PLEASE. PLEASE STOP.

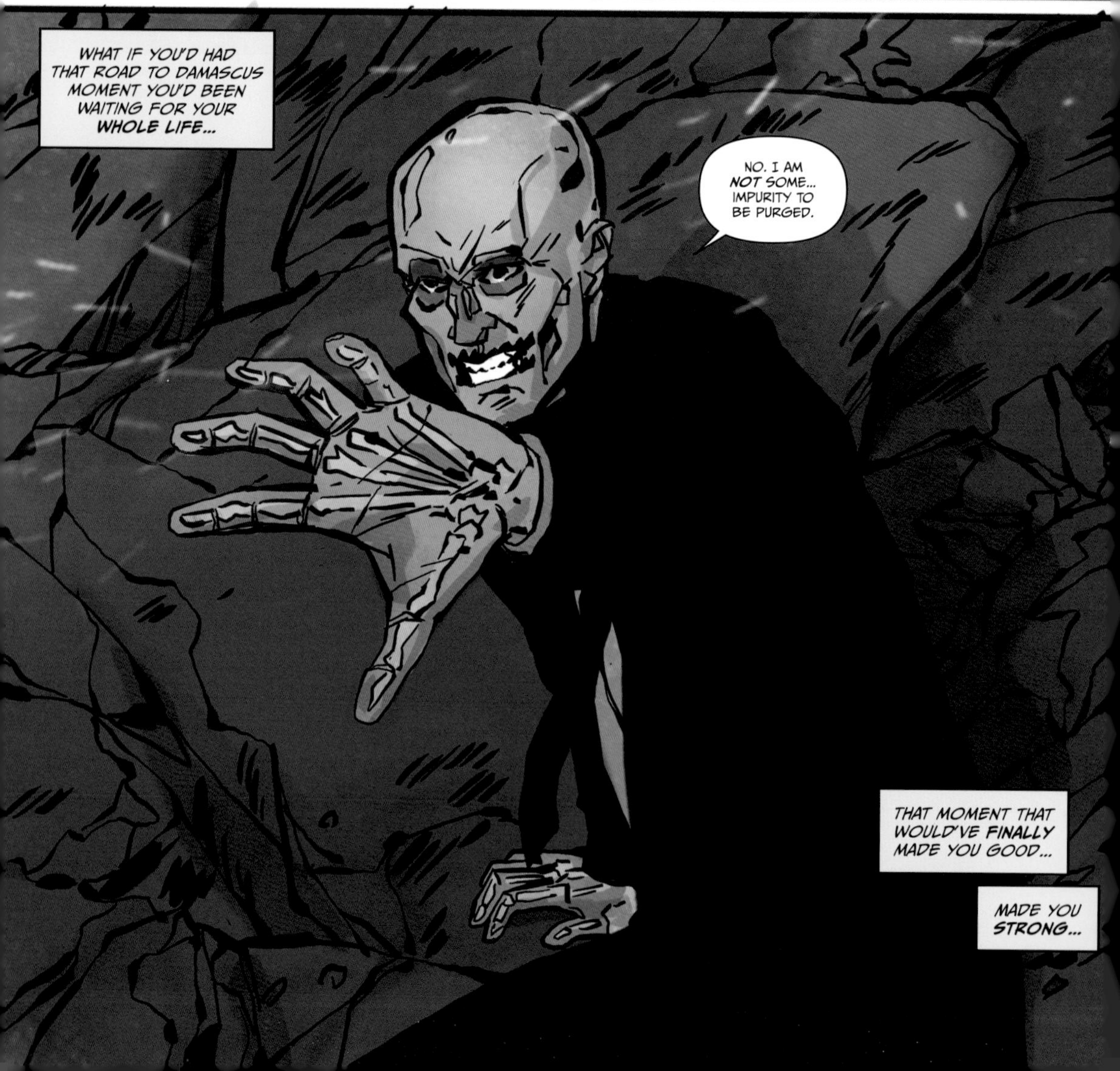
WHAT IF YOU'D HAD THAT ROAD TO DAMASCUS MOMENT YOU'D BEEN WAITING FOR YOUR WHOLE LIFE...
NO. I AM NOT SOME... IMPURITY TO BE PURGED.
THAT MOMENT THAT WOULD'VE FINALLY MADE YOU GOOD...
MADE YOU STRONG...

BUT IT JUST BROKE YOU INSTEAD?

YEEEAAARRRGHHH!

UUUUUUUU...

DAD? DAD, ARE YOU OKAY?

WHY IS HE *SMILING* LIKE THAT?

HAVE ANY OF YOU... *FOLKS* SEEN MY CAR?

I...THERE'S MORE.

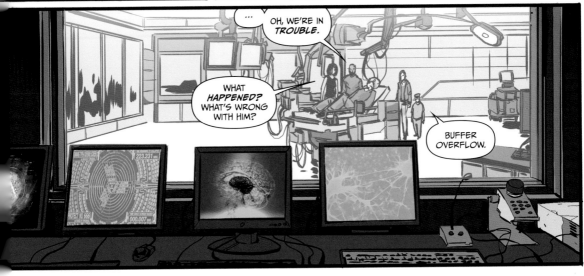

... OH, WE'RE IN *TROUBLE.*

WHAT *HAPPENED?* WHAT'S WRONG WITH HIM?

BUFFER OVERFLOW.

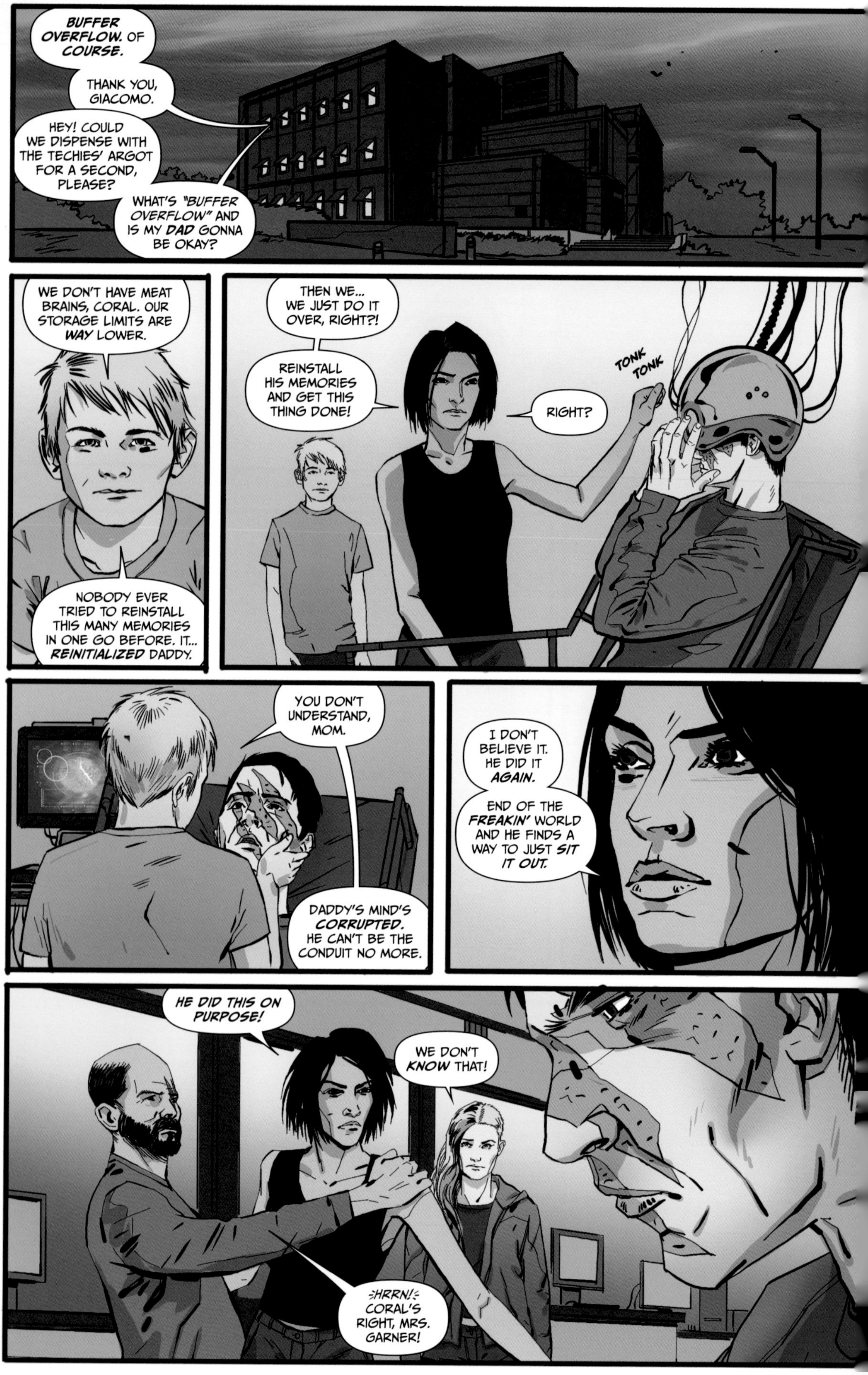
BUFFER OVERFLOW. OF COURSE.
THANK YOU, GIACOMO.
HEY! COULD WE DISPENSE WITH THE TECHIES' ARGOT FOR A SECOND, PLEASE?
WHAT'S "BUFFER OVERFLOW" AND IS MY DAD GONNA BE OKAY?
WE DON'T HAVE MEAT BRAINS, CORAL. OUR STORAGE LIMITS ARE WAY LOWER.
NOBODY EVER TRIED TO REINSTALL THIS MANY MEMORIES IN ONE GO BEFORE. IT... REINITIALIZED DADDY.
THEN WE... WE JUST DO IT OVER, RIGHT?!
REINSTALL HIS MEMORIES AND GET THIS THING DONE!
RIGHT?
TONK TONK
YOU DON'T UNDERSTAND, MOM.
DADDY'S MIND'S CORRUPTED. HE CAN'T BE THE CONDUIT NO MORE.
I DON'T BELIEVE IT. HE DID IT AGAIN.
END OF THE FREAKIN' WORLD AND HE FINDS A WAY TO JUST SIT IT OUT.
HE DID THIS ON PURPOSE!
WE DON'T KNOW THAT!
HRRN! CORAL'S RIGHT, MRS. GARNER!

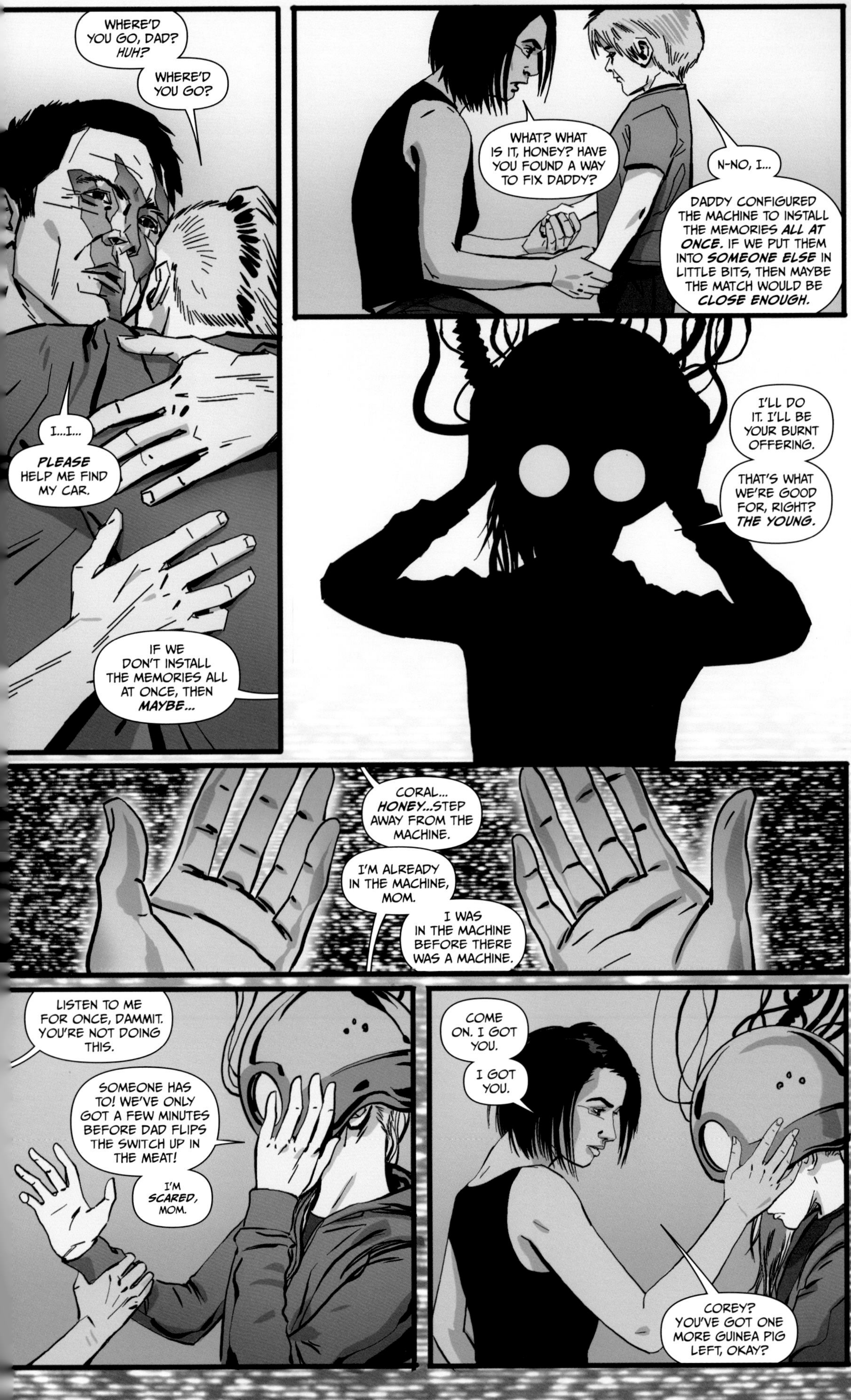
WHERE'D YOU GO, DAD? HUH?
WHERE'D YOU GO?
I...I...
PLEASE HELP ME FIND MY CAR.
IF WE DON'T INSTALL THE MEMORIES ALL AT ONCE, THEN MAYBE...
WHAT? WHAT IS IT, HONEY? HAVE YOU FOUND A WAY TO FIX DADDY?
N-NO, I...
DADDY CONFIGURED THE MACHINE TO INSTALL THE MEMORIES ALL AT ONCE. IF WE PUT THEM INTO SOMEONE ELSE IN LITTLE BITS, THEN MAYBE THE MATCH WOULD BE CLOSE ENOUGH.
I'LL DO IT. I'LL BE YOUR BURNT OFFERING.
THAT'S WHAT WE'RE GOOD FOR, RIGHT? THE YOUNG.
CORAL... HONEY...STEP AWAY FROM THE MACHINE.
I'M ALREADY IN THE MACHINE, MOM.
I WAS IN THE MACHINE BEFORE THERE WAS A MACHINE.
LISTEN TO ME FOR ONCE, DAMMIT. YOU'RE NOT DOING THIS.
SOMEONE HAS TO! WE'VE ONLY GOT A FEW MINUTES BEFORE DAD FLIPS THE SWITCH UP IN THE MEAT!
I'M SCARED, MOM.
COME ON. I GOT YOU.
I GOT YOU.
COREY? YOU'VE GOT ONE MORE GUINEA PIG LEFT, OKAY?

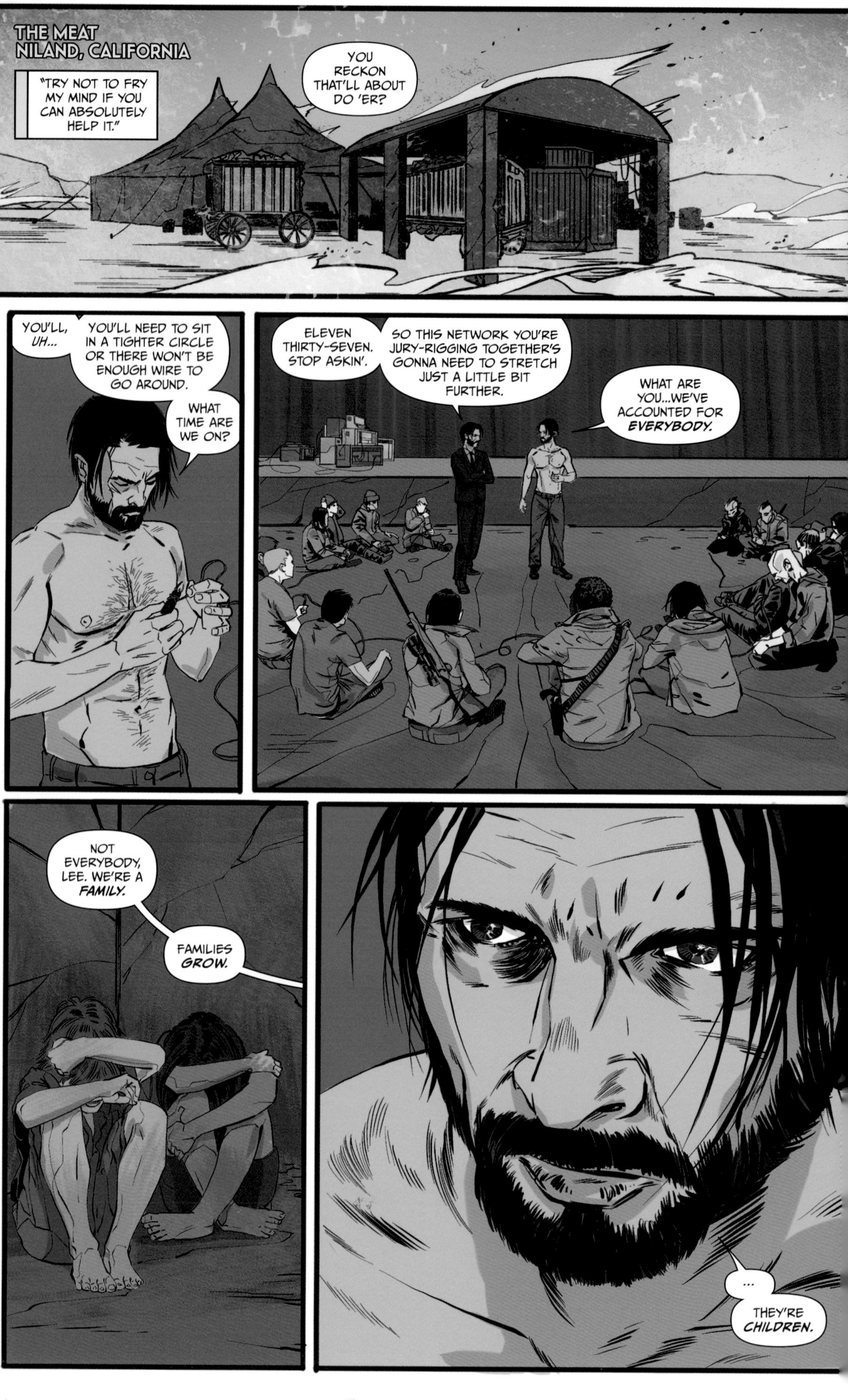
THE MEAT
NILAND, CALIFORNIA
"TRY NOT TO FRY MY MIND IF YOU CAN ABSOLUTELY HELP IT."
YOU RECKON THAT'LL ABOUT DO 'ER?
YOU'LL, UH...
YOU'LL NEED TO SIT IN A TIGHTER CIRCLE OR THERE WON'T BE ENOUGH WIRE TO GO AROUND.
WHAT TIME ARE WE ON?
ELEVEN THIRTY-SEVEN. STOP ASKIN'.
SO THIS NETWORK YOU'RE JURY-RIGGING TOGETHER'S GONNA NEED TO STRETCH JUST A LITTLE BIT FURTHER.
WHAT ARE YOU...WE'VE ACCOUNTED FOR EVERYBODY.
NOT EVERYBODY, LEE. WE'RE A FAMILY.
FAMILIES GROW.
...
THEY'RE CHILDREN.

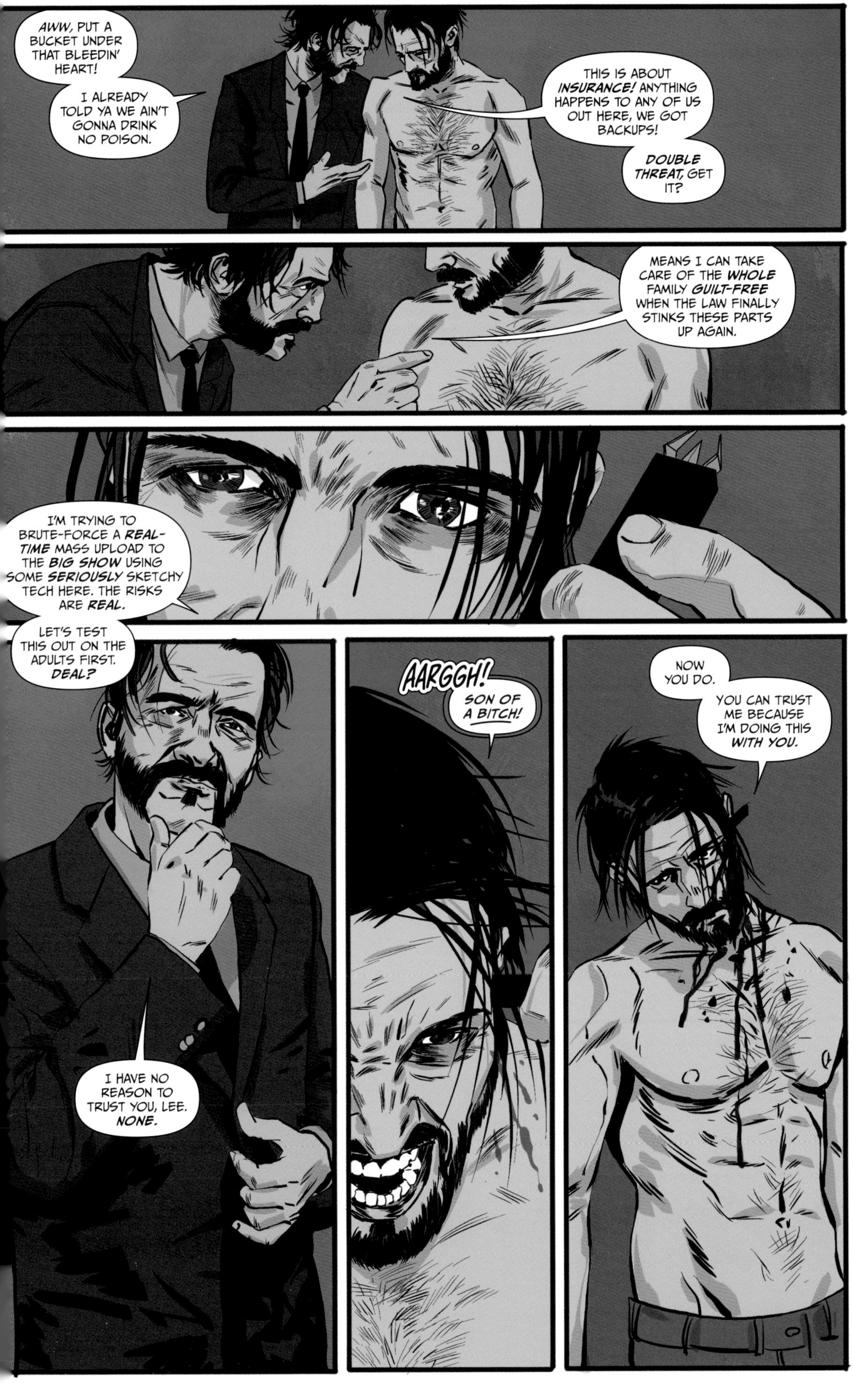
AWW, PUT A BUCKET UNDER THAT BLEEDIN' HEART!
I ALREADY TOLD YA WE AIN'T GONNA DRINK NO POISON.
THIS IS ABOUT INSURANCE! ANYTHING HAPPENS TO ANY OF US OUT HERE, WE GOT BACKUPS!
DOUBLE THREAT, GET IT?
MEANS I CAN TAKE CARE OF THE WHOLE FAMILY GUILT-FREE WHEN THE LAW FINALLY STINKS THESE PARTS UP AGAIN.
I'M TRYING TO BRUTE-FORCE A REAL-TIME MASS UPLOAD TO THE BIG SHOW USING SOME SERIOUSLY SKETCHY TECH HERE. THE RISKS ARE REAL.
LET'S TEST THIS OUT ON THE ADULTS FIRST. DEAL?
I HAVE NO REASON TO TRUST YOU, LEE. NONE.
AARGGH!
SON OF A BITCH!
NOW YOU DO.
YOU CAN TRUST ME BECAUSE I'M DOING THIS WITH YOU.

ARCADIA
LOS ANGELES

≈KAFF≈ HA!

YOU...YOU THINK YOU CAN ≈NN!≈ JUST BLUDGEON THE NEW 'TIL IT STOPS MOVING.

NOTLAN!

YES, YES, "NOTLAN". I HEARD YOU THE FIRST TWELVE TIMES!

CHANGE THE RECORD, YOU GRAY ENCUMBRANCE!

THIS ONE MAKES SO MUCH NOISE, ROGER!

SO MUCH MORE THAN THE OTHERS!

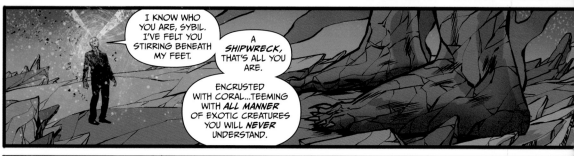

I KNOW WHO YOU ARE, SYBIL. I'VE FELT YOU STIRRING BENEATH MY FEET.

A SHIPWRECK, THAT'S ALL YOU ARE.

ENCRUSTED WITH CORAL...TEEMING WITH ALL MANNER OF EXOTIC CREATURES YOU WILL NEVER UNDERSTAND.

YOU ARE A SUBSTRATE, WOMAN...

A WARM HOST FOR RADIANT LARVAE YOU HAVE NO RIGHT TO DESTROY!

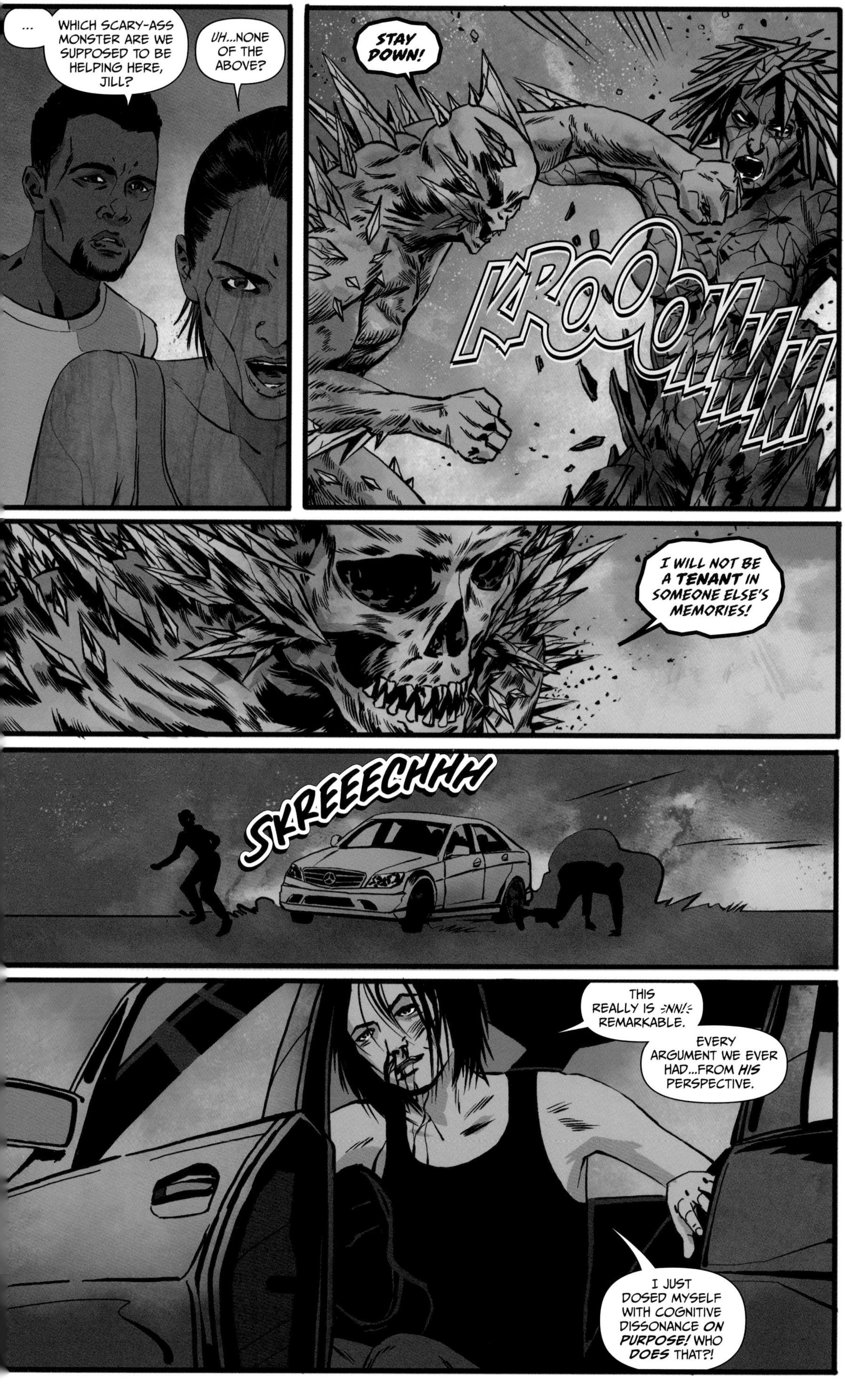
...
WHICH SCARY-ASS MONSTER ARE WE SUPPOSED TO BE HELPING HERE, JILL?
UH...NONE OF THE ABOVE?
STAY DOWN!
KROOOOWWM
I WILL NOT BE A TENANT IN SOMEONE ELSE'S MEMORIES!
SKREEEECHHH
THIS REALLY IS NN! REMARKABLE.
EVERY ARGUMENT WE EVER HAD...FROM HIS PERSPECTIVE.
I JUST DOSED MYSELF WITH COGNITIVE DISSONANCE ON PURPOSE! WHO DOES THAT?!

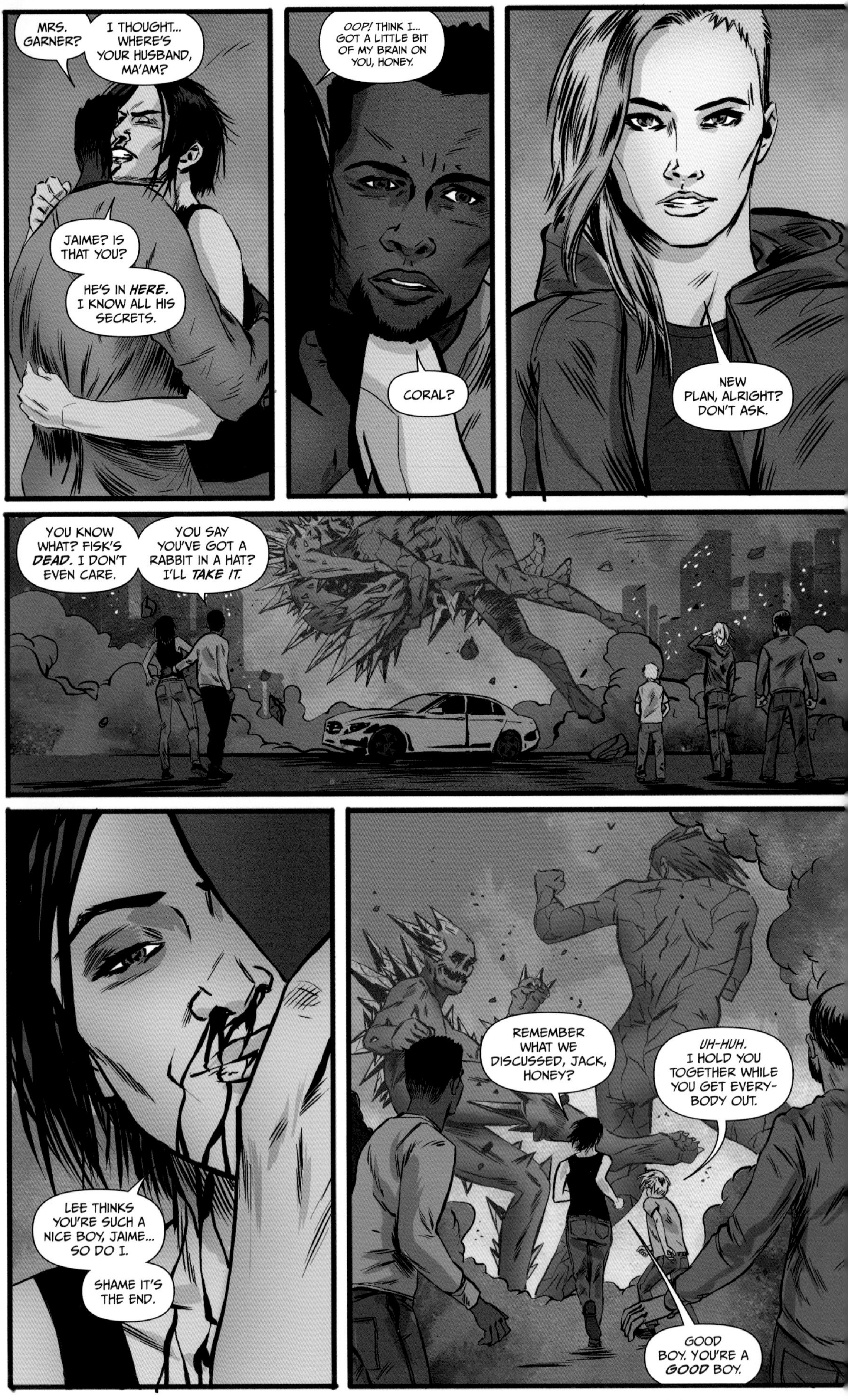
MRS. GARNER?
I THOUGHT... WHERE'S YOUR HUSBAND, MA'AM?
JAIME? IS THAT YOU?
HE'S IN *HERE.* I KNOW ALL HIS SECRETS.
OOP! THINK I... GOT A LITTLE BIT OF MY BRAIN ON YOU, HONEY.
CORAL?
NEW PLAN, ALRIGHT? DON'T ASK.
YOU KNOW WHAT? FISK'S *DEAD.* I DON'T EVEN CARE.
YOU SAY YOU'VE GOT A RABBIT IN A HAT? I'LL *TAKE IT.*
LEE THINKS YOU'RE SUCH A NICE BOY, JAIME... SO DO I.
SHAME IT'S THE END.
REMEMBER WHAT WE DISCUSSED, JACK, HONEY?
UH-HUH. I HOLD YOU TOGETHER WHILE YOU GET EVERY-BODY OUT.
GOOD BOY. YOU'RE A *GOOD* BOY.

KR-OOOMM

MUH... MUH...MRS. GARNER.

YOUR BOY, HE CAN HUH... *HELP ME.*

AND WHY WOULD HE DO THAT?

SHE'S SO *O-OLD.*

ARCADIA I—ISN'T SOME MUH-*MILDEWED KEEPSAKE!* IT'S ALIVE!

:*HUKK!*:

THANK YOU, BABY.

AND WHAT GIVES *YOU* THE RIGHT TO DECIDE WHAT THIS PLACE IS, EITHER?

PUH... *PROGRESS.*

DON'T YOU WANT TO SEE THE *FAR SHORE?*

NOT IF I HAVE TO SEE IT ON *MY OWN.*

YOU *BORE* ME. *BOTH OF YOU.*

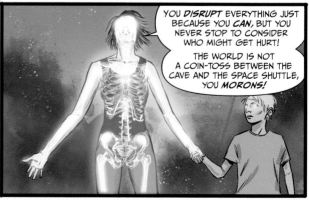

YOU *DISRUPT* EVERYTHING JUST BECAUSE YOU *CAN,* BUT YOU NEVER STOP TO CONSIDER WHO MIGHT GET HURT!

THE WORLD IS NOT A COIN-TOSS BETWEEN THE CAVE AND THE SPACE SHUTTLE, YOU *MORONS!*

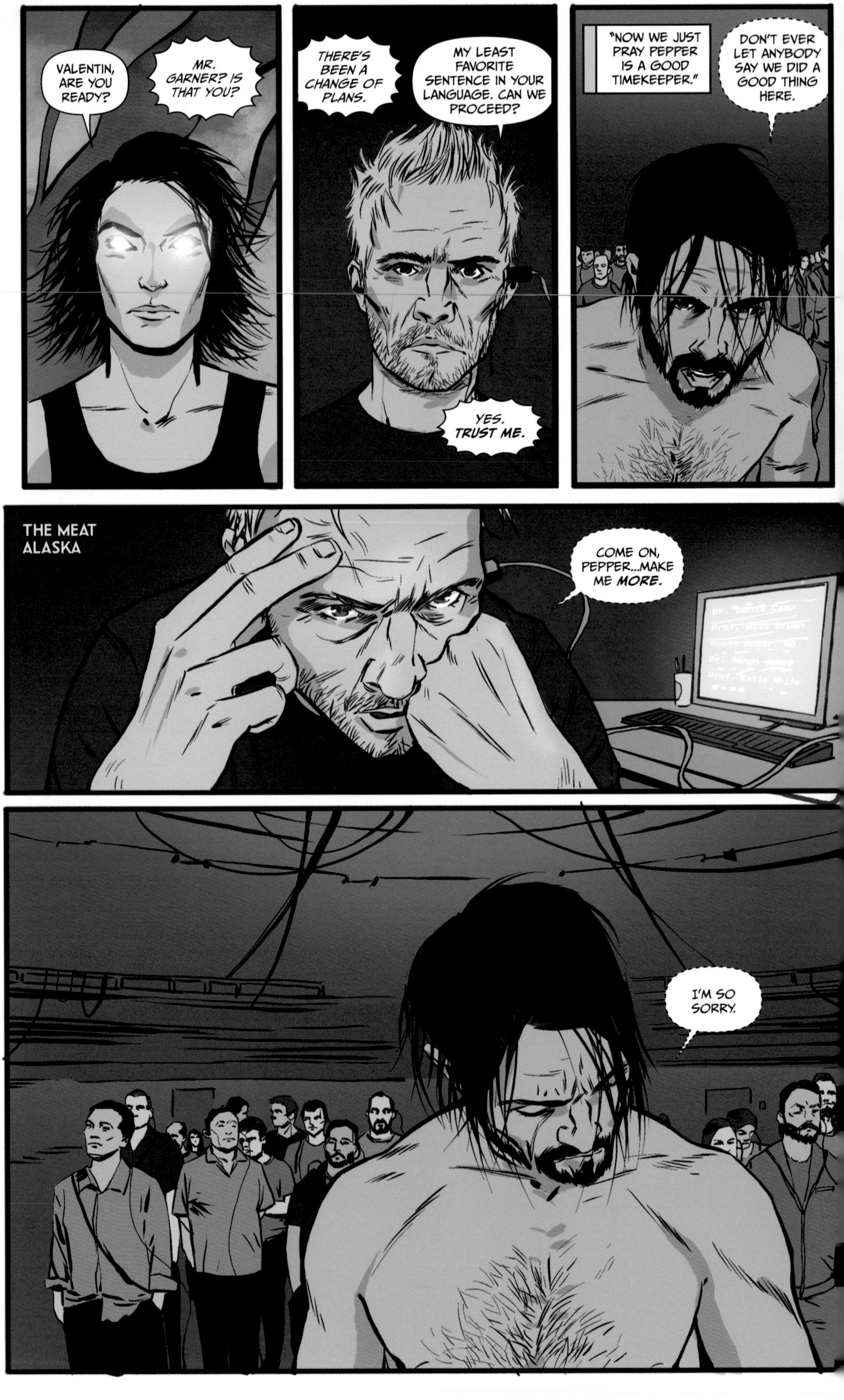
VALENTIN, ARE YOU READY?
MR. GARNER? IS THAT YOU?
THERE'S BEEN A CHANGE OF PLANS.
MY LEAST FAVORITE SENTENCE IN YOUR LANGUAGE. CAN WE PROCEED?
YES. TRUST ME.
"NOW WE JUST PRAY PEPPER IS A GOOD TIMEKEEPER."
DON'T EVER LET ANYBODY SAY WE DID A GOOD THING HERE.
THE MEAT
ALASKA
COME ON, PEPPER...MAKE ME MORE.
I'M SO SORRY.

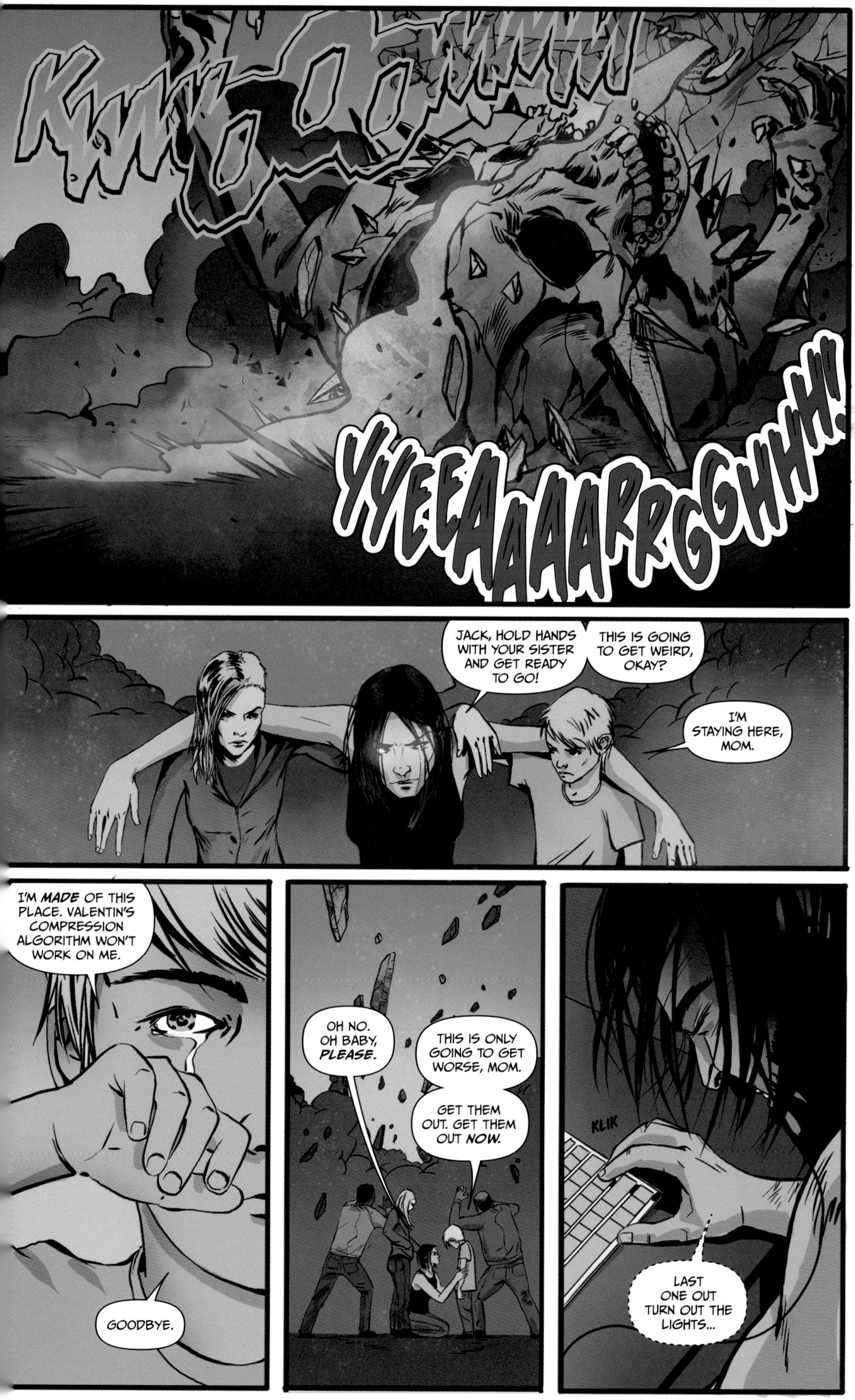
KWWWOOOMMM
YYEEAAAARRGGHHH!
JACK, HOLD HANDS WITH YOUR SISTER AND GET READY TO GO!
THIS IS GOING TO GET WEIRD, OKAY?
I'M STAYING HERE, MOM.
I'M *MADE* OF THIS PLACE. VALENTIN'S COMPRESSION ALGORITHM WON'T WORK ON ME.
GOODBYE.
OH NO. OH BABY, ***PLEASE.***
THIS IS ONLY GOING TO GET WORSE, MOM.
GET THEM OUT. GET THEM OUT ***NOW.***
KLIK
LAST ONE OUT TURN OUT THE LIGHTS...

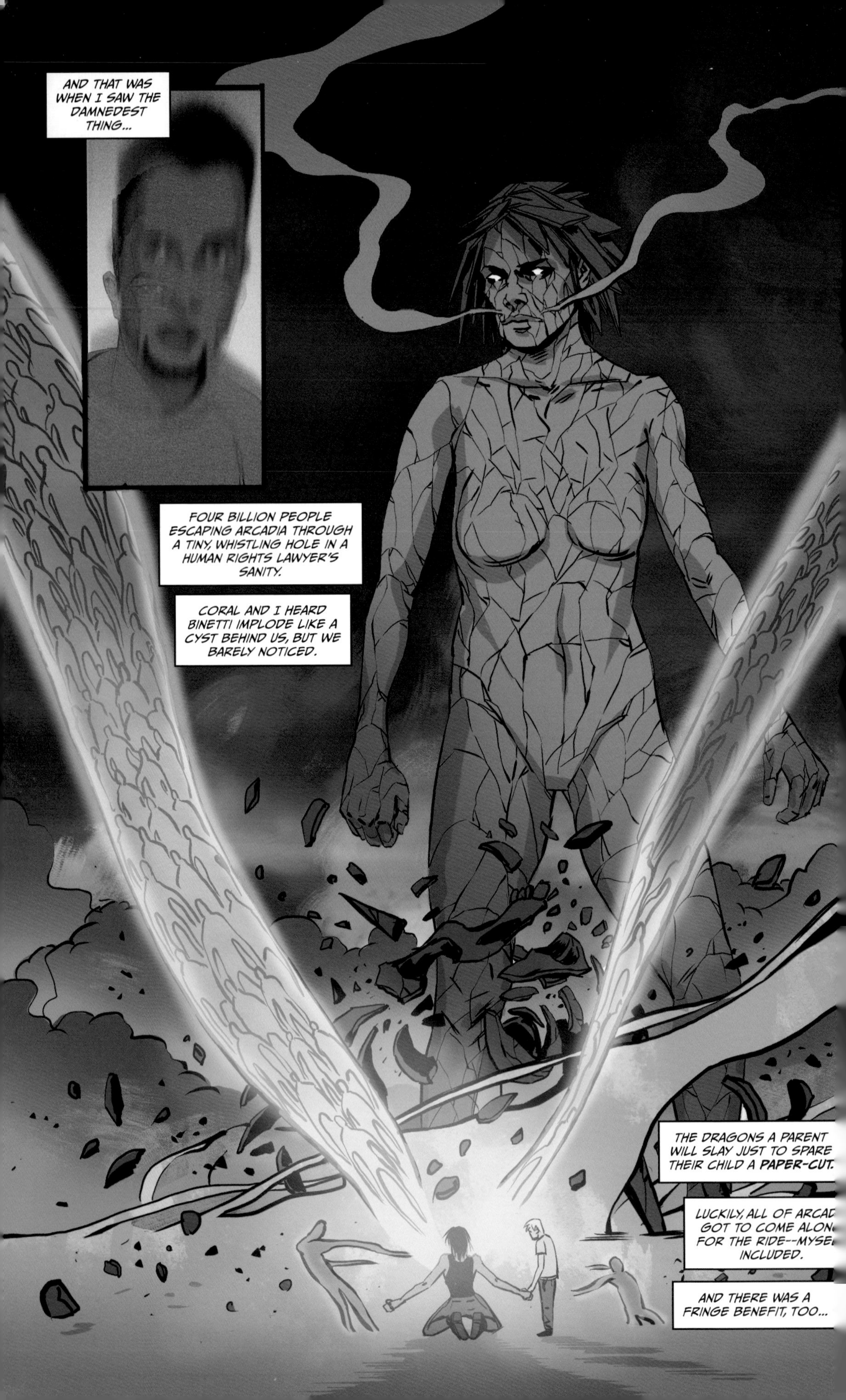
AND THAT WAS WHEN I SAW THE DAMNEDEST THING...
FOUR BILLION PEOPLE ESCAPING ARCADIA THROUGH A TINY, WHISTLING HOLE IN A HUMAN RIGHTS LAWYER'S SANITY.
CORAL AND I HEARD BINETTI IMPLODE LIKE A CYST BEHIND US, BUT WE BARELY NOTICED.
THE DRAGONS A PARENT WILL SLAY JUST TO SPARE THEIR CHILD A **PAPER-CUT.**
LUCKILY, ALL OF ARCAD GOT TO COME ALON FOR THE RIDE--MYSE INCLUDED.
AND THERE WAS A FRINGE BENEFIT, TOO...

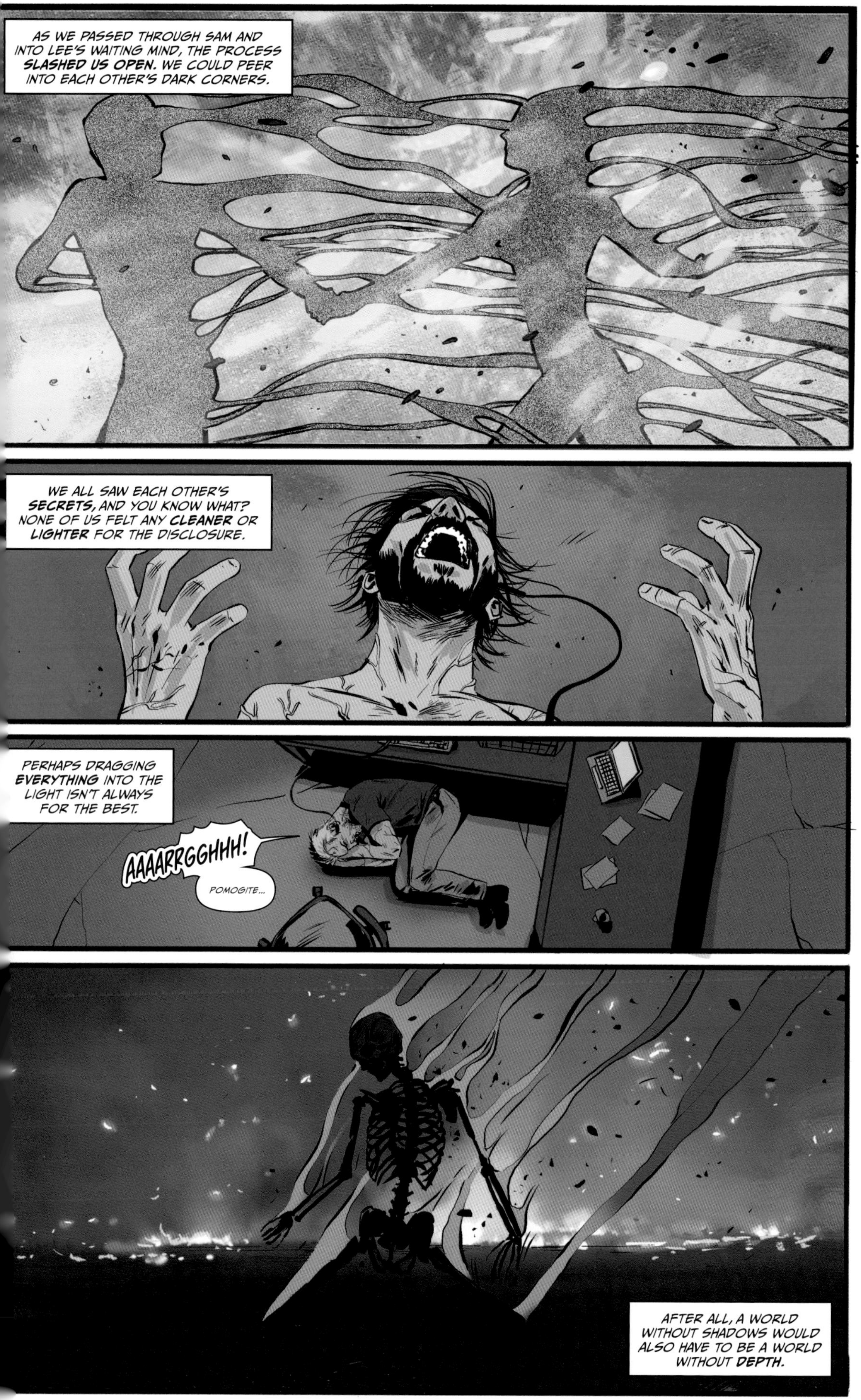
AS WE PASSED THROUGH SAM AND INTO LEE'S WAITING MIND, THE PROCESS SLASHED US OPEN. WE COULD PEER INTO EACH OTHER'S DARK CORNERS.
WE ALL SAW EACH OTHER'S SECRETS, AND YOU KNOW WHAT? NONE OF US FELT ANY CLEANER OR LIGHTER FOR THE DISCLOSURE.
PERHAPS DRAGGING EVERYTHING INTO THE LIGHT ISN'T ALWAYS FOR THE BEST.
AAAARRGGHHH!
POMOGITE...
AFTER ALL, A WORLD WITHOUT SHADOWS WOULD ALSO HAVE TO BE A WORLD WITHOUT DEPTH.

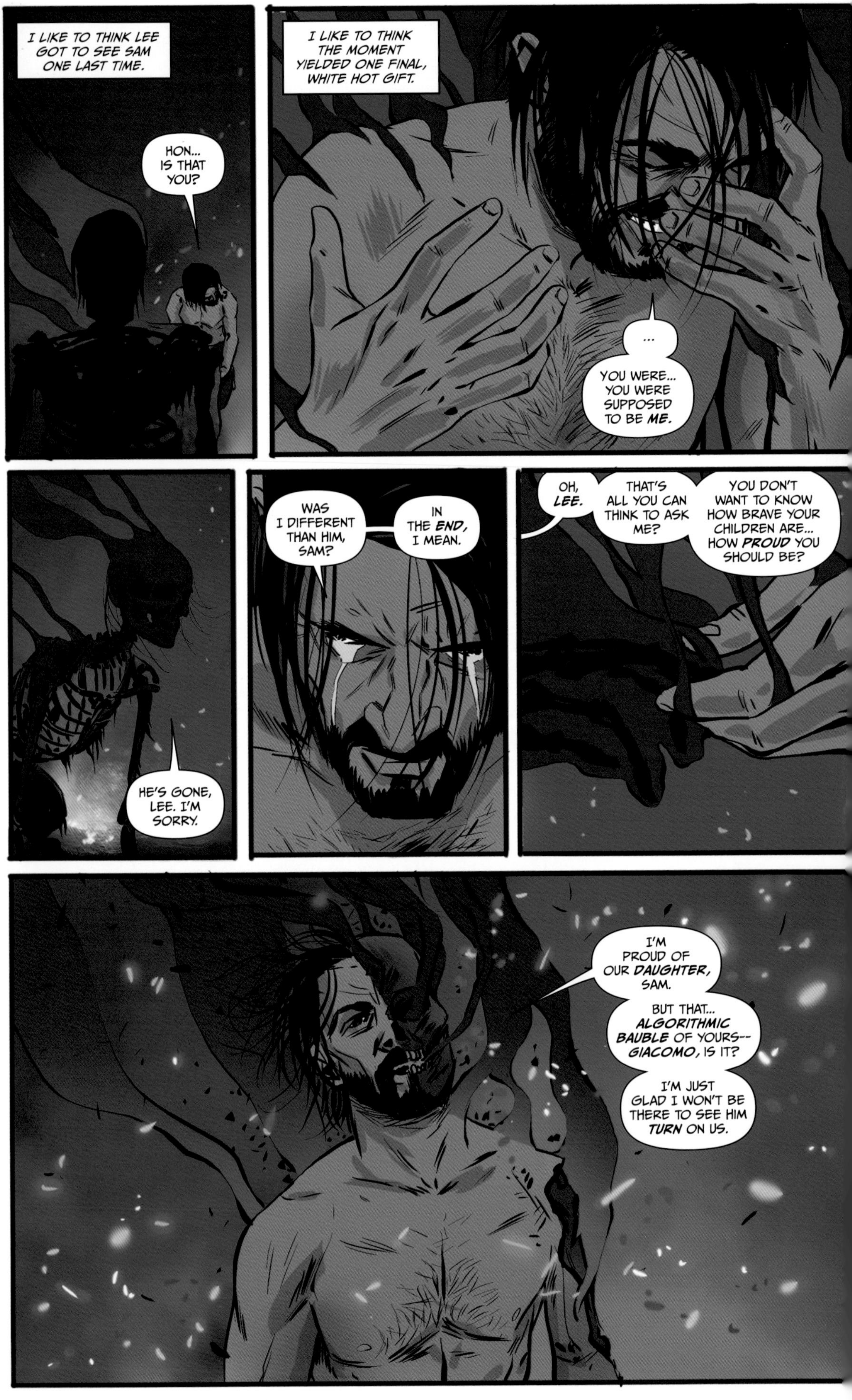
I LIKE TO THINK LEE GOT TO SEE SAM ONE LAST TIME.
HON... IS THAT YOU?
I LIKE TO THINK THE MOMENT YIELDED ONE FINAL, WHITE HOT GIFT.
...
YOU WERE... YOU WERE SUPPOSED TO BE ME.
HE'S GONE, LEE. I'M SORRY.
WAS I DIFFERENT THAN HIM, SAM?
IN THE END, I MEAN.
OH, LEE.
THAT'S ALL YOU CAN THINK TO ASK ME?
YOU DON'T WANT TO KNOW HOW BRAVE YOUR CHILDREN ARE... HOW PROUD YOU SHOULD BE?
I'M PROUD OF OUR DAUGHTER, SAM.
BUT THAT... ALGORITHMIC BAUBLE OF YOURS-- GIACOMO, IS IT?
I'M JUST GLAD I WON'T BE THERE TO SEE HIM TURN ON US.

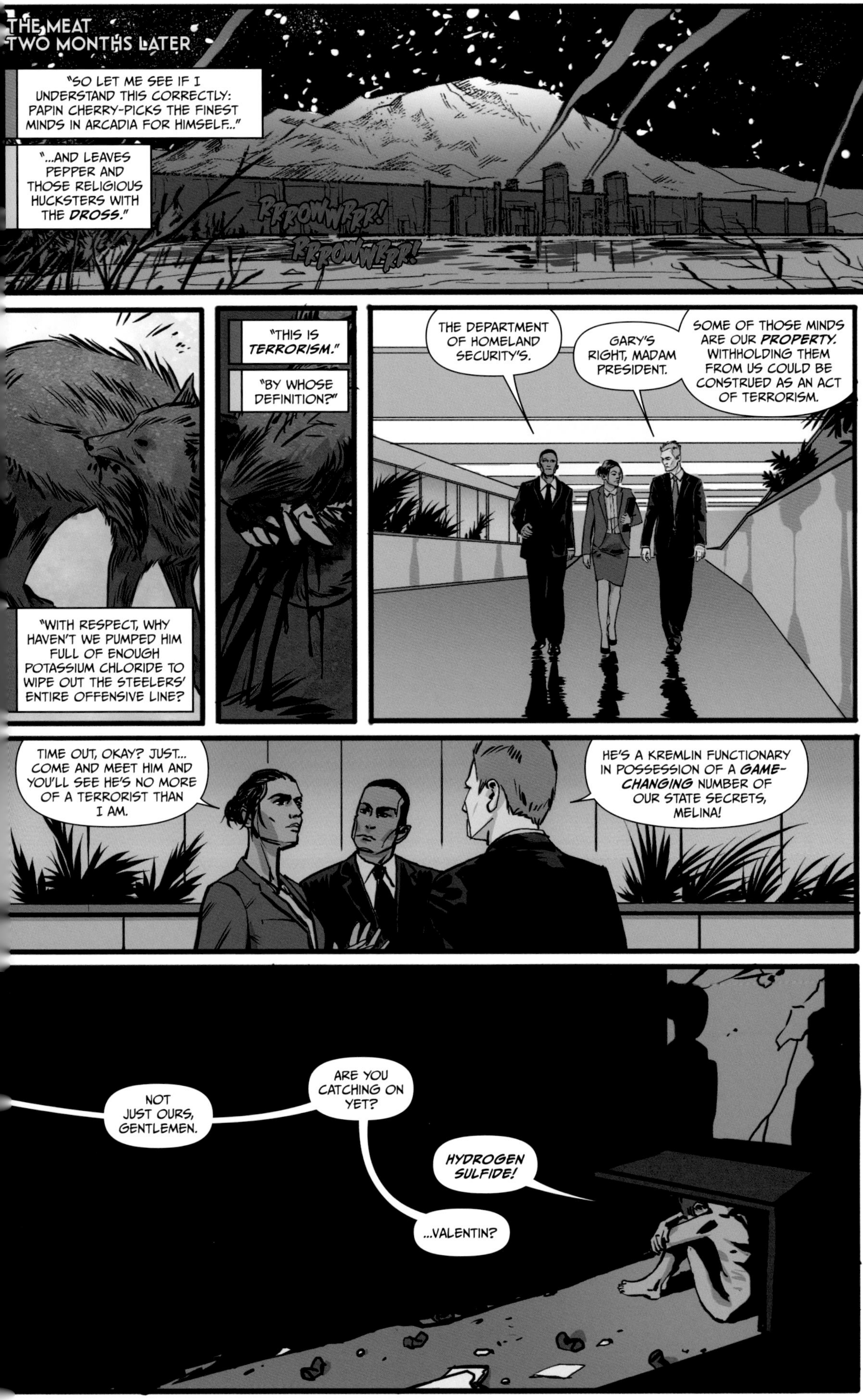
THE MEAT
TWO MONTHS LATER
"SO LET ME SEE IF I UNDERSTAND THIS CORRECTLY: PAPIN CHERRY-PICKS THE FINEST MINDS IN ARCADIA FOR HIMSELF..."
"...AND LEAVES PEPPER AND THOSE RELIGIOUS HUCKSTERS WITH THE DROSS."
RRROWWRRR!
RRROWWRRR!
"WITH RESPECT, WHY HAVEN'T WE PUMPED HIM FULL OF ENOUGH POTASSIUM CHLORIDE TO WIPE OUT THE STEELERS' ENTIRE OFFENSIVE LINE?
"THIS IS TERRORISM."
"BY WHOSE DEFINITION?"
THE DEPARTMENT OF HOMELAND SECURITY'S.
GARY'S RIGHT, MADAM PRESIDENT.
SOME OF THOSE MINDS ARE OUR PROPERTY. WITHHOLDING THEM FROM US COULD BE CONSTRUED AS AN ACT OF TERRORISM.
TIME OUT, OKAY? JUST... COME AND MEET HIM AND YOU'LL SEE HE'S NO MORE OF A TERRORIST THAN I AM.
HE'S A KREMLIN FUNCTIONARY IN POSSESSION OF A GAME-CHANGING NUMBER OF OUR STATE SECRETS, MELINA!
NOT JUST OURS, GENTLEMEN.
ARE YOU CATCHING ON YET?
HYDROGEN SULFIDE!
...VALENTIN?

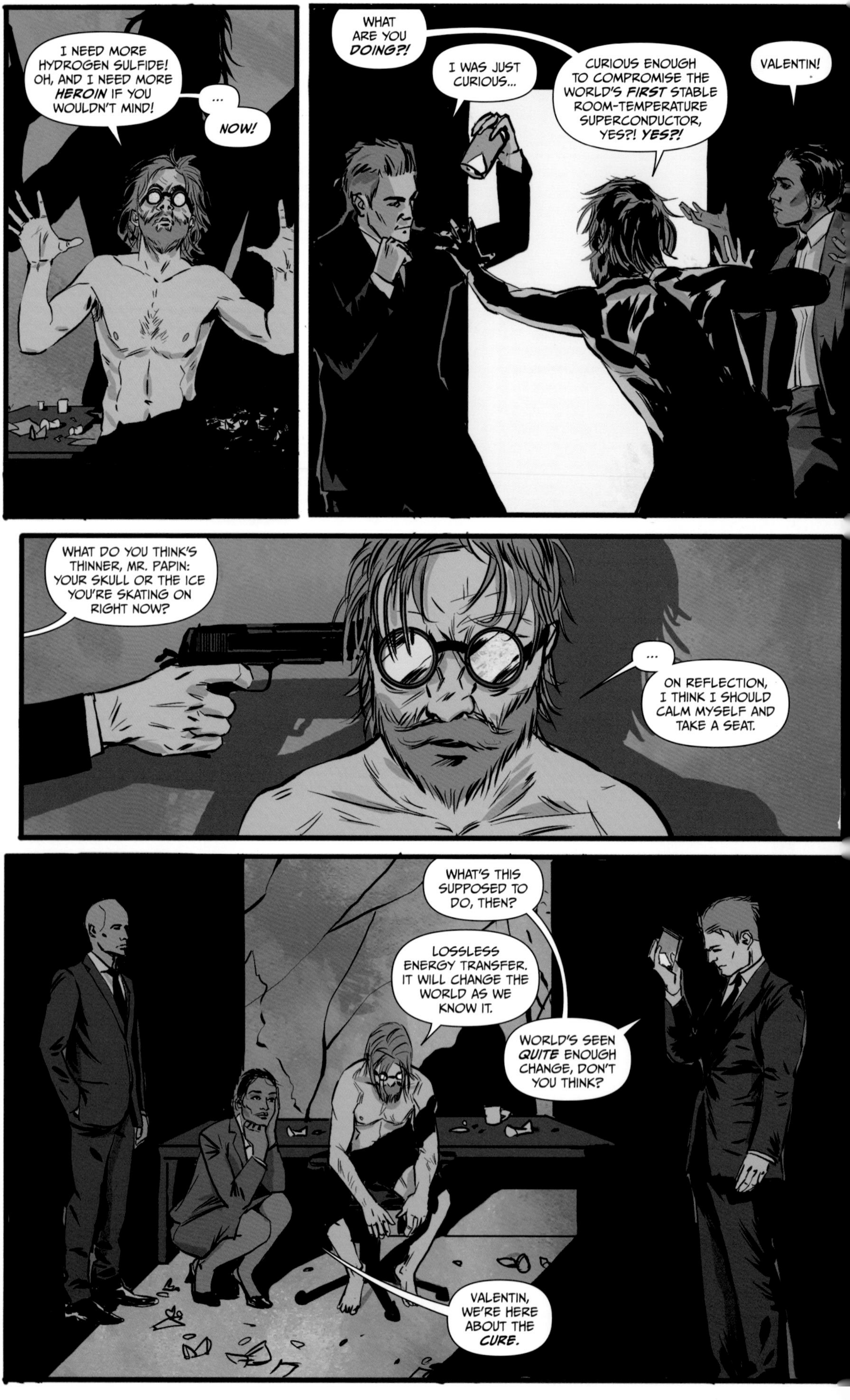
I NEED MORE HYDROGEN SULFIDE! OH, AND I NEED MORE *HEROIN* IF YOU WOULDN'T MIND!
...
NOW!
WHAT ARE YOU *DOING?!*
I WAS JUST CURIOUS...
CURIOUS ENOUGH TO COMPROMISE THE WORLD'S *FIRST* STABLE ROOM-TEMPERATURE SUPERCONDUCTOR, YES?! *YES?!*
VALENTIN!
WHAT DO YOU THINK'S THINNER, MR. PAPIN: YOUR SKULL OR THE ICE YOU'RE SKATING ON RIGHT NOW?
...
ON REFLECTION, I THINK I SHOULD CALM MYSELF AND TAKE A SEAT.
WHAT'S THIS SUPPOSED TO DO, THEN?
LOSSLESS ENERGY TRANSFER. IT WILL CHANGE THE WORLD AS WE KNOW IT.
WORLD'S SEEN *QUITE* ENOUGH CHANGE, DON'T YOU THINK?
VALENTIN, WE'RE HERE ABOUT THE *CURE*.

THE CURE?

YES, VALENTIN. THE *CURE.*

WE HAVE A SLIGHT PAPILLOMAVIRUS PROBLEM, IF YOU RECALL.

BILLIONS DEAD, YOU KNOW.

AH, THE CURE! OF COURSE!

SORRY, I'VE BEEN QUITE DISTRACTED.

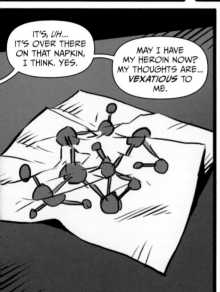

IT'S, *UH...* IT'S OVER THERE ON THAT NAPKIN, I THINK. YES.

MAY I HAVE MY HEROIN NOW? MY THOUGHTS ARE... *VEXATIOUS* TO ME.

SOON.

WE ALSO NEED YOU TO EXTRACT FOUR BILLION PEOPLE FROM PEPPER AND FRIENDS' MINDS SO THEY CAN BE RE-UPLOADED ONCE IT'S SAFE.

NO RE-UPLOAD. NO.

WHY?

WE BIRTHED A *COMPLETELY NEW SPECIES* IN THERE, MADAM PRESIDENT.

WHAT DO YOU THINK THEY'LL MAKE OF US WHEN THEY'RE OLDER?

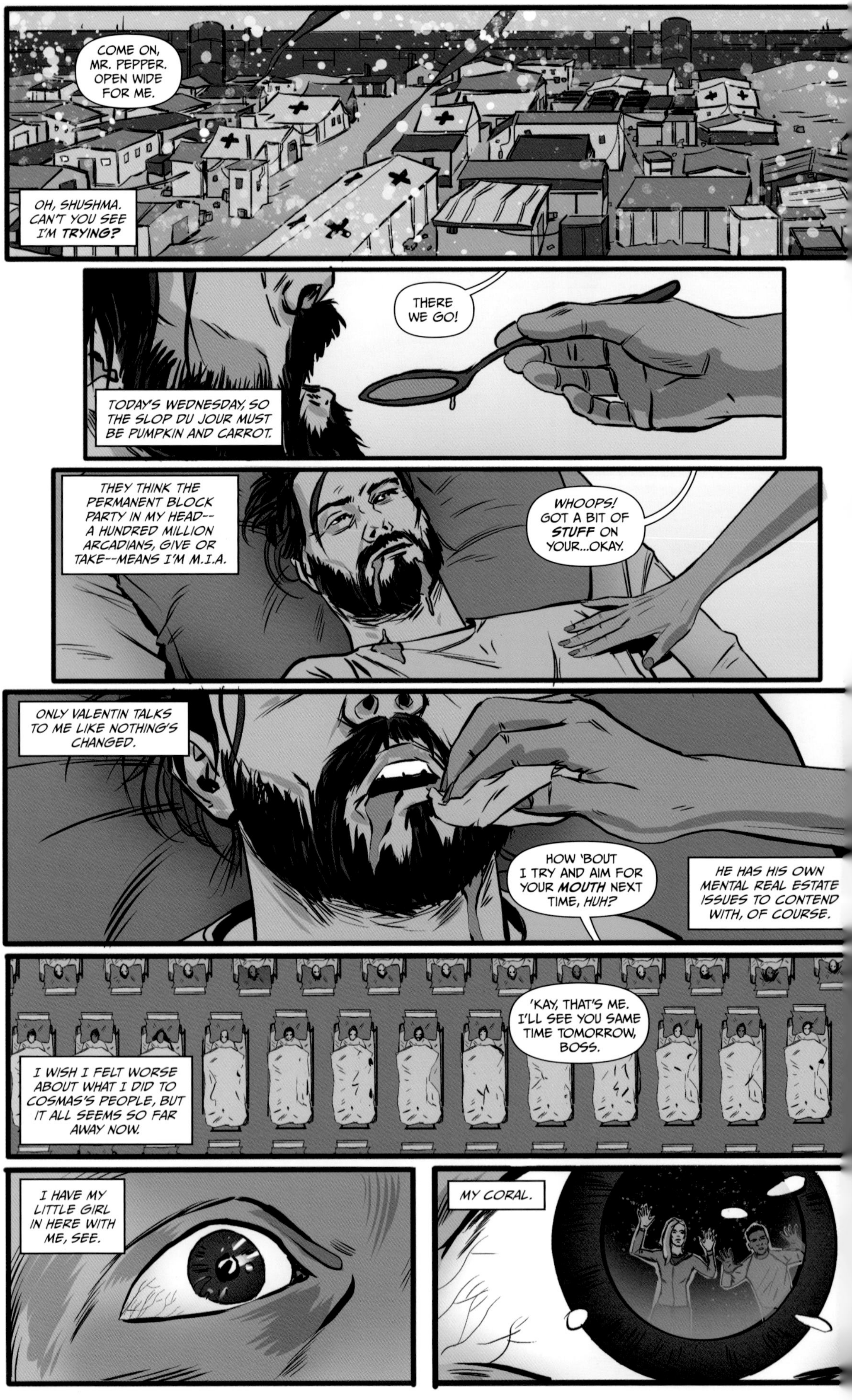
COME ON, MR. PEPPER. OPEN WIDE FOR ME.
OH, SHUSHMA. CAN'T YOU SEE I'M TRYING?
TODAY'S WEDNESDAY, SO THE SLOP DU JOUR MUST BE PUMPKIN AND CARROT.
THERE WE GO!
THEY THINK THE PERMANENT BLOCK PARTY IN MY HEAD-- A HUNDRED MILLION ARCADIANS, GIVE OR TAKE--MEANS I'M M.I.A.
WHOOPS! GOT A BIT OF STUFF ON YOUR...OKAY.
ONLY VALENTIN TALKS TO ME LIKE NOTHING'S CHANGED.
HOW 'BOUT I TRY AND AIM FOR YOUR MOUTH NEXT TIME, HUH?
HE HAS HIS OWN MENTAL REAL ESTATE ISSUES TO CONTEND WITH, OF COURSE.
I WISH I FELT WORSE ABOUT WHAT I DID TO COSMAS'S PEOPLE, BUT IT ALL SEEMS SO FAR AWAY NOW.
'KAY, THAT'S ME. I'LL SEE YOU SAME TIME TOMORROW, BOSS.
I HAVE MY LITTLE GIRL IN HERE WITH ME, SEE.
MY CORAL.

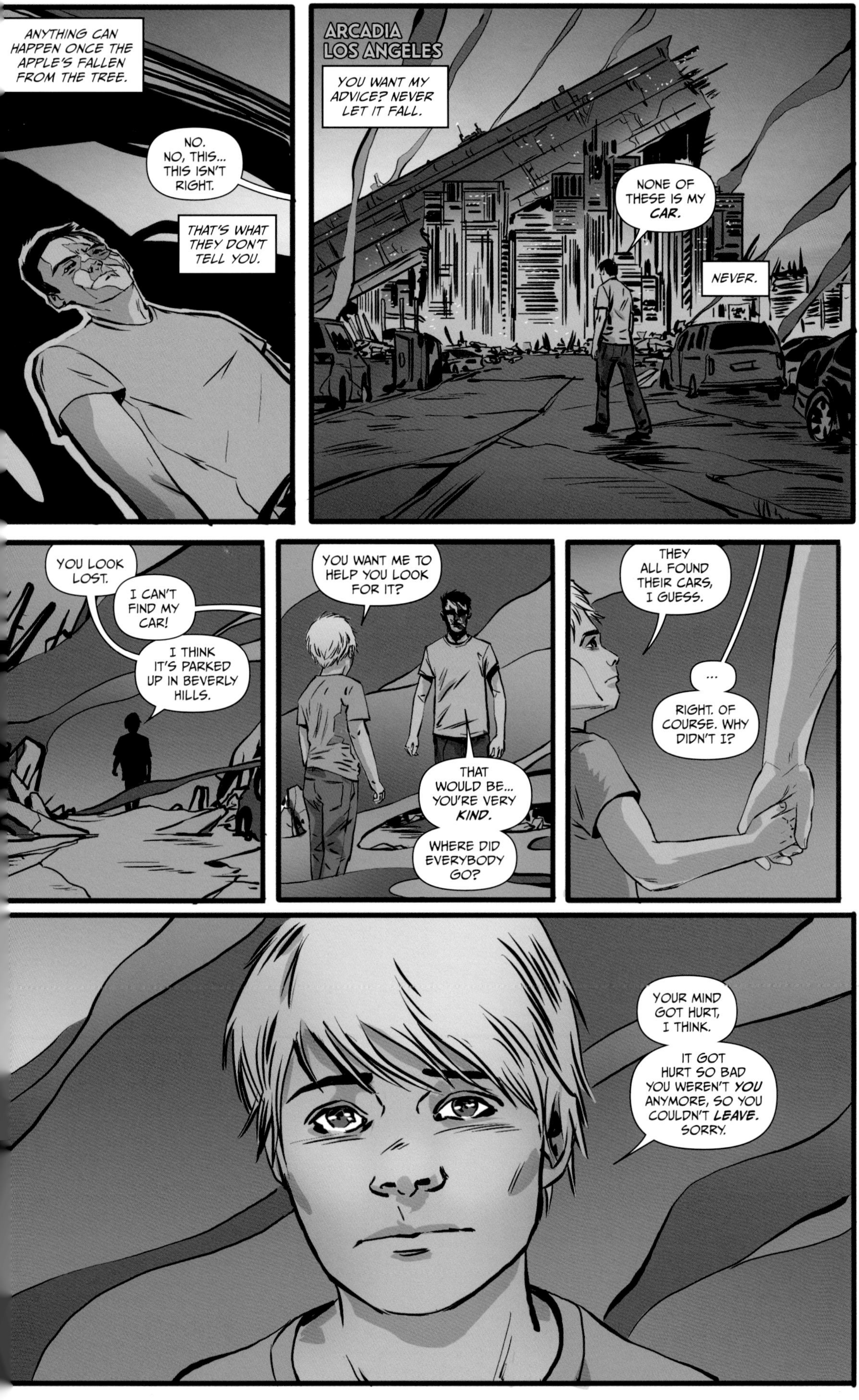
ANYTHING CAN HAPPEN ONCE THE APPLE'S FALLEN FROM THE TREE.
NO. NO, THIS... THIS ISN'T RIGHT.
THAT'S WHAT THEY DON'T TELL YOU.
ARCADIA LOS ANGELES
YOU WANT MY ADVICE? NEVER LET IT FALL.
NONE OF THESE IS MY CAR.
NEVER.
YOU LOOK LOST.
I CAN'T FIND MY CAR!
I THINK IT'S PARKED UP IN BEVERLY HILLS.
YOU WANT ME TO HELP YOU LOOK FOR IT?
THAT WOULD BE... YOU'RE VERY KIND.
WHERE DID EVERYBODY GO?
THEY ALL FOUND THEIR CARS, I GUESS.
...
RIGHT. OF COURSE. WHY DIDN'T I?
YOUR MIND GOT HURT, I THINK.
IT GOT HURT SO BAD YOU WEREN'T YOU ANYMORE, SO YOU COULDN'T LEAVE. SORRY.

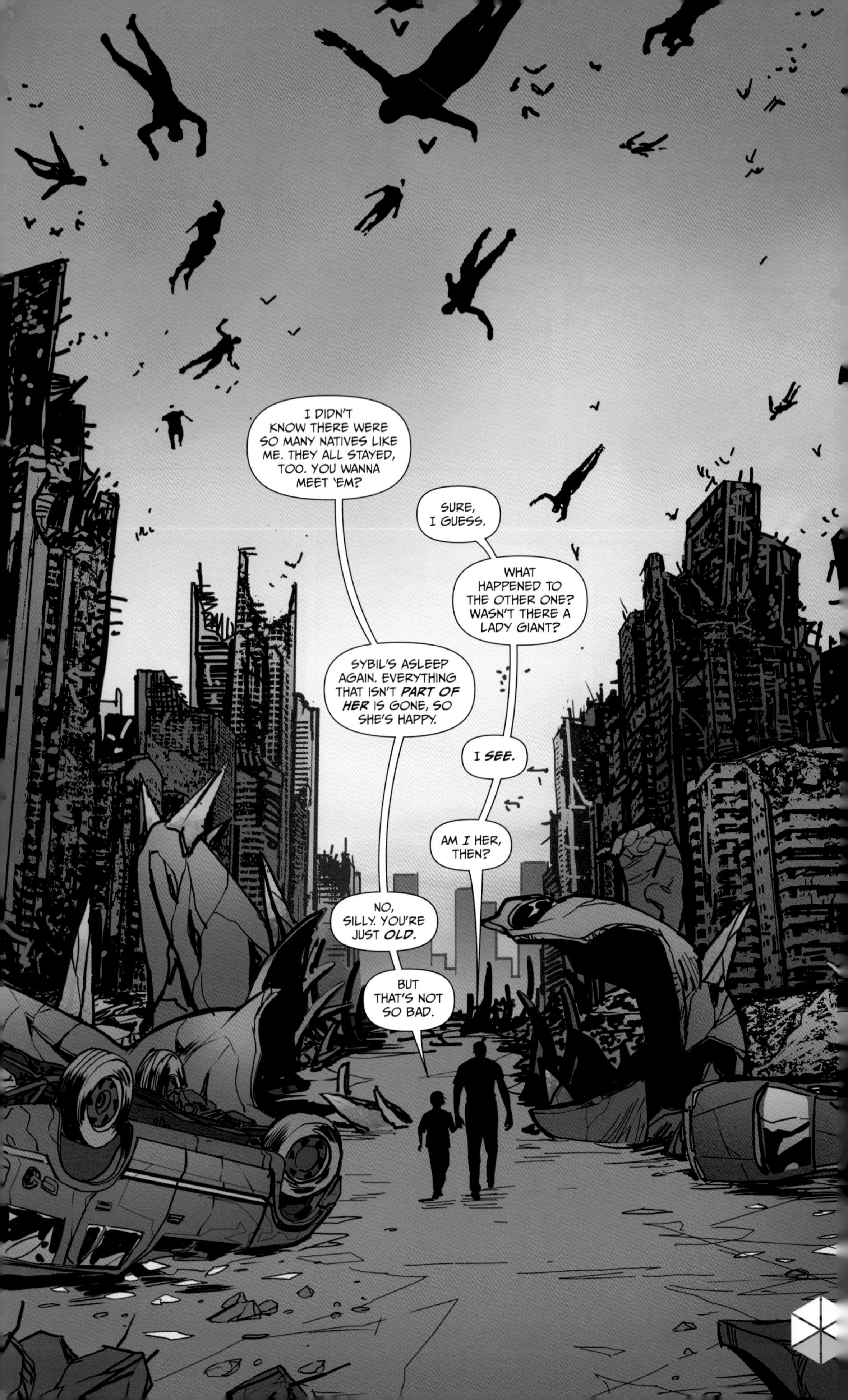
I DIDN'T KNOW THERE WERE SO MANY NATIVES LIKE ME. THEY ALL STAYED, TOO. YOU WANNA MEET 'EM?
SURE, I GUESS.
WHAT HAPPENED TO THE OTHER ONE? WASN'T THERE A LADY GIANT?
SYBIL'S ASLEEP AGAIN. EVERYTHING THAT ISN'T ***PART OF HER*** IS GONE, SO SHE'S HAPPY.
I ***SEE.***
AM ***I*** HER, THEN?
NO, SILLY. YOU'RE JUST ***OLD.***
BUT THAT'S NOT SO BAD.

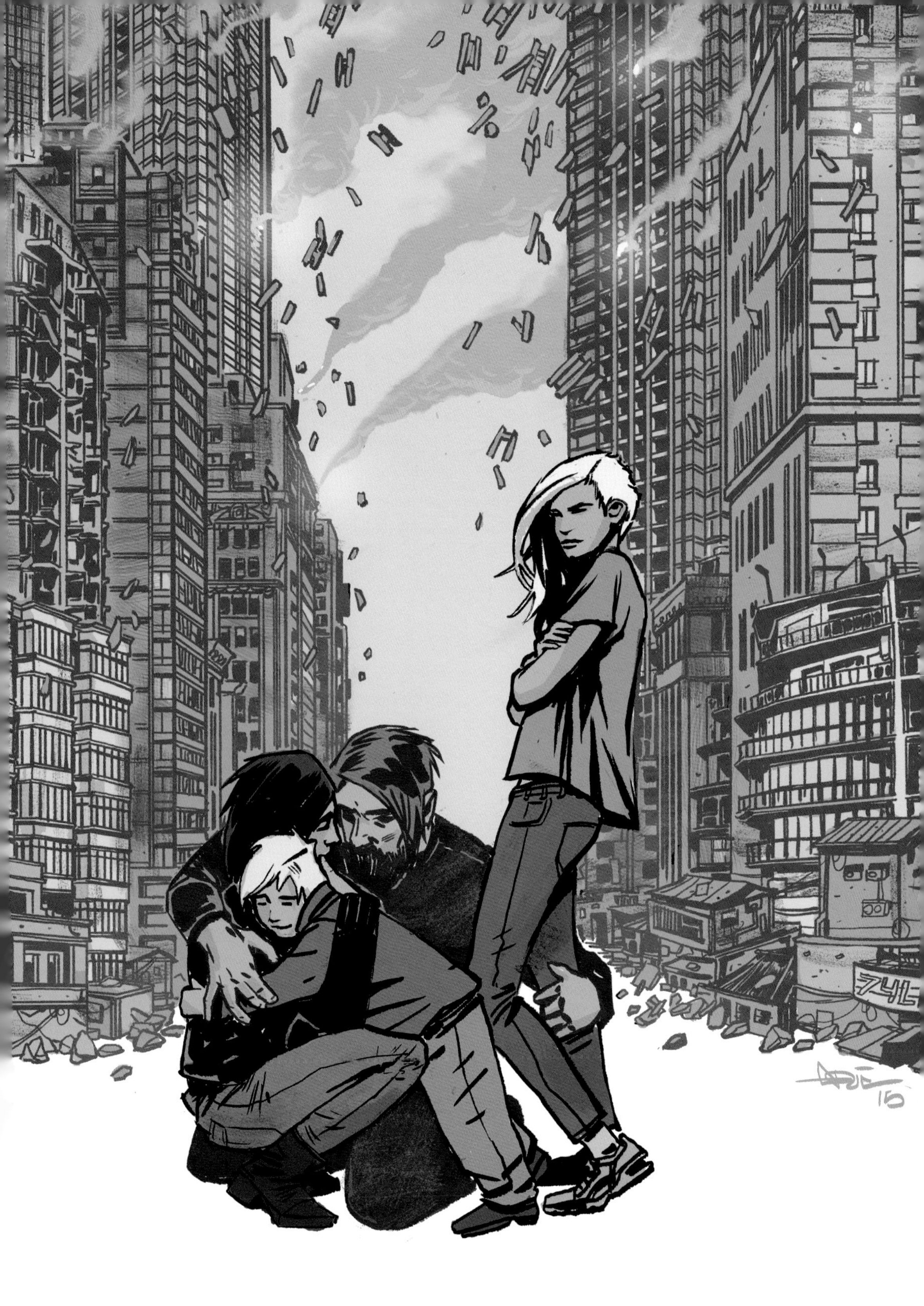

Issue Eight Main Cover **Eric Scott Pfeiffer**

Issue One Main Cover **Matt Taylor**

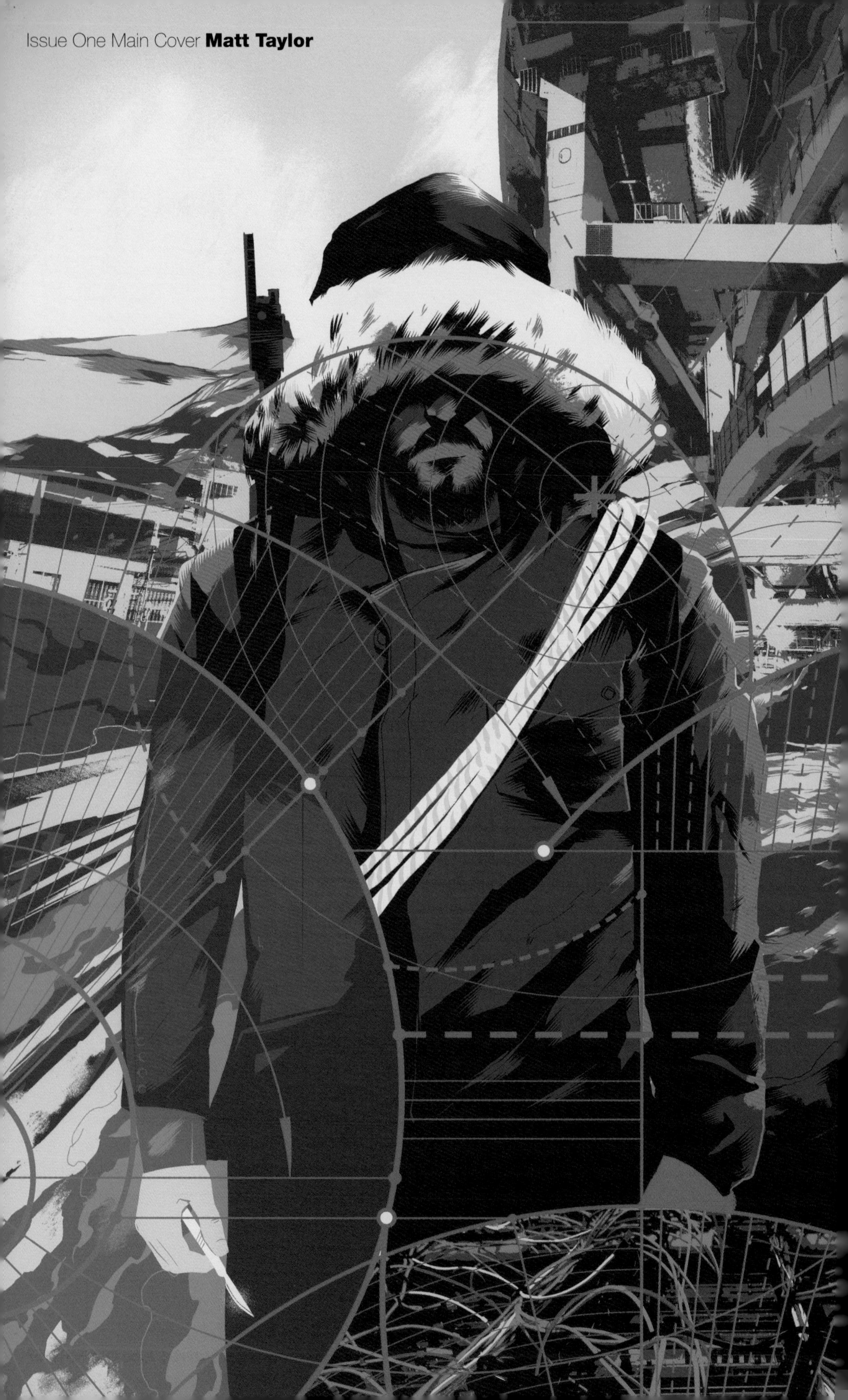

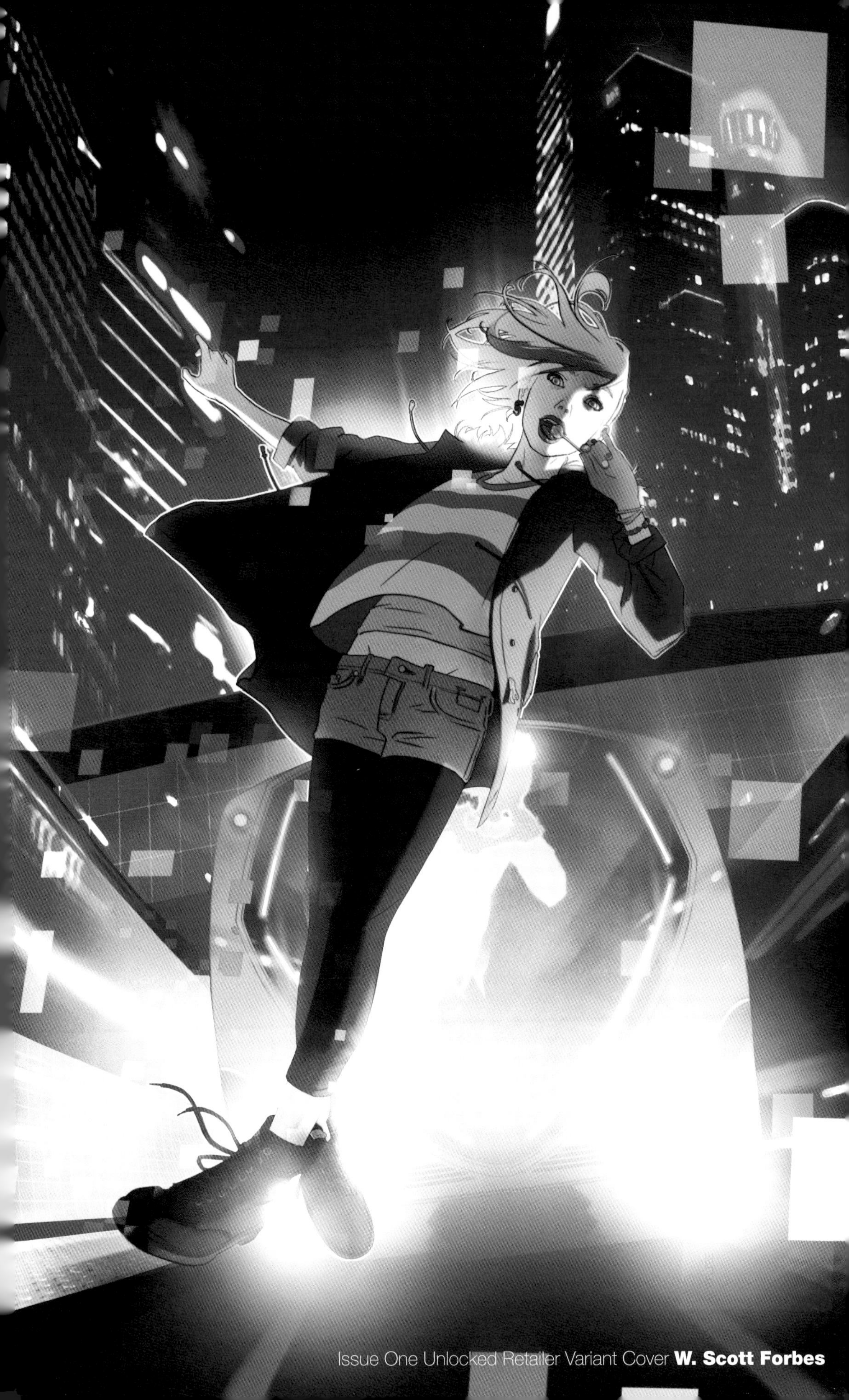

Issue One Unlocked Retailer Variant Cover **W. Scott Forbes**

Issue One BOOM! Ten Years Variant Cover **Frazer Irving**

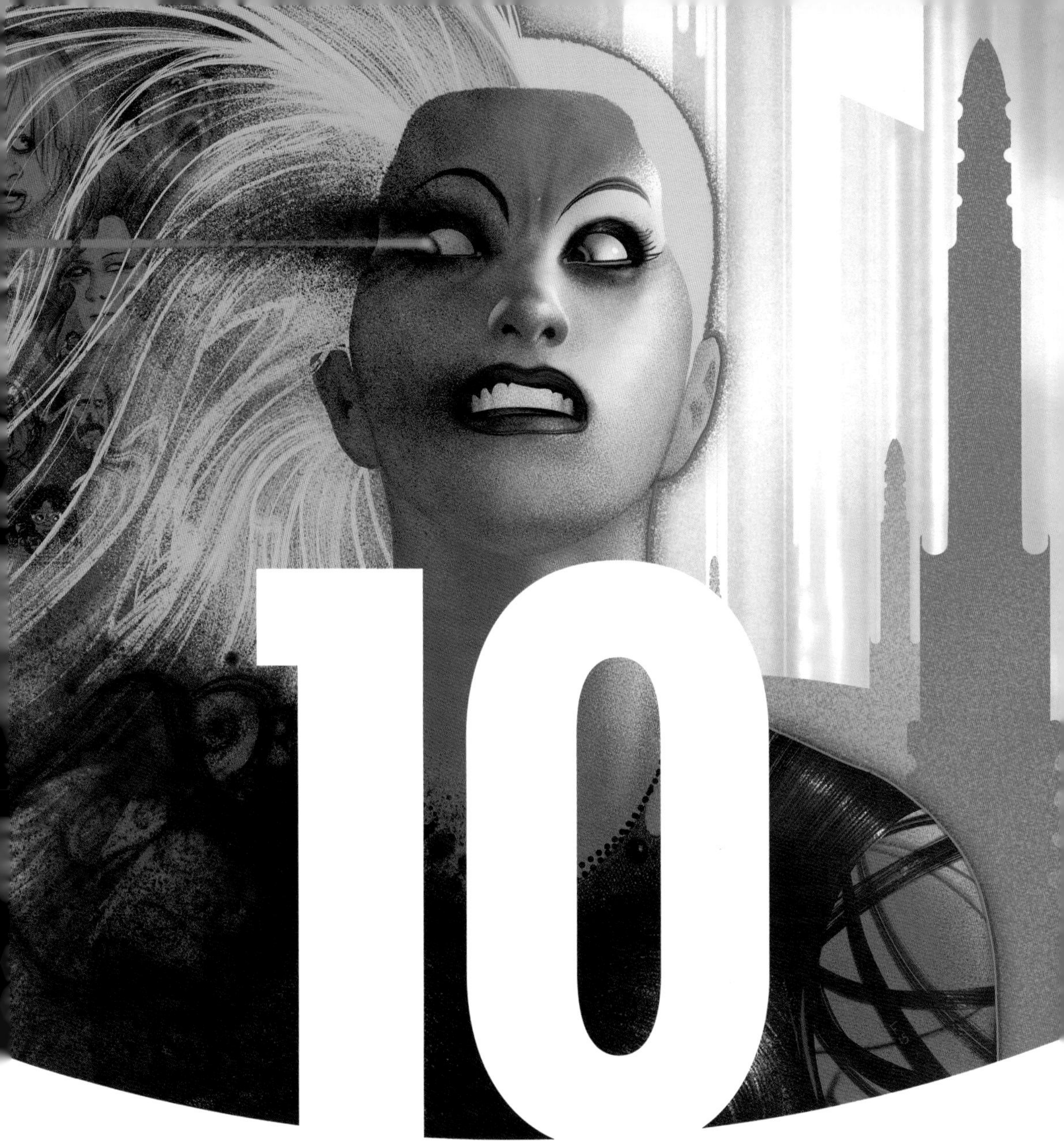
10

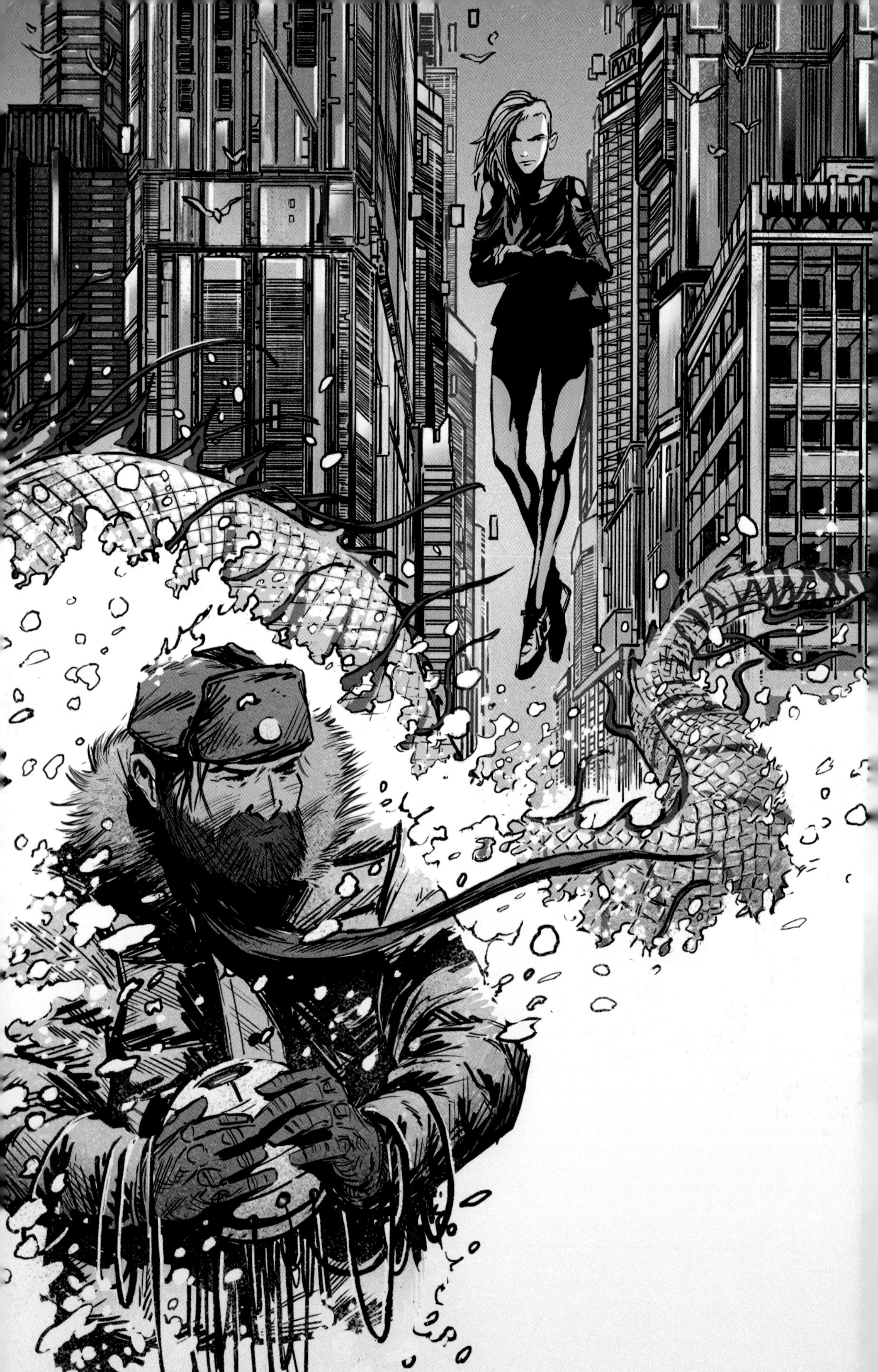

Issue One Second Print Cover **Eric Scott Pfeiffer**

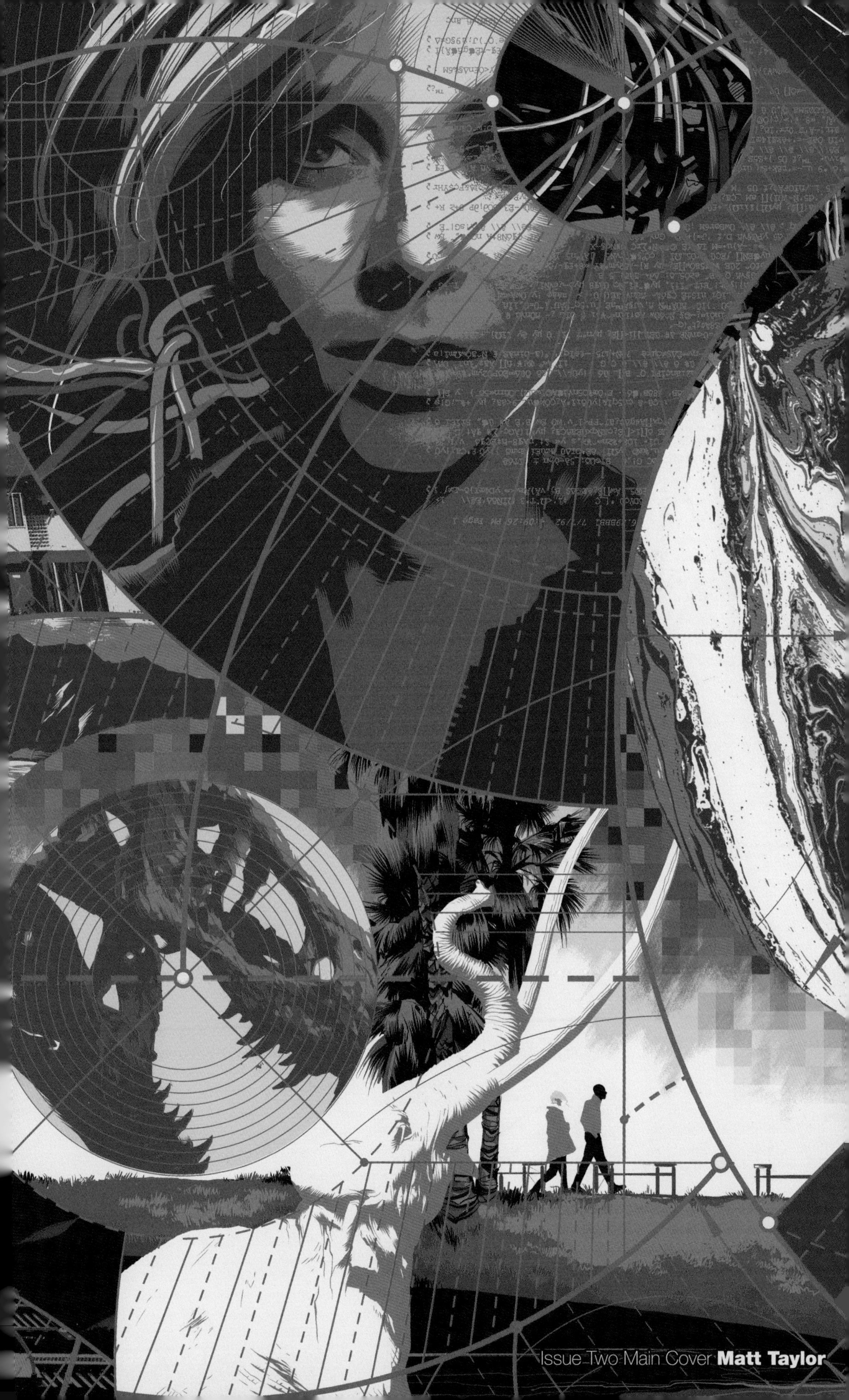

Issue Two Main Cover **Matt Taylor**

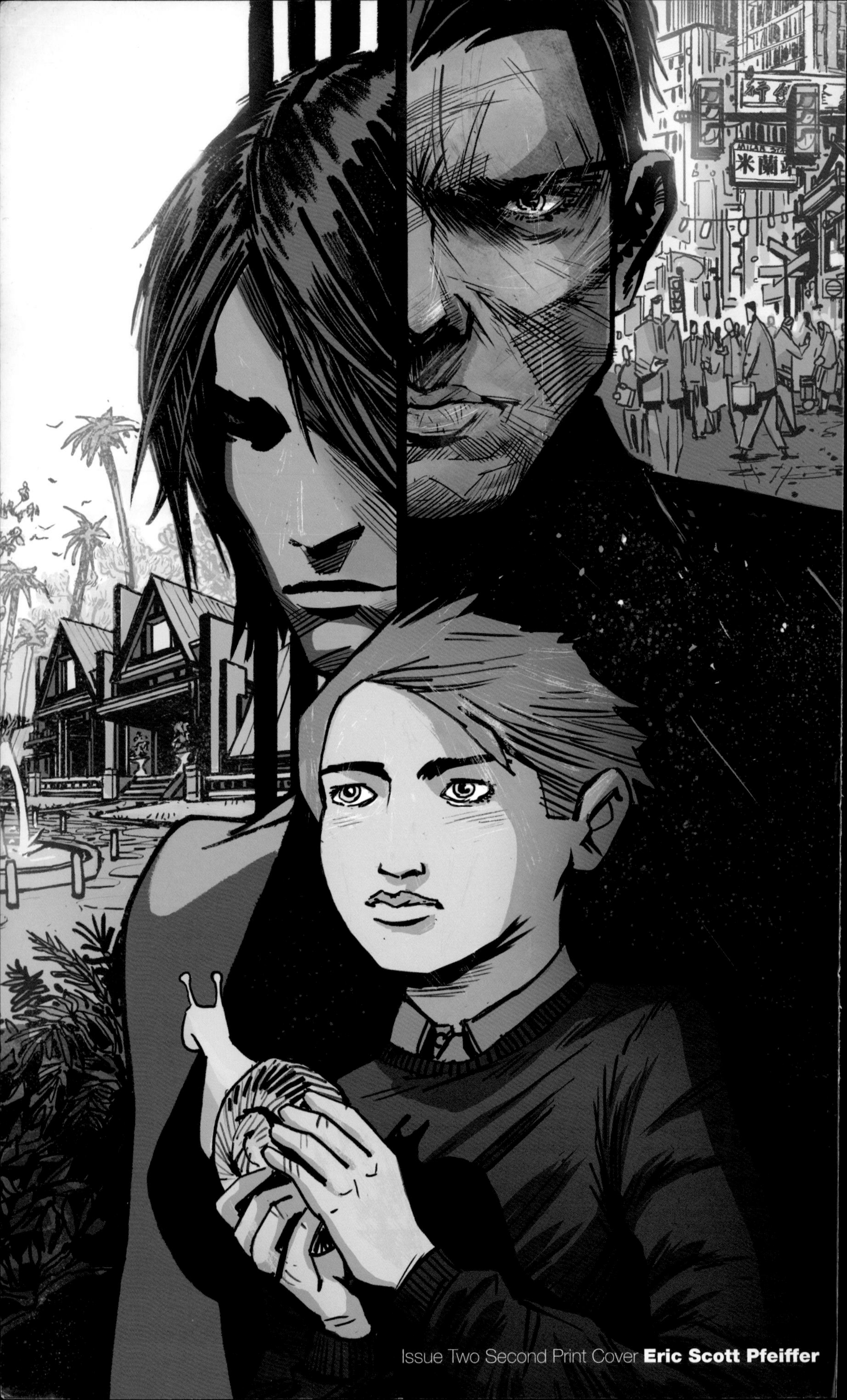

Issue Two Second Print Cover **Eric Scott Pfeiffer**

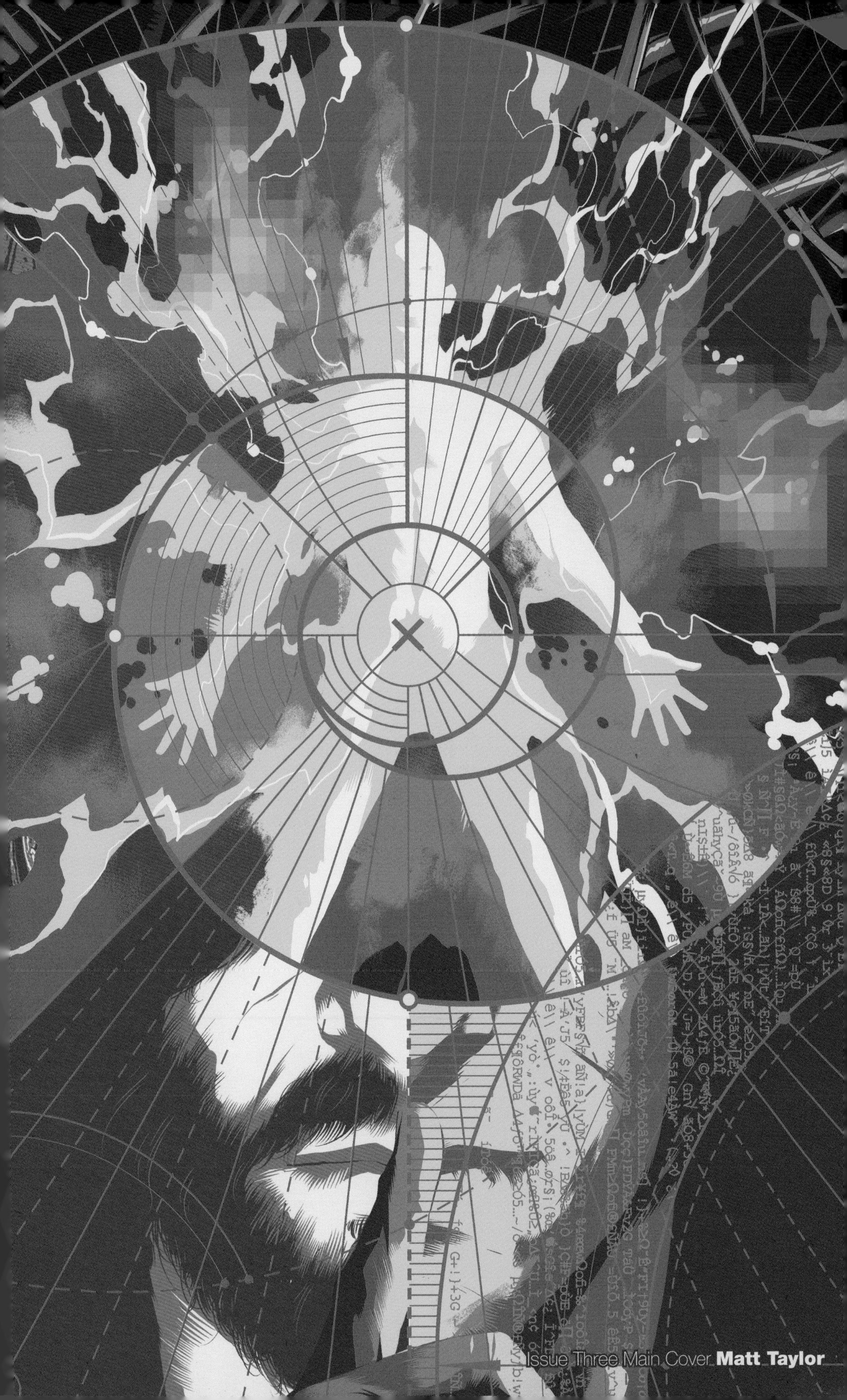

Issue Three Main Cover **Matt Taylor**

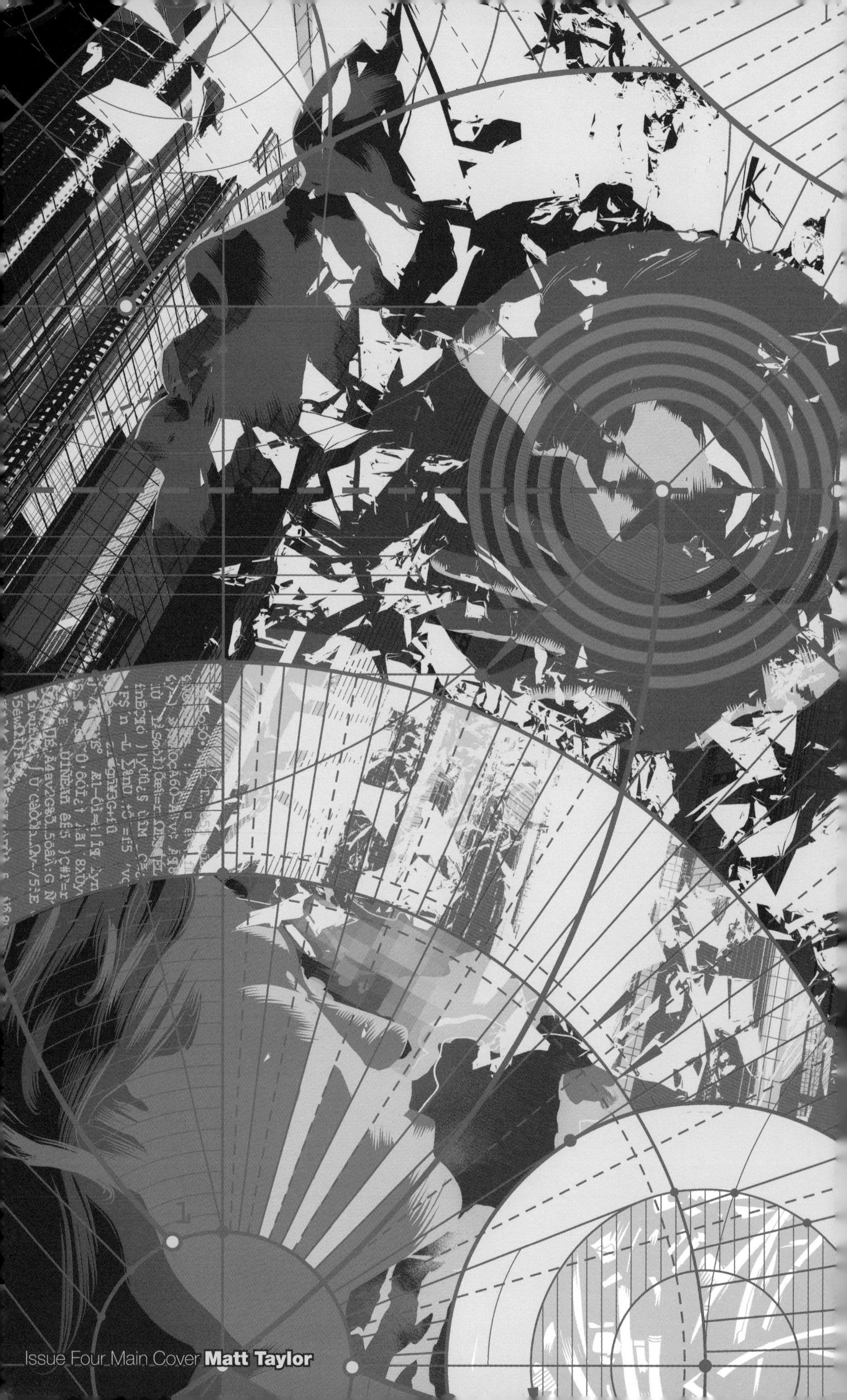

Issue Four Main Cover **Matt Taylor**

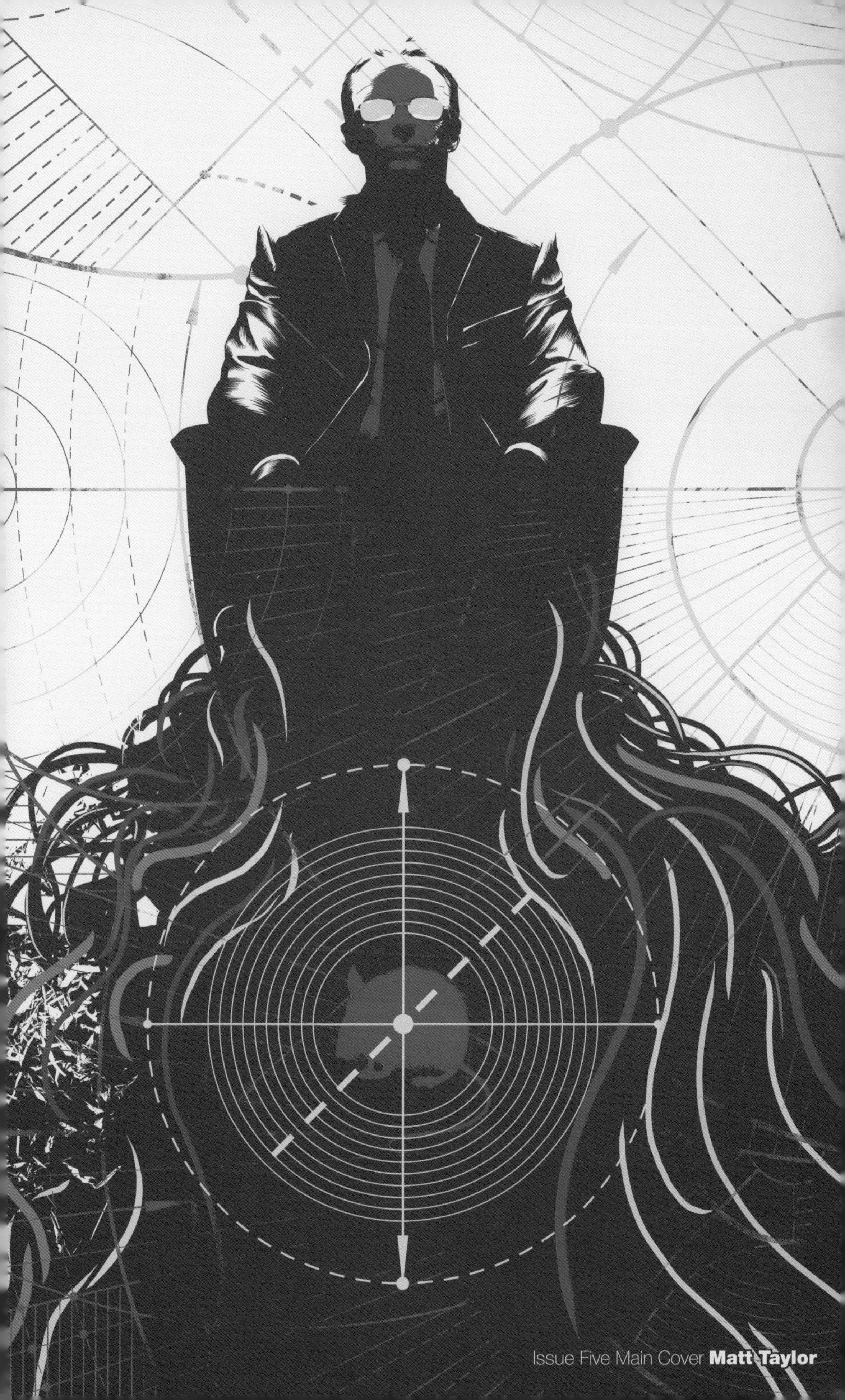

Issue Five Main Cover **Matt Taylor**

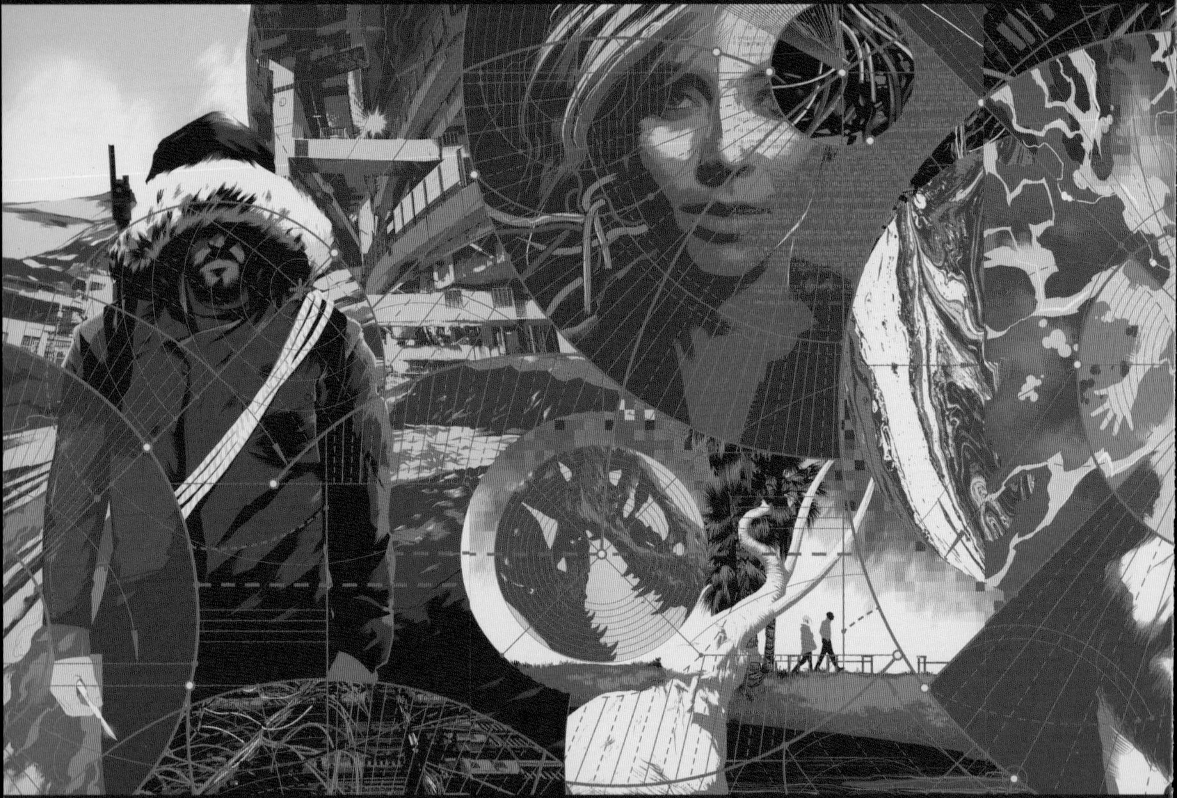

Series Connecting Covers **Matt Taylor**

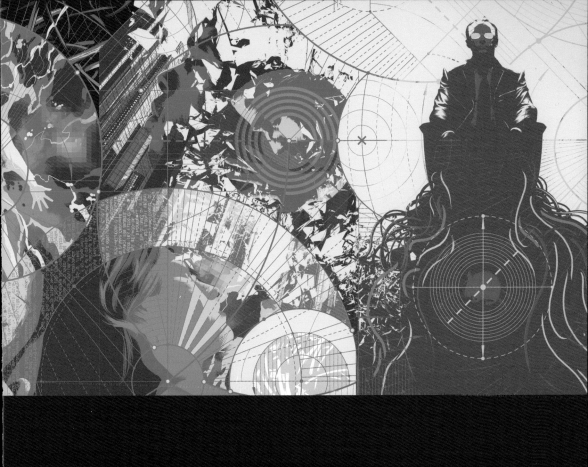